Melbourne, Australia

Dave Knight

Contents

Articles

Attractions

Transportation

References

Overview of Melbourne

Melbourne

Melbourne	
Victoria	

Top: Melbourne city centre,
centre left: Flinders Street Station,
centre right: Shrine of Remembrance,
centre: Federation Square,
bottom left: Melbourne Cricket Ground,
bottom right: Royal Exhibition Building.

Melbourne

Population:	4.00 million (Metropolitan area) (2nd)
• Density:	1566/km² (4055.9/sq mi) (Urban area; 2006)
Established:	30 August 1835
Coordinates:	37°48′49″S 144°57′47″E
Elevation:	31 m (102 ft)

Area:	8806 km² (3400.0 sq mi) (LGAs total)
Time zone: • Summer (DST)	AEST (UTC+10) AEDT (UTC+11)
LGA:	31 Municipalities across Greater Melbourne
County:	Bourke
State District:	54 electoral districts and regions
Federal Division:	23 Divisions

Mean Max Temp	Mean Min Temp	Annual Rainfall
19.8 °C 68 °F	10.2 °C 50 °F	646.9 mm 25.5 in

Melbourne (pronunciation: /ˈmɛlbərn/, locally also [ˈmælbən, -bn̩][citation needed]) is the capital and most populous city in the state of Victoria, and the second most populous city in Australia. The Melbourne City Centre (also known as the "Central Business District" or "CBD") is the hub of the greater geographical area (or "metropolitan area") and the Census statistical division—of which "Melbourne" is the common name. As of June 2009, the greater geographical area had an approximate population of 4.00 million. Inhabitants of Melbourne are called Melburnians.

The metropolis is located on the large natural bay known as Port Phillip, with the city centre positioned at the estuary of the Yarra River (at the northern-most point of the bay). The metropolitan area then extends south from the city centre, along the eastern and western shorelines of Port Phillip, and expands into the hinterland. The city centre is situated in the municipality known as the City of Melbourne, and the metropolitan area consists of a further 30 municipalities.

It was founded in 1835 (47 years after the European settlement of Australia) by settlers from Van Diemen's Land. It was named by governor Richard Bourke in 1837, in honour of William Lamb—the 2nd Viscount Melbourne. Melbourne was officially declared a city by Queen Victoria in 1847. In 1851, it became the capital city of the newly created colony of Victoria. During the Victorian gold rush of the 1850s, it was transformed into one of the world's largest and wealthiest cities. After the federation of Australia in 1901, it then served as the interim seat of government of the newly created nation of Australia until 1927.

Today, it is a centre for the arts, commerce, education, entertainment, sport and tourism. It is the birthplace of cultural institutions such as Australian film (as well as the world's first feature film), Australian television, Australian rules football, the Australian impressionist art movement (known as the Heidelberg School) and Australian dance styles (such as New Vogue and the Melbourne Shuffle). It is also a major centre for contemporary and traditional Australian music. It is often referred to as the "cultural capital of Australia".

Melbourne has been ranked as one of the top three World's Most Livable Cities by the Economist Group's Intelligence Unit (since 2002), top 10 Global University Cities by RMIT's Global University Cities Index (since 2006) and top 20 Global Innovation Cities by the 2thinknow Global Innovation Agency (since 2007). The metropolis is also home to the world's largest tram network. The main airport serving Melbourne is Melbourne Airport.

History

For more details on this topic, see History of Melbourne.

See also: Timeline of Melbourne history and History of Victoria

Early history and foundation

Further information: Foundation of Melbourne

Before the arrival of European settlers, the area was occupied for an estimated 31,000 to 40,000 years by under 20,000 hunter-gatherers from three indigenous regional tribes: the Wurundjeri, Boonwurrung and Wathaurong. The area was an important meeting place for the clans of the Kulin nation alliance, as well as a vital source of food and water. The first European settlement in Victoria was established in 1803 on Sullivan Bay, near present-day Sorrento, but this settlement was abandoned due to a perceived lack of resources. It would be 30 years before another settlement was attempted.

Melbourne Landing, 1840; watercolour by W. Liardet (1840)

In May and June 1835, the area that is now central and northern Melbourne was explored by John Batman, a leading member of the Tasmanian Port Phillip Association, who negotiated a "purchase" of 600000 acres (2400 km^2) with eight Wurundjeri elders. Batman selected a site on the northern bank of the Yarra River, declaring that "this will be the place for a village", and returned to Launceston in Tasmania (then known as Van Diemen's Land). However, by the time a settlement party from the Association arrived to set up the new village, a separate group organised and financed by John Pascoe Fawkner had already arrived (on 30 August 1835) aboard his ship the *Enterprize* and established a settlement at the same location. The two groups ultimately agreed to share the settlement.

It is not known what Melbourne was called before the arrival of Europeans. Early European settlers mistranslated the words "Doutta-galla" which are believed to have been the name of a prominent tribal member, but said by some to also translate as "treeless plain". This was nevertheless used as one of the early names for the colony.

Batman's Treaty with the Aborigines was annulled by the New South Wales government (which at the time governed all of eastern mainland Australia), which compensated the Association. Although this meant the settlers were now trespassing on Crown land, the government reluctantly accepted the settlers' *fait accompli* and allowed the town (known at first by various names, including 'Batmania') to remain.

In 1836, Governor Bourke declared the city the administrative capital of the Port Phillip District of New South Wales, and commissioned the first plan for the city, the Hoddle Grid, in 1837. Later that year the settlement was named Melbourne after the current British prime minister William Lamb, 2nd Viscount Melbourne, who resided in the village of Melbourne in Derbyshire. The General Post Office opened under that name on 13 April 1837. Melbourne was declared a city by letters patent of Queen Victoria, issued on 25 June 1847.

The Port Phillip District became the separate Colony of Victoria in 1851, with Melbourne as its capital.

Victorian gold rush

Further information: Victorian gold rush

The discovery of gold in Victoria in the same year led to the Victorian gold rush, and Melbourne, which provided most service industries and served as the major port for the region, experienced rapid growth. Migration to Melbourne, particularly from overseas including Ireland and China, caused a massive population increase. Slums developed including a temporary "tent city" established on the southern banks of the Yarra, the Little Lonsdale district and at Chinatown. In the aftermath of the Eureka Rebellion, mass public support for the plight of the miners in Melbourne resulted in major political changes to the colony.

"Canvas Town", South Melbourne in the 1850s. Temporary accommodation for the thousands who poured into Melbourne each week during the gold rush.

The population growth and flow of gold into the city helped stimulate a program of grand civic building beginning with the design and construction of many of Melbourne's surviving institutional buildings including Parliament House, the Treasury Building and Treasury Reserve, the Old Melbourne Gaol, Victoria Barracks, the State Library, Supreme Court, University, General Post Office, Government House, Customs House the Melbourne Town Hall, St Paul's, St Patrick's cathedrals and several major markets including the surviving Queen Victoria Market. The city's inner suburbs were planned, to be linked by boulevards and gardens. Melbourne had become a major finance centre, home to several banks, the Royal Mint to Australia's first stock exchange in 1861.

Before the arrival of white settlers, the indigenous population in the district was estimated at 15,000, but following settlement the number had fallen to less than 800, and continued to decline with an estimated 80% decrease by 1863, due primarily to introduced diseases, particularly smallpox.

The land boom and bust

The economic boom of the Victorian gold rush peaked during the 1880s and Melbourne had become the richest city in the world and the largest city after London in the British Empire. Melbourne hosted five international exhibitions at the large purpose-built Exhibition Building between 1880 and 1890[citation needed] spurring the construction of several prestigious hotels including the Menzies, Federal and the Grand (Windsor).

Lithograph of the Royal Exhibition Building (now a World Heritage site) built to host the World's Fair of 1880

During an 1885 visit, English journalist George Augustus Henry Sala coined the phrase "Marvellous Melbourne", which stuck long into the twentieth century and is still used today by Melburnians. Growing building activity culminated in a "land boom" which, in 1888, reached a peak of speculative development fuelled by consumer confidence and escalating land value. As a result of the boom, large commercial buildings, coffee palaces, terrace housing and palatial mansions proliferated in the city. The establishment of a hydraulic facility in 1887 allowed for the local manufacture of elevators which, in turn resulted in the first construction of high-rise buildings. This period also saw the expansion of a major radial rail-based transport network.

A brash boosterism that had typified Melbourne during this period ended in 1891 with a severe depression of the city's economy, sending the local finance and property industries into a period of chaos during which 16 small banks and building societies collapsed and 133 limited companies went into liquidation. The Melbourne financial crisis was a contributing factor in the Australian economic depression of the 1890s and the Australian banking crisis of 1893. The effects of the depression on the city were profound, although it recovered enough to grow slowly during the early twentieth century.

Federation of Australia

Further information: Federation of Australia

At the time of Australia's federation on 1 January 1901, Melbourne became the temporary seat of government of the federation. The first federal parliament was convened on 9 May 1901 in the Royal Exhibition Building, where it was located until 1927, when it was moved to Canberra. The Governor-General of Australia resided at Government House in Melbourne until 1930 and many major national institutions remained in Melbourne well into the twentieth century. Flinders Street Station was the world's busiest passenger station in 1927 and Melbourne's tram network overtook

Melbourne and the Yarra in 1928

Sydney's to become the world's largest in the 1940s. During World War II, Melbourne industries thrived on wartime production and the city became Australia's leading manufacturing centre.[citation needed]

Post-war period

After World War II, Melbourne expanded rapidly, its growth boosted by Post war immigration to Australia. While the "Paris End" of Collins Street began Melbourne's boutique shopping and open air cafe cultures, the city centre was seen by many as stale, the dreary domain of office workers, something expressed by John Brack in his famous painting *Collins St., 5 pm* (1955). Height limits in the Melbourne CBD were lifted after the construction ICI House, transforming the city's skyline with the introduction of skyscrapers. The eyes of the world were on the city when it hosted the 1956 Summer Olympics.

Suburban expansion intensified, serviced by new indoor malls beginning with Chadstone Shopping Centre. The post-war period also saw a major renewal of the CBD and St Kilda Road which significantly modernised the city. New fire regulations and redevelopment saw most of the taller pre-war CBD buildings demolished. Many of the larger suburban mansions from the boom era were also either demolished or subdivided.

Eastern skyline and the Yarra River in 1959

To counter the trend towards low-density suburban residential growth, the government began a series of controversial public housing projects in the inner city by the Housing Commission of Victoria, which resulted in demolition of many neighbourhoods and a proliferation of high-rise towers. In later years, with the rapid rise of motor vehicle ownership, the investment in freeway and highway developments greatly accelerated the outward suburban sprawl and declining inner city population. The Bolte government sought to rapidly accelerate the modernisation of Melbourne. Major road projects including the remodelling of St Kilda Junction, the widening of Hoddle Street and then the extensive 1969 Melbourne Transportation Plan changed the face of the city into a car-dominated environment.

Australia's financial and mining booms between 1969 and 1970 resulted in establishment of the headquarters of many major companies (BHP Billiton and Rio Tinto, among others) in the city. Nauru's then booming economy resulted in several ambitious investments in Melbourne, such as Nauru House.[citation needed] Melbourne remained Australia's main business and financial centre until the late 1970s, when it began to lose this primacy to Sydney.

As the centre of Australia's "rust belt", Melbourne experienced an economic downturn between 1989 to 1992, following the collapse of several local financial institutions. In 1992 the newly elected Kennett government began a campaign to revive the economy with an aggressive development campaign of public works coupled with the promotion of the city as a tourist destination with a focus on major events and sports tourism. During this period the Australian Grand Prix moved to Melbourne from Adelaide. Major projects included the construction of a new facility for the Melbourne Museum, Federation Square, the Melbourne Exhibition and Convention Centre, Crown Casino and the CityLink tollway. Other strategies included the privatisation of some of Melbourne's services, including power and public transport, and a reduction in funding to public services such as health, education and public transport infrastructure.

Contemporary Melbourne

Since 1997, Melbourne has maintained significant population and employment growth. There has been substantial international investment in the city's industries and property market. Major inner-city urban renewal has occurred in areas such as Southbank, Port Melbourne, Melbourne Docklands and more recently, South Wharf. According to the Australian Bureau of Statistics, Melbourne sustained the highest population increase and economic growth rate of any Australian capital city in the three years ended June 2004. These factors have led to population growth and further suburban expansion through the 2000s.

Melbourne's CBD in 2005 from Docklands at twilight.

In 2008, Melbourne was named as a UNESCO City of Literature.

From 2006, the growth of the city extended into "green wedges" and beyond the city's Urban growth boundary. Predictions of the city's population reaching 5 million people pushed the state government to review the growth boundary in 2008 as part of its Melbourne @ Five Million strategy. Melbourne survived the financial crisis of 2007-2010 better than any other Australian city. In 2009, more new jobs were created in Melbourne than any other Australian capital - almost as many as the next two fastest growing cities, Brisbane and Perth, combined. and Melbourne's property market remained strong, resulting in historically high property prices and widespread rent increases.

Geography

Topography

Further information: Geology of Victoria

Melbourne is located in the south-eastern part of mainland Australia, within the state of Victoria. Geologically, it is built on the confluence of Quaternary lava flows to the west, Silurian mudstones to the east, and Holocene sand accumulation to the southeast along Port Phillip. The southeastern suburbs are situated on the Selwyn fault which transects Mount Martha and Cranbourne.

Map of greater Melbourne and Geelong

Melbourne extends along the Yarra towards the Yarra Valley toward the Dandenong Ranges and Yarra Ranges to the east. It extends northward through the undulating bushland valleys of the Yarra's tributaries − Moonee Ponds Creek (toward Tullamarine Airport), Merri Creek, Darebin Creek and Plenty River to the outer suburban growth corridors of Craigieburn and Whittlesea. The city sprawls south-east through Dandenong to the growth corridor of Pakenham towards West Gippsland, and southward through the Dandenong Creek valley, the Mornington Peninsula and the city of Frankston taking in the peaks of Olivers Hill, Mount Martha and Arthurs Seat, extending along the shores of Port Phillip as a single conurbation to reach the exclusive suburb of Portsea and Point Nepean. In the west, it extends along the Maribyrnong River and its tributaries north towards Sunbury and the foothills of the Macedon Ranges, and along the flat volcanic plain country towards Melton in the west, Werribee at the foothills of the You Yangs granite ridge and Geelong as part of the greater metropolitan area to the south-west.

Melbourne's major bayside beaches are located in the south-eastern suburbs along the shores of Port Phillip Bay, in areas like Port Melbourne, Albert Park, St Kilda, Elwood, Brighton, Sandringham, Mentone and Frankston although there are beaches in the western suburbs of Altona and Williamstown. The nearest surf beaches are located 85 kilometres (53 mi) south-east of the Melbourne CBD in the back-beaches of Rye, Sorrento and Portsea.

Climate

Further information: Extreme Weather Events in Melbourne

Melbourne has a moderate oceanic climate (Köppen climate classification *Cfb*) and is well known for its changeable weather conditions. This is mainly due to Melbourne's location situated on the boundary of the very hot inland areas and the cold southern ocean. This temperature differential is most pronounced in the spring and summer months and can cause very strong cold fronts to form. These cold fronts can be responsible for all sorts of severe weather from gales to severe thunderstorms and hail, large temperature drops, and heavy rain. Port Phillip is often warmer than the surrounding

Autumn in suburban Canterbury

oceans and/or the land mass, particularly in spring and autumn; this can set up a kind of "bay effect" similar to the "lake effect" seen in the United States where showers are intensified leeward of the bay. Relatively narrow streams of heavy showers can often affect the same places (usually the eastern suburbs) for an extended period of time, whilst the rest of Melbourne and surrounds stays dry. Melbourne is also prone to isolated convective showers forming when a cold pool crosses the state, especially if there is considerable daytime heating. These showers are often heavy and can contain hail and squalls and significant drops in temperature, but they pass through very quickly at times with a rapid clearing trend to sunny and relatively calm weather and the temperature rising back to what it was before the shower. This occurs often in the space of minutes and can be repeated many times in a day, giving Melbourne a reputation for having "four seasons in one day", a phrase that is part of local popular culture and familiar to many visitors to the city.

Melbourne is colder than other mainland Australian state capital cities in the winter. The lowest temperature on record is –2.8 °C (27 °F), on 4 July 1901. However, snowfalls are rare: the most recent occurrence of sleet in the CBD was on 25 July 1986 and the most recent snowfalls in the outer eastern suburbs and Mount Dandenong were on 10 August 2005, More commonly, Melbourne experiences frosts and fog in winter.

During the spring, Melbourne commonly enjoys extended periods of mild weather and clear skies. Melbourne and Sydney's average January and February daily highs are similar. However, Melbourne's summers are notable for days of extreme heat, with Melbourne holding the Australian capital city extreme temperature record of 46.4°C, set on 7 February 2009.

Climate data for Melbourne												
Month	Jan	Feb	Mar	Apr	May	Jun	Jul	Aug	Sep	Oct	Nov	Dec	Year
Record high °C (°F)	45.6 (114.1)	46.4 (115.5)	41.7 (107.1)	34.9 (94.8)	28.7 (83.7)	22.4 (72.3)	23.1 (73.6)	26.5 (79.7)	31.4 (88.5)	36.9 (98.4)	40.9 (105.6)	43.7 (110.7)	46.4 (115.5)
Average high °C (°F)	25.9 (78.6)	25.8 (78.4)	23.9 (75)	20.3 (68.5)	16.7 (62.1)	14.0 (57.2)	13.4 (56.1)	14.9 (58.8)	17.2 (63)	19.6 (67.3)	21.9 (71.4)	24.2 (75.6)	19.8 (67.6)
Average low °C (°F)	14.3 (57.7)	14.6 (58.3)	13.2 (55.8)	10.7 (51.3)	8.6 (47.5)	6.9 (44.4)	6.0 (42.8)	6.7 (44.1)	7.9 (46.2)	9.5 (49.1)	11.1 (52)	12.9 (55.2)	10.2 (50.4)
Record low °C (°F)	5.5 (41.9)	4.5 (40.1)	2.8 (37)	1.5 (34.7)	−1.1	−2.2	−2.8	−2.1	−0.5	0.1 (32.2)	2.5 (36.5)	4.4 (39.9)	−2.8
Precipitation mm (inches)	47.6 (1.874)	47.3 (1.862)	50.2 (1.976)	57.3 (2.256)	56.2 (2.213)	49.2 (1.937)	47.7 (1.878)	50.2 (1.976)	57.9 (2.28)	66.2 (2.606)	59.5 (2.343)	59.2 (2.331)	648.5 (25.531)
Avg. precipitation days	8.3	7.4	9.3	11.4	13.9	14.1	15.1	15.6	14.7	14.1	11.7	10.4	146.0
Sunshine hours	279	228.8	210.8	168	120.9	108	114.7	145.7	171	195.3	210	232.5	2184.7
Source: Bureau of Meteorology.												

Urban structure

See also: Melbourne city centre, List of heritage listed buildings in Melbourne, Lanes and Arcades of Melbourne, and Parks and gardens of Melbourne

A 180 degree panoramic image of Melbourne's CBD: with the Hoddle Grid (left) and Southbank (right), as seen from the Rialto Observation Deck (2008)

The centre of the CBD is formed by the Hoddle Grid (dimensions of 1 by 0.5 miles (1.6 by 0.80 km)). The grid's southern edge fronts onto the Yarra River. Office, commercial and public developments in the adjoining districts of Southbank and Docklands have made these redeveloped areas into extensions of the CBD in all but name.

The city centre is well known for its historic and attractive lanes and arcades (the most notable of which are Block Place and Royal Arcade) which contain a variety of shops and cafés and are a byproduct of the city's layout.

Melbourne is known for the "laneway culture" of its extensive network of lively city lanes which include Centre Place (pictured).

The Melbourne CBD, compared with other Australian cities, has comparatively unrestricted height limits and as a result of waves of post-war development contains five of the six tallest buildings in Australia, the tallest of which is the Eureka Tower, situated in Southbank. It has an observation deck near the top from where you can see above all of Melbourne's structures. The Rialto tower, the city's second tallest, remains the tallest building in the old CBD; its observation deck for visitors has recently closed. The CBD and surrounds also contain many significant historic buildings such as the Royal Exhibition Building, the Melbourne Town Hall and Parliament House. Although the area is described as the *centre*, it is not actually the demographic centre of Melbourne at all, due to an urban sprawl to the south east, the demographic centre being located at Glen Iris.

Melbourne's urban structure features large parks and gardens and wide avenues

Melbourne is typical of Australian capital cities in that after the turn of the 20th century, it expanded with the underlying notion of a 'quarter acre home and garden' for every family, often referred to locally as the *Australian Dream*. This, coupled with the popularity of the private automobile throughout much of the 20th century, led to the auto-centric urban structure now present today in the middle and outer suburbs. Much of metropolitan Melbourne is accordingly characterised by low density sprawl, whilst its inner city areas feature predominantly medium-density, transit-oriented urban forms. The city centre, Docklands, St.Kilda Road and Southbank areas feature high-density forms.

Melbourne is often referred to as Australia's garden city, and the state of Victoria was once known as *the garden state*. There is an abundance of parks and gardens in Melbourne, many close to the CBD with a variety of common and rare plant species amid landscaped vistas, pedestrian pathways and tree-lined avenues. There are also many parks in the surrounding suburbs of Melbourne, such as in the municipalities of Stonnington, Boroondara and Port Phillip, south east of the CBD.

The extensive area covered by urban Melbourne is formally divided into hundreds of suburbs (for addressing and postal purposes), and administered as local government areas 31 of which are located within the metropolitan area.

Housing

Main article: Housing in Victoria, Australia

Pin Oak Court, Vermont South (famous as the fictional "Ramsay Street" in the cult soap opera Neighbours) is typical of the majority of suburban Melbourne.

"Melbourne Style" Victorian terrace houses are common in the inner suburbs and have been the subject of gentrification

Housing in Melbourne is characterised by high rates of private housing ownership[citation needed], minimal and lack of public housing and high demand for, and largely unaffordable, rental housing.[citation needed] Public housing is usually provided by the Housing Commission of Victoria and operates within the framework of the Commonwealth-State Housing Agreement, by which funding for public housing is provided by both federal and state governments.[citation needed] Public housing can be difficult to obtain with many residents forced to wait on waiting lists.[citation needed]

At present, Melbourne is experiencing high population growth, generating high demand for housing. This has created a housing boom, pushing housing prices up and having an effect on rental prices as well as availability of all types of housing. Subdivision regularly occurs in the far outer areas of Melbourne with Display homes from numerous developers offering house and land packages.

Environment

See also: Environmental issues in Australia

Like many urban environments, Melbourne faces some significant environmental issues, many of them relating to the city's large urban footprint and urban sprawl and the demand for infrastructure and services.

One such issue is water usage, drought and low rainfall. Drought in Victoria, low rainfalls and high temperatures deplete Melbourne water supplies and climate change will have a long-term impact on the water supplies of Melbourne. Melbourne has been in a drought since 1997. In response to low water supplies and low rainfall due to drought, the

A Parks Victoria litter trap on the river catches floating rubbish on the Yarra at Birrarung Marr

government implemented water restrictions and a range of other options including: water recycling schemes for the city, incentives for household water tanks, greywater systems, water consumption awareness initiatives, and other water saving and reuse initiatives; also, in June 2007, the Bracks Government announced that a $3.1 billion Wonthaggi desalination plant would be built on Victoria's south-east coast, capable of treating 150 billion litres of water per year, as well as a 70 km (43 mi) pipeline from the Goulburn area in Victoria's north to Melbourne and a new water pipeline linking Melbourne and Geelong. Both projects are being conducted under controversial Public-Private Partnerships and a multitude of independent reports have found that neither project is required to supply water to the city and that Sustainable Water Management is the best solution and in the meantime, the drought must be weathered.

Many of Melbourne's inner city councils have a higher than average supporter and voter base for the Australian Greens, however, the average is lower in the outer suburbs.

In response to Attribution of recent climate change, the City of Melbourne, in 2002, set a target to reduce carbon emissions to net zero by 2020 and Moreland City Council established the Zero Moreland program, however not all metropolitan municipalities have followed, with the City of Glen Eira notably deciding in 2009 not to become carbon neutral.

Melbourne has one of the largest urban footprints in the world due to its low density housing, resulting in a vast suburban sprawl, with a high level of car dependence and minimal public transport outside of inner areas. Much of the vegetation within the city are non-native species, most of European origin, and in many cases plays host to invasive species and noxious weeds. Significant introduced urban pests include the Common Myna, Feral Pigeon, Brown Rat, European Wasp, Common Starling and Red Fox. Many outlying suburbs, particularly towards the Yarra Valley and the hills to the north-east and east, have gone for extended periods without regenerative fires leading to a lack of saplings and undergrowth in urbanised native bushland. The Department of Sustainability and Environment partially addresses this problem by regularly burning off. Several national parks have been designated around the urban area of Melbourne, including the Mornington Peninsula National Park, Port Phillip Heads Marine National Park and Point Nepean National Park in the south east, Organ Pipes National Park to the north and Dandenong Ranges National Park to the east. There are also a number of significant state parks just outside Melbourne.

Responsibility for regulating pollution falls under the jurisdiction of the EPA Victoria and several local councils. Air pollution, by world standards, is classified as being good, however summer and autumn are the worst times of year for atmospheric haze in the urban area.

Another recent environmental issue in Melbourne was the Victorian government project of channel deepening Melbourne Ports by dredging Port Phillip Bay – the Port Phillip Channel Deepening Project. It was subject to controversy and strict regulations among fears that beaches and marine wildlife could be affected by the disturbance of heavy metals and other industrial sediments. Other major pollution problems in Melbourne include levels of bacteria including E. coli in the Yarra River and its tributaries caused by septic systems, as well as litter. Up to 350,000 cigarette butts enter the storm water runoff every day. Several programs are being implemented to minimise beach and river pollution.

In February 2010, *The Transition Decade*, an initiative to transition human society, economics and environment towards sustainability, was launched in Melbourne.

Culture

Main article: Culture of Melbourne

Melbourne is an international cultural centre, with cultural endeavours spanning major events and festivals, drama, musicals, comedy, music, art, architecture, literature, film and television. It is a UNESCO City of Literature and has thrice shared top position in a survey by *The Economist* of the *World's Most Livable Cities* on the basis of a number of attributes which included its broad cultural offerings.

The stained glass ceiling of the Great Hall of the National Gallery of Victoria

The city celebrates a wide variety of annual cultural events and festivals of all types, including the Melbourne International Arts Festival, Melbourne International Film Festival, Melbourne International Comedy Festival and the Melbourne Fringe Festival.

The Australian Ballet is based in Melbourne, as is the Melbourne Symphony Orchestra. Melbourne is the second home of Opera Australia after it merged with 'Victoria State Opera' in 1996. The Victorian Opera had its inaugural season in 2006 and operates out of various venues in Melbourne.

Princess Theatre

Notable theatres and performance venues include: The Victorian Arts Centre (which includes the State Theatre, Hamer Hall, the Playhouse and the fairfax Studio), Melbourne Recital Centre, Sidney Myer Music Bowl, Princess Theatre, Regent Theatre, Forum Theatre, Palace Theatre, Comedy Theatre, Athenaeum Theatre, Her Majesty's Theatre, Capitol Theatre, Palais Theatre and the Australian Centre for Contemporary Art.

There are more than 100 galleries in Melbourne. Most notably it is home to Australia's oldest and largest art gallery, the National Gallery of Victoria.

Melbourne is the birthplace of Australian film and television (as well as the world's first feature film), Australian rules football, Australian impressionist art movement known as the Heidelberg School, and

Australian contemporary dance (including the Melbourne Shuffle and New Vogue styles).

Street Art in Melbourne is becoming increasingly popular with the *Lonely Planet* guides listing it as a major attraction.

The city is also admired for its exciting mix of vigorous modern architecture which intersects with an impressive range of nineteenth and early twentieth century buildings.

Sport

Main article: Sport in Victoria

Melbourne is a notable sporting location as the host city for the 1956 Summer Olympics games, the first Olympic Games ever held in Australia and the southern hemisphere, along with the 2006 Commonwealth Games.

Docklands Stadium (known as Etihad Stadium) has a retractable roof

Melbourne is home to three major annual international sporting events in the Australian Open (one of the four Grand Slam tennis tournaments), Melbourne Cup (horse racing), and the Australian Grand Prix (Formula One). In recent years, the city has claimed the SportsBusiness title "World's Ultimate Sports City". The city is home to the National Sports Museum, which until 2003 was located outside the members pavilion at the Melbourne Cricket Ground and reopened in 2008 in the Olympic Stand.

Australian rules football and cricket are the most popular sports in Melbourne and also the spiritual home of these two sports in Australia and both are mostly played in the same stadia in the city and its suburbs. The first ever official cricket Test match was played at the Melbourne Cricket Ground in March 1877 and the Melbourne Cricket Ground is the largest cricket ground in the world [citation needed]. The first Australian rules football matches were played in Melbourne in 1859 and the Australian Football League is headquartered at Docklands Stadium. Nine of its teams are based in the Melbourne metropolitan area and the five Melbourne AFL matches per week attract an average 40,000 people per game. Additionally, the city annually hosts the AFL Grand Final.

The city is also home to several professional franchises in national competitions including Football (Soccer) clubs Melbourne Victory and Melbourne Heart who play in the A-league competition, the rugby league club Melbourne Storm who play in the NRL competition, the rugby union club Melbourne Rebels who play in the Super 15 competition, the netball club Melbourne Vixens who play in the trans-Tasman trophy ANZ Championship, and the basketball club Melbourne Tigers who play in the NBL competition. A second Melbourne-based NBL team may be established for the 2011-2012 season. In November 2008, it was announced that the Victorian Major Events Company had informed the Australian Olympic Committee that Melbourne was considering making bids for either the 2024 or 2028 Summer Olympics.

Economy

Melbourne has a highly diversified economy with particular strengths in finance, manufacturing, education and research, IT, logistics and transportation, and conventions and tourism.

NAB world headquarters (right) at Melbourne Docklands

The city is headquarters for many of Australia's largest corporations, including five of the ten largest in the country (based on revenue), and five of the largest six in the country (based on market capitalization) (ANZ, BHP Billiton (the world's largest mining company), the National Australia Bank, Rio Tinto and Telstra); as well as such representative bodies and thinktanks as the Business Council of Australia and the Australian Council of Trade Unions.

Melbourne is home to Australia's largest and busiest seaport which handles more than $75 billion in trade every year and 39% of the nation's container trade. Melbourne Airport provides an entry point for national and international visitors, and is Australia's second busiest airport.

The Australian Synchrotron in Melbourne is an important scientific research tool enhancing the contribution of education and research to Melbourne's economy

Melbourne is an important financial centre. Two of the big four banks, NAB and ANZ, are headquartered in Melbourne. The city has carved out a niche as Australia's leading centre for superannuation (pension) funds, with 40% of the total, and 65% of industry super-funds including the $40 billion-dollar Federal Government Future Fund. The city was rated 34th within the top 50 financial cities as surveyed by the Mastercard Worldwide Centers of Commerce Index (2007), between Barcelona and Geneva, and second only to Sydney (14th) in Australia.

The city is the centre of Australia's automotive industry, which includes Ford and Toyota manufacturing facilities, and the engine manufacturing facility of Holden, as well as the Australian headquarters of those three companies. It is home to many other manufacturing industries.

Melbourne is a major technology hub, with an ICT industry that employs over 60,000 people (one third of Australia's ICT workforce), has a turnover of $19.8 billion and export revenues of $615 million.

Tourism also plays an important role in Melbourne's economy, with approximately 7.6 million domestic visitors and 1.88 million international visitors in 2004. In 2008, Melbourne overtook Sydney with the amount of money that domestic tourists spent in the city. Melbourne has been attracting an increasing share of domestic and international conference markets. Construction began in February 2006 of a $1 billion 5000-seat international convention centre, Hilton Hotel and commercial precinct adjacent to the Melbourne Exhibition and Convention Centre to link development along the Yarra River with the Southbank precinct and multi-billion dollar Docklands redevelopment.

Main article: Tourism in Melbourne

Demographics

Main article: Demographics of Melbourne

See also: Melbourne population growth

Melbourne is a diverse and multicultural city.

Almost a quarter of Victoria's population was born overseas, and the city is home to residents from 233 countries, who speak over 180 languages and dialects and follow 116 religious faiths. Melbourne has the second largest Asian population in Australia (16.2%), which includes the largest Indian and Sri Lankan communities in the country. The cultural diversity is also reflected by the fact that the city is home to restaurants serving cuisines from all over the world.

The first European settlers in Melbourne were British and Irish. These two groups accounted for nearly all arrivals before the gold rush, and supplied the predominant number of immigrants to the city until World War II.

Melbourne was transformed by the 1850s gold rush; within months of the discovery of gold in August 1852, the city's population had increased by nearly three-quarters, from 25,000 to 40,000 inhabitants. Thereafter, growth was exponential and by 1865, Melbourne had overtaken Sydney as Australia's most populous city.

Large numbers of Chinese, German and United States nationals were to be found on the goldfields and subsequently in Melbourne. The various nationalities involved in the Eureka Stockade revolt nearby give some indication of the migration flows in the second half of the nineteenth century.

In the aftermath of the World War II, Melbourne experienced unprecedented inflows from Southern Europe, primarily Greece, Italy, Macedonia, Malta, Croatia, Serbia, and Bosnia and Herzegovina also West Asia mostly from Lebanon and Turkey. In 2006 149,195 persons in the Melbourne Statistical District claimed Greek ancestry, either alone or in combination with another ancestry; only four Greek cities have larger populations. Melbourne and the Greek city of Thessaloniki became sister cities in 1984, as commemorated by a marble stele (pillar) from the Prefecture of Thessaloniki, unveiled 11 November 2008. Ethnic Chinese and Vietnamese also maintain significant presences.

Melbourne exceeds the national average in terms of proportion of residents born overseas: 34.8% compared to a national average of 23.1%. In concordance with national data, Britain is the most commonly reported overseas country of birth, with 4.7 %, followed by Italy (2.4%), Greece (1.9 %) and then China (1.3 %). Melbourne also features substantial Vietnamese, Indian and Sri Lankan-born communities, in addition to recent South African and Sudanese influxes.

Over two-thirds of people in Melbourne speak only English at home (68.8%). Italian is the second most common home language (4.0%), with Greek third and Chinese fourth, each with over 100,000 speakers.

Although Victoria's net interstate migration has fluctuated, the Melbourne statistical division has grown by approximately 50,000 people a year since 2003. Melbourne has now attracted the largest proportion of international overseas immigrants (48,000) finding it outpacing Sydney's international migrant intake, along with having strong interstate migration from Sydney and other capitals due to more affordable housing and cost of living, which have been two recent key factors driving Melbourne's growth.

In recent years, Melton, Wyndham and Casey, part of the Melbourne statistical division, have recorded the highest growth rate of all local government areas in Australia. Despite a demographic study stating that Melbourne could overtake Sydney in population by 2028, the ABS has projected in two scenarios that Sydney will remain larger than Melbourne beyond 2056, albeit by a margin of less than 3% compared to a margin of 12% today. However, the first scenario projects that Melbourne's population overtakes Sydney in 2039, primarily due to larger levels of internal migration losses assumed for Sydney.

After a trend of declining population density since World War II, the city has seen increased density in the inner and western suburbs aided in part by Victorian Government planning blueprints, such as Postcode 3000 and Melbourne 2030 which have aimed to curtail the urban sprawl.

Religion

St Paul's Anglican Cathedral

Melbourne is home to a wide range of religious faiths, the most widely held faith of which is Christian (64%) with a large Catholic population (28.3%). However Melbourne and indeed Australia are highly secularised, with the proportion of people identifying themselves as Christian declining from 96% in 1901 to 64% in 2006 and those who did not state their religion or declared no religion rising from 2% to over 30% over the same period. Nevertheless, the large Christian population is signified by the city's two large cathedrals – St Patrick's (Roman Catholic), and St Paul's (Anglican). Both were built in the Victorian era and are of considerable heritage significance as major landmarks of the city.

Other responses included no religion (20.0%, 717,717), Anglican (12.1%, 433,546), Eastern Orthodox (5.9%, 212,887) and the Uniting Church (4.0%, 143,552). Buddhists, Muslims, Jews, Hindus and Sikhs collectively account for 7.5% of the population.

Melbourne has the largest Jewish population in Australia, the community currently numbering approximately 60,000. The city is also home to the largest number of Holocaust survivors of any Australian city, indeed the highest per capita concentration outside Israel itself. Reflecting this vibrant and growing community, Melbourne has a plethora of Jewish cultural, religious and educational institutions, including over 40 synagogues and 7 full-time parochial day schools, along with a local Jewish newspaper.

St Patrick's Roman Catholic Cathedral

Media

Main article: Media in Melbourne

Three daily newspapers serve Melbourne: the Herald Sun (tabloid), The Age (broadsheet) and The Australian (national broadsheet). The free mX is also distributed weekday afternoon at railway stations and on the streets of central Melbourne.

Six television stations serve Melbourne: HSV-7, which broadcasts from the Melbourne Docklands precinct; GTV-9, which broadcasts from their Richmond studios; and ATV-10, which broadcasts from the Como Complex in South Yarra. National stations that broadcast into Melbourne include the

SBS studios at Federation Square

Australian Broadcasting Corporation (ABC), which has two studios, one at Ripponlea and another at Southbank; and Special Broadcasting Service (SBS), which broadcasts from their studios at Federation Square in central Melbourne. C31 Melbourne is the only local community television station in Melbourne, and its broadcast range also branches out to regional centre Geelong. Melbourne also receives Pay TV, largely through cable and satellite services. Foxtel and Optus are the main Pay TV providers.

A long list of AM and FM radio stations broadcast to greater Melbourne. These include 'public' (i.e. state owned ABC & SBS) and community stations. Many commercial stations are networked-owned: DMG has Nova 100 and Classic Rock; ARN controls Gold and Mix; and Austereo runs both Fox and Triple M. Stations from towns in regional Victoria may also be heard (e.g. Star FM, Warragul). Youth alternatives include ABC Triple J and youth run SYN. Triple J, and similarly PBS and Triple R, strive to play under represented music. JOY caters for gay and lesbian audiences. For fans of classical music there are 3MBS and ABC Classic FM. AM stations include ABC: 774, Radio National, and News Radio; and also Fairfax affiliates 3AW (talk) and Magic (easy listening). Melbourne has many community run stations that serve alternative interests, such as 3CR and 3KND (Indigenous). Many suburbs have low powered community run stations serving local audiences.

Melbourne can be seen on the small screen through TV shows such as Rush (2008 TV series), Offspring (TV series), Neighbours and City Homicide. Past productions include Kath & Kim and Blue Heelers.

Governance

The Melbourne City Council governs the City of Melbourne, which takes in the CBD and a few adjoining inner suburbs. However the head of the Melbourne City Council, the Lord Mayor of Melbourne, is frequently treated as a representative of greater Melbourne (the entire metropolitan area), particularly when interstate or overseas. Robert Doyle, elected in 2008, is current Lord Mayor.

The Parliament of Victoria meets in Parliament House

The rest of the metropolitan area is divided into 31 local government areas. All these are designated as Cities, except for five on the city's outer fringes which are classified as Shires. Local government authorities have elected councils and are responsible for a range of functions set out in the Local Government Act 1989, such as urban planning and waste management.

Most non-local government services are provided or regulated by the Victorian state government, which governs from Parliament House in Spring Street. These include public transport, main roads, traffic control, policing, education above preschool level, health and planning of major infrastructure projects.

Melbourne City Council meets in Melbourne Town Hall

Education

Main article: Education in Victoria

See also: List of schools in Victoria and List of universities and research institutions in Melbourne

Education is overseen statewide by the Department of Education and Early Childhood Development (DEECD), whose role is to 'provide policy and planning advice for the delivery of education'. It acts as advisor to two state ministers, that for Education and for Children and Early Childhood Development.

State Library of Victoria, Melbourne's largest public library. (La Trobe Reading Room – 5th floor view)

Preschool, primary and secondary

The Littlejohn Memorial Chapel at Scotch College, the oldest secondary school in Melbourne

Melbourne schools are predominant among Australian schools whose alumni are listed in *Who's Who in Australia*, a listing of notable Australians. In the top ten boys schools in Australia for *Who's Who*-listed alumni, Melbourne schools are Scotch College (first in Australia - it is also Melbourne's oldest secondary school), Melbourne Grammar School (second), Melbourne High School (third), Geelong Grammar School (fourth - has a junior campus in suburban Toorak) and Wesley College (sixth). In the top ten girl's schools for *Who's Who*-listed alumni Melbourne schools are Presbyterian Ladies College (first in Australia), Methodist Ladies College (third), Melbourne Girls Grammar School (fifth), Mac.Robertson Girls' High School (sixth) and University High School (tenth).

There are five selective public schools in Melbourne (entry based on examination/audition): Melbourne High School, MacRoberston Girls' High School, Nossal High School, John Monash Science School and the Victorian College of the Arts Secondary School, but all public schools may restrict entry to students living in their regional 'zone'.

Primary and secondary assessment, curriculum development and educational research initiatives throughout Melbourne and Victoria is undertaken by the Victorian Curriculum and Assessment Authority (VCAA), which offers the Victorian Essential Learning Standards (VELS) and Achievement Improvement Monitor (AIM) certificates from years Prep through Year 10, and the Victorian

Certificate of Education (VCE) and Victorian Certificate of Applied Learning (VCAL) as part of senior secondary programs (Years 11 to 12).

Although non-tertiary public education is free, 35% of students attend a private primary or secondary school. The most numerous private schools are Catholic, and the rest are independent (see Public and Private Education in Australia).

Tertiary, vocational and research

Melbourne's two largest universities are the University of Melbourne and Monash University, the largest university in Australia. Both are members of the Group of Eight. Melbourne University ranked second among Australian universities in the 2006 THES international rankings. *The Times Higher Education Supplement* ranked the University of Melbourne as the 36th best university in the world, Monash University was ranked the 38th best university in the world. The city of Melbourne was ranked the world's fourth top university city in 2008 after London, Boston and Tokyo.

Other prominent universities include the Royal Melbourne Institute of Technology and La Trobe University which have also placed in the THES rankings. Other universities include Swinburne University of Technology based in the inner city Melbourne suburb of Hawthorn. The Geelong based Deakin University also has a significant campus in Melbourne. Victoria University has nine campuses across Melbourne's western region, including three in the heart of Melbourne's Central Business District (CBD) and another four within ten kilometers of the CBD. Some of the nation's oldest educational institutions and faculities are located in Melbourne, including the oldest Engineering (1860), Medical (1862), Dental (1897) and Music (1891) schools, all at the University of Melbourne. The University of Melbourne is the oldest university in Victoria and the second-oldest university in Australia.

In recent years, the number of international students at Melbourne's universities has risen rapidly, a result of an increasing number of places being made available to full fee paying students.

Infrastructure

Health

The Government of Victoria's Department of Human Services oversees approximately 30 public hospitals in the Melbourne metropolitan region, and 13 health services organisations.

There are many major medical, neuroscience and biotechnology research institutions located in Melbourne: St. Vincent's Institute of Medical Research, Australian Stem Cell Centre, the Burnet Institute, Australian Regenerative Medicine Institute, Victorian Institute of Chemical Sciences, Brain Research Institute, Peter MacCallum Cancer Centre, the Walter and Eliza Hall Institute of Medical Research, and the Melbourne Neuropsychiatry Centre.

Other institutions include the Howard Florey Institute, the Murdoch Children's Research Institute, Baker IDI Heart and Diabetes Institute and the Australian Synchrotron. Many of these institutions are associated with and are located near universities.

Transport

Main article: Transport in Melbourne

Melbourne has a very high dependency on the automobile for transport particularly in the outer suburban areas with a total of 3.6 million private vehicles using 22320 km (13870 mi) of road, and one of the highest lengths of road per capita in the world. It is served by an extensive network of freeways and arterial roadways. The largest number of cars are bought in the outer suburban area. Major highways feeding into the city include the Eastern Freeway, Monash Freeway and West Gate Freeway (which spans the large Westgate Bridge), whilst other freeways circumnavigate the city or lead to other major cities, including CityLink (which spans the large Bolte Bridge), Eastlink, the Western Ring Road, Calder Freeway, Tullamarine Freeway (main airport link) and the Hume Freeway which links Melbourne and Sydney.

The Bolte Bridge is part of the CityLink tollway system

Southern Cross Station - Melbourne's main inter-urban train station

A Melbourne tram

Melbourne has an integrated public transport system based around extensive train, tram and bus networks. Its tram network is the largest in the world, while the rail network is one of the largest in the world, hosting 15 lines, the Paris Metro is a third smaller, while San Francisco's BART system is less than half the size. Its train and tram networks were originally laid out late in the 19th century assisted by wealth from the gold rush. The early 20th century saw an increase in popularity of the private automobile, resulting in unsustainable outward suburban expansion. Public transport usage declined between the 1940s, when 25% of travelers used public transport, and 2003, where it bottomed out at

Melbourne's suburban public transport hub – Flinders Street Station – as seen from the observation deck on Rialto Tower

7.6%. The public transport system was privatised in 1999, symbolising the peak of the decline. Despite privatisation and successive governments persisting with auto-centric urban development into the 21st century, there has been large increases in public transport patronage since, bringing the figure back up to 9% by 2006. In 2006, the State Government tentatively announced a goal of 20% public transport mode share by 2020 and since 2006, public transport patronage has grown by over 20%.

The Melbourne rail network consists of 16 suburban lines which radiate from the City Loop, a partially underground metro section of the network beneath the Central Business District (Hoddle Grid). Flinders Street Station is Melbourne's busiest railway station, and was the world's busiest passenger station in 1926. It remains a prominent Melbourne landmark and meeting place. The city has rail connections with regional Victorian cities, as well as interstate rail services to Sydney and Adelaide, which depart from Melbourne's other major rail terminus, Southern Cross Station in Spencer Street. In the 2008–2009 financial year, the Melbourne rail network recorded 213.9 million passenger trips, the highest in its history.

Melbourne has the largest tram network in the world. The tram network carries approximately 178 million passenger trips a year. Melbourne's is Australia's only tram network to comprise more than a single line. Sections of the tram network are on roads, while others are separated or are light rail routes. Melbourne's trams are recognised as iconic cultural assets and a tourist attraction. Heritage trams operate on the free City Circle route, intended for visitors to Melbourne, and heritage restaurant trams travel through the city during the evening.

Melbourne's bus network consists of almost 300 routes which mainly service the outer suburbs fill the gaps in the network between rail and light rail services. In 2007, a total of 86.7 million passenger trips were recorded on Melbourne's buses .

Melbourne is also a major shipping port. The Port of Melbourne is Australia's largest container and general cargo port and also its busiest. In 2007, the port handled two million shipping containers in a 12 month period, making it one of the top five ports in the Southern Hemisphere. Station Pier in Port Phillip Bay handles cruise ships and the Spirit of Tasmania ferries which cross Bass Strait to Tasmania.

Swanston Dock, Port of Melbourne

Melbourne Airport

Melbourne has four airports. Melbourne Airport, at Tullamarine, is the city's main international and domestic gateway and second busiest in Australia. The airport is home base for passenger airlines Jetstar and Tiger Airways Australia and cargo airlines Australian air Express and Toll Priority and is a major hub for Qantas and Virgin Blue. Avalon Airport, located between Melbourne and Geelong, is a secondary hub of Jetstar. It is also used as a freight and maintenance facility. Air Ambulance facilities are available for domestic and international transportation of patients.

Melbourne also has a significant general aviation airport, Moorabbin Airport in the city's south east as well as handling a limited number of passenger flights. Essendon Airport, which was once the city's main airport also handles passenger flights, general aviation and some cargo flights.

Utilities

Main article: Energy in Victoria

Water storage and supply for Melbourne is managed by Melbourne Water, which is owned by the Victorian Government. The organisation is also responsible for management of sewerage and the major water catchments in the region and will be responsible for the Wonthaggi desalination plant and North–South Pipeline. Water is stored in a series of reservoirs located within and outside the Greater Melbourne area. The largest dam, the Thomson River Dam,

Sugarloaf Reservoir (in 2007) at Christmas Hills in the metropolitan area is one of Melbourne's closest water supplies.

located in the Victorian Alps, is capable of holding around 60% of Melbourne's water capacity, while smaller dams such as the Upper Yarra Dam and the Cardinia Reservoir carry secondary supplies.

Gas and electricity are provided by private companies.

Numerous telecommunications companies provide Melbourne with terrestrial and mobile telecommunications services and wireless internet services.

Sister cities

Melbourne

Boston

Milan

Saint Petersburg

Thessaloniki

Tianjin

Osaka

The City of Melbourne has six sister cities. They are:

- ● Osaka, Japan, 1978
- ▨ Tianjin, China, 1980
- ≣ Thessaloniki, Greece, 1984
- Boston, United States, 1985
- ▬ Saint Petersburg, Russia, 1989
- ▮ ▮ Milan, Italy, 2004

Some other local councils in the Melbourne metropolitan area have sister city relationships; see Local Government Areas of Victoria.

Melbourne is a member of the C40: Large Cities Climate Leadership Group and the United Nations Global Compact – Cities Programme.

See also

- Timeline of Melbourne history
- Melbourne tourism
- Crime in Melbourne
- Melway – the native street directory and general information source in Melbourne.
- Hook turn – driving manoeuvre that is common in the inner city area.
- City of Literature – Melbourne was named a City of Literature by UNESCO in 2008.
- The Southern Star (observation wheel)
- 2am Lockout
- Melbourne population growth
- Neighbours

Lists:

- List of Melburnians

- List of Melbourne suburbs
- List of Mayors and Lord Mayors of Melbourne
- List of songs about Melbourne
- List of heritage listed buildings in Melbourne
- Local Government Areas of Victoria
- List of Australian capital cities

Notes

[a] The variant spelling 'Melbournian' is sometimes found but is considered grammatically incorrect. The term 'Melbournite' is also sometimes used.

[b] Legislation passed in December 1920 resulted in the formation of the SECV from the Electricity Commission. (State Electricity Commission Act 1920 (No.3104))

Further reading

- Bell, Agnes Paton (1965). *Melbourne: John Batman's Village*. Melbourne, Vic: Cassell Australia,. p. 178.
- Boldrewood, Rolf (1896). *Old Melbourne Memories*. Macmillan and Co. pp. 259 pages.
- Borthwick, John Stephen; David McGonigal (1990). *Insight Guide: Melbourne*. Prentice Hall Travel. p. 247. ISBN 0134677137, 9780134677132.
- Briggs, John Joseph (1852). *The History of Melbourne, in the County of Derby: Including Biographical Notices of the Coke, Melbourne, and Hardinge Families*. Bemrose & Son. p. 205.
- Brown-May, Andrew; Shurlee Swain (2005). *The Encyclopedia of Melbourne*. Melbourne, Vic: Cambridge University Press,. p. 820.
- Carroll, Brian (1972). *Melbourne: An Illustrated History*. Lansdowne. p. 128. ISBN 0701801956, 9780701801953.
- Cecil, David (1954). *Melbourne*. Bobbs-Merrill. p. 450.
- Collins, Jock; Letizia Mondello; John Breheney; Tim Childs (1990), *Cosmopolitan Melbourne. Explore the world in one city*, Big Box Publishing, Rhodes, New South Wales. ISBN 0957962401
- Coote, Maree (2009,2003). *The Melbourne Book: A History of Now*. Melbournestyle Books. p. 356. ISBN 9780975704745.
- Davidson, Jim (ed.)(1986), *The Sydney-Melbourne Book*, Allen and Unwin, North Sydney, New South Wales. ISBN 0868618195
- Lewis, Miles Bannatyne; Philip Goad, Alan Mayne (1994). *Melbourne: The City's History and Development* (2nd ed.). City of Melbourne. ISBN 0949624713, 9780949624710.
- McClymont, David; Mark Armstrong (2000). *Lonely Planet Melbourne* [1]. Lonely Planet. pp. 200 pages. ISBN 1864501243, 9781864501247.
- Newnham, William Henry (1956). *Melbourne: The Biography of a City*. F. W. Cheshire. pp. 225 pages.
- O'Hanlon, Seamus and Tanja Luckins (eds.)(2005), *Go! Melbourne. Melbourne in the Sixties*, Melbourne Publishing Group, Beaconsfield, Victoria. ISBN 0975780204

- Priestley, Susan (1995). *South Melbourne: A History*. Melbourne University Press. p. 455. ISBN 0522846645, 9780522846645.

External links

- Encyclopedia of Melbourne official website [2]
- City of Melbourne official site [3]
- Melbourne travel guide from Wikitravel
- Official tourist board site of Melbourne [4]
- Victorian Division of the United Nations Association of Australia [5]

pnb:نروبلیم

History

History of Melbourne

See also: Timeline of Melbourne history

History of Australia
This article is part of **a series**
Chronological
Prehistory
1606–1787
1788–1850
1851–1900
1901–1945
Since 1945
Timeline
Topical
Monarchy · Exploration
Constitution · Federation
Economic · Railway
Immigration · Indigenous
Military · Diplomatic
States, Territories and cities
New South Wales · Sydney · Newcastle
Victoria · Melbourne
Queensland · Brisbane
Western Australia · Perth
South Australia · Adelaide

Tasmania · Hobart
Australian Capital Territory · Canberra
Northern Territory · Darwin
Australia Portal

The **history of Melbourne** details the city's growth from a fledging settlement into a modern commercial and financial centre as Australia's second largest city.

Pre-European settlement

The area around Port Phillip and the Yarra valley, on which the city of Melbourne now stands, was the home of the Kulin nation, an alliance of several language groups of Indigenous Australians, whose ancestors had lived in the area for up to 40,000 years. The Kulin lived by fishing, hunting and gathering, and made a good living from the rich food sources of Port Phillip and the surrounding grasslands.

Aborigines on Merri Creek by Charles Troedel

Many of the Aboriginal people who live in Melbourne today are descended from aboriginal nations from other parts of Victoria and Australia, however there are still people who identify as Wurundjeri and Boon warung descendants of the original nations who occupied the area of Melbourne prior to European settlement. While there are few overt signs of the Aboriginal past in the Melbourne area, there are a wealth of sites of cultural and spiritual significance.

European exploration

In 1797, George Bass was the first European to enter what came to be called Bass Strait, the passage between the Australian mainland and Van Diemen's Land (Tasmania), when he sailed as far west as Western Port. In 1802 John Murray in the *Lady Nelson* entered Port Phillip Bay, and he was followed shortly after by Matthew Flinders. In 1803 Charles Grimes found the mouth of the Yarra River, and hiked as far inland as Keilor.

The Enterprize, the ship of John Pascoe Fawkner landing at Melbourne

Later in 1803 the British Governor of New South Wales, fearful that the French might try to occupy the Bass Strait area, sent Colonel David Collins with a party of 300 convicts to establish a settlement at Port Phillip. Collins arrived at the site of Sorrento, on the Mornington Peninsula, in October 1803, but was put off by the lack of fresh water.

In May 1804 he moved the settlement to Tasmania, and thus became the founder of Hobart. Among the convicts at Sorrento was a boy called John Pascoe Fawkner, who would later come back to settle in the Melbourne area.

The northern shores of Bass Strait were then left to a few whalers and sealers for another 20 years. In 1824 Hamilton Hume and William Hovell came overland from New South Wales, failing to find Western Port, their destination, but instead reaching Corio Bay, where they found good grazing land. But it was another ten years before Edward Henty, a Tasmanian grazier, established an illegal sheep-run on crown land at Portland, in what is now western Victoria, in 1834.

1835 Foundation of Melbourne

Main article: Foundation of Melbourne

John Batman, a successful farmer in northern Tasmania, also desired more grazing land. In April 1835, he sailed across the Strait and up Port Phillip to the mouth of the Yarra. He explored a large area in what is now the northern suburbs of Melbourne.

On 6 June Batman, as part of a Tasmanian business syndicate known as the Port Phillip Association signed a treaty with the local Aboriginal people, in which he purported to buy

1880s Artist impression of Batman's Treaty being signed

2,000 km² of land around Melbourne and another 400 km²
around Geelong, on Corio Bay to the south-west. On 8 June
he wrote in his journal: "So the boat went up the large river...
and... I am glad to state about six miles up found the River all
good water and very deep. *This will be the place for a
village.*" This last sentence later became famous as the
"founding charter" of Melbourne.

Collins Street, Melbourne, 1839.
Watercolour by W. Knight

Batman returned to Launceston and began plans to mount a
large expedition to establish a settlement on the Yarra. But
John Pascoe Fawkner, by now a businessman in Launceston,
had the same idea. He bought a ship, the schooner *Enterprize*,
which sailed on 4 August, with a party of intending settlers.
When his party reached the Yarra on 2 September, they were
dismayed and angry to find Fawkner's people already in
possession.

The two groups decided that there was plenty of land for
everybody, and when Fawkner arrived on 16 October with
another party of settlers, he agreed that they should start
parcelling out land and not dispute who was there first. Both
Batman and Fawkner settled in the new town, which had
several interim names—such as Batmania, Bearbrass,

Melbourne Landing,1840; watercolor by W.
Liardet (1840)

Bareport, Bareheep, Barehurp and Bareberp (in June 1835) -- before being officially named Melbourne
in honour of the British Prime Minister, Lord Melbourne, in March 1837.

Early settlement

Melbourne began as a collection of tents and huts on the banks of the Yarra, yet within ten years,
because of its economic position as a centre of pastoralism and land speculation it had established
many stone and brick public and financial buildings. From September 1836 it was the administrative
centre of the Port Phillip District of New South Wales.

Government was represented first by a police magistrate, William Lonsdale, and then from October
1839 by a Superintendent, Charles La Trobe, a gifted man with artistic and scientific interests who did
much to lay the foundations of Melbourne as a real city. La Trobe's most lasting contribution to the city
was to reserve large areas as public parks: today these are the Treasury Gardens, the Carlton Gardens,
the Flagstaff Gardens, Royal Park and the Royal Botanic Gardens.

Another important early figure was Robert Hoddle, who laid out the square grid on which the town was
built, and which still marks the streets of Melbourne's central business district. On October 22, 1841,

with the incorporation of the town of Melbourne, this area was divided into the four wards of Bourke, Gipps, La Trobe and Lonsdale.[1]

In 1851 the white population of the whole Port Phillip District was still only 77,000, although it had already become a centre of Australia's wool export trade, and only 23,000 people lived in Melbourne. Until the building boom which followed the gold rushes, most of Melbourne was built of timber, and almost nothing from this period survives. Two exceptions are St James Old Cathedral (1839) in Collins St (now relocated to the Flagstaff Gardens), and St Francis Catholic Church (1841) in Elizabeth St. Suburban development had already begun, with the wealthy building houses by the seashore at St Kilda, and a port developing at Williamstown. In 1848 Melbourne acquired an Anglican bishop.

In July 1851 the successful agitation of the Port Phillip settlers led to the establishment of Victoria as a separate colony, and La Trobe became its first Lieutenant-Governor. A few months later gold was discovered at several locations around the colony, most notably at Ballarat and Bendigo. The ensuing gold rush radically transformed Victoria, and particularly Melbourne.

With the arrival of Europeans in the area, the local indigenous people were hard hit by introduced diseases, and their decline was hastened by mistreatment, alcohol and venereal disease. There were also frontier conflicts such as the Battle of Yering in 1840. Simon Wonga made moves to reclaim land for Kulin people to settle on in 1859, but they were not successful until 1863 when the surviving members of the Wurundjeri and other Woiwurrung speakers were given 'permissive occupancy' of Coranderrk Station, near Healesville and forcibly resettled.

1850s Gold Rush

See also: Victorian Gold Rush

The discovery of gold led to a huge influx of people to Victoria, most of them arriving by sea at Melbourne. The town's population doubled within a year. In 1852 75,000 people arrived in the colony and this, combined with a very high birthrate, led to rapid population growth (as well as the equally rapid dispossession of the Aboriginal populations in those areas of inland Victoria which had not already been cleared for sheep runs).

Victoria's population reached 400,000 in 1857 and 500,000 in 1860. As the easy gold ran out many of these people flooded

Lithograph of the original plans for Parliament House, Melbourne.

into Melbourne or became a pool of unemployed in cities around Ballarat and Bendigo. There arose a huge wave of social unrest urging the opening of the lands in rural Victoria for small yeoman farming. In 1857 a 'Land Convention held in Melbourne. Later a provisional government was formed by land hungry miners demanding land reform.

The accelerated population growth and the enormous wealth of the goldfields fuelled a boom which lasted for forty years, and ushered in the era known as "marvellous Melbourne." The city spread eastwards and northwards over the surrounding flat grasslands, and southwards down the eastern shore of Port Phillip. Wealthy new suburbs like South Yarra, Toorak, Kew and Malvern grew up, while the working classes settled in Richmond, Collingwood and Fitzroy.

The influx of educated gold seekers from England led to rapid growth of schools, churches, learned societies, libraries and art galleries. The first railway in Australia was built in Melbourne in 1854. The University of Melbourne was founded in 1855 and the State Library of Victoria in 1856. The foundation stone of St Patrick's Catholic Cathedral was laid in 1858 and that of St Paul's Anglican Cathedral in 1880. The Philosophical Institute of Victoria received a Royal Charter in 1859 and became the Royal Society of Victoria. In 1860 this Society assembled Victoria's only attempt at inland exploration, the Burke and Wills expedition.

A Melbourne Town Council had been created in 1847, and one by one other suburbs also gained town status, complete with town councils and mayors. In 1851 a party-elected Legislative Council, dominated by squatter interests, opposed the notion of universal suffrage and the role of the Legislative Assembly. In December 1854 discontent with the licensing system on the goldfields led to the rising at the Eureka Stockade, one of only two armed rebellions in Australian history (the other being the Castle Hill convict rebellion of 1804).

In November 1856, Victoria was given a constitution and in the following year full responsible government with a two house Parliament. For Melbourne, the major consequence was the magnificent edifice of Parliament House, Melbourne, which was started in December 1855 and completed in stages between 1856 and 1929.

The boom fuelled by gold and wool lasted through the 1860s and '70s. Victoria suffered from an acute labour shortage despite its steady influx of migrants, and this pushed up wages until they were the highest in the world. Victoria was known as "the working man's paradise" in these years. The Stonemasons Union won the eight-hour day in 1856 and celebrated by building the enormous Melbourne Trades Hall in Carlton.

1880s and 1890s expansion

Melbourne's population reached 280,000 in 1880 and 490,000 in 1890. For a time it was the second-largest city in the British Empire, after London. In terms of area, Melbourne was already one of the largest cities in the world. Rather than building high-density apartment blocks like European cities, Melbourne expanded in all directions in the characteristic Australian suburban sprawl.

Lithograph of the building hosting the World's Fair of 1880 showing the rear wings which no longer exist.

The middle classes lived in detached villas on large blocks of land, while the working class lived in reasonably comfortable cottages in the northern and western suburbs, and older areas like Fitzroy and Collingwood became slums. Most of the new heavy industry was concentrated in the western suburbs. The wealthy built huge mansions beside the sea or in the picturesque Yarra Valley.

The new suburbs were serviced by networks of trains and trams which were among the largest and most modern in the world. Melbourne's civic pride was demonstrated by the huge edifice of the Royal Exhibition Building, built in 1880 to house the Melbourne International Exhibition.

In the 1880s the long boom culminated in a frenzy of speculation and rapid inflation of land prices known as the Land Boom. Governments shared in the wealth and ploughed money into urban infrastructure, particularly railways. Huge fortunes were built on speculation, and Victorian business and politics became notorious for corruption. English banks lent

The Federal Coffee Palace, a temperance hotel was the largest and tallest building in Melbourne - one of many built in 1888.

freely to colonial speculators, adding to the mountain of debt on which the boom was built.

1891 economic bust

In 1891 the inevitable happened: a spectacular crash brought the boom to an abrupt end. Banks and other businesses failed in large numbers, thousands of shareholders lost their money, tens of thousands of workers were put out of work. Although there are no reliable statistics, there was probably 20 percent unemployment in Melbourne throughout the 1890s.

A map dating to the 1880s shows the well-established suburbs of Melbourne.

Melbourne had 490,000 people in 1890, and this figure scarcely changed for the next 15 years as a result of the crash and subsequent long slump. Immigration dried up, emigration to the goldfields of Western Australia and South Africa increased, and the high birthrate of the mid 19th century fell sharply and the city's growth continued, but very slowly.

Australia's capital: 1901-1927

Melbourne's status as Australia's largest city lasted long enough, however, for it to become the seat of government of the new Commonwealth of Australia when the six colonies federated in 1901. Parliament House in Spring St was lent to the Parliament of Australia, while Victoria's Parliament found temporary accommodation in the Royal Exhibition Building.

The city's growth stalled, and by 1905 Sydney had resumed its place as Australia's largest city.

Not until about 1910 did economic growth resume, and Melbourne's population reached 670,000 by 1914. But the boom years did not return, and the level of wages remained far lower than it had been in the 1880s. As a result urban poverty became a feature of city life, and the slum areas of the inner industrial suburbs spread.

Due to long delays in establishing permanent capital at Canberra, Melbourne remained Australia's capital until 1927. This had important long-term consequences. Melbourne became the centre of the Commonwealth Public Service, the Australian Defence Forces, the diplomatic corps (very small until World War II), and also to a large extent of the legal profession, all of which reinforced the supremacy of Melbourne University and exclusive schools such as Scotch College, Melbourne Grammar School and Xavier College.

Although Sydney gradually surpassed Melbourne as a financial centre, Melbourne retained its intellectual and cultural dominance.

Interwar period

Melbourne's mood was also darkened by the terrible sacrifices of World War I, in which 112,000 Victorians enlisted and 16,000 were killed. There were bitter political divisions during the war, with Melbourne's Irish-born Catholic Archbishop Daniel Mannix leading opposition to conscription for the war and the Labor Party suffering a traumatic split. Another 4,000 Victorians died in the Spanish flu epidemic which followed the war. There was a modest revival of prosperity in the 1920s, and the population reached 1 million in 1930, but in 1929 the Wall Street Crash ushered in another Depression, which lasted until World War II.

Flinders Street Station, intersection of Swanston and Flinders Streets in 1927 when it was the world's busiest passenger station.

During these years Melbourne acquired another great landmark, the Shrine of Remembrance in St Kilda Road, largely built by unemployed workers during the Depression. The population stagnated again, and was still only 1.1 million in 1940.

World War two

Main articles: Australian home front during World War II, and Military history of Australia during World War II

Melbourne and the Yarra in 1928.

During World War II, although Canberra was officially the capital, most of the military and civilian administration was centered in Melbourne, and the city's economy benefited from wartime full employment and the influx of American service personnel (including General Douglas MacArthur, who made his headquarters in Collins St).

Organised crime was rife, with gang fights in the streets of Collingwood and underworld figures like Squizzy Taylor legendary. The Labor Party was much less successful in Melbourne than it was in Sydney and other Australian cities. Labor did not form a majority government in Victoria until 1952.

Post World War Two

After World War II, a new era of increasing prosperity arrived, fuelled by high prices for Victoria's wool, increased government spending on transport and education, and the stimulus of renewed high immigration. Unlike prewar immigration, which had been mostly from the British Isles, the postwar program brought an influx of Europeans, at first mostly refugees from eastern and central Europe. A large proportion of these immigrants were Jews, and the Jewish population of Melbourne became the largest population proportionally of any Australian city, at about 1.4% in 1970. [2] They were followed by migrants from Italy, Greece and the Netherlands.

Swanston Street from Princes Bridge in 1959

Later, in the 1960s, migrants came from Yugoslavia, Turkey and Lebanon. These inflows rapidly transformed the city's demographic profile and many aspects of its life. This new growth required new spending on infrastructure such as roads, schools and hospitals, which had been neglected during the long decades of recession and low growth between 1890 and 1940. Henry Bolte, Premier from 1955 to 1972, was responsible for much of this rapid development of infrastructure. Under Bolte, some of the old inner-city slums were bulldozed and the dislocated tenants were housed in high-rise blocks of state-owned apartments.

Since the 1970s, the pace of change in Melbourne has been increasingly rapid. The end of the White Australia Policy brought the first significant Asian migration to Melbourne since the gold rushes, with large numbers of people from Vietnam, Cambodia and China arriving. For the first time, Melbourne acquired a large Muslim population, and the official policy of multiculturalism encouraged Melbourne's various ethnic and religious minorities to maintain and celebrate their identities. At the same time, the practice of mainstream Christianity largely declined, leading to a secularisation of public life.

ICI House, commenced in 1955, was a powerful symbol of the Olympic city's modern aspirations.

State patronage of the arts led to a boom in festivals, theatre, music and the visual arts. Tourism became a major industry, bringing still more foreign faces to Melbourne's streets. Two new universities opened, Monash University in 1961 and La Trobe University in 1967, followed by others in the 1980s, maintaining Melbourne's place as a leader in tertiary education.

By the end of the 20th century Melbourne had 3.8 million people. The urban sprawl spread from Werribee in the south-west to Healesville in the north-east and encompassing the whole of the Mornington Peninsula and Dandenong Ranges to the south and east. A program of freeway construction was fast tracked in the 1970s and 1980s, while the expansion of rail and tram networks were neglected. These factors led to the rapid growth of the number and use of private cars.

Partly as a result of the increasing difficulty of traveling across the city, the central business centre declined, and satellite suburbs such as Frankston, Dandenong and Ringwood, and further out Melton, Sunbury and Werribee, became centres of manufacturing, retailing and administration. As a result, industrial employment in the old working class inner suburbs declined, with these areas rapidly gentrifying in the 1990s and 2000s.

1989 financial crash

These trends, along with cyclical recession and poor governance contributed to a financial crash in 1989, leading to the forced sale of one of Victoria's best-known symbols, the State Bank of Victoria. This was followed by a deep recession. Melbourne's population growth slowed during the early 1990s as employment contracted, with a rise in migration to other states such as Queensland.

In turn this recession contributed to the fall of Joan Kirner's Labor government and the election in 1992 of a radical free-market Liberal government under Jeff Kennett. Kennett's team restored Victoria's finances by making sweeping cuts to public expenditure, closing many schools, privatising the tramways and electricity production, and reducing the size of the public service. These reforms came at a high social cost, but ultimately restored confidence in Melbourne's economy and led to a resumption of growth. By 1999 Kennett was voted out, but key landmarks that his government commissioned, such as the Crown Casino, the Melbourne Exhibition and Convention Centre and the new Melbourne Museum, remain.

2000s

In the early years of the 21st century, Melbourne entered a new period of high economic and population growth under the more cautious Labor government of Steve Bracks, which restored public expenditure on health and education. As the city's suburbs continued to sprawl outwards, the Bracks government sought to restrict new suburban growth to designated growth corridors and encourage higher-density apartment living in the city's main transport hubs.

A view of the Yarra River at twilight, with Melbourne's central business district on the left and Southbank on the right

The city's Central Business District experienced a major resurgence in the 2000s, aided by a large increase in inner-city apartment living, the opening of new public spaces such as Federation Square and the new Southern Cross railway station, a determined marketing campaign by Lord Mayor John So's City Council and continuing development of the Southbank and Docklands precincts.

Since the late 2000s, population growth in Melbourne has been accelerating. Since the early 20th century, the city has been expanding outwards with low-density suburban urban forms to accommodate population growth. As this urban form is unsustainable, many sustainable alternatives have been proposed and implemented into policy to limit suburban sprawl, create transit-oriented urban environments and affordable housing and rent. However, in 2009 the Victorian Government announced plans to extend the city's urban growth boundary, potentially rezoning green wedges and agricultural land for housing development.

Since 1997, Melbourne has maintained significant population and employment growth. There has been substantial international investment in the city's industries and property market. Major inner-city urban renewal has occurred in areas such as Southbank, Port Melbourne, Melbourne Docklands and more recently, South Wharf. According to the Australian Bureau of Statistics, Melbourne sustained the highest population increase and economic growth rate of any Australian capital city in the three years ended June 2004. The city survived the Global Financial Crisis better than any other

Melbourne's CBD from Docklands at twilight

Australian city, adding more jobs in 2009 than any other Australian city, almost as much as Brisbane and Perth combined, the 2nd and 3rd fastest growing cities.

These factors combined has led to yet further suburban expansion through the 2000s into Green Wedges and beyond Urban Growth Boundaries, to accommodate the large population growth. Melbourne's property market is currently in a bubble, with property largely expensive and unaffordable, and widespread rent increases. The most recent generation of Melburnians are expected to see a sharp decline in housing and property ownership in line with unaffordability.

Despite lack of a progressive economy, general lack of government funding for public services such as public transport, and continued unsustainable urban growth, the city has seen sustained growth in its cultural institutions such as art, music, literature, performance, etc, as many contributors to and patrons of the arts relocate to Melbourne amongst excellent independent community support structures such as press and radio and a thriving cultural community. In 2003, Melbourne was named as a UNESCO City of Literature and the city hosts the majority of Australia's contemporary festivals, events and institutions, new galleries, music venues, museums, of all shapes and sizes are opening across the city. In February 2010, *The Transition Decade*, an initiative to transition human society, economics and environment towards sustainability, was launched in Melbourne.

See also

- History of Victoria
- Melbourne
- Melbourne population growth

External links

- Local History of the city of Melbourne [3]
- http://www.whitehat.com.au
- http://www.museum.vic.gov.au
- http://www.enterprize.org.au

Cityscape

Melbourne City Centre

Melbourne	
Melbourne, Victoria	
Aerial view of the Melbourne CBD	
Population:	20,360 (suburb)
Established:	1835
Postcode:	3000, 3004, 3006
Location:	• 35 km (22 mi) from Belgrave • 29 km (18 mi) from Dandenong • 18 km (11 mi) from Glen Waverley
LGA:	• Melbourne • Port Phillip
State District:	Melbourne
Federal Division:	Melbourne

Suburbs around Melbourne:		
North Melbourne	Carlton	Fitzroy
Docklands	**Melbourne**	East Melbourne
St Kilda	South Melbourne	South Yarra

Melbourne City Centre is the common name for the central locality (suburb) (officially known simply as "Melbourne") within Greater Melbourne metropolitan area (the capital city of the state of Victoria, Australia of which "Melbourne" is also the common name) that also forms the majority an area known as the **Capital City Zone** (known as the "Central Business District" (CBD) or "Central Activities District" (CAD)) .

It is the administrative centre of the City of Melbourne Local Government Area and a major administrative centre (along with East Melbourne) for the State government of Victoria.

Its area consists of the original settlement is known as the Hoddle Grid - a one mile long (1.6 km) by half mile wide (0.80 km) grid of streets and lane ways, located on the northern bank of the Yarra River (approx 10 km upstream from the river estuary) and several adjoining areas stretching south along St Kilda Road.

The Central Activities District, of which the Melbourne City Centre is a part includes the Hoddle Grid, as well as some bordering areas such as Melbourne Docklands and Southbank. Major cultural icons include Federation Square, the State Library of Victoria, Melbourne Immigration Museum, and St Pauls Cathedral and Chinatown and the Queen Victoria Market.

It is also a major financial hub being the corporate headquarters of two of the world's largest mining companies: BHP Billiton and Rio Tinto, two largest gaming companies: Crown and Tabcorp, largest communications company: Telstra, largest transport company: Toll, and the iconic brewery: Foster's. Two of Australia's "big four" banks: ANZ and NAB are headquartered nearby at Docklands. It is currently home to five of the ten tallest buildings in Australia (Eureka Tower is located nearby in Southbank).

It has played host to a number of significant single national and international events, which include: the first sitting of the Parliament of Australia in 1901, 1956 Summer Olympics, Commonwealth Heads of Government Meeting in 1981, World Economic Forum in 2000, 2006 Commonwealth Games and 2006 G20 Ministerial Meeting. The city centre is also renowned for hosting a large number of annual events, many being the biggest in Australia and the World.

It is notable for its distinct blend of contemporary and Victorian architecture, expansive parks and gardens, alleyway and arcade culture It is also the starting point of Melbourne's metropolitan rail and Victoria's regional rail networks (at Flinders Street and Southern Cross stations respectively), and the most dense section of Melbourne's tram network — which is the largest in the World.

History

Further information: History of Melbourne

Melbourne's central grid patterned layout, known as the Hoddle grid, was first laid out in 1837. From the 1870s to 1920s, the central part of Melbourne was home to mostly medical professionals who had established practices along Collins Street and Spring Street and before the 1960s, only a handful of permanent residents lived in the Spring Street area and St Kilda Road. The area was largely unpopular for residents and council policies did not permit development of apartment style housing in the area.

St Kilda Road was annexed in the 1960s and given the postcode of Melbourne 3004 to stimulate office development along the strip and reduce pressure on overdevelopment of the Hoddle Grid. The result was the demolition of many of the street's grand mansions.

Things changed somewhat due to the Kennett government's Postcode 3000 planning policy in the 1990s, which provided incentives for living in the central area.

Although the city centre now includes St Kilda Road, it competes for office space with Southbank, Docklands and the major outer suburban centres such as Box Hill, Glen Waverley, Ringwood, Belgrave, Ferntree Gully and increasingly South Yarra.

Geography

Officially, the city centre is bordered by Spencer Street to the west and extends north as far as Grattan Street which borders Carlton. The border extends along La Trobe Street, William Street, Peel Street, Grattan Street, taking in the Queen Victoria Market, Berkeley Street, Victoria Street. To the east it is bordered by Spring Street, however the area extends east to take in parts of Wellington Parade, Brunton Avenue, Punt Road and the Yarra River. It borders South Yarra to the south east at Anderson Street, Domain Road, Domain Street, Arnold Street, Fawkner Park, Commercial Road, High Street. It also borders both St Kilda along St Kilda Road and Albert Park along Queens Road, Lakeside Drive and South Melbourne along Albert Road, Kings Way, Palmerston Crescent, Wells Place and finally Southbank along St Kilda Road and the south side of Flinders Street (Northbank) which includes Flinders Street Station and the Melbourne Aquarium.

Map of Melbourne City Centre (with some inner suburbs)

Although these are the borders on official maps, there are several adjoining areas that function as part of the Central Activities District. This includes Melbourne Docklands (with Docklands Stadium), Southbank, Victoria and East Melbourne/Jolimont (with the Melbourne Cricket Ground).

Although the area is described as the *centre*, it is neither the geographic or demographic centre of Melbourne, due to an urban sprawl to the south east; the geographic centre is currently located at Bourne St, Glen Iris.

Demographics

Central Melbourne has one of the fastest growing residential populations in Australia. Residents of the city centre are of mixed social status. On one hand, living in the centre of the city offers proximity to work and the best access to public transport. On the other hand, there are many strata titled studio apartments that have no carparks and limited space. As a result there is a mix of students and young urban professionals living in the locality of Melbourne.

Transport

The Melbourne City Centre is the transport hub of the city.

Despite a wide range of public transport options, the automobile still remains the primary method of getting around in the Melbourne City Centre. The main arterial is Kings Street There are major taxi termini in the CBD.

Flinders Street Station

The city is serviced by five railway stations as part of the Melbourne Underground Rail Loop: Flinders Street (the busiest), Southern Cross Station (the hub of the regional network in Spencer Street at Melbourne Docklands) also an interstate terminal and three underground stations - Parliament, Melbourne Central and Flagstaff (not open on weekends) stations. Flinders Street Station is also the hub for Melbourne's suburban train network.

Trams run down the main streets Flinders, Collins, Bourke and Latrobe as well as Spencer Street, Market Street, Elizabeth Street, Swanston Street, Spring Street, Swan Street and St Kilda Road. There are several large accessibility tram superstops located in Flinders Street, Collins Street, Swanston Street and Bourke Street mall.

Trams on Spencer Street

The city is also well connected by bus services, with majority of buses running down Lonsdale street. Major bus stops include Melbourne Central and QV. Most bus routes service suburbs north and east of the city given the lack of train lines to these areas.

Major bicycle trails lead to the CBD and a main bicycle path down Swanston Street.

Ferries dock along the northbank of the Yarra at Federation Wharf and the turning basin at the Aquatic Centre. There is also a water taxi service to Melbourne and Olympic Parks.

Culture and sport

3 major buildings of Melbourne Park: 1.
Melbourne Cricket Ground (MCG) 2. Rod Laver
Arena (Australian tennis stadium) 3. Vodafone
Arena (sports & entertainment venue)

Most professional sporting clubs represent Greater Melbourne (e.g. Melbourne Victory, Melbourne Storm). An exception is the Melbourne Cricket Club and Melbourne Football Club (its offshoot) both based at the Melbourne Cricket Ground which was built in Jolimont, adjacent to the city but a locality of the suburb of East Melbourne. Both were the first clubs of their respective sports and established in a time when the city's population was still very small and limited to a handful of inner suburbs. As a result, the Melbourne Cricket Club has a fairly exclusive membership, whilst the Melbourne Football Club, although bearing the name Melbourne, is associated by the supporters of other suburban clubs as representing the central suburb and perceive its supporters to represent the locality and not the entire city. As a result, despite its rich tradition and early success, it is one of the least supported clubs in the VFL/AFL. The lack of identity resulted in a push for the Melbourne Hawks, which was stopped by intervention from Joseph Gutnick and the majority of the Hawthorn Football Club members. It has had intense rivalries with younger clubs from the adjacent inner suburbs such as the Collingwood Football Club and early inter-town rival Geelong Football Club. The Melbourne Football Club has recently made efforts to shed its suburban tag and be embraced by the whole metropolitan area. In line with this, the club recently employed strategies such as establishing *Team Melbourne*, (a group of sporting teams which bear the name "Melbourne"), and a strategy for promoting the brand as representing the city in China through club supporter and former Lord Mayor John So.

Golf is played at the course of the Albert Park Golf Club on Queens Road.

External links

- Local history of Melbourne CBD [3]
- Melbourne City Centre is at coordinates 37°49′05″S 144°58′34″E

Hoddle Grid

A ~180 degree panoramic image of the eastern side of Melbourne's Hoddle Grid, the original CBD (or "the city"), and the new CBD area of Southbank, on the right side. Photographed from the Rialto Observation Deck

The **Hoddle Grid** is the layout of the streets in the centre of the central business district of Melbourne. Named after its designer, Robert Hoddle, the Grid was laid out in 1837, and later extended. It covers the area from Flinders Street to Queen Victoria Market, and from Spencer Street to Spring Street.

Schematic plan of Hoddle's allotments for the village of Melbourne, March, 1837

History

While the survey plan has proved, in time, to be far-sighted for public utility, serving Melbourne to this day, at the time Hoddle's instructions from Governor Gipps were more prosaic.

Land allotments for sale at public auction were to be produced as quickly as possible to deliver to the market. Gipps also insisted that all towns laid out during his term of office should have no public squares included within their boundaries, being convinced that they only encouraged democracy.

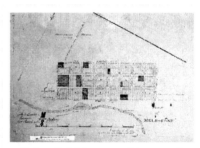

Robert Hoddle's survey of the town of Melbourne in 1837.

The grid was defined largely by the geography of the area. It was planned to span a gently sloping valley between small hills (knolls) (Batman's Hill, Flagstaff Hill and Eastern Hill) and roughly parallel to the course of the Yarra River. Elizabeth Street, Melbourne in the centre of the grid was built over a gully and has therefore been prone to flooding.

Trees surrounded by buildings - King St. Melbourne

The wide main streets were also to accommodate the large number of bullock carts that would ride through the centre of town preventing them from holding up horse drawn traffic when making right turns.

In the 1860s, surveys extended the district, incorporating the region of similarly laid out streets bounded by Victoria Street, Dudley Street and the Queen Victoria Market.

Specifications

See also: Lanes and Arcades of Melbourne

All major streets are one and half chains (99 ft or 30 m) in width, while all blocks are exactly 10 chains square (10 acres, 201 m × 201 m). It is one mile (1.6 km) long by half a mile wide (0.80 km). The grid's longest axis is oriented 70 degrees clockwise from true north, to align better with the course of the Yarra River. The majority of Melbourne is oriented at 8 degrees clockwise from true north - noting that magnetic north was 8° 3' E in 1900, increasing to 11° 42' E in 2009.

North-south streets

Parallel to the Yarra River:

- Flinders Street *(southernmost)*
- Flinders Lane[1]
- Collins Street
- Little Collins Street[2]
- Bourke Street, incorporating Bourke Street Mall
- Little Bourke Street[3]
- Lonsdale Street
- Little Lonsdale Street[4]
- La Trobe Street (also written Latrobe) *(northernmost)*

[1] One-way westbound, except two-way between Market and Spencer Streets

[2] One-way westbound, except two-way between King and Spencer Streets

[3] One-way westbound

[4] One-way eastbound

East-west streets

Perpendicular to the Yarra River:

- Spring Street *(easternmost)*
- Exhibition Street
- Russell Street
- Swanston Street
- Elizabeth Street
- Queen Street
- Market Street[1]
- William Street
- King Street
- Spencer Street *(westernmost)*

[1] Runs only between Flinders and Collins Streets, and is the single major deviation from the Grid.

Docklands, Victoria

Docklands

Melbourne, Victoria

View toward Docklands from high above the Melbourne CBD in 2008. From left to right - Batmans Hill & Southern Cross Station; Victoria Harbour; Stadium Precinct; New Quay; Waterfront City; Digital Harbour

Population:	3939 (2006)
Established:	2000
Postcode:	3008
Area:	3 km² (1.2 sq mi)
Location:	2 km (1 mi) from Melbourne CBD
LGA:	City of Melbourne
State District:	Melbourne
Federal Division:	Melbourne

Suburbs around Docklands:		
Footscray	West Melbourne	North Melbourne
Yarraville	**Docklands**	Melbourne
Port Melbourne	Port Melbourne	Southbank

Docklands (also known as **Melbourne Docklands** to differentiate it from London Docklands) is an inner city suburb in Melbourne, Victoria, Australia occupying an area extending up to 2 km west of and adjacent to Melbourne's Central Business District (CBD). Its Local Government Area is the City of Melbourne. Demographically, Docklands has a population, according to the 2006 Census, of 3,939.

Docklands is bounded by Spencer Street, Wurundjeri Way and Charles Grimes Bridge to the east, CityLink to the west and Lorimer Street across the Yarra to the south.

Docklands is a primarily waterfront area centred around the banks of the Yarra River. The area is the product of an ongoing urban renewal project to extend the area of the CBD (excluding Southbank and St Kilda Road) by over a third when completed around 2015.

Docklands includes the Melbourne landmarks Etihad Stadium, Southern Cross Station and The Southern Star Ferris wheel.

From the 1880s, the Docklands were used for docks, rail infrastructure and industry but mostly fell out of use following the containerisation of shipping traffic. The space remained vacant and unused during the 1980s and it fell in to disrepair. Docklands became notable during the 1990s for its underground rave dance scene, a dance culture which survives through popular organised events held at Docklands Stadium.

The stadium (then known as Colonial Stadium) in 1996 was built as a centrepiece to kick-start developer interest in Docklands as a viable renewal area. Urban renewal began in earnest 2000 as a collection of several independent but themed developments with staged development milestones. The project was tendered out and overseen by VicUrban, an agency of the State government of Victoria. The brief for the master plan was for wide open water promenades and road boulevards with contributions of landscaping and public art commissions to be made by each developer. VicUrban promotes its vision of Docklands as being a major tourist attraction with projections of over 20 million visitors a year and having a future (2015) residential population of over 20,000.

Despite being almost completely redeveloped, Docklands does retain a handful of significant heritage buildings mostly related to the area's industrial and maritime history. Most of the heritage buildings remaining on the site have been redeveloped and integrated into the development or will be in future.

Docklands has become a sought-after business address, attracting the national headquarters of National Australia Bank, ANZ, Medibank Private, Bureau of Meteorology, Myer, National Foods as well as the regional headquarters for AXA Asia Pacific, Ericsson and Bendigo Bank. The Business Park model of large low-rise campus -style office buildings combined with transport and proximity to city centre is seen by many in the real estate industry to be one of the reasons behind the success of the Docklands office market.

While still incomplete, Docklands developer-centric planning has been widely criticised and many Melbourne politicians and media commentators lament its lack of green open space, pedestrian activity, transport links and culture.

History

Before the Foundation of Melbourne, Docklands was a wetlands area consisting of a large salt lake (on the current site of Victoria Harbour) and a giant swamp (known as West Melbourne Swamp) the at the mouth of Moonee Ponds Creek. It was one of the open hunting grounds of the Wurundjeri people who created middens around the edges of the lake.

At Melbourne's foundation, John Batman set up his home on Batman's Hill at Docklands, marking the westernmost point of the settlement. However the rest of Docklands remained largely unused for decades.

The advent of rail infrastructure in the late 1860s saw the city's industry gradually expand into the Docklands area.

The earliest plans to redevelop Docklands came in the 1870s when a plan was prepared to extend the Hoddle Grid westward , following the curve of the Yarra River effectively doubling its size. The plan included several gridlike blocks with an ornamental garden and lake in the shape of the United Kingdom to occupy the site of the salt lake.

However the proposal was abandoned in favour of extending the city northward and a major engineering project began in the 1880s to reroute the course of the Yarra River and this resulted in the widening of the river for shipping and the creation of Victoria Docks. Light industry grew to surround the western rail yards of Spencer Street railway station (Now Southern Cross railway station.)

By the 1920s, with shipping moved from the Yarra turning basin at Queensbridge, Docklands had become the busiest port of the city.

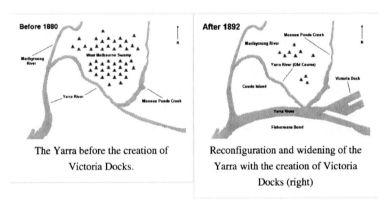

The Yarra before the creation of Victoria Docks.

Reconfiguration and widening of the Yarra with the creation of Victoria Docks (right)

Disuse

With the introduction of containerisation in the shipping industry, the docks along the Yarra River east of the modern Bolte Bridge, and within Victoria Harbour immediately to the west of the central business district, became inadequate for the new container ships. The principal docking area shifted closer to the mouth of the Yarra, creating a vast amount of vacant inner-city land.

Early renewal proposals

Docklands was seen as a large urban blight by the Cain state government. Property consultants JLW Advisory carried out a market demand assessment of the site in the mid 1980s.[citation needed]

The size of the Melbourne Docklands area meant that political influences were unescapable. The Docklands project was on top of the government's agenda, however, due to the poor condition of the wharf infrastructure, much investment was required to initiate the project which the government at the time could not afford. Nevertheless, the Docklands project stayed on the drawing board, but with little progress.[citation needed] In 1990, the Docklands Task Force was established to devise an infrastructure strategy and conduct the public consultation process. The Committee For Melbourne, a not for profit organisation that brought together the private sector of Melbourne for a public good, was pursuing another planning strategy. It involved a bid for the Olympic Games and another proposal to turn the Docklands into a technology city known as the Multifunction Polis (MFP). Both bids fell through in late 1990. Nevertheless, the Committee For Melbourne's approach became the preferred model in the proceeding strategies for the Docklands development, leading to the formation of the Docklands Authority in July 1991.

Kennett Era - wheels set in motion

With a government running in budget deficits, not much progress was made on the Docklands project. In Late 1992, Jeff Kennett was elected Premier. Kennett instituted many changes and turned the government's financial position around. He then embarked on a multitude of projects, which included Docklands. It was politically imperative to get the project rolling, the Docklands Authority opted for the concept of having leaving all design and funding of infrastructure to the developers. The development industry supported this, and claimed that the project would be more efficient. May 1996 saw the relaunch of the tender process. Few restrictions were applied to the bids from developers, and as the vision was to make Docklands 'Melbourne's Millennium Mark', the key criterion for a successful bid was to get projects going by 2000. It did not take long for the realisation that the lack of government coordination in infrastructure planning would create problems. Developers would not invest into public infrastructure where benefits would flow on to an adjacent property. This was corrected by allowing developers to negotiate for infrastructure funding with the government. The Docklands Village precinct was planned for a residential and commercial mixed development, but in late 1996 that plan was scrapped when it was announced a private football stadium would be built on the site. The site was chosen for its easy access to the then Spencer Street Station (now Southern Cross Station), and it was intended to be an anchor for the entire project and provide for a clear signal to the long awaited start of the Docklands project. However, this would create a huge barrier between the city and Docklands.

In 1989 several architectural firms were invited to discuss how the area could best serve the Melbourne public.

The commission to design the overall plan was granted to Ashton Raggatt McDougall by the Docklands Authority.

During 1998 and 1999, with the exception of Yarra Waters (Yarra's Edge) bid by Mirvac, bid for every other precinct fell through, the reasons are often unclear due to secrecy provisions. The Kennett government at the same time was voted out.

Docklands rave history

Docklands became notable during the 1990s for its underground rave dance scene.

The site was host to a number of dance parties hosted by Future Entertainment and Hardware Corporation during the 1990s.[citation needed] DJs and performers such as Paul van Dyk, Carl Cox, Jeff Mills, Frankie Knuckles, David Morales, Marshall Jefferson and BT headlined these events. The biggest event hosted, in terms of attendance, was the "Welcome 2000" New Year's Eve dance party hosted on December 31, 1999.[citation needed]

The dance tradition has continued through events such as Earthdance and Sensation held in 2008 at Etihad Stadium.

Tendering Process

The independent developments put out to tender out by the State Government and overseen by the Docklands Authority (then Vic Urban), a division of the State government in 2000.

Through the tendering process for the sites, Business Park was split once more and awarded to two consortia, becoming Entertainment City (renamed Paramount Studios) - a movie theme park with film studios, to be developed by a Viacom led consortium, and Yarra Nova (which later evolved into NewQuay) to the MAB Corporation consortium. The Paramount Studios proposal fell through, and the site was put to tender once more, as Studio City, and later awarded as two parts, becoming what is now the Central City Studios and Waterfront City.

Yarra Waters/Yarra Quays was awarded to Mirvac later becoming Yarra's Edge, while Technology Park was renamed Commonwealth Technology Port before finally becoming Digital Harbour.

A number of other sites also encountered false starts, with Victoria Harbour originally being awarded to Walker Corporation, before being put out to tender again and finally being awarded to Lend Lease in April 2001. Batman's Hill was originally awarded to Bruno Grollo's Grocon, which had plans for what would have been the world's tallest building rising 560 m, dubbed Grollo Tower and featuring a mix of office, apartment, hotel and retail. This deal also fell through with the site being subdivided into 15 parcels as well as Rail Goods Shed No.2:

- Site 1/753 Bourke Street - awarded to Pan Urban.
- Site 2a/737 Bourke Street - Equiset.
- Site 2b/750 Collins Street - Grocon.

- Goods Shed North/733 Bourke Street - Equiset/Pan Urban JV.
- Site 3a/700 Collins Street - Leighton Holdings.
- Site 3b/717 Bourke Street - Global Campus Management/Babcock & Brown.
- Goods Shed South/735 Collins Street/Village Docklands -Kuok Group/Walker Corp JV.
- Site 4a/Village Docklands - Kuok Group/Walker Corp JV.
- Site 4b/Village Docklands - Kuok Group/Walker Corp JV.
- Site 4c/Village Docklands - Kuok Group/Walker Corp JV.
- Site 4d/Village Docklands - Kuok Group/Walker Corp JV.
- Site 4e/Village Docklands - Kuok Group/Walker Corp JV.
- Site 4f/Village Docklands - Kuok Group/Walker Corp JV.
- Site 5a - Kangan Batman TAFE.
- Site 5b - Under negotiation, Sama Dubai.
- Site 6 - Under negotiation, Sama Dubai.
- Site 7/643 Collins Street - Grocon.

The Stadium Precinct was divided into four corner blocks:

- North West Stadium Precinct (NWSP) - Channel 7/Pacific Holdings.
- North East Stadium Precinct (NESP) -Pan Urban.
- South West Stadium Precinct (SWSP) - Devine Limited/RIA Property Group.
- South East Stadium Precinct (SESP) - Bourke Junction Consortium

City of Melbourne - gradual handover

On July 1, 2007 Docklands became part of the City of Melbourne local government authority however VicUrban retains planning authority until 2010.

Heritage

Significant heritage buildings include 67 Spencer Street, former railway offices (adaptively reused as the "Grand Hotel" apartments), the railway goods sheds (adaptively reused as an indoor market), The Mission to Seafarers building, Victoria Dock and Central Pier, Queens Warehouse (adaptively reused as a vintage car museum), Docklands park shipping crane and a small number of warehouses and container sheds.

Districts

The area is broken up into a number of precincts, which are each being designed and built by a different development company.

Batman's Hill

The **Batman's Hill** precinct is adjacent to the western edge of the city and bordered by the Yarra River to the south, Spencer Street to the east, Etihad Stadium to the north and Victoria Harbour to the west. The precinct is named after the historical landmark Batman's Hill, which was once situated within the area.

Batman's Hill is a mixed-use precinct including commercial and retail space, entertainment, hotels, residential sections, restaurants, cultural sites and educational institutions as well as the historic Rail Goods Shed No. 2, which was split in half to allow for the extension of Collins Street into Docklands, providing businesses with an address that is considered to be prestigious. The area is 100,000 square metres.

More than half the precinct is already built, committed or under construction, and includes the Watergate/Site One apartment and small office complex, 700 Collins Street (home to the Bureau of Meteorology and Medibank Private), 750 Collins Street (the headquarters of AXA Asia Pacific), Kangan Institute's Automotive Centre for Excellence (ACE) and the Fox Classic Car Museum. Currently under construction are 717 Bourke Street (consisting of a 294 room Travelodge Hotel and Esmod fashion and design college) and 737 Bourke Street (the new home of National Foods).

On August 2, 2007, it was reported that a $1.5 billion scheme had been earmarked for Collins Street by Middle Eastern investment company Sama Dubai, to be designed by architect Zaha Hadid and Melbourne firm Ashton Raggatt McDougall. The plan would consist of four buildings, including Docklands' tallest tower as well as civic spaces spanning two sites to be built on decking over Wurundjeri Way. The proposed tower will be between 50 to 60 storeys tall and would attract an eight-to-12-star energy rating. However, no formal announcement has been made by Vic Urban or the State Government.

Construction has also begun on the new offices of Fairfax Media at 643 Collins Street. The new building, to be known as Media House, will comprise 16,000 m^2 of office space accommodating 1,400 staff, on decking over railway lines opposite Southern Cross Station. The $110 million eight-storey facility has been designed by architects Bates Smart to achieve a 5-star Green Star rating, and will feature a news ticker, outdoor screen and grassy plaza. It is being developed by Grocon and is due to be completed in 2009.

Village Docklands

Village Docklands is a 3ha precinct, within the larger Batman's Hill area, being developed jointly by the Kuok Group and Walker Corporation. A masterplan prepared by Marchese + Partners in conjunction with Bligh Voller Nield architects was approved in early 2002, it included a 60 storey Shangri La hotel with a Collins Street address and a mix of commercial and residential towers, as well as the refurbishment of the southern half of Goods Shed No. 2 into a night market and food hall.

In mid 2007, a new, more commercially orientated masterplan was prepared by Bates Smart. In it a new 38 storey office tower replaces the Shangri La on Collins Street and the number of streets is reduced from four to three, replaced by pedestrian thoroughfares. Overall there will now be four office buildings, ranging in height from 155m (to roof) to 36 m and two residential towers, as well as a child care centre and the refurbishment of the Goods Shed with a 'lantern' structure addressing Collins Street. The entire precinct is aiming for a 6 Star Green Star rating.

On December 17, 2007, Walker Corporation launched the next phase of construction, beginning with demolition works and site preparation.

Stadium Precinct

The Stadium precinct, which sits on the eastern edge of Docklands, consists of Etihad Stadium, Seven Network's Melbourne Digital Broadcast Centre, Victoria Point apartments, Bendigo Bank offices, and Quest serviced apartments. It is linked to Southern Cross Station and the Melbourne CBD by the Bourke Street pedestrian bridge, built over railway lines.

Stadium precinct plaza and Harbour Esplanade

Etihad Stadium (originally Colonial Stadium) was opened in March 2000. The ability for the structure to have both open and closed roof configurations has seen it host many sports events, including Australian Rules Football, soccer, cricket and rugby as well as concerts.

The complex is managed by Stadium Operations Ltd, which is owned by the Seven Network, with ownership transferring to the Australian Football League in 2025.

Developer Pan Urban has announced plans for a $300 million twin-tower apartment development known as Lacrosse Docklands for the North East Stadium Precinct with the towers set to rise 21 and 18 storeys respectively, above the stadium concourse, with restaurants and bars opening out on to the concourse, forming a retail plaza.

A consortium made up of ISPT, CBUS Property and EPC Partners, has been awarded the rights for the South East Stadium Precinct. Plans for the site to be known as Bourke Junction include office towers of 29 and 21 storeys on the north-eastern and south-western corners of the site, as well as three lower-rise buildings housing a 250 room hotel, a pub, medical centre, retail facilities, a business club and a two-level gymnasium

Digital Harbour @ Comtechport Precinct

Digital Harbour is a waterfront has an area of 44,000 square metres, with development intended to expand to include 220,000 square metres of commercial, residential, SOHO units and retail space. At present only two buildings have been completed; 1010 LaTrobe Street/Port 1010 (home to VicTrack, Australian Customs Service), and the Innovation Building (home of the Telstra Learning Academy and Innovation Centre). A third building, Life.lab is currently under construction, while a fourth, 1000 LaTrobe Street, is expected to commence shortly.

Port 1010 received the Commercial Architecture Award at the 2007 Victorian Architecture Awards held on Friday 13 July.

Victoria Harbour

The **Victoria Harbour** Precinct is the centrepiece of Docklands. The precinct includes a proposed extension of Collins and Bourke Streets to meet at the water's edge. It has an area of 280,000 square metres with 3.7 kilometres of waterfront; the 12-year construction plans for Victoria Harbour include residential apartments, commercial office space, retail space, community facilities and the development of public spaces such as Grand Plaza, Harbour Esplanade, Docklands Park and Central Pier.

View toward Victoria Harbour National Australia Bank HQ (centre) Erricson building and Dock 5 tower (right) from the stadium terrace

One of the first completed office buildings in the precinct was the colourful National Australia Bank headquarters, located at 800 Bourke Street, which accommodates approximately 3,600 staff. The building features large, open flexible floor plates, sunny atria in the heart of the building, a campus-style workplace and a four-star energy rating.

Almost 1,000 Ericsson employees also call Victoria Harbour home, with the company's new Melbourne offices at 818 Bourke Street. Ericsson House sits on the water's edge next door to National Australia Bank HQ and Dock 5 apartments

The first residential tower to be built at Victoria Harbour was Dock 5. Rising 30 storeys, it was designed by award-winning Melbourne firm John Wardle Architects and HASSELL, derives its name from its location which was known as Dock 5.

The Gauge, at 825 Bourke Street will house the new offices of developer Lend Lease and Fujitsu. The eight-storey building was designed to achieve a six-star energy rating, becoming the second building in Docklands to do so.

A Safeway supermarket opened in Merchant Street (opposite The Gauge) in 2008 , along with a number of other retail tenancies at street level including an optometry practice called Kaleyedoscope, Australia Post, a childcare centre, and offices above.

In September 2006, plans were unveiled for ANZ's new world headquarters to be located at Victoria Harbour. The complex will feature a vast low rise office building, shops, car parking facilities and a YMCA. The new complex will enable 6500 ANZ staff to work in one integrated area, however ANZ will maintain its flagship building, 100 Queen Street Melbourne. The new ANZ headquarters designed by award-winning firm HASSELL, developed by Lend Lease, will be the largest office complex in Australia. Construction commenced in late 2006 with completion expected in 2009. The building will rise at 833 Collins Street, after the extension of Collins Street to meet Bourke Street is completed. It has been designed to achieve a six-star energy rating.

On Tuesday 7 August 2007, Myer announced that it had chosen Victoria Harbour as the location for its new Corporate Store Support Offices. The new offices are being built at 800 Collins Street opposite ANZ.

NewQuay

NewQuay, opened in 2002 was one of the first residential and commercial developments in Docklands. It currently has five residential towers and a podium building developed by MAB Corporation. Looking at the development from the water, the buildings are the Nolan, Arkley, Palladio, Sant'Elia, Boyd, and Conder.

View of New Quay from the Central Pier.
From the left the Nolan, Arkley, Palladio
and Boyd.

The flagship building Palladio - which is shaped like the prow of a ship - is named after Italian architect Andrea Palladio.The podium building, Sant'Elia is named after another Italian architect Antonio Sant'Elia. The rest are named after Australian artists: Sidney Nolan, Howard Arkley, Arthur Boyd, and Charles Conder.

Aquavista, completed in May 2007, is a strata office development and the first commercial building to be completed in NewQuay as part of the HQ NewQuay development. Another, the seven-storey 370 Docklands Drive is currently under construction with a further two buildings - Lots 5 & 9 - currently under design development.

On October 17, 2007, MAB Corporation launched 'The Avenues at NewQuay' development, comprising of three-storey townhouse residences, with park and waterfront frontages, to be built as part of NewQuay's western precinct. The development is being designed by Plus Architecture.

There is also harbourside dining at cafés in the precinct. The types of cuisines include Italian, Indian, Middle Eastern, Cantonese, Moroccan, Cambodian and Modern Australian.

Yarra's Edge

Yarra's Edge is a residential precinct, and the only Docklands precinct south of the Yarra River being developed by Mirvac. When complete, it will consist of 11 apartment towers, costing AU$1.3 billion, and cover 0.15 km^2.

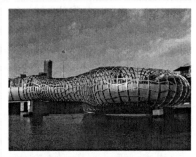

Webb Bridge from the Yarra's Edge marina

Yarra's Edge was one of the first developments in the Docklands, with construction of Tower 1 commencing in 2000. It is divided into 3 smaller precincts:

The Marina Precinct: Comprising the marina and boardwalk with six residential towers ranging in height from 25 to 47 storeys

The Park Precinct: Comprising Point Park and two residential towers

The River Precinct: Comprising a mix of lower level less, intense terrace-style developments and three high-rise towers towards the Bolte Bridge.

To date only five apartment towers have been completed as well as the RekDek (located in the podium of Tower 1 and featuring a gymnasium and 25 metre lap pool), a public promenade, Point Park (with an outlook towards the CBD) and mix of restaurants, cafes and retail including a day spa and convenience store. Yarra's Edge also has a 175-berth marina, giving boat owners previously unavailable proximity to Crown Casino and the city.

Webb Bridge is an award winning bridge designed by Denton Corker Marshall in collaboration with artist Robert Owen, forming a cycling and pedestrian link to the main part of Docklands through Docklands Park. It is the conversion of the former Webb Bridge rail link. The bridge is near the **Charles Grimes Bridge** over the Yarra.

Waterfront City

Waterfront City is a shopping and entertainment area that includes The Southern Star Ferris wheel, Icehouse ice sports and entertainment centre, and the Black Light Glow in the Dark Indoor Mini Gol Believed to be the first of its kind in Australia, shops and cafes will also be centred around this area.

The precinct on Victoria Harbour features an integration of retail, waterfront entertainment, tourism, dining, commercial and urban community. It has an area of 193,000 square metres.

Stage One was completed in December 2005 in time for the Melbourne Stopover of the Volvo Ocean Race in January – February 2006 and the Commonwealth Games in March 2006. The precinct currently features a large circus tent which hosts the International Circus Spectacular as well as mosaic of local entertainers and a number of bronze statues of including

Waterfront City and Southern Star wheel (in 2008 before disassembly)

John Farnham, Graham Kennedy, Kylie Minogue, Nellie Melba and Dame Edna.

Stage Two includes a public entertainment area incorporating The Southern Star, a 120-metre (390 ft) tall Ferris wheel in the shape of a seven-pointed star and a brand direct outlet centre, Harbour Town. Harbour Town is home to Australia's first Costco Warehouse Store. Waterfront City also features restaurants, cafes, bars as well as cinemas, bowling and other family entertainment options.

Docklands Studios Melbourne

See also: List of films shot in Melbourne

Opened in 2004, Docklands Studios Melbourne [1] is Melbourne's largest film and television studio complex. The site is located approximately 1.5 km from the city's Central Business District. It has an area of 60,000 square metres and currently consists of five film and television sound stages.

The first major contract for the new studios was the American film *Ghost Rider* in 2005; with a budget of nearly $120 million, at the time it was the biggest feature film to be made in Victoria and features scenes involving Melbourne landmarks. Since then the studios have housed international productions such as Spike Jonze's *Where The Wild Things Are*, *Knowing* with Nicolas Cage and The Pacific the companion to the mini series *Band of Brothers*. *Don't Be Afraid of the Dark* starring Katie Holmes and Guy Pearce is due for release in early 2011.

Television series that have been produced at the studios include *Project Runway* series 2, *Australia's Got Talent*, *Are You Smarter Than a 5th Grader?*, *Satisfaction* series 2 & 3. *Beat the Star (Australia)*,

Australia's Got Talent, *Iron Chef Australia* and *Winners & Losers* .

In 2010 feature films *The Eye of the Storm*, directed by Fred Schepisi and starring Geoffrey Rush, Judy Davis and Charlotte Rampling; and *Killer Elite*, starring Jason Statham, Clive Owen and Robert De Niro were housed by the studios.

In 2009 the Government of Victoria, together with the Studios, undertook the Future Directions project. This has resulted in the State Government committing the Studios to focus on both the international and domestic film and television industries. Further developments to the infrastructure of the site are planned for 2010, including a refurbishment of Stage 5 as a television studio and redevelopment to the workshop.[citation needed]

Long term plans for the Studios include a large sound stage, mess hall, workshop and retail spaces, production offices, and permanent commercial tenancies.[citation needed]

On 11 October 2010 the studios were re-branded as Docklands Studios Melbourne (formerly Melbourne Central City Studios), formally adopting the name by which the Studios were commonly known.[citation needed]

Transportation

Melbourne Docklands is serviced by car, rail, trams, bicycle and ferry.

Docklands Highway and Wurundjeri Way are the main roads going through Docklands. These connect to the nearby Westgate Freeway on the southern end. Links to the CBD include Flinders Street extension and La Trobe Street.

Docklands' Southern Cross Railway Station from Spencer Street in the Melbourne City Centre.

Docklands is serviced by Southern Cross Station to the far east. North Melbourne railway station is close by to the north of Docklands.

In 2003 the free City Circle Tram was rerouted through Docklands along Flinders Street, Harbour Esplanade and Latrobe Street, instead of running along Spencer Street. From May 2009 City Circle trams have run along Docklands Drive to and from Waterfront City. Tram route 70 was extended to Waterfront City in September 2009 when route 48 was rerouted to run along the newly-extended Collins Street to Victoria Harbour. Tram route 30 enters Docklands via Latrobe Street, terminating at the north end of Harbour Esplanade. Route 86 runs along Latrobe Street and Docklands Drive, terminating at Waterfront City.

Several offroad bicycle paths run through Docklands, all of which connect through the central spine of Webb Bridge, Docklands park and Harbour Esplanade, connecting Melbourne to the inner western suburbs and the Capital City Trail.

There are also three ferry terminals which connect Docklands to the CBD and inner bayside suburbs. One at Victoria Harbour, one at New Quay and one at Yarra's Edge.

Demographics and industry

Docklands residents are almost solely housed in high density housing.

In 2009, there were just under 10,000 working mostly in office and retail industries.

Notable residents

- Sam Newman
- Troy de Haas (athlete)

Local media

The precinct has two publications, Docklands Community News and 3008 Docklands Magazine.

The Docklands Community News' first edition was published in 2003, and both DCN & 3008 Docklands Magazine have grown with the Docklands precincts' population. Both publications are printed and distributed to all businesses and residences within Docklands, which allows for a regular readership of over 10,000. The DCN paper informs the community of relevant news relating to Docklands, also supplying residents, business owners and workers with a platform for community discussion.

3008 Docklands Magazine also covers all matters relating to the Docklands Community and businesses but also covers events and news pertaining to Melbourne City and the surrounding suburbs as Docklands is under the jurisdiction of the City of Melbourne. 3008 Docklands Magazine is a glossy, well produced, stylish publication which is both informative and interesting and has been well received by its reader base since its first issue back in May 2006. 3008 Docklands Magazine has a significant online following.

Panorama

Docklands as seen from Yarra's Edge at night in 2005

Critical response

The planning of Docklands has raised a large amount of public debate and the area has created significant controversy, particularly the failed Ferris wheel.

In 1999, Melbourne City Council Director of Projects criticised the disconnection of the precinct to the CBD, claiming that the lack of transport links, particularly pedestrian meant Docklands was "seriously flawed".

The problem was exacerbated in 2005, when the pedestrian link between Lonsdale Street and Docklands proposed in 2001 was cut from the final design design of Southern Cross Station development due to budget blowouts.

Sculpture group *Shoal Fly By* (2003) by Bellemo & Cat at Docklands

In 2006, Royce Millar of The Age referred to it as a "wasted opportunity.

In 2008, the City of Melbourne released a report which criticised Docklands lack of transport and wind tunnel effect, lack of green spaces and community facilites.

In 2009, Neil Mitchell wrote for The Age declaring Docklands as a planning "dud". The Lord Mayor Robert Doyle has been openly critical of Docklands, claiming in 2009 that it lacks any form of "social glue".

However despite the local criticism in 2009, Sydney travel writer Mal Chenu described Melbourne Docklands as "the envy of Sydneysiders"

In 2010, VicUrban's general manager David Young acknowledged that Harbour Esplanade "doesn't stack up". Kim Dovey, professor of architecture and design at the University of Melbourne added that Harbour Esplanade was "too big" and claimed that Docklands was "so badly done" that it required a "major rethink".

External links

- Docklands, Victoria is at coordinates 37°48′50″S 144°56′35″E
- Official website [2]
- 3008 Docklands Magazine Website [3]
- Docklands Community News [4]
- NewQuay website [5]
- Waterfront City website [6]
- Victoria Harbour website [7]
- Yarra's Edge website [8]
- Digital Harbour website [9]
- Victoria Online - Docklands Authority [10]
- Australian Places - Docklands [11]
- How public is your private? Article about Docklands by Martin Musiatowicz [12]

Southbank, Victoria

Southbank	
Melbourne, Victoria	
 The Southbank skyline and Princes Bridge viewed from Federation wharf on the opposite side of the Yarra River	
Population:	9364 (2006)
Established:	1990
Postcode:	3006
Area:	1.7 km² (0.7 sq mi)
Property Value:	AUD $411,250
Location:	1 km (1 mi) from Melbourne
LGA:	• City of Port Phillip • City of Melbourne
State District:	Albert Park
Federal Division:	Melbourne Ports

Suburbs around Southbank:		
Docklands	Melbourne	Melbourne
South Wharf	**Southbank**	Melbourne
South Melbourne	Albert Park	Melbourne

Southbank is a suburb in Melbourne, Victoria, Australia, on the south side of the Yarra River, opposite Melbourne's central business district. Its Local Government Area are the Cities of Melbourne and Port Phillip. At the 2006 Census, Southbank had a population of 9,364.

Bordered to the north by the Yarra River, and to the east by St Kilda Road, Southbank's southern and western borders are bounded by Dorcas Street, Kings Way, West Gate Freeway and Montague Street.

Southbank was formerly an industrial area and part of South Melbourne. It was transformed into a densely populated district of high rise apartment and office buildings beginning in the early 1990s as part of an urban renewal program. Though few buildings built before this time have been spared redevelopment, Southbank does retain some significant heritage including many buildings in the major cultural precinct at the St Kilda Road end and some warehouses and wharves towards the area now known as "South Wharf".

The central feature of Southbank is Southgate Arts and Leisure Precinct, a retail, eating, and entertainment precinct on the southern bank of the Yarra River. Southgate features the iconic sculpture *Ophelia* by Deborah Halpern, which is the big Y symbol (representing Melbourne) that stands at Bear Brass cafe. The entertainment precinct extends along the Yarra and includes Crown Casino. The suburb also includes an office precinct and a hi-density residential precinct which has many skyscrapers, the tallest of which is the Eureka Tower. The Queensbridge Precinct includes Queensbridge Square, a pedestrian plaza and meeting place.

Heritage

Despite being dominated by modern apartments and office towers Southbank has a number of significant heritage buildings existing Arts precinct on the eastern end and along St Kilda Road which includes Victorian Arts Centre and National Gallery of Victoria (1960s), parts of the Victorian College of the Arts campus as well as the Victoria Barracks and Malthouse Theatre. Rare pockets of heritage on the western side includes the James Bond Store (25-43 Southbank Boulevarde) built in 1888.

Promenade

Southbank promenade

The Southbank promenade, designed by architects Denton Corker Marshall, runs from Princes Bridge along to Queens Bridge street and Queens Bridge which also incorporates Queensbridge Square and continuing to the west of the Bridge is "Yarra Promenade", which runs underneath Kings Way and Kings Bridge to Clarendon Street, Spencer Street Bridge including Crown Entertainment Complex and promenade restaurants.

The Southbank art and craft market occurs on the promenade near the Arts Centre every Sunday. The promenade is also home to several buskers and a pavement chalk artists.

History

Before British settlement, the area now called South Melbourne was a series of low lying swamps inhabited by Aboriginal tribes.

From British settlement the area which is now Southbank consisted of some old factories, warehouses and wharves mostly built between the 1860s-1920s when the area was part of the first port of Melbourne. It had a few old bridges, the first being the first Princes Bridge and later the Sandridge Bridge which was formerly part of the Port Melbourne railway line from 1888 to 1987, and the Arts centre precinct which opened in the 1980s on a former parkland.

The suburb was the subject of urban renewal in the early 1990s aimed at stimulating development in a period when Melbourne was experiencing an economic downturn.

Denton Corker Marshall designed and oversaw the original Southbank Promenade in 1990 which paved the way for development of apartments.

Southgate, Sheraton towers and new tall office buildings for The Herald and Weekly Times Ltd and IBM were built along with an award winning pedestrian footbridge at about the same time in late 1992, and combined with a new Sunday arts and crafts market, attracted local and tourist visitors to the area. At the eastern end of the area is the Victorian Arts Centre.

Further buildings including the Esso headquarters were built between 1992 and 1995. Development expanded along the Yarra westward with the Melbourne Convention and Exhibition Centre ("Jeff's Shed") in 1996 and Crown Casino in 1997, stimulating the first residential towers. In 2001, the boutique "Melburnian" apartments, designed by Bates Smart were one of the first to be aimed at the owner occupier market and included the most expensive penthouse sold in Melbourne at the time. Clarendon Towers also attracted the owner occupiers. Beginning with Southbank Towers in 2001 and the Centurion in 2002, Central Equity began a swathe of apartment towers and at the same time the neighbouring Yarra's Edge precinct of the new Melbourne Docklands began to kick off.

The arts precinct was extended with the construction of the award winning buildings for the Australian Centre for Contemporary Art in 2002 and the Victorian College of the Arts school of drama. At around the same time a new headquarters for the State Emergency Service was built.

Central Equity continued construction of several blocks of apartment buildings on much of the Southbank land which it had acquired including Riverside Place, The Summit, Melbourne Tower and City Tower. Most of them are aimed at the rental market and managed by Melbourne Inner City Management (MICM) a division of Central Equity.

With a boom in apartment building and the success of the Melburnian, the areas closer to the river began to attract developers. The 91 floor Eureka Tower was begun in 2002, aimed at being the tallest residential tower in the world and was completed in 2006.

The Queensbridge Precinct began development in 2005 with Freshwater Place. A plaza linked to the north bank and Flinders Street Station via a pedestrian and cycle path developed from the Sandridge

Bridge. The formerly disused bridge was opened to the public on 12 March 2006, just in time for the 2006 Commonwealth Games. The Northbank promenade was completed later in 2006 to link the sections.

An increasing number of corporations began opening their offices in Southbank. PricewaterhouseCoopers relocated their office from Spring Street to Freshwater Place in 2005. Other names on the list include Fujitsu, and Foster's Group.

In May 2008 the Victorian Government created the new suburb place and name 'South Wharf', in the western end of Southbank (encompassing the Melbourne Exhibition and Convention Centre and Polly Woodside National Trust museum). South Wharf is home to several large apartment buildings, along with a completed convention centre, a hotel and a large shopping centre precinct. Southbank and South Wharf share the same postcode (3006).

Media

Southank features some radio & television studios owned by the Australian Broadcasting Corporation, The studios are serviced by shows like 774 ABC Melbourne, 621 ABC Radio National, ABC Classic FM 105.9, Triple J 107.5, & television programs such as Stateline VIC, ABC News Victoria, also with other programs such as Spicks & Specks, East of Everything, as well as entertainment, arts, documentaries & more. as well as international broadcasts Radio Australia & Australia Network.

Transport

A number of tram lines run through Southbank.

Although Southbank promenade forms part of the Capital City Bicycle Trail, the large number of pedestrians in the area means bicycle riding at high speed is hazardous; advisory signs have been posted to try to keep cyclists at speeds of 10 km/h or less.

Gallery

View from Southgate promenade across the Yarra River

Historic Victoria Barracks

Elisabeth Murdoch Building of the Victorian College of the Arts

PriceWaterHouseCoopers & Freshwater Place in Southbank

Eureka
Tower

Melbourne
Southbank

Southgate
Footbridge

The ACCA and the
Malthouse Theatre in the
Ngargee arts precinct

Malthouse Theartre
(Contemporary Australian
Theatre) & Plaza in
Southbank,

See also

- City of South Melbourne - the former local government area of which Southbank was a part.

External links

- Local history of Southbank [1]
- Denton Corker Marshall Official website [2]
- Southbank, Victoria is at coordinates 37°49′44″S 144°57′25″E

South Melbourne, Victoria

South Melbourne
Melbourne, Victoria

South Melbourne Town Hall

Population:	8790 (2006)
Established:	1840s
Postcode:	3205
Area:	2.5 km² (1.0 sq mi)
Property Value:	AUD $1,000,000
Location:	3 km (2 mi) from Melbourne
LGA:	City of Port Phillip
State District:	Albert Park
Federal Division:	Melbourne Ports

Suburbs around South Melbourne:		
Docklands	Southbank	Southbank
Port Melbourne	**South Melbourne**	Melbourne
Albert Park	Albert Park	Melbourne

South Melbourne is a suburb in Melbourne, Victoria, Australia, 2 km south from Melbourne's central business district. Its Local Government Area are the Cities of Port Phillip and Melbourne. At the 2006 Census, South Melbourne had a population of 8790.

The suburb is notable as it was one of the first of Melbourne's suburbs to adopt full municipal status and is, along with Fitzroy, one of Melbourne's oldest suburbs. Historically, it was known as **Emerald Hill**.

History

"Canvas Town", South Melbourne in the 1850s. Temporary accommodation for the thousands who poured into Melbourne each week during the gold rush.

South Melbourne Town Hall in 1880.

Before European settlement, the area now called South Melbourne featured a single hill (where the Town Hall now stands) surrounded by swamps. The Hill was a traditional social and ceremonial meeting place for Aboriginal tribes.

The area was first settled by Europeans in the 1840s and became known as Emerald Hill.

During the Victorian Gold Rush of 1851 a tent city, known as *Canvas Town* was established. The area soon became a massive slum, home to tens of thousands of migrants from around the world.

Land sales at Emerald Hill began in 1852 and independence from Melbourne was granted when Emerald Hill was proclaimed a borough on 26 May 1855. Many of the residents of Canvas Town moved to prefabricated cottages in suburbs like Collingwood and South Melbourne and some of these early homes remain in South Melbourne's Coventry Street.

The new municipality developed rapidly, and by 1872 Emerald Hill was proclaimed a town. During the late 1870s, South Melbourne became a favoured place of residents for Melbourne's middle class with fashionable terraced housing becoming the norm including some English style squares, the best example of which was St Vincent Gardens. The South Melbourne Town Hall was built between 1879-1880 and designed in suitable grandeur to evoke the city's booming status establishing a civic heart at Bank Street bordered by Clarendon, Park, Cecil and Dorcas streets. In 1883 Emerald Hill became a city, changing its official name to South Melbourne.

South Melbourne experienced a decline in the 1950s as Melbourne sprawled outwards. Like many other Melbourne inner city suburbs, during the 1960s the Housing Commission of Victoria stepped in and erected several high-rise public housing towers, the tallest and largest of which, *Park Towers* (c.1969) is in South Melbourne. 'Emerald Hill Court' is the other housing commission building located in South Melbourne (c.1962). The result was an injection of migrants adding to the multicultural flavour of the area.

In the 1980s, South Melbourne experienced one of Melbourne's biggest waves of gentrification. [citation needed] Many of the terrace homes were restored and renovated and a new middle class moved in. As a result of the development of Southbank in the 1990s, Clarendon Street has become one of the highest rental yielding commercial streets [citation needed] in the entire city of Melbourne, attracting many of the residents from the apartment buildings to shop.

Recently, there has been some new developments within South Melbourne and at the Southbank end of Clarendon Street, including Australia's largest hotel.

Features

The main commercial district is centred around Clarendon Street, and includes the vibrant South Melbourne market. Along Clarendon Street there are many retailers, cafes and eateries.

Like Melbourne CBD, there are many small laneways in South Melbourne.

The town hall precinct is home to some of Melbourne's best examples of Victorian architecture.

In recent years, South Melbourne has seen an increase in population density due to apartment development in nearby Southbank, Victoria, where development has spilled over from the Melbourne CBD. To the east, towards St Kilda Road complex are many high rise office buildings.

The South Melbourne market is bordered by Cecil Street, York Street, and Coventry Street.

South Melbourne features some television production studios owned by the Seven Network and Global Television, in the south of the suburb, but Seven's news programs are broadcast from the Melbourne Docklands's Digital Broadcast Centre. The studios are serviced by Channel Seven shows like *Wheel of Fortune*, *Deal or No Deal*, *Dancing with the Stars* and *It Takes Two*

There are many galleries in South Melbourne, most of which are located in the streets off Clarendon Street.

Seeyup Temple (c.1856) is located in South Melbourne.

Sport

It was once home to the South Melbourne Swans team which played in the Victorian Football League (VFL/AFL), which played out of the Lake Oval (now Bob Jane Stadium) in nearby Albert Park before relocating to Sydney in 1982 in a radical move which eventually spawned the national Australian Football League.

South Melbourne FC is regarded as one of Australia's most successful football (soccer) club with four national titles to their name. They currently play in the Victorian Premier League at Bob Jane Stadium, a rectangular stadium built on Lake Oval, the former home ground of the South Melbourne Swans. Historically, they have been known as South Melbourne Hellas, a tribute to the migrant Greek founders of the club, and traditionally played at Middle Park.

Gallery

See Yup Temple off Raglan
Street

Famous former residents

- Dally Messenger
- Gentleman Jack McGowan
- William John Wills

See also

- City of South Melbourne - the former local government area of the same name.

External links

- SouthMelbourne.com [1] Business directory and travel information

Geographical coordinates: 37°50'06"S 144°57'36"E

Fitzroy, Victoria

Fitzroy	
Melbourne, Victoria	
Aerial view looking south over Fitzroy. Victoria Parade (top); Atherton gardens Housing Commission of Victoria estate (tall buildings top); Fitzroy Town Hall (centre); Brunswick Street commercial centre (right)	
Population:	8814 (2006)
Established:	1850s
Postcode:	3065
Area:	1.4 km² (0.5 sq mi)
Property Value:	AUD $921,125
Location:	3 km (2 mi) from Melbourne CBD
LGA:	City of Yarra
State District:	Richmond
Federal Division:	Melbourne

Suburbs around Fitzroy:		
Carlton North	Fitzroy North	Clifton Hill
Carlton	**Fitzroy**	Collingwood
Melbourne	East Melbourne	Richmond

Fitzroy is an inner city suburb of Melbourne, Victoria, Australia, 2 km north-east from Melbourne's central business district. Its Local Government Area is the City of Yarra. At the 2006 Census, Fitzroy had a population of 8,814.

Fitzroy has two of the 82 designated Major Activity Centres in the Melbourne 2030 Metropolitan Strategy - the commercial strips of Brunswick Street and Smith Street.

Fitzroy was Melbourne's first suburb, and is bordered by Victoria St/Parade, Nicholson St, Smith St, and Alexandra Parade. The heart of Fitzroy can be found in Brunswick Street, which is one of Melbourne's major retail, eating, and entertainment strips. Fitzroy is inhabited by a wide variety of ethnicities and socio-economic groups.

Fitzroy is characterised by a fairly tightly-spaced rectangular grid of medium-sized and narrow streets with numerous back lanes. There are many one-way streets. Fitzroy is Melbourne's smallest suburb in terms of area, being approximately 100 Ha.

Fitzroy takes its name from Sir Charles Augustus FitzRoy, the Governor of New South Wales from 1846-1855.

History

Fitzroy was Melbourne's first suburb, created when the area between Melbourne and Alexandra Parade (originally named Newtown) was subdivided into vacant lots and offered for sale. Newtown was later renamed Collingwood, and the area now called Fitzroy (west of Smith Street) was made a ward of the Melbourne City Council. On 10 September 1858, Fitzroy became a municipality in its own right, separate from the City of Melbourne. Surrounded as it was by a large number of factories and industrial sites in the adjoining suburbs, Fitzroy was ideally suited to working men's housing, and from the 1860s to the 1880s, Fitzroy's working class population rose dramatically. The area's former mansions became boarding houses and slums, and the heightened poverty of the area prompted the establishment of several charitable, religious and philanthropic organisations in the area over the next few decades. A notable local entrepreneur was Macpherson Robertson, whose confectionery factories engulfed several blocks and stand as heritage landmarks today.

The establishment of the Housing Commission of Victoria in 1938 saw swathes of new residences being constructed in Melbourne's outer suburbs. With many of Fitzroy's residents moving to the new accommodation, their places were taken by post-war immigrants mostly from Italy and Macedonia, and the influx of Italian and Irish immigrants saw a marked shift towards Catholicism from Fitzroy's traditional Methodist and Presbyterian roots. The Housing Commission would build two public housing estates in Fitzroy in the 1960s: one in Hanover Street and one at the southern end of Brunswick Street.

Before World War I, Fitzroy was a working-class neighborhood, even back then it had a concentration of political radicals living there. Postwar immigrants to the suburb resulted in the area becoming largely diverse. Many working-class Chinese immigrants also settled in Fitzroy due to its proximity to Chinatown, with also a noticeable Viatamese community; a small enclave of Africans exist there, and has been coined the centre of Melbourne's Hispanic community (particurly Johnston Street), with many Spanish and Latin American-themed resurants, clubs, bars and some stores.

Like other inner-city suburbs of Melbourne, Fitzroy underwent a process of gentrification during the 1980s and 1990s. The area's manufacturing and warehouse sites were converted into apartments, and the corresponding rising rent prices in Fitzroy saw many of the area's residents move to Northcote and Brunswick. In June 1994, the City of Yarra was created by combining the cities of Fitzroy, Collingwood and Richmond.

Local Landmarks

Non-Residential Architecture

The Moran and Cato warehouse designed by R.A. Lawson is considered to be of high architectural merit. The Old Tramways sheds are on the Victorian Heritage Register. The Champion Hotel is notable for its fanciful Edwardian design.

Residential Architecture

Fitzroy's architecture is very diverse and features some of the finest Victorian era architecture in Melbourne. The entire suburb is a heritage precinct with many individual buildings covered by heritage controls. Among the earliest homes, Royal Terrace (1853–1858) on Nicholson Street overlooking the Carlton Gardens was one of the first terrace houses in Melbourne.

Fitzroy's architecture is a legacy of its early history when a mixture of landuses was allowed to develop close to each other, producing a great diversity of types and scales of building. While many of Fitzroy's streets have examples of fine Victorian houses, there are also many examples of workers cottages, terraces, corner shops and pubs, warehouses and factories rubbing shoulders in the space of few metres. Additionally, there are examples of infill development from the 1970s such as 'six-pack' style flats and units, along with the large-scale results of 'slum clearance' programs of the Housing Commission of Victoria in the 1960s that bestowed some of Melbourne's most well-known and visible high-rise public housing in the form of the Atherton Gardens 37°48′16″S 144°58′44″E estate on the corner of Brunswick and Gertrude Streets that houses about 3,000 people, or a third of Fitzroy's population. [*citation needed*]

Due to its desirability as a place to live, Fitzroy faces increasing pressure for residential development. Recent residential projects in Fitzroy have sought to express a sense of Fitzroy's urban character in various ways and have been hotly contested in some cases.

Culture and sport

Art

Fitzroy is considered one of the centres of contemporary art in Melbourne. There are many small commercial art galleries, artist-run spaces and artist studios located within the suburb. Fitzroy has a thriving street art community and is also the home of Gertrude Contemporary Art Spaces and the Centre for Contemporary Photography.

Live performance

Fitzroy is a hub for live music in Melbourne, and plays host to several prominent venues: the Old Bar, Bar Open, the Evelyn Hotel, Gertrudes Brown Couch, Cape Live and the Empress Hotel (in Fitzroy North). The well-known Punters Club was also located in the area; however, it was forced to close in 2002.

Pubs

Fitzroy has a large number of pubs for such a small suburb. The former Devonshire Arms hotel was located in Fitzroy Street and remains the oldest building in Fitzroy. There are many other pubs in Fitzroy.

Cafes

The tiny suburb of Fitzroy has many cafes with good kitchens. Only one of the original three cafes is still standing - Marios. Bakers relocated North, and closed in 2007 while The Black Cat has transformed itself into a bar, but still retains its

The Devonshire Arms; the oldest extant building in Fitzroy

onstreet garden. With the advance of gentrification, a variety of cafes in different styles have opened up and down Brunswick Street, on Smith Street, parts of Gertrude Street and in some of the back streets in former milk bars and warehouse sites.

Sport

The Fitzroy Football Club (the Fitzroy Lions) was formed in 1883 as part of the VFL/AFL. The club had some early success before relocating its home games several times and finally running into financial difficulties in the 1980s, forcing it to merge with the Brisbane Bears in 1996 to form the Brisbane Lions. After sponsoring various local clubs, it returned as a playing club in its own right to play in the 2009 Victorian Amateur Football Association season and play out of the Brunswick Street Oval.

The Fitzroy Stars Football Club are an Indigenous club that joined the Northern Football Leaguein 2008. They currently play their home games at Crispe Park in Reservoir.

The Melbourne Chess Club, the oldest chess club in the southern hemisphere (est. 1866), is located at the corner of Leicester and Fitzroy St.

Social and community services

The health needs of Fitzroy residents and other Melburnians is served by St Vincent's Hospital.

A long tradition of community activism and civil society with many social and community service organisations having been based there. Organisations currently operating in the suburb include: the Fitzroy Legal Service, Yarra Community Housing Limited, Society of Saint Vincent de Paul, Brotherhood of St Laurence and the Tenants Union of Victoria, a free legal service for residential tenants.

Organisations which were formed in Fitzroy and have since moved their base include: Hanover Housing Services

Transport

There are no railway stations located in Fitzroy itself, with the nearest train stations being Rushall in North Fitzroy, Collingwood station and Parliament station. An underground railway line running between the City Loop and Clifton Hill with stations located beneath Brunswick Street and Smith Street has been proposed, although this is unlikely to be constructed in the short to medium term.

Three tram lines pass through Fitzroy or its boundaries:

- **Route 86 (Bundoora-Docklands):** travels along Nicholson Street, Gertrude Street and Smith Street.
- **Route 96 (East Brunswick-St Kilda):** travels along Nicholson Street.
- **Route 112 (West Preston-St Kilda):** bisects Fitzroy along Brunswick Street.

The City of Yarra also supports a car sharing service, Flexicar [1], which has several locations in Fitzroy:

Kerr Street - Corner of Kerr & Smith Streets on the south side of Kerr.

Victoria Street - On the corner of Victoria Street and Brunswick Street. Opposite Red Tongue Cafe. Napier Street - Outside Fitzroy Town Hall.

Westgarth Street (NEW) - In the first space on the north side of Westgarth Street to the west of Brunswick Street. Outside Retro Cafe.

Hotham Street (Collingwood) - Near the intersection with Smith Street. The first park on the north side of the street.

Heritage places

Being Melbourne's oldest suburb, Fitzroy has many old buildings and a large number that have been classified as having heritage significance. There are many individual buildings with a heritage listing and almost the entire suburb is subject to heritage protection in the City of Yarra planning scheme.

See also

- City of Fitzroy - the former local government area of the same name.

External links

- Fitzroy, Victoria is at coordinates 37°48′04″S 144°58′44″E
- Fitzroyalty [2] Fitzroy based local blog
- Fitzroy local news site [3] Fitzroy local news written by local experts
- Local History of Fitzroy [4]
- ⊛ Chisholm, Hugh, ed (1911). "Fitzroy". *Encyclopædia Britannica* (Eleventh ed.). Cambridge University Press.

Carlton, Victoria

Carlton	
Melbourne, Victoria	
Aerial view looking south over Carlton. The Royal Exhibition Building and Carlton Gardens (left), Rathdowne Street (centre), Drummond Street (right) and Lygon Street (far right)	
Population:	12,050 (2006)
• Density:	6694.4/km² (17338.4/sq mi)
Established:	1851
Postcode:	3053
Area:	1.8 km² (0.7 sq mi)
Property Value:	AUD $682,500
Location:	2 km (1 mi) from Melbourne
LGA:	City of Melbourne
State District:	Melbourne
Federal Division:	Melbourne

Suburbs around Carlton:		
Parkville	Carlton North	Fitzroy North
North Melbourne	**Carlton**	Fitzroy
West Melbourne	Melbourne	East Melbourne

Carlton is an inner city suburb of Melbourne, Victoria, Australia, 2 km north from Melbourne's central business district. Its Local Government Area is the City of Melbourne. At the 2006 Census, Carlton had a population of 12,050.

Its boundaries are roughly Elizabeth Street to the West, Princes Street to the North, Victoria Street to the south, and Nicholson Street to the East.

The suburb well known for its "Little Italy" precinct on Lygon Street, for its Victorian architecture and its European-style squares (University Square, Lincoln Square, Argyle Place and MacArthur Place) and the Carlton Gardens, the latter being the location of the Royal Exhibition Building, one of Australia's few man-made sites with World Heritage status.

Carlton is thought to have been named after Carlton House, London.

History

Carlton was founded in 1851 at the beginning of the Victorian Gold Rush. Carlton Post Office opened on 19 October 1865.

Demographics

The area is noted for its diverse population that has been the home in earlier days of Jewish and Italian immigrants

A large number of low-income residents live in the substantial public housing estates that were built during the 1960s. The two main estates are between Lygon and Rathdowne Sts, and between Nicholson and Canning Sts. These are configured as a mixture of 4 and 5-storey walk-up flats and 22-storey high-rise towers which are in the process of being redeveloped as mixed-tenure housing.

Carlton also has a sizeable tertiary student population, local and international, due to its proximity to the University of Melbourne and RMIT University. While much of the student housing has traditionally been in the older Victorian terraces common throughout the area, the new residential buildings developed during the 1990s and early 2000s targeted at the international student market have transformed the once low-rise skyline of Swanston Street so that its predominant height is about 10-11 storeys.

Local Landmarks

Further information: Little Italy, Melbourne

Lygon Street, which runs through the heart of Carlton is a centre of Italian culture and cuisine. It is popular among Melburnians and foreigners alike for its numerous restaurants, especially Italian restaurants. Lygon Street has six specialist gelaterias, and several continental cake cafes.

Royal Exhibition Building located on Rathdowne Street.

Carlton is home to some of Melbourne's most historically significant buildings such as Melbourne Trades Hall and the World Heritage Site of the Carlton Gardens, the Royal Exhibition Building and the ruins of the old Carlton brewery, a collection of buildings constructed between 1864 and 1927, all listed on the Victorian Heritage Register. The Carlton Gardens are also home to the Melbourne Museum.

Carlton has many 19th century public buildings. The Carlton Club, which was built in 1889 by Inskip & Robertson, is notable for its decorative Australian native kangaroo gargoyles and polychrome

Florentine arches. The Carlton Post Office and Police Station are both fine Renaissance Revival styled buildings. The Carlton Court House on Drummond Street was designed in the Gothic style by G.B.H Austin and constructed between 1888 and 1889. The Lygon Buildings on Lygon Street were built in 1888 in the Mannerist style. Carlton Gardens Primary School, on Rathdowne Street, opened in 1884.

Residential

Many heritage registered Victorian terrace houses can be found on Drummond Street, a long wide boulevard flanked by grand homes, including Rosaville (no46 built 1883), Medley Hall (no48 built 1892-93), Drummond Terrace (no 93-105 built 1890-91), Lothian Terrace (no175-179 built 1865-69), Terraces at 313&315 (1889), Police Station (no330 built 1878) and Court House (no345-355 built 1887-88).

Notable Public Spaces

The Bali Memorial, which commemorates the victims of the 2002 Bali bombings, is situated in Lincoln Square. It was officially opened on 12 October 2005, the third anniversary of the explosion that killed 202 innocent people, including 88 Australians.

The northern part of Argyle Square, adjacent to Lygon Street, has been redeveloped into an Italian piazza, known as Piazza Italia, in a joint project between the City of Melbourne and its twin city, Milan. A giant sundial is the main feature of the piazza.

Politics

Carlton falls within the federal electorate of Melbourne (currently held by the Adam Bandt of the Greens) and the state electorate of Melbourne (currently held by the ALP's Bronwyn Pike).

A traditional working-class suburb, it has typically seen a high vote for the ALP. However, like many other inner-city suburbs undergoing a process of gentrification, the Greens have been gaining an increasing share of the vote.

The suburb contains two polling booths, which collectively produced the following primary-vote results at the 2007 federal election: 53.29% ALP, 22.60% Greens, 20.13% Liberal, 1.57% Democrat, and 0.83% Family First.

Education

Due to Carlton's close proximity to the Parkville campus of The University of Melbourne, many university-owned buildings can be found around Carlton as a result of the university's expansion through the years. This includes the University Square redevelopment, where the state-of-the-art Law and ICT buildings and a new underground carpark is located. However, the university's continued expansion into Carlton are opposed by some residents. Two of the university's residential colleges are situated in Carlton. Medley Hall is located on Drummond Street, while Graduate House is on Leicester Street. Graduate House is a residential college for graduate students only and does not admit any undergraduate students.

Melbourne Business School and part of RMIT University's City Campus is also situated in Carlton.

Victoria and Tasmania's Catholic seminary, Corpus Christi College, is located on Drummond Street. The college accommodates forty seminarians who are studying to become priests.

Primary education is provided by two schools; Carlton Gardens Primary School [1] and Carlton Primary School. CGPS was founded in 1884 and is one of Melbourne's oldest schools and the closest to the cbd.

Transport

Carlton is served by many of Melbourne's tram routes, running along Swanston street and terminating at Melbourne University. Tram routes 8 and 1 trams continues through Carlton North and beyond via Lygon Street.

Buses serve Carlton via Lygon, Elgin, and Rathdowne Streets. There are currently no trains to Carlton, with the closest station being Melbourne Central Station. There were talks and proposals of extending the city train loop to service Carlton, but no concrete plans have been proposed.

Rod Eddington's East West Link Needs Assessment does mention however, that there will be subway(s) in Carlton, as a part of the proposed 17 km metro tunnel.

Health

Carlton is also very well serviced by the health sector. The Royal Women's Hospital and the new Royal Dental Hospital provide high quality health care. It is also a centre of biomedical research. The Cancer Council Victoria, Cancer Research Institute and Victorian College of Optometry all have their premises in Carlton. Carlton is the home of NETS (Victoria) which provides emergency transport of sick newborns between hospitals throughout Victoria and from Tasmania.

Culture

The famous La Mama Theatre is located in Carlton. It is noted for its energy, which is typical of the early Australian theatre scene in the 1970s. Besides that, Cinema Nova on Lygon Street shows many international arthouse films, while Readings bookstore has been a hub for literary and musical connoisseurs since the 1970s. Carlton is also home to the renowned Dracula Nightclub, which is on the corner of Cardigan Street and Victoria Street, which is famous for its cabaret shows.

Religion

There are a number of churches in Carlton, which serve the spiritual needs of Carlton residents. St Jude's Anglican Church, on Lygon Street, is one of the most active and well attended Anglican churches in the Greater Melbourne area. Other churches in the area include a Romanian Orthodox Church on Queensberry Street, a Salvation Army Church, the Sacred Heart Catholic Church, Chinese Church of Christ and the Christian Chapel of the Church of Christ built in 1865. The Catholic seminary is situated on the site of St George's Catholic Church, Carlton's oldest surviving building, dating from 1855.

Sport

Carlton is the home of the Australian rules football club, the Carlton Blues, who are based at their former home ground, the Princes Park Football Ground in nearby North Carlton. The club plays home games at the Docklands Stadium and The Melbourne Cricket Ground.

Lygon Street, Grattan Street and Queensberry Street were part of the route of the marathon in the 2006 Commonwealth Games which was hosted by Melbourne. Lygon and Cardigan streets are part of the seventh course of the annual cycling tour, Jayco Herald Sun Tour.

Melbourne University Regiment

- The Melbourne University Regiment (MUR) is based on Grattan Street, Carlton. MUR serves to train potential Officers in the Australian Army Reserve. MUR was founded in 1884 as D company, 4th Battalion of the Victorian Rifles, and changed to its current name and role in 1948. Famous alumni include Sir John Monash, Sir Robert Menzies, Sir Ninian Stephen, Barry Humphries, and Andrew Peacock.

External links

- Carlton, Victoria is at coordinates 37°48′00″S 144°58′01″E
- Australian Places: Carlton [2]
- Melbourne University Regiment [3]
- Carlton Residents Association [4]

Caulfield North, Victoria

Caulfield North	
Melbourne, Victoria	
Labassa, Manor Grove	
Population:	14,034 (2006)
Postcode:	3161
Area:	4.2 km² (1.6 sq mi)
Property Value:	AUD $1,080,000
Location:	11 km (7 mi) from Melbourne
LGA:	City of Glen Eira
State District:	Caulfield
Federal Division:	Melbourne Ports

Suburbs around Caulfield North:		
Prahran	Armadale	Malvern
St Kilda East	**Caulfield North**	Caulfield East
Elsternwick	Caulfield	Caulfield East

Caulfield North is a suburb in Melbourne, Victoria, Australia, 9 km south-east from Melbourne's central business district. Its Local Government Area is the City of Glen Eira. At the 2006 Census, Caulfield North had a population of 14,034.

It is bounded by Orrong Road in the west, Glen Eira Road in the south, Dandenong Road in the north and Kambrook Road in the east. The suburb contains Caulfield Park - a park of approximately 26 hectares in size, bounded by Balaclava Road, Inkerman Road, Hawthorn Road and Park Crescent.

History

Caulfield North was once home to many large Victorian mansions, most of which were demolished and subdivided, however a few remain, the most notable of which is **Labassa**, which is owned by the National Trust. The mansion was one of the filming locations for the 2002 film *Queen of the Damned*.

Many streets in the suburb were named in the late 1850s after Crimea War locations and people, for example, Cardigan, Canrobert, Inkerman, Alma, Raglan.

The Caulfield North Post Office was opened on 26 March 1915.

Public transport

Trams service Caulfield North extensively, with a major tram interchange at Balaclava Junction. Tram routes 3, 16 and 64 all service Caulfield North. Caulfield North also contains, Balaclava Junction, the only extant grand union in the Southern Hemisphere, a junction where trams can go in all directions from all directions.

Trains connect the suburb to the city via the major transport interchange, Caulfield railway station at Caulfield East (via tram route 3). Trains also connect the suburb to the city through Balaclava railway station (via tram routes 3 and 16).

Notable people

Australian television personality Graham Kennedy went to the Caulfield North State School (now Caulfield Junior College), in Balaclava Road.

Gallery

See also

- City of Caulfield - the former local government area of which Caulfield North was a part.

External links

- Caulfield North, Victoria is at coordinates 37°52′23″S 145°01′30″E

Things to See and Do

Heide Museum of Modern Art

Heide Museum of Modern Art	
Heide I, a former farm house, now houses some of the museum's works and artefacts from the Heide Circle era	
Established	1981
Location	Bulleen, Manningham, Melbourne, Australia
Type	Contemporary art museum, Historic site, Sculpture park
Visitor figures	70,000
Public transit access	291 & 283 Bus routes, nearest train; Heidelberg Station
Website	www.heide.com.au [1]

Heide Museum of Modern Art, more commonly just **Heide**, is a contemporary art museum located in Bulleen, east of Melbourne, Australia. Established in 1981, the museum comprises several detached buildings and surrounding gardens & parklands of historical importance that are used as gallery spaces to exhibit works in various mediums by contemporary Australian artists.

The museum occupies the site of a former dairy farm that was purchased by the prominent Melbourne art collectors John and Sunday Reed in 1934 and became home to a collective known as the Heide Circle, which included many of Australia's best-known modernist painters, such as; Albert Tucker, Sidney Nolan, Laurence Hope Joy Hester and others, who lived and worked in the former farm house (Heide I).

Between 1964 and 1967, a new residence was built (Heide II). It is considered to be one of the finest examples of modernist architecture in Victoria. In 1981, the museum was established on the site, incorporating the existing buildings and surrounding gardens & parklands as exhibition and gallery spaces. A dedicated gallery building (Heide III) was constructed in 1993 and the museum continued to broaden its collection of works to include all forms of contemporary Australian art, including some by contemporary Indigenous artists.

The museum underwent major redevelopment in 2005-06 which included the installation of several sculptural and installation art pieces, landscaping & redesign of the gardens, construction of a new education centre & gallery space, extension of the Heide III building and various other works.

In 2009 after 19 months of redevelopment, the cafe reopened in November as Cafe Vue at Heide. This completed building works at Heide.

History

See also: Heide Circle

Early history

The museum is situated on a site that was originally occupied by a dairy farm, the farm house was built in the 1880s-1890s. The Yarra River and surrounding hills east of Melbourne provided an ideal setting for many artists, writers, poets, etc, exemplified in the formation of the Heidelberg School at Heidelberg, Montsalvat in Eltham and various artist camps in locations such as Box Hill and Warrandyte.

Heide I and front gardens.

Thus, the area was frequented by artists since the mid-19th century.

In 1934, the farm was purchased by John and Sunday Reed, passionate supporters and collectors of Australian art and culture, and named after the nearby town of Heidelberg. The Reeds established one of the finest private libararies in Melbourne at Heide, containing many of the most important and lavish art magazines and journals from Europe and America. Access was open to all Heide visitors and provided much inspiration for visitng artists, writers, musicians and the Reeds' other creative friends. A loose grouping of Australian artists who became known as the "Heide Circle", began living and working at Heide, counting amongst their number many of Australia's best-known modernist painters.

A number of modernist artists came to live and work at various times through the 1930s, 40s and 50s at Heide, and as such it became the place where many of the most famous works of the period were painted. Albert Tucker, Sidney Nolan, Laurence Hope and Joy Hester, amongst others, all worked at Heide. Nolan painting 26 of his original 27 Ned Kelly works in the dining room of Heide I.

The Heide Circle continued in their primary commitment to Figurative Modernism through the 1950s and 60s, with several of the artists forming the Antipodeans Group and taking a stand against the new abstract art. The Heide Circle became well known for the intertwined personal and professional lives of the people involved. Sunday Reed conducted affairs with a number of them, with the knowledge of her husband.

In 1964, the Reeds commissioned Victorian architect David McGlashan to design a new residence, initially intended to be "a gallery to be lived in". It is designed with simple L-shaped walls that interlink to form a sequence of internal and external 'rooms' in Mount gambier limestone, white terrazzo, treated pine and glass. The Reeds moved into Heide II in 1967 and it served as their residence for some time.

In the mid 1960s Heide's much loved kitchen garden was created by Sunday Reed in a bare cow paddock.

Museum establishment

The Reeds sold Heide II, most of the adjoining land and a body of their art collection (113 works) to the Victorian Government in August 1980 for the creation of a public art gallery, then named Heide Park and Art Gallery. The Reeds returned to live in Heide I. Dr Norman Wettenhall was appointed the first Chairman and the then Premier of Victoria, Sir Rupert Hamer was honoured as the inaugural Patron. Maudie Plamer was appointed the inaugural Director in 1981. After six months of converting the modern Heide II into a public space, Heide Park and Art Gallery opened in November.

Recent history

The museum underwent major redevelopment in 2005-06 which included the installation of several sculptural and installation art pieces, landscaping & redesign of the gardens, construction of a new education centre & gallery space, extension of the Heide III building to incorporate works from the Barbara Tucker Gift and various other works. On July 13, 2006 the museum officially re-opened after its $3 million dollar renovation and extension. The new buildings were designed by O'Connor + Houle Architecture.

Buildings, features, and layout

Heide is situated on a former floodplain of the Yarra River in Bulleen. It is bordered to the north-east and east by the Yarra Valley Country Club, to the west and south by Banksia Park, and to the south-east by Templestowe Road. The site borders the Yarra River, at Fannings Bend, in its north-west corner. The museum itself comprises several detached buildings and surrounding gardens and parklands on the site, described in further detail below, all of which are used in various capacities as exhibition spaces.

Heide II, viewed from the northeast side.

Buildings and facilities

- **Heide I** - built 1880s

  A former dairy farm house, purchased by the Reeds in 1934 and became home to members of the Heide Circle who also completed various in the building. Restored at various times in the late 20th century, it currently houses various works and artifacts from its Heide Circle residents and is used as an exhibition space.

- **Heide II** - built 1963

  Designed by Victorian architect David McGlashan, who was commissioned by the Reeds, it was initially intended to be "a gallery to be lived in" and served as their residence for some time. The building is considered one of the best examples of modernist architecture in Victoria and is currently used as an exhibition space.

- **Heide III** - built 1993, extended 2005

  Originally designed by Andrew Andersens of Peddle Thorp Architects and later extended to create additional exhibition spaces, both indoors and outdoors, and to extend the existing visitor amenities. It houses the largest gallery spaces of the museum including: the Central Galleries; the Albert & Barbara Tucker Gallery, Tucker Study Centre; Kerry Gardner & Andrew Myer Project Gallery; and the Heide Store.

- **Sidney Myer Education Centre** - built 2005

  Designed by O'Connor and Houle Architecture, its purpose is expressed as "a dynamic learning and thinking space for teachers, students, and community groups." The centre offers innovative and diverse education and public programs based on Heide's changing exhibitions, architecture, landscape and collection.

- **Heide Cafe** - completed in November 2009

After a 19 month redevelopment program Cafe Vue at Heide opened to the public on 24 November 2009. The $1.5 million redevelopment was designed by Chris Connell Design (CCD). Inspired by the award winning architecture of Heide and its beautiful gardens, Café Vue at Heide is a sleek and elegant addition to this iconic site. The café's glass pavilion seats 55 patrons inside and an outdoor area seats an additional 55 patrons.

The building has recycled existing granite and limestone and incorporates new materials including - anodised lso aluminium, glass, steel and additional timber sourced from sustainable forests. Sustainable elements have been incorporated in the design.

Gardens/Parklands

The gardens at Heide cover sixteen acres surrounding the buildings and host a diverse environment of trees, shrubs, flowering plants and paddocks that extend down over the river flats to the banks of the Yarra River. On purchasing the Heide property in 1934, John and Sunday Reed commenced the planting of hundreds of European and exotic trees. Friend and artist, Neil Douglas, among other friends, was instrumental in helping the Reeds establish Heide's early gardens. The gardens surrounding Heide I were restored in 2001 as the first part of Heide's current Redevelopment Program and the gardens surrounding Heide II were restored in 2006.

Major gardens include; the Sir Rupert Hamer Garden, constructed as a sculptural park and to reduce noise from nearby Manningham Road; Kitchen Garden, established by the Heide Circle to provide vegetables, herbs and fruit for its residents; and Karakarook's Garden, a sculptural garden bed with edible native vegetation. The surrounding parklands also include formal perennial walks, parterre gardens, woodlands and parkland dotted with contemporary sculptural installations dotted throughout. The gardens utilise extensive water management systems.

Some of the more notable works in the gardens and parklands include:

- *Helmet*, Tanya Court & Cassandra Chilton, 2008 (painted white by street artists in late 2008)
- *Rings of Saturn*, Inge King, 2005–06
- *Karakarook's Garden*, Lauren Berkowitz, 2005–06
- *Cows*, Jeff Thomson, 1987

Access

- **Heide I** - Closed to the general public, however guided tours run from 2pm.
- **Heide II** - Various rooms open during exhibitions.
- **Heide III** - Various spaces open during exhibitions.

    Heide Shop (In Heide III) - Open to general public, free.

- **Gardens & Sculpture Park** - Open to the general public, free.

The installation on the lawns to the north of the museum, entitled *Cows*, by Jeff Thomson, 1987

Collection

The museum's collection includes works in various mediums by many contemporary Australian artists conducted since the 1930s. These include works by artists such as; Moya Dyring, Sidney Nolan, Albert Tucker, Joy Hester, John Perceval, Arthur Boyd, Howard Arkley, Charles Blackman, Peter Booth, Mike Brown, Richard Larter, Wolfgang Sievers, Sweeney Reed, Sam Atyeo and Jenny Watson.

In Media

The museum, its works and the surrounding gardens and parklands has served as subject matter for various photographers and have also featured in many Australian television programs:

- The courtyard of Heide III was the setting for an art school graduation in *Very Small Business*, ABC TV series, 2008
- The museum's gardens were featured in an episode of *Gardening Australia* in 2007.

Gallery

See also

- Art of Australia
- **Associated Galleries:**
- National Gallery of Victoria
- National Gallery of Australia
- **Related Topics:**
- Heidelberg School
- Montsalvat
- Box Hill artists' camp
- Heide Circle

External links

- Heide Museum of Modern Art Website [2]
- Heide Museum of Modern Art Artabase page [3]
- Peddle Thorp Melbourne [4]

Geographical coordinates: 37°45′39″S 145°04′59″E

Melbourne Museum

Melbourne Museum	
Melbourne Museum in the Carlton Gardens	
Established	1854
Location	Melbourne, Australia
Type	History museum
Website	[1]

Melbourne Museum is located in the Carlton Gardens in Melbourne, Australia, adjacent the Royal Exhibition Building.

It is the largest museum in the Southern Hemisphere, and is a venue of Museum Victoria, which also operates the Immigration Museum and Scienceworks Museum.

The museum has seven main galleries, a Children's Gallery and a temporary exhibit gallery on three levels, Upper, Ground and Lower Level and was constructed by Baulderstone Hornibrook.

The Touring Hall is where temporary exhibits are displayed. Past exhibits include mummies from Egypt and dinosaurs from China. The Big Box is part of the Children's Gallery.

In addition, the museum has other facilities such as the Sidney Myer Amphitheatre and The Age Theatre. The Discovery Centre, on the Lower Level, is a free public research centre. The museum also has a cafe and a souvenir shop.

The IMAX Theatre, which is situated on the Lower Level is also part of the museum complex. It shows movies, usually documentary films, in 3-D format.

History

The museum had its earliest beginnings in the Government Assay Office which on 9 March 1854, opened some displays in La Trobe Street. In 1858, Frederick McCoy who was Professor of Natural History at the University of Melbourne was appointed Director of the National Museum.[2]

The Melbourne Museum was originally located (along with the State Library and the old state gallery) in the city block between La Trobe, Swanston, Little Lonsdale and Russell Streets - the nearby Museum underground railway station was originally named after it, although following the move the station was renamed Melbourne Central. The State Library now uses all the space in that building, the gallery also having moved to the NGV site.

Main permanent exhibits

The main permanent exhibits include:

- Science and Life Gallery - including a skeleton of a *Diprotodon* (a giant wombat-like creature), and skeletons of dinosaurs such as:

Natural history exhibit at Melbourne Museum (center specimen is an Orange Roughy)

  - *Tarbosaurus* (Giant meat eater, Tyrannosauridae)
  - *Mamenchisaurus* (Giant Sauropod)
  - *Tsintaosaurus*
  - *Hadrosaurid*
  - *Pteranodon*
  - *Gallimimus*
  - *Hypsilophodon*

In 2010 a new exibit called 600 million years of Victoria that includes some more prehistoric animals such as:

  - *Muttaburrasaurus*
  - *Tiktaalik*
  - *Anomalocaris*
  - and many other prehistoric animals.
  - The Science & Life Gallery also contains the exhibitions: Bugs Alive!, Marine Life: Exploring our seas and two more exhibitions soon to open in 2010.
- Melbourne Gallery - where the mounted hide of Phar Lap, a race horse that won the Melbourne Cup during the depression era, is exhibited.
  - It also features an exhibition about the history of Melbourne from the early 1800s through to present day (called The Melbourne Story).
- Large skeleton of a Pygmy Blue Whale
- Mind and Body Gallery - a gallery regarding the human body. It also features a world first exhibition about the mind (called The Mind: enter the labyrinth).
- Evolution Gallery - the upper level features the exhibition 'Darwin to DNA'. The lower level feature Wild: Amazing animals in a changing world exhibition.
- Forest Gallery - a living temperate Victorian forest environment, complete with live birds, reptiles, and other fauna
- Bunjilaka Aboriginal Cultural Centre - a gallery with exhibitions about the Aborigines of Victoria
- Te Pasifika Gallery - an exhibition which highlights the history and watercrafts of Pacific Islanders
- Children's Gallery - exhibitions aimed at 3 to 8 year olds.
- Touring Hall - is where international touring exhibitions are displayed. A Day In Pompeii which was on display at Melbourne Museum from 26 June - 25 October 2009 was Melbourne Museum's

most popular temporary exhibition. Past Touring Hall exhibitions include Hatching the Past: Dinosaur Eggs and Babies (30 May 2008 to 24 August 2008), The Great Wall of China: Dynasties, dragons and warriors (23 March 2007 to 22 July 2007), Spirit of the Games: the Opening Ceremony revealed (18 March to 23 July 2006), Dinosaurs from China (2005).

- Public spaces - Outside the main galleries are various displays relating to Victoria's and Australia's history, including CSIRAC (an early computer built in Australia) and a Pygmy Blue Whale.

Festival Melbourne 2006

Melbourne Museum was one of the venues of Festival Melbourne 2006, a city-wide art festival held in conjunction of the 2006 Commonwealth Games, which was held in Melbourne. Among the exhibitions held in the museum were 'Common Goods:Cultures Meet Through Craft', which featured crafts made by artists from various Commonwealth countries and 'CARVE:Indigenous carving practices', a series of demonstrations of traditional indigenous carving practices and techniques from Australia, New Zealand and Canada.

Besides that, there was a producers' market, 'Victorian Producers' Market', where the best produces from regional Victoria such as wine, cheese and others were sold. A cooking competition, 'Culinary Pro Am of the Commonwealth' was also held between top Melbourne chefs, each representing a Commonwealth country.

Another crowd drawer was the large screen on museum grounds where live actions of the Games were shown.

Gallery

Melbourne Museum

Museum hall

Melbourne Museum (Modern Architecture)

CSIRAC, Australia's first digital computer

External links / References

- Melbourne Museum [1]
- Disability information [3]
- Melbourne Food and Wine during the 2006 Commonwealth Games [4]
- Reference of Museum items [5]

Geographical coordinates: 37°48′12″S 144°58′17″E

Immigration Museum, Melbourne

Geographical coordinates: 37°49′09″S 144°57′38″E

Immigration Museum, Melbourne	
Immigration Museum in Old Customs House	
Established	1998
Location	Melbourne, Australia
Type	Culture museum
Website	[1]

The **Immigration Museum** is a museum primarily displaying Australia's immigration history. It is located on Flinders Street in Melbourne, Victoria, in the Old Customs House. It is famous for its most important space, the Long Room, which is a magnificent piece of Renaissance revival architecture.

The museum was founded in 1998, and is a division of Museum Victoria which administers the cultural and scientific collections of the State of Victoria. Its sister museums are Melbourne Museum (including the Royal Exhibition Building) and Scienceworks Museum.

In addition to its work on documenting immigraton history, the museum also hosts various travelling exhibitions, and also provides educational programs.

External links

• Immigration Museum website [2]

Australian Centre for Contemporary Art

The **Australian Centre For Contemporary Art** (ACCA) is a contemporary art gallery in Melbourne, Australia. The gallery is located on Sturt Street in the Melbourne Arts Precinct, in the inner suburb of Southbank.

The Australian Centre for Contemporary Art. The Malthouse Theatre is on the right.

The ACCA is housed in a distinctive brown metallic building (made of COR-TEN weathering steel) designed by Melbourne architects Wood Marsh. The building has won Australian architectural awards for its monolithic sculptural form and has been compared to a Sandcrawler from Star Wars. The interior has vast spaces with the capacity to display a variety of works.

The adjacent Malthouse Theatre shares a courtyard and is a venue for contemporary performing arts. The combined complex goes by the name of Ngargee, which is a Bunurong - that is, local Aboriginal tribe and guardians - word describing gathering for celebration.

External links

- ACCA website [1]

Geographical coordinates: 37°49′35″S 144°58′01″E

Gertrude Contemporary Art Spaces

Gertrude Contemporary Art Spaces is a contemporary art complex located in the suburb of Fitzroy, Melbourne Australia.

The complex was founded in 1985 and contains 3 exhibition spaces and 16 studio facilities.

External links

- Official website [1]
- Gertrude CAS Artabase page [2]

The Arts Centre (Melbourne)

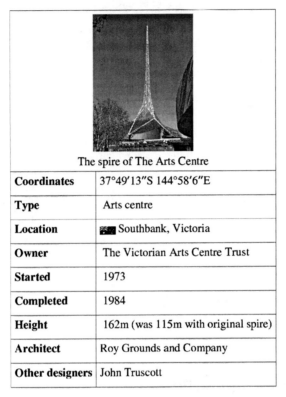

The spire of The Arts Centre

Coordinates	37°49′13″S 144°58′6″E
Type	Arts centre
Location	Southbank, Victoria
Owner	The Victorian Arts Centre Trust
Started	1973
Completed	1984
Height	162m (was 115m with original spire)
Architect	Roy Grounds and Company
Other designers	John Truscott

The Arts Centre is a performing arts centre consisting of a complex of theatres and concert halls in the Melbourne Arts Precinct, located in the inner Melbourne suburb of Southbank in Victoria, Australia.

It was designed by architect Sir Roy Grounds, the masterplan for the complex (along with the National Gallery of Victoria) was approved in 1960, and construction of the Arts Centre began in 1973 following some delays. The complex opened in stages, with **Hamer Hall** opening in 1982, and the **Theatres Building** opening in 1984.

The Arts Centre is located by the Yarra River and along St Kilda Road, one of the city's main thoroughfares, and extends into the Melbourne Arts Precinct.

Major companies regularly performing in the theatres include Opera Australia and The Australian Ballet, the Melbourne Theatre Company and Melbourne Symphony Orchestra. The Arts Centre also hosts a large number of Australian and international performances and production companies.

The Arts Centre is listed on the Victorian Heritage Register.

History

The Arts Centre site has long been associated with arts and entertainment and has previously been home to circus, theatre, roller and ice skating, cinema and dance.

After World War II it was decided that Melbourne needed a cultural centre. After many years of discussion, a master plan was approved in 1960, with Sir Roy Grounds as the chosen architect.

During the ensuing years, and to accommodate difficulties associated with the geology of the site, changes to the original plans were made and eventually the Arts Centre emerged as two buildings - now known as the Theatres Building and Hamer Hall, with interiors designed by John Truscott.

Work commenced on the Theatres in 1973 and land was acquired for the Hamer Hall (formerly the Melbourne Concert Hall) in 1975. The building now known as Hamer Hall opened in 1982. The Theatres Building opened two years later.

The Centre is unusual in that its theatres and concert hall are built largely underground. Hamer Hall, situated closest to the river, was initially planned to be almost entirely underground, thus providing a huge open vista between the theatre spire, the river and Flinders Street Station. However, construction problems with the foundations, including water seepage, meant the structure had to be raised to three storeys above ground.

Similarly, budget constraints meant that Grounds' design for the Theatres Building, which included a copper-clad spire, were shelved, and a shortened un-clad design was substituted. This was eventually replaced with the current 'full-height' un-clad spire.[citation needed]

Performance venues and facilities

The Arts Centre is a complex of distinct venues. **Hamer Hall** is a separate building and the largest of the venues - the building also houses the small experimental theatre BlackBox. The other venues (the State Theatre, Playhouse and Fairfax Studio) are housed in the **Theatres Building** (under the spire).

The Sidney Myer Music Bowl, situated in nearby King's Domain, is an outdoor arena also managed by The Arts Centre. It seats 12,000 on the lawn area and 2,150 in reserved seating, and is used for music concerts.

Hamer Hall

Hamer Hall (formerly the Melbourne Concert Hall) is a 2,661 seat concert hall - the largest venue in the Arts Centre complex, used for orchestra and contemporary music performances. It was opened in 1982, and was later renamed

The interior of Hamer Hall as seen from the back of the stage.

Hamer Hall in honour of Sir Rupert Hamer (the 39th Premier of Victoria) shortly after his death in 2004.

State Theatre

The **State Theatre** is located in the Theatres Building of the Arts Centre complex, under the spire, and is a 2,077 seat theatre used for opera and theatre performances. It was opened in 1984, and has one of the largest stages in the World.

Playhouse

The **Playhouse** is also located in the Theatres Building of the Arts Centre complex, and is a 822 seat theatre used for plays and dance performances. It was also opened in 1984.

Fairfax Studio

The **Fairfax Studio** is also located in the Theatres Building of the Arts Centre complex, and is a 376 seat theatre. It was also opened in 1984.

Galleries

The Arts Centre also houses dedicated gallery spaces including Gallery 1 (formally the George Adams Gallery) on Level 6 (Ground level), Gallery 2 on Level 7, the St Kilda Road Foyer Gallery and the Smorgan Family Plaza, whose walls and central areas are used for exhibitions, in the Theatres Building.

Arts Centre Spire

The complex retains landmark status due to its massive steel spire and its wrap-around base.

The original spire envisaged by Roy Grounds was 115 metres tall and because of its complexity was one of the first structures in Australia to rely on computer-aided-design (CAD). By the mid-1990s, signs of deterioration became apparent on the upper spire structure, and the Arts Centre Trust decided to replace the spire.

The Arts Centre spire, a Melbourne landmark

The new spire was completed in 1996, and reaches 162 metres, though it is still based on Grounds' original design. The spire is illuminated with roughly 6,600 metres (21,653 feet) of optic fibre tubing, 150 metres (492 feet) of neon tubing on the mast and 14,000 incandescent lamps on the spire's skirt.

The metal webbing of the spire is influenced by the billowing of a ballerina's tutu and the Eiffel Tower.

A Wedge-tailed Eagle and Peregrine Falcon were utilised in early 2008 to deter groups of Sulphur-crested Cockatoos from damaging the spire's electrical fittings and thimble-sized lights.

Redevelopment

Hamer Hall is to undergo a A$128.5 million redevelopment which will make the facility even more accessible, providing a better experience for audiences, and ensuring that it can continue to attract and present a wide range of top international and local performers.

The project will help Victoria maintain its competitive advantage well into the future by providing a cultural precinct where all Victorians and visitors can experience the best arts and cultural activities from Australia and around the world.

The redevelopment of Hamer Hall will provide a better experience for audiences and performers alike through improved acoustics, better box office facilities, staging systems and technology, and new auditorium seating for patrons to enjoy a greater range of performances.

The renovation will create a new outward facing venue that aims to enhance the unique heritage character of the building, making it more accessible and inviting to the public.

Planned improvements include: new and expanded foyer spaces, new connections with the city, St Kilda Road and the river, with new stairs, improved disability access, escalators and lifts, improved acoustics, new auditorium seating and cutting edge staging systems and technology, innovative approaches to sustainability including power generation and waste and water management.

The A$128.5 million redevelopment is first stage of the Southbank Cultural Precinct redevelopment which aims to deliver an increased cultural presence for the state by enhancing public connectivity and accessibility, linking Victoria's major arts venues and companies via a new urban space, and providing exceptional public amenity for the community and burgeoning residential population of Southbank and the CBD.

Disability Access

There are accessible seating options in all of Arts Centre venues with companion seating available in most venues. Seating maps for Fairfax [1], Hamer Hall (stalls [2] and circle [3]), Playhouse (circle [4]) and State Theatre (circle [5] and boxes [6]) and Sidney Myer Music Bowl (stalls [7] and boxes [8]) indicate accessible seating.

A TTY phone system operates to allow direct access to the Arts Centre by phone for people with hearing disabilities. The dedicated number for this service is (03) 9281 8441.

A hearing system is available in all Arts Centre venues except BlackBox and the ANZ Pavilion. The system utilises a FM signal, providing coverage to all seats in the venues via headphones or neckloops, and is available from the venue ushers.

Patrons may seek assistance into the auditorium from any of the front of house staff either at the St Kilda Road Level Concierge Desk in The Theatres Building or in the theatre foyer. There are a small number of wheelchairs available for in-house use (i.e. from carpark to seats) but these must be booked by calling the Concierge in advance. Accessible car parking is available in the Arts centre car park, however, limited spaces are available. There is also some disabled street parking around the Sydney Myer Music Bowl on a first come, first serve basis.

See also

- List of concert halls

External links

- The Arts Centre [9]

National Gallery of Victoria

Geographical coordinates: 37°49′21″S 144°58′07″E

<table>
<tr><td colspan="2" align="center">National Gallery of Victoria</td></tr>
<tr><td colspan="2" align="center"></td></tr>
<tr><td>Established</td><td>1861</td></tr>
<tr><td>Location</td><td>Southbank, Victoria, Australia</td></tr>
<tr><td>Type</td><td>Art gallery</td></tr>
<tr><td>Visitor figures</td><td>1,650,000 (2006/2007) [1]</td></tr>
<tr><td>Director</td><td>Gerard Vaughan</td></tr>
<tr><td>Public transit access</td><td>Flinders Street Station
Tram routes 1, 3, 5, 6, 8, 16, 64, 67, 72</td></tr>
<tr><td>Website</td><td>http://www.ngv.vic.gov.au</td></tr>
</table>

The **National Gallery of Victoria** is an art gallery and museum in Melbourne, Australia. Founded in 1861, it is the oldest and the largest public art gallery in Australia. The main gallery is located in St Kilda Road, in the heart of the Melbourne Arts Precinct of Southbank, with a branch gallery at Federation Square.

National Gallery Of Victoria (NGV)

At the time when the gallery opened, Victoria was an independent colony for just ten years, but in the wake of the Victorian gold rush, it was easily the richest part of Australia, and Melbourne the largest city. Generous gifts from wealthy citizens, notably industrialist Alfred Felton, made it possible for the National Gallery to start purchasing large collections of overseas works from both old and modern masters. It currently holds 63,000 works of art.

The National Gallery of Victoria Art School, associated with the gallery, was founded in 1867. It was the leading centre for academic art training in Australia until about 1910. The School's graduates went on to become some of Australia's most significant artists.

Heidelberg era

In the late 19th and early 20th century, domestic art began to thrive (particularly with the "Heidelberg School" in what was then an outer suburb of Melbourne) and the National Gallery was well-placed to add an excellent collection of key Australian works, which trace the metamorphosis of imported European styles into distinctively Australian art. One of the most famous works at the gallery is *The pioneer* by Frederick McCubbin (1904).

Collection

The International Collection includes works by Gian Lorenzo Bernini, Marco Palmezzano, Rembrandt, Peter Paul Rubens, Giovanni Battista Tiepolo, Tintoretto, Paolo Uccello, and Paolo Veronese, amongst others. In the Modern collection, the gallery has continued to expand into new areas, becoming an early leader in textiles, fashion, photography, and Australian Aboriginal art. Today it has strong collections in areas as diverse as old masters, Greek vases, Egyptian artifacts and historical European ceramics, and the largest and most comprehensive range of artworks in Australia.[citation needed]

The latest addition to the collection is "The Rest on the Flight Into Egypt with Saint Catherine and Angels" by Paris Bordone. The purchase price was $3.8 million from

The view looking south towards the entrance to the gallery

The pioneer by Frederick McCubbin (1904) at the National Gallery of Victoria

National Gallery of Victoria entrance sign carved by Walter Langcake, 180 St Kilda Road

a private dealer, one-third funded by NGV Council of Trustees Allan and Maria Myers. This is the largest amount ever paid for a painting in the NGV collection.

As a "National Gallery"

The gallery's name has caused some confusion over the years, as Victoria is not, and never has been a nation, but a state of Australia, and there is also the National Gallery of Australia (NGA) in Canberra. Some people, such as the chairman of the NGA, have called for the NGV to be renamed, perhaps to "Melbourne Gallery". However, the NGV was founded some 40 years before the founding of the Commonwealth of Australia, when Victoria was a self governing British colony; the name alludes to that period, when Victoria was a discrete political entity. It was also established more than a century before the National Gallery in Canberra. According to former Victorian Premier Steve Bracks, "We won't be renaming the National Gallery of Victoria. It has a great tradition. It is the biggest and best gallery in the country and it's one of the biggest and best in the world."

Ian Potter Centre and NGV International

In 1959, the commission to design a new gallery and cultural centre was awarded to the architectural firm Grounds Romberg Boyd. In 1962, Roy Grounds split from his partners Frederick Romberg and Robin Boyd, retained the commission, and designed the gallery at 180 St Kilda Road (now known as **NGV International**). The building was completed in December 1967 and opened on 20 August 1968. One of the features of the gallery buildings are famous for is the Leonard French ceiling, one of the world's largest pieces of suspended stained glass. The

The "mousehole" entrance features a "water wall", the first in Melbourne.

Leonard French ceiling, conference rooms and upper gallery

ceiling casts colourful light on the floor below. Grounds subsequently designed the adjacent Victorian Arts Centre with its iconic spire.

The gallery is now spread over two buildings a short distance from each other at the southern end of the CBD. A new space, **The Ian Potter Centre**, in Federation Square opened in 2003 and houses the Australian art collection. Grounds' building just south of the Yarra River now houses the international collection. It reopened in December 2003 after four years of renovations by architect Mario Bellini.

The iconic *Angel* sculpture by Deborah Halpern was removed to be restored and relocated to Birrarung Marr. The Australian collection includes a large number of works donated by Dr. Joseph Brown in 2004, which forms the Joseph Brown Collection.

Picasso theft

A famous event in the history of the gallery was the theft of Pablo Picasso's painting "The Weeping Woman" in 1986 by a person or group who identified themselves as the "Australian Cultural Terrorists". The group took the painting to protest the perceived poor treatment of the arts by the state government of the time and sought as a ransom the establishment of an art prize for young artists. The painting was returned in a railway locker a week later.

Blockbusters

The National Gallery of Victoria has held several large exhibitions known as "blockbusters", starting with *Impressionists: Masterpieces from the Musee d'Orsay* in 2004, and an exhibition of Dutch masters in winter 2005 with Vermeer's painting The Love Letter from the Rijksmuseum in Amsterdam exhibited among many others. It was the first time a Vermeer painting had been exhibited in Australia. There was also an exhibition of Caravaggio paintings in 2004.

The 2006 Melbourne Winter Masterpieces exhibition was titled *Picasso: Love and War 1935-1945* and ran from 30 June 2006 and 8 October 2006. The exhibition of over 300 Picasso drawings and paintings from the years 1935-1945 was curated by Anne Baldassari, Director of the Musée Picasso, Paris.

The 2007 Melbourne Winter Masterpieces exhibition was titled "Guggenheim Collection 1940s to now" (30 June to 7 October 2007) and showed more than 85 works by 68 artists, mainly from the Solomon R. Guggenheim Museum, New York City, but also from other Guggenheim Museums in Venice, Bilbao, and Berlin. The exhibition did not travel to any other city; it was seen by more than 180,000 visitors.

The 2008 Melbourne Winter Masterpieces exhibition was titled "Art Deco 1910—1939" and ran from 28 June to 5 October 2008. The exhibition was organized by the Victoria and Albert Museum, London.

The 2009 Melbourne Winter Masterpieces exhibition was titled "Salvador Dalí Liquid Desire" and ran from 13 June to 4 October 2009.

Directors of the NGV

Directors of the NGV since its inception:

- G. F. Folingsby, 1882–91
- L. Bernard Hall, 1891-35
- W. B. McInnes, (acting) 1935-36
- P. M. Carew-Smyth, (acting) 1937
- J. S. Macdonald, 1936–41
- Daryl Lindsay, 1942–55
- Eric Westbrook, 1956–73
- Gordon Thomson (administrator), 1973–74
- Eric Rowlison, 1975–80
- Patrick McCaughey, 1981–87
- Rodney Wilson, 1988
- James Mollison, 1989–95
- Timothy Potts, 1995–98
- Gerard Vaughan, 1999-

External links

- NGV Official website [2]
- Archive [3] of William Blake exhibit
- Egyptian objects in the National Gallery of Victoria [4]

State Library of Victoria

State Library of Victoria	
Established	1854
Location	Melbourne, Victoria, Australia
Collection	
Size	2M books
Other information	
Budget	$48.7M (FY 2008-09)
Director	John Cain (President)
Staff	295
Website	http://www.slv.vic.gov.au

The **State Library of Victoria** is the central library of the state of Victoria, Australia, located in Melbourne. It is on the block bounded by Swanston, La Trobe, Russell, and Little Lonsdale Streets, in the northern centre of the central business district. The library holds over 1.5 million books and 16,000 serials, including the diaries of the city's founders, John Batman and John Pascoe Fawkner, and the folios of Captain James Cook.

History

In 1853 the decision to build a state library was made at the instigation of Lieutenant-Governor Charles La Trobe and Sir Redmond Barry. A competition was held to decide who would design the new building; local architect Joseph Reed, who later designed the Melbourne Town Hall and the Royal Exhibition Building, won the commission.

A panoramic view of the library facade, forecourt and lawns from Swanston Street

On 3 July 1854, the recently inaugurated Governor Sir Charles Hotham laid the foundation stone of both the new library and the University of Melbourne. The library opened in 1856, with a collection of 3,800 books chosen by Sir Redmond, the President of Trustees. Augustus H. Tulk, the first librarian, was appointed three months after the opening.

The first reading room was the Queen's Reading Room (now Queen's Hall), which opened in 1859. Temporary buildings built in 1866 for the Intercolonial Exhibition remained in use by the library until 1909, when work began on a new annexe building to mark the library's Jubilee. This new building was the landmark Domed Reading Room, which opened in 1913 and was designed by Norman G. Peebles.

Plans for the original annexe were scaled back due to the money running out and the annexe, to house a new museum were gradually built during the Interwar years in an austere stripped classical style.

The reading dome's original skylights were modified and covered in copper sheets in 1959 due to water leakage.

The library complex also held the State's Gallery and Museum until the National Gallery of Victoria moved to St Kilda Road in the late 1960s, and the current Melbourne Museum was built in the Carlton Gardens in the 1990s.

The library underwent major refurbishments between 1990 and 2004, designed by architects Ancher Mortlock & Woolley. The project cost approximately AU$200 million. The reading room closed in 1999 to allow for renovation, during which natural light was returned. The renamed La Trobe Reading Room reopened in 2003.

The redevelopment included the construction of a number of exhibition spaces which are used to house the permanent exhibitions The Mirror of the World: Books and Ideas and The Changing Face of Victoria as well as a display from the Pictures Collection in the Cowen Gallery. As a result of the redevelopment the State Library of Victoria could now be considered one of the largest exhibiting libraries in the world.

In 2009 work began to re-develop the southern wing of the library on Little Lonsdale St to create the Wheeler Centre, part of Melbourne's city of literature initiative. The centre officially opened in February 2010.

Front lawn, forecourt and statues

The grassy lawn in front of the library's grand entrance on Swanston Street is a popular lunch-spot for the city's workers and students at the adjacent RMIT University. Originally enclosed by a picket fence, then by a wrought iron fence and gates in the 1870s, the space was opened with the removal of the fence in 1939.

A number of statues are in the entrance area. A pair of bronze lions graced the park from the 1860s until 1937. There are statues of Sir Redmond Barry, designed by James Gilbert and built by Percival Ball, installed in 1887;

A view of the library from the left side facing Swanston Street

Saint George and the Dragon, by the English sculptor Sir Joseph Edgar Boehm, installed in 1889; Jeanne d'Arc (Joan of Arc), a replica of the statue by French sculptor Emmanuel Frémiet, installed in 1907; and Charles La Trobe, by Australian sculptor Peter Corlett, installed in 2006.

On Sundays between 2.30pm and 5.30pm a speakers' forum takes place on the library forecourt, where orators take turns in speaking on various subjects.

Interior

Reading Room and Dome

The landmark Domed Reading Room, which opened in 1913 and was designed by Norman G. Peebles. Its octagonal space was designed to hold over a million books and up to 500 readers. It is 34.75 m in both diameter and height, and its oculus is nearly 5 m wide. The dome was the largest of its type in the world on completion.

In 1965, the La Trobe Building annex was opened to house the Library's Australiana collection, which has since moved to the La Trobe Reading Room.

Australian band Faker recorded their music video for 'Hurricane' inside the reading room in 2005.

The La Trobe Reading Room

Arts Library

The library maintains an extensive, world-class collection of books, periodicals, recordings and other materials pertaining to art, music and the performing arts.

Chess room

The library has a chess room that houses a wide range of materials dedicated to the history, study and practice of chess. It contains a collection of items from the Anderson Chess Collection, one of the three largest public chess collections in the world. In addition to bookshelves containing an extensive range of books and periodicals relating to chess, the room has game tables with chessboards and pieces, and a few glass cabinets containing historical chess paraphernalia. The room is a multi-purpose room intended also for reading and studying.

Collections

Databases

Many of the library's electronic databases are available from home to any Victorian registered as a State Library User. Databases include the full Encyclopædia Britannica; Oxford Reference dictionaries and encyclopaedias; multi-subject magazine and journal article databases; newspaper archives of most major Australian and international papers from 2000 onwards; and specialist subject databases.

Gallery

The library from Melbourne Central, showing the whole roof, including the renowned dome, and the left-side street entry

Panoramic view of the La Trobe Reading Room

The Redmond Barry Reading Room

State Library of Victoria (Cowen Gallery - Stawell Room)

State Library of Victoria (Cowen Gallery - McArthur Room)

State Library of Victoria (Cowen Gallery)

State Library of Victoria (Exhibition of Stained Glass - William Shakespeare in the Dome Gallery)

References

- "State Library of Victoria" [1]. *Libraries*. National Library of Australia. Retrieved 2008-10-21.

External links

- State Library of Victoria's Official Website [1]
- Wheeler Centre [2]

Geographical coordinates: 37°48′35″S 144°57′53″E

St Paul's Cathedral, Melbourne

St Paul's Cathedral, Melbourne

St. Paul's Cathedral Interior (Arcade)

Archbishop of Melbourne	The Most Revd Philip Freier
Dean of Melbourne	The Rt Revd Dr Mark Burton
Precentor	The Revd Rachel McDougall
Associate Clergy	The Revd Jim Brady, The Revd Christopher Carolane, The Revd Dr Ray Cleary
Healing Ministry	The Revd Lawrence Turnbull
Director of Music + Organist	Dr June Nixon
Affiliations	Anglican Church
Cathedral Location	Cnr Flinders Street + Swanston Street
Website	St Paul's Cathedral [1]

St Paul's Cathedral, Melbourne, is the metropolitical and cathedral church of the Anglican Diocese of Melbourne, Victoria in Australia. It is the seat of the Anglican Archbishop of Melbourne and Metropolitan of the Province of Victoria. The cathedral, which was built in stages, is a major Melbourne landmark.

Location

The cathedral is located in the centre of Melbourne, on the eastern corner of Swanston Street and Flinders Street. It is diagonally opposite Flinders Street Station, which was the transport hub of 19th century Melbourne and is still an important centre. Immediately to the south of the cathedral across Flinders Street is the new public heart of Melbourne, Federation Square. Continuing south down Swanston Street is Princes Bridge which crosses the Yarra River, leading to St Kilda Road. The cathedral therefore commands the southern approaches to the city.

History

Although there was no established church in colonial Victoria, most of the colony's establishment were Anglicans and the Church of England, (as it was then called), was given the best site in Melbourne for its cathedral. At the time of its construction St Paul's was the tallest building in central Melbourne and dominated the city's skyline. The growth of multi-storey buildings in central Melbourne during the 20th century robbed St Paul's of its commanding position and restricted views from many angles. The recent construction of Federation Square, which involved the demolition of a pair of adjacent highrise buildings, the Gas and Fuel Buildings, has improved the Cathedral's visibility from the south.

St Paul's is built on the site of Melbourne's first Christian service, conducted on the banks of the Yarra a few months after Melbourne was founded in 1835. The area was a market until 1848, when St Paul's Parish Church, a bluestone church, was built on the site.

In 1885, as Melbourne grew rapidly, this church was demolished to make way for the new cathedral. It replaced St James Old Cathedral, which then stood on the corner of William Street and Collins Street, but was later removed to a site near the Flagstaff Gardens.

Papal Visit

On 28 November 1986 on arrival in Melbourne Pope John Paul II made a brief visit to the cathedral in recognition of the dialogue between the Anglican and Roman Catholic churches in Melbourne fostered by respective former archbishops, the Most Reverend Sir Frank Woods (Anglican) and the Most Reverend Sir Frank Little (Roman Catholic).

The cathedral choir sang *Ecce vicit Leo* as His Holiness entered the cathedral, after which His Holiness prayed for Christian Unity, and lit a metre-long candle. A memorial chapel (see below) commemorates this historic occasion: the third time in four centuries where a Pope had entered an Anglican Cathedral.

Architecture

St Paul's is built in a revival of the style known as Gothic transitional, being partly Early English and partly Decorated. It was designed by the distinguished English architect William Butterfield, who was noted for his ecclesiastical work. The foundation stone was laid in 1880. Butterfield never saw the site and the building work was frequently delayed by disputes between Butterfield, in England, and the Church authorities on the spot. Butterfield resigned in 1884 and the building was finished by a local architect, Joseph Reed. Consequently the design of the spires differs greatly from those originally planned (similar to those built at Christ Church, South Yarra). The Cathedral Chapter has a scale model of the original completed design.

The Cathedral was consecrated on 22 January 1891, but the building of the spires did not begin until 1926. The spires were designed by John Barr of Sydney. An organ was imported from England and is acknowledged as the finest surviving work of T. C. Lewis, one of the greatest organ-builders of the 19th century. Besides Sunday and weekday Mass the cathedral also has a tradition of a daily choral evensong, one of the few Anglican cathedrals outside the British Isles to do so.

St Paul's Cathedral: the north face and the spire

St Paul's in unusual among Melbourne's great 19th century public buildings in that it is not made from bluestone, the city's dominant building material. Instead it is made from sandstone from the Barrabool Hills and limestone embellishments of Waurn Ponds limestone, both from near Geelong, giving the cathedral a warm yellow-brown colouring rather than Melbourne's characteristic cold blue-grey. This gives it a strikingly different appearance to the bluestone Gothic of St Patrick's Catholic cathedral on the eastern edge of the city. Because the spires are made from Sydney sandstone and are thirty years newer, they are of a darker tone than the older parts of the building. St Paul's Moorhouse Tower is the second highest Anglican spire in the world, the tallest being Salisbury Cathedral's.

By the 1990s the constant traffic vibration of central Melbourne had led to concerns about the structural soundness of the cathedral, particularly the spires. A public appeal, led by the then Dean, the Very Reverend David Richardson, raised AU$18 million to restore the spires and improve the interior of the building. The seven-year restoration project is almost complete under the guidance of Falkinger Andronas Architects and Heritage Consultants. The restoration works were undertaken by Cathedral Stone. The Restoration Works were acknowledge by the Australian Institute of Architects with the Llachlan Macquarie National Award for Heritage Architecture 2009.

As part of the work, stone heads of Dean David Richardson and philanthropist Dame Elisabeth Murdoch, created by Melbourne sculptor Smiley Williams were added to the spires, and new dalle de verre glass was created by Janusz and Magda Kuszbicki for the new west doors and the 'Eighth Day' lantern in the Moorhouse Tower.

Dean

Deans of Melbourne

- Hussey Burgh Macartney (1852–1894)
- George Oakley Vance (1894–1910)
- Reginald Stephen (1910–1914)
- Charles John Godby (1914–1919)
- John Stephen Hart (1919–1927)
- George Ellis Aickin (1927–1932)
- Frederick Waldegrave Head (1934–1941)

Night view

- Henry Thomas Langley (1942–1947)
- Alfred Roscoe Wilson (1947–1953)
- Stuart Barton Babbage (1953–1962)
- Tom William Thomas (1962–1984)
- James Alexander Grant (1985–1999)
- David John Leyburn Richardson (1999–2008) Dean Emeritus
- Mark Gregory Burton (2009-)

Music

Director of Music + Organists of St Paul's Cathedral

- Ernest Wood (1888–1914)
- A. E. Floyd (1914–1947)
- C. C. Campbell Ross (1947–1951)
- Lance Hardy (1951–1973)
- June Nixon (1973–present)

Dr June Nixon was awarded a Lambeth Doctorate by the Archbishop of Canterbury in recognition of her long contribution to choral and organ music; the first female to be so honoured.

Organ

The cathedral's pipe organ which was built by T. C. Lewis and
Co of Brixton, England. Over six and half thousand pounds
were spent on its construction, shipping and installation
before it was played at the cathedral's opening in 1891.
Various modifications and maintenance works have been
carried out since then, culminating in a $726,000 restoration
which was completed in 1990 with the help of a National
Trust appeal. In its restored state the organ has four manuals
with 44 stops and pedals with nine stops, all with
electro-pneumatic action. It is housed in the cathedral's south
transept behind newly-stencilled facade pipes.

Organ

Choir

Originally formed in 1888 in conjunction with the choir of All Saints' St Kilda, the cathedral choir led
the procession for the official opening in 1891.

The choir today consists of 20 boys (on scholarships) and 16 men. It sings weekday evensong (Tuesday
- Friday) and two regular services on Sunday. However the choir is also called upon for special events
and is known to sing at chapter evensongs, synod services, state funerals, concerts and carol services.

Stained glass

The robes worn by the choir have evolved over time.
Originally, the choir wore traditional black cassocks and
white surplices. With the introduction of the *Australian
Prayer Book* in the late 1970s new cassocks of a green colour
approximating that of the new prayer book cover (and
coincidentally, that of the visible organ pipework at the time)
were introduced and surplices were discontinued. On a visit to
the cathedral in 1985 by the then Archbishop of Canterbury, a
somewhat astonished Robert Runcie exclaimed that he had
"never seen a cathedral choir wearing *green* robes before".

With the restoration of the organ in the early 1990s, surplices were restored and cassocks of a deep
burgundy were introduced matching the new stencil design hue on the organ pipes.

Currently the boys' choir has a leadership team consisting of the Head Chorister (Head Boy), assisted
by a Deputy Head Chorister. The Head Chorister (and Deputy Head Chorister) perform the leadership
and ceremonial roles common throughout the Anglican Church. However the role of "Dean's Chorister"
was created by the previous Dean of Melbourne, David Richardson, which at the level between Senior
Chorister/s and Deputy Head Chorister, primarily has the role of leading the choir procession with the

'virge', or ceremonial mace.

On 28 November 2007, a carol service featuring the choir was recorded by the Australian Broadcasting Corporation and telecast Australia-wide on Christmas Eve.

Belfry

St Paul's has one of the few peals of thirteen bells outside the British Isles. The bells were donated by Thomas Dyer Edwardes. They are rung regularly, with practice sessions held on Wednesday and Friday evenings.

Music foundation

Established in 1993, the cathedral's music foundation is solely responsible for paying the lay clerks (men singers) and music staff (including the director of music), as well maintaining the organ, purchasing music and funding promotions.

As seen from Flinders Street Station

Services

Sundays

- 8.00am Holy Communion (1662 Book of Common Prayer)
- 9:15am Sung Eucharist (First Sunday of the month: Family Eucharist)
- 10.30am Choral Eucharist
- 6.00pm Choral Evensong (First Sunday of the month: Choral Eucharist)

Mondays to Fridays

- 7.45am Eucharist (Wednesday)
- 12.15pm Eucharist (Monday to Saturday)
- 5.10pm Evening Prayer (Monday)
- 5.10pm Choral Evensong (Tuesday - Friday during school term, otherwise Evening Prayer)
- 6.00pm Healing Service (Tuesday)

Saturdays and Public Holidays

- 12.15pm Said Eucharist

Image gallery

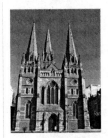

Spires (Gothic Revival)

Sanctuary

Interior (Commemorates the visit of Pope John Paul II)

Chapel

West End

Interior

See also

- List of Anglo-Catholic Churches

External links

- St Paul's Cathedral, Melbourne [1]
- Anglican Diocese of Melbourne
- Disability information [2]
- St Paul's Cathedral [3] at Culture Victoria
- Falkinger Andronas Architects, Heritage Consultants [4]

Geographical coordinates: 37°49′01″S 144°58′03″E

Collins Street Baptist Church

Collins Street Baptist Church is a Baptist church in central Melbourne, Australia. Founded on this site in 1845, it is the oldest Baptist church in Victoria. It is best known as the former church of the outspoken minister Tim Costello, brother of the former Treasurer of Australia, Peter Costello.

The first Baptist service in Melbourne was held in 1838 in a tent on a vacant allotment of land opposite the present church. The first chapel was built on the

Collins Street Baptist Church

current site in 1845. In the late 1850s it was decided to enlarge the building. The current church was designed Joseph Reed, the architect who designed the Melbourne Town Hall and several other prominent Melbourne churches, and the new church was opened in 1862. Unlike most Melbourne churches of the period, which are either Gothic or Romanesque, Collins St Baptist is in the form of a classical temple, with four Corinthian columns facing the street. According to the church's website, this "reflects the Baptist understanding of the church as a gathered community of believers rather than as a special building."

In conformity with the Baptist dislike of decoration in churches, the interior has plain plastered walls. It has arched moulded windows, a double aisle and side seats facing the pulpit. A central raised pulpit emphasises the stress in Baptist theology on the Word of God being read and preached as central features of the services of worship. Seating is arranged in a "U" shape around the central axis determined by the pulpit and the Communion table. There is no form of decoration other than some detail in the windows and carving on the pulpit and Communion furniture. No cross or symbol appears in the church.

Baptist tradition also disapproved of music in churches, but in 1854 a small organ was installed. In 1885 the a larger organ was installed. This was restored and expanded in 1974.

Jim Barr was appointed a minister of Collins Street Baptist Church in 1991, when he established the Urban Mission Unit (now known as Urban Seed), recruited the first group of mission interns and implemented the SEEDS training program. This time was followed by his appointment as the Pastor at

Collins Street Baptist Church from 1994 to 2000. During this time Jim was responsible for the pastoral and liturgical leadership of the Church community as well as taking a keen interest in the world around the Collins Street church.

Tim Costello, a lawyer, republican activist and former Mayor of St Kilda as well as a Baptist Minister, was appointed a Pastor of the Collins Street Baptist Church and Director of the Urban Mission Unit in 1995, the year before his brother, Peter Costello, became Federal Treasurer. Tim Costello's outspoken comments on many social and political issues brought new attention to the church. Under his leadership, the Urban Mission Unit rose to prominence as a leading voice on urban, business, social and political issues including homelessness, drug addiction, problem gambling and poverty. The Urban Mission Unit changed its name to Urban Seed in 2001. Tim Costello left the position in 2004 on being appointed chief executive officer of World Vision Australia. The Senior Pastor is now Rev Rowena Curtis.

Several historically notable individuals were members of the church. During the early 20th century the numerous women active in the Victorian women's movement were members including Cecilia Downing, Margaret McLean and Bessie Rees. Politicians Denis Lovegrove, Robert Reid were members as were prominent Melbourne Syme family, including owner of *The Age* David Syme.

External links

- Collins Street Baptist Church [1]
- Urban Seed [2]

Geographical coordinates: 37°48′53″S 144°58′04″E

East Melbourne Hebrew Congregation

East Melbourne Hebrew Congregation	
Basic information	
Location	488 Albert St, East Melbourne, Victoria, ⚑ Australia
Geographic coordinates	37°48′33″S 144°58′27″E
Affiliation	Orthodox Judaism
Year consecrated	1877
Status	Active
Leadership	Rabbi Dovid Gutnick
Website	melbournecitysynagogue.com [1]
Architectural description	
Architect(s)	Crouch & Wilson
Architectural style	Renaissance Revival
Direction of facade	South
Groundbreaking	20th March, 1877
Completed	1877
Construction cost	£7000
Specifications	
Capacity	470
Length	22.2m (73 ft)
Width	12.8m (42 ft)
Height (max)	9.4m (31 ft)
Dome(s)	2

Materials	Brick

The **East Melbourne Hebrew Congregation** (Hebrew: ק"ק מקוה ישראל), also known as **East Melbourne Shule**, **East Melbourne Synagogue**, **Melbourne City Synagogue** or **City of Melbourne Synagogue** is a historical Jewish congregation in East Melbourne, Victoria, Australia. The synagogue, consecrated in 1877, is the oldest in Melbourne.

History

The congregation was formed in 1857 under the leadership of Reverend Moses Rintel following his leave from the Melbourne Hebrew Congregation. Initially named Mikveh Israel Melbourne Synagogue, it was provided with a government land grant in 1859 on the corner of Little Lonsdale Street and Stephen Street (today Exhibition Street) in Melbourne's City Centre. A small synagogue was erected on the site in 1860. The congregation consisted primarily of Rintel's followers, including German and Eastern-European Jews who lived in Melbourne's inner-city suburbs within walking distance of the synagogue.

Seeking new premises, the congregation received government permission to sell its property in 1870. It moved to a new site on Albert Street, East Melbourne, where a new synagogue building was consecrated in 1877. Rintel served the congregation until his death in 1880.

In March 1977 the synagogue's centenary was celebrated with a special service led by Rabbi M. Honig.

Architecture

Continuously in use since 1877, the East Melbourne Synagogue is the oldest in Melbourne and the largest 19th-century synagogue in Victoria. It is listed on the Victorian Heritage Register and is classified by the National Trust of Australia due to its historical, social, and architectural significance.

The two-storeyed synagogue was designed by noted Melbourne architects Crouch & Wilson. The internal space is surrounded on three sides by a gallery carried by cast iron columns, each surmounted by an unusual arrangement of an impost block flanked by consoles. The main ceiling is paneled, with a row of large and unusual ventilators marking the location of former suspended gas lights. The original interior, particularly the Bimah and Torah ark, remain in an intact state.

The building's facade, constructed in the style of Renaissance Revival, was completed in 1883. It comprises five bays. Tuscan pilasters divide the bays of the lower floor, and Corinthian pilasters divide the upper floor bays. Two dome-like mansard roofs flank the central pediment.

Today

Led by Rabbi Dovid Gutnick since November 2007, the congregation has a current membership of around 200 families. It is currently the only synagogue in Melbourne's inner-city area.

See also

- History of the Jews in Australia
- List of synagogues in Australia and New Zealand
- Oldest synagogues in the world

External links

- East Melbourne Hebrew Congregation website [1]
- East Melbourne Synagogue on the Victorian Heritage Register [2]
- East Melbourne Synagogue at the National Trust [3]

Further reading

- History of the East Melbourne Hebrew Congregation "Mickva Yisrael", 1857–1977, By Morris C. Davis, East Melbourne Hebrew Congregation, 1977

ISBN 0959689907, 9780959689907

- Historical Sketch of the Two Melbourne Synagogues Together with Sermons Preached, by Dattner Jacobson and Moses Rintel (1877), By Maurice Brodzky, Dattner Jacobson, Moses Rintel, Kessinger Publishing LLC, 2009

ISBN 1104177714

Scots' Church, Melbourne

Scots' Church, Melbourne	
 The Scots' Church, Melbourne	
Location	Collins Street, Melbourne
Country	Australia
Denomination	Presbyterian Church of Australia
Website	Scotschurch.com [1]
History	
Founder(s)	Rev James Forbes
Architecture	
Architect(s)	Joseph Reed
Style	Neo-Gothic
Administration	
Division	Presbyterian Church of Victoria
Subdivision	Presbytery of Melbourne West
Clergy	
Senior pastor(s)	Rt Rev Douglas Robertson
Pastor(s)	Rev Richard O'Brien Rev John Diacos Rev Geoffrey Blackburn

The Scots' Church, a Presbyterian church in Melbourne, Australia, was the first Presbyterian Church to be built in the Port Phillip District (now the state of Victoria). It is located in Collins Street and is a congregation of the Presbyterian Church of Australia.

Background

The Rev James Forbes was recruited to come to Australia as a Presbyterian Minister by the Rev John Dunmore Lang, arriving in Melbourne from Sydney by boat on 20 January 1838. He found that retired Church of Scotland minister Rev James Clow had arrived on 25 December 1837 and had commenced an afternoon service between 2 and 4 according to Presbyterian forms in a basic building constructed west of William Street and north of Little Collins Street (now the site of the AMP centre). Clow had been a Church of Scotland chaplain in Bombay but had retired and was of independent means. He had intended to settle in South Australia but when he stopped en route in Hobart the positive reports about Port Phillip led him to visit in October 1837 and then settle permanently.

Original church

The Olderfleet Buildings, near the site of the first Scots' Church

Forbes continued the Presbyterian services commenced by Clow on 31 December 1837 in the Pioneers Church near the north west corner of William Street and Little Collins Street. The Church of England soon made exclusive claims to this communal building and so Forbes held services in Craig and Broadfoot's store in Collins Street until a temporary timber building called Scots Church was opened on the adjoining land loaned by David Fisher in July 1838. The site was between where the Olderfleet and Rialto buildings were subsequently erected (Lot 14 Section 2). It was essentially a large room with a fireplace.

On Saturday 3 February 1838 a meeting of members and friends of the Church of Scotland was held with James Clow in the chair. It was resolved to build a church and that £300 be raised in order to obtain the matching grant available under the Church Act. This is regarded as the official birthday of Presbyterianism in Victoria and of the beginning of Scots' Church. A committee of James Clow (treasurer), James Forbes and Skene Graig (secretaries) was appointed to collect subscriptions and to take the steps to obtain a church site. The sum of £139.19.0 was subscribed on the spot.

Scots Church secured a 2.0-acre (8100 m^2) site on the corner of Collins and Russell Streets as a Government grant. When the site was allocated, the elders objected that it was "too far out of town".

The temporary building also served as the Scots' Church School which relocated to new brick premises in September 1839 on the western part of the 2-acre (8100 m^2) site on the corner of Collins and Russell

Streets adjoining the present Baptist Church and on which the George's department store was later erected.

First Scots' Church

The foundation stone of the first purpose built church building was laid on 22 January 1841 and it was opened on 3 October 1841. It was designed to seat 500 and the contract sum was £2,485 without plastering, gallery, vestry or fittings. The building was opened with temporary seating. Plastering was carried out the following year, proper pews, gallery and vestry were added in 1849 and a spire some years later.

The Assembly Building, adjoining the site of the first Scots' Church in Collins Street

James Forbes built a two-story manse (minister's house) on the site where the Assembly Hall now stands and was later reimbursed. The manse was sold to the General Assembly of the Presbyterian Church of Victoria for 5,000 pounds in about 1913. In 2007 the Assembly Hall was bought by the Scots' Church Properties Trust to be renovated for use as congregational offices and meeting halls following the demolition of the Scots' Church Hall in Russell Street and the heritage listed Scots' Church Car Park and the redevelopment of the site with a 10 story building.

This first church building was demolished partly because of concerns that the tower and spire would collapse after it developed huge cracks and became crooked.[citation needed] The congregation had outgrown the building during Gold Rush of 1850s & 1860s as the population of Melbourne expanded.

Current Building

One of the stained glass windows at Scots, depicting the Parable of the Hidden Treasure and the Parable of the Pearl

Construction of the current building took place between 1871 and 1874, during the ministry of Rev Irving Hetherington and his assistant Rev Peter Menzies, and was opened on 29 November 1874 with seating for 1000. It was designed by Joseph Reed of the firm Reed and Barnes, and built by David Mitchell, the father of Dame Nellie Melba. Reed and Barnes also designed the Melbourne Town Hall, the State Library of Victoria, Trades Hall, the Royal Exhibition Building, the Wesley Church in Lonsdale Street, the original Presbyterian Ladies' College in East Melbourne, and Collins Street Independent Church, now St. Michael's Uniting Church, on the opposite corner of Russell Street.

Scots' is in the Neo-Gothic style and built of Barrabol freestone, with dressings in Kakanul stone from New Zealand . During the last decades of the nineteenth century the spire of Scots' Church was the tallest structure in Melbourne. The interior features the large stained glass window depicting the Last Supper, basalt asile columns, timber beamed roof and an elevated floor for a good view of the pulpit.

Laid up in the church are two sets of Regimental Colours of the Australian 5th Battalion, The Victorian Scottish Regiment, which include the honour LANDING at ANZAC.

The crest & flag of Australian Prime Minister Sir Robert Menzies are located near lectern. Queen Elizabeth II was present for the presentation by Dame Pattie Menzies in 1983. Queen Elizabeth had been accompanied by Sir Robert in 1961 when they visited Scots' to unveil a war memorial mosaic in the vestibule near the entrance.

Music

Organ

The first pipe organ at Scots' was built in 1883 by Hill and Son. It was rebuilt and enlarged in 1910 by George Fincham and Sons and rebuilt again in 1959. The organ was removed for storage in 1999. The present organ was built in 1998 by Orgelbau, Schwarzach, Austria.

Choir

The Choir of Scots' Church has been under the Director of Music Douglas Lawrence since 1984. He had started the Choir of Ormond College (University of Melbourne) in 1982 and raised the standard at

Scot's considerably. The Choir released their first recording in 1987: *Joy my Heart Outpoured*. Scots' Choir consists of four principals, eight choral scholars and other members. Dame Nellie Melba reputedly started and finished her singing career in the choir at Scot's Church, and her funeral was taken from Scots' in February 1931.

Ministers

The first minister of Scots' Church was Rev James Forbes, who, as well as being involved in the foundation of Scots' Church, was instrumental in the establishment of John Knox Free Presbyterian Church on Swanston Street (now housing a Church of Christ congregation), Scotch College, Royal Melbourne Hospital, and the Melbourne Mechanics' Institute.

Rev Charles Strong became the minister in 1875. His theology was questioned after the publication of an article in the Victorian Review entitled "The Atonement", but he resigned from Scots' Church before the Presbyterian Church of Victoria heard the case.

Scots' Church is currently served by a senior minister, Rev Douglas Robertson, and a minister to the central business district, Rev Richard O'Brien. Rev Geoffrey Blackburn serves as the pastoral care minister.

Scots' Church tower in the gothic revival style

Historically, most of the senior ministers at Scots' Church have been trained or served in the Church of Scotland, including Robertson, who first worked at Scots' as an assistant minister between 1991 and 1994. He returned to Scotland to take up the position of Parish Minister in Appin And Lismore, North Argyll, but was then called by the congregation of Scots' Church to come back to Melbourne and serve as senior minister from February 2001. Robertson recently served as moderator of the Presbyterian Church of Victoria.

As in any church with a Presbyterian structure, the ministers of Scots' govern and care for the congregation with a body of Church Elders called the Session.

Services

Services are held on every Sunday of the year. A traditional service is held at 11:00am and a contemporary service known as *engage city church* (formerly known as *sevententhirty*) at 5pm at 156 Collins Street. Communion is held on the first Sunday of each season (Autumn, Winter, Spring and Summer) and on Easter Sunday. A lunchtime service for innercity workers is held at 1pm every

Wednesday. From time to time prominent members of the community are invited preach at this service. In 2006 one such speaker was Australian golfer Aaron Baddeley. On the Wednesday before the AFL Grand Final, Scots' hosts a Grand Final Service. The speaker at this service in 2009 was Shaun Hart.

An Indonesian language service is held every Sunday at 5:15pm. On April 1, 2007, the congregation known as the Indonesian Christian Church [2] officially joined Scots'.

Theology

As a congregation of the Presbyterian Church of Australia, the ministers and elders of Scots' Church are required to ascribe to the Westminster Confession of Faith, the major English statement of Calvinistic Christianity.

Members are not required to ascribe to the Westminster Confession, but, if they are not already a member of a Christian church, are admitted to membership by making a public declaration of faith in Jesus Christ and their commitment to the church.

Ecumenism

Scots' Church has participated in a number of ecumenical activities. Two Catholics have preached from the pulpit of Scots' Church: Archbishop of Melbourne Sir Frank Little in 1974 and Bishop Mark Coleridge in May 2005.

Francis Macnab & the Ten Commandments

In September 2008, Francis Macnab of St Michael's Uniting Church launched what he called a "new faith" with a $120,000 advertising campaign including posters reading, "The Ten Commandments, one of the most negative documents ever written."

The Session of Scots' Church published a reply defending the Ten Commandments from "[t]he most incredible publicity war... being waged against the historic Christian faith." They installed a poster on their Russell Street frontage facing towards St. Michael's, outlining the influence of the Ten Commandments and calling it "the most positive and influential document ever written."

A poster published and displayed by Scots' Church in response to a poster from St. Michael's Uniting Church describing the Ten Commandments as "one of the most negative documents ever written".

External links

- Scots' Church home page [3]
- The Choir of Scots' Church at Move Records [4]
- Catholic bishop preaches at Scots' [5]

Photos

- Design for the new Presbyterian Church, Collins Street, 1872 from wood engraving. From the State Library of Victoria [6]
- Scots' Church in 1877 by Nicholas J. Caire. From the National Library of Australia [7]
- Scots' in situ, Collins Street 1880s. From the National Library of Victoria [8]
- Original pulpit from the State Library of Victoria [9]
- Scots' Church today. Exterior from east [10]
- Scots' Church today. Exterior from east II [11]
- Scots' Church today. Exterior from west [12]
- Scots' Church today. Exterior from west at night [13]

37°48′53″S 144°58′08″E

St Francis Catholic Church (Melbourne)

St Francis' Church is the oldest Catholic church in Victoria, Australia. Located on the corner of Lonsdale Street and Elizabeth Street, it is one of only three buildings in central Melbourne which predates the Gold Rush of 1851.

History

The church's foundation stone was laid on 4 October 1841, the feast day of St Francis of Assisi, to whom the church is dedicated. It was commissioned by Fr Patrick Geoghegan, the first Catholic priest in the Port Phillip District of New South Wales, which became Victoria in 1851. In 1848 St Francis' became the cathedral church of the first Catholic Bishop of Melbourne, James Goold, and continued as a Cathedral until 1868, when the diocesan seat was moved to the still unfinished St Patrick's Cathedral (which was not formally consecrated until 1897).

Centrally located in the Melbourne's CBD, St Francis' has never lost its place as one of the city's most popular and widely-used churches, and today is the busiest church in Australia, with more than 10,000 worshippers attending each week. Since 1929 it has been a Centre of Eucharistic Life in the care of the Congregation of the Blessed Sacrament. The church is listed with Victorian Heritage Register, the National Trust of Australia (Victoria) and the Australian Heritage Commission. Although there have been many changes made to the building, including the erection of a new tower, a gift from the Grollo family, to house the original 1853 bell imported from Dublin, the church remains essentially as it was designed by Samuel Jackson.

External links

- St Francis Church [1]

Geographical coordinates: 37°48′42″S 144°57′45″E

St Patrick's Cathedral, Melbourne

St. Patrick's Cathedral	
	The Gothic Revival Central Tower of St Patrick's Cathedral
Basic information	
Location	Melbourne, Australia
Geographic coordinates	37°48′36″S 144°58′34″E
Affiliation	Roman Catholic
District	Archdiocese of Melbourne
Year consecrated	1897
Ecclesiastical or organizational status	Minor basilica
Leadership	Archbishop Denis James Hart
Website	www.stpatrickscathedral.org.au [1]
Architectural description	
Architect(s)	William Wardell
Architectural style	Gothic Revival
Completed	1939

St Patrick's Cathedral is the cathedral church of the Roman Catholic Archdiocese of Melbourne in Victoria, Australia, and seat of its archbishop, currently Denis J. Hart. It is known internationally as a leading example of the Gothic Revival style of architecture.

In 1974 Pope Paul VI conferred the title and dignity of minor basilica on it. In 1986 Pope John Paul II visited the Cathedral and addressed clergy during his Papal Visit.

The Cathedral is built on a traditional east-west axis, with the altar at the eastern end, symbolising belief in the resurrection of Christ. The plan is in the style of a Latin cross, consisting of a nave with side aisles, transepts with side aisles, a sanctuary with seven chapels, and sacristies. It is 103.6 metres long on its long axis, 56.4 metres wide across the transepts and 25.3 metres wide across the nave. The nave and transepts are 28.9 metres high. The central spire is 105 metres high and the flanking towers and spires are 61.9 metres high.

History

In 1848, James Goold, an Augustinian friar, was appointed the first bishop of Melbourne, and became the fourth bishop in Australia, after Sydney, Hobart and Adelaide.

Negotiations with the colonial government for the grant of five acres of land for a church in the Eastern Hill area began in 1848. On 1 April 1851, only 16 years after the foundation of Melbourne, the Colonial Secretary of Victoria finally granted the site to the Roman Catholic Church.

Goold decided to build his Cathedral on the Eastern Hill site. Since the Catholic community of Melbourne was at the time almost entirely Irish, the Cathedral was dedicated to St Patrick, the patron saint of Ireland.

View of the main entrance to the cathedral

William Wardell, Melbourne's foremost ecclesiastical architect was commissioned to prepare plans for a Cathedral, but the project was delayed by severe labour shortages during the Gold Rush of 1851, which drew almost every able-bodied man in the colony to the goldfields, and the foundation stone was not laid until 1858. The Cathedral was designed in the [Gothic] style [of early Fourteenth Century England], based on the great mediæval cathedrals of England, a style at the height of its popularity in the mid 19th century. The nave [exhibits 'curvilinear traceries' in the principal windows of circa 1300 to 1350is; the transepts have traceries] in Geometric Decorated, a style [of the immediately previous thirty years in England.][The eastern arm with its chevet of chapels in the French manner is still principally in the English late Thirteenth Century style, giving the most complete essay attempted in that style during the Nineteenth Century. William] Wardell [was a remarkably ambitious and capable architect; he went on] to design the second St Mary's Cathedral, Sydney in a similar style, [even larger than St Patrick's, but with a completely English square East End].

In 1974 Pope Paul VI conferred the title and dignity of minor basilica on it. In 1986 Pope John Paul II visited the Cathedral and addressed clergy during his Papal Visit.

Construction

Although the nave was completed within ten years, construction proceeded slowly, and was further delayed by the severe depression which hit Melbourne in 1891. Under the leadership of Archbishop Thomas Carr the Cathedral was consecrated in 1897 and even then it was not finished. Given the size of the Catholic community at the time, the massive bluestone Gothic cathedral was an immense and very expensive undertaking, and there were long delays while funds were raised. St Patrick's was [one of] the [two] largest church[es] brought to substantial completion anywhere in the world in the 19th century. ADD [The other is St Patrick's Cathedral, New York, USA]

St Patrick's Cathedral, Melbourne. The statue in the foreground is of the Irish nationalist leader Daniel O'Connell

Daniel Mannix, who became Archbishop of Melbourne in 1917, maintained a constant interest in the cathedral, which he was determined to see finished after the long delays during the previous 30 years. He oversaw the addition of the spires and other elements in the late 1930s. The building was officially completed in 1939.

Restoration

To celebrate the centenary of its consecration in 1997, the Cathedral was closed throughout 1994 to be upgraded. Nothing was added to the main building. Rather, it underwent significant conservation work, with funds contributed by the federal and Victorian governments, corporate and philanthropic donors and the community of Melbourne.

The Cathedral's stained glass windows had buckled and cracked, and required the full year to restore to their original state. Teams of stonemasons and stained-glass craftsmen used "lime mortars and materials long-forgotten by the building trade — like medieval times." The 1992-97 restoration works were undertaken under the guidance of Falkinger Andronas Architcts and Heritage Consultants. The Works were awarded the Royal Australian Institute of Architects (Victorian Chapeter) John George Knight Award for Heritage Architecture 1996.

Music

Cathedral choir

There has been music at St Patrick's since 1858, but the present cathedral choir was founded in 1939, when the Vienna Mozart Boys Choir found itself stranded in Australia at the outbreak of war. The choir has between 50-60 members who are all students of St Kevin's College in Toorak, through a scholarship program from the archdiocese. The choir has made commercial recordings in the past, mainly from 1950s to 1990s. Selected recording before the 80s have been deposited with the National Film and Sound Archive (Screensound Australia).

Cathedral singers

Formed in May 1996, the St Patrick's Cathedral Singers supplement the musical resources of the Cathedral. They sing weekly at the Sunday evening mass. Entrance is by audition, and some scholarship are available to eligible students from the Australian Catholic University. Its current musical director is Dr Geoffrey Cox.

Pipe organs

The cathedral's original pipe organ was built in the late 1870s by Robert Mackenzie and completed in 1880 by George Fincham. The current installation built by George Fincham & Sons, Melbourne in 1962-64 and incorporates a substantial part of the original. Installed in the west gallery of the cathedral, it comprises 81 speaking stops spread over four manuals and pedals. Some of the stops can be dated to 1880 or 1896, when the instrument was enlarged.The organ was refurbished in 1996-97 for the centenary of the cathedral. In addition to serving the liturgical needs of the cathedral, the organ is occasional used for recitals and recordings.

Bells

The bells of the cathedral were acquired by Bishop Goold, Melbourne's Roman Catholic leader at that time, when he visited Europe in 1851-1852. He bought a peal of eight bells for £500 (with some records showing that it cost £700). They arrived in Australia in 1853. The peal of eight is in F natural, with the tenor weighing approximately 700 kilograms. The peal set weights around 3556 kilograms or 3.556 metric tons.

The bells were hung in a low frame at ground level in the western aisle in 1868. The consecration service was attended by around 5,000 people. The eight bell bears the coat of arms of Bishop Goold. The bells were eventually hung at the south-eastern tower.

The ringers of St Patrick's began the custom of ringing in the New Year in 1871. And by the 1880s, St Patrick's Cathedral became the leading tower for Australian change ringing. The bells were rung for the requiem mass of Pope Pius X in 1914. by 1959 the belfry fell into disrepair and the bells became unringable. The bells remained silent until in 1988, when the peal was sent to Eayre and Smith Bell foundry in England as the major Victorian project among Bicententennial bell restorations. Upon their return, a ninth bell, an Angelus bell, was added. An electronic chiming mechanism was also installed at this time for all the bells. The original manual method was retained by the electronic mechanism, in order to replicate how the bells would have sounded if they were rung by hand. The entire eight headstocks had to be replaced just ten years after this installation.

The bells are unique in that they were cast untuned, they ring anti-clockwise instead of clockwise, and they are thought to be the only ring of eight bells cast by Murphy which are still in operation today.

Photo Gallery of St Patrick's Cathedral

St Patrick's Cathedral - Gothic Revival Architecture

St Patrick's Cathedral - Gothic Revival Architecture

St Patrick's Cathedral - Gothic Revival (East Side)

St Patrick's Cathedral East Side

St Patrick's Cathedral – St Catherine of Siena (1347-1380) Statue

St Patrick's Cathedral – St Francis of Assisi (1181-1226) Statue

St Patrick's Cathedral – River from the throne of God & of the Lamb

St Patrick's Cathedral – River Fall

St Patrick's Cathedral Entrance Interior

St Patrick's Cathedral Interior

St Patrick's Cathedral Interior

St Patrick's Cathedral - Music Organ

See also

- Media related to St Patrick's Cathedral, Melbourne at Wikimedia Commons

References

- O'Farrell, Patrick (1977). *The Catholic Church and Community in Australia*. Thomas Nelson (Australia), west Melbourne.

External links

- St Patrick's Cathedral website [1]

Wesley Church, Melbourne

Wesley Church is a Uniting Church in the centre of Melbourne, in the State of Victoria, Australia.

Wesley Church was originally built as the central church of the Wesleyan movement in Victoria. It is named after John Wesley (1703–1791), the founder of Methodism. Today Wesley Church is the home of two Uniting Church congregations, the English-speaking Wesley Church, and the Chinese-speaking Gospel Hall.

In 1902, the Wesleyan Church in Australia combined with four other churches to form the Methodist Church of Australasia. In 1977, the Methodist, Presbyterian and Congregational Churches further combined to form the Uniting Church.

History

Wesleyans were part of the life of Melbourne from the beginning of European settlement. The first Christian worship service in Melbourne was led by Henry Reed [1], a businessman and Wesleyan lay preacher from Launceston, Tasmania. The first service by an ordained Christian minister in Melbourne was led by Joseph Orton [2], Wesleyan Superintendent of Tasmania, on 24 April 1836. Joseph Orton had been a strong opponent of slavery in Jamaica, where he was imprisoned for his views. In Tasmania, he was an equally strong critic of mistreatment of aboriginal people.

A small chapel was built in 1838, and then replaced with a larger one in Collins Street, able to seat 600 people, opened in June 1841. The organ imported for that church in 1842 is still in use in the present church.

The present Wesley Church, in Lonsdale Street was built in 1858. The Superintendent, Daniel Draper [3], strongly proposed a grand gothic design with high quality architecture. This design was criticised by many Wesleyans as too ornate, too Gothic and too Anglican for a Wesleyan Church. However, Draper's design prevailed. The foundation stone was laid on 2 December 1857, and the Church was opened on 26 August 1858.

This Church was the central congregation of the Wesleyan Church for Victoria, where the Conferences met, and where ministers were ordained. It was located in a poor part of Melbourne, and pioneered many initiatives in Community Service. In the 1880s, a team of Biblewomen were appointed to work with people experiencing serious poverty. One of these was Mrs Varcoe, who established Livingstone House, a home for homeless boys in Drummond St, Carlton.

In 1869, Wesley Church appointed Moy Ling [4] to begin a Chinese-speaking congregation in Little Bourke Street. He named it the "Gospel Hall".

In 1893, during the acute depression which followed the bank crash of 1891, Alexander Edgar [5] was appointed as minister, with an expectation that he would develop a city mission and be its first

Superintendent. So Wesley became the base for the Central Methodist Mission, now called Wesley Mission Victoria, which grew into one of Melbourne's largest non-profit social welfare agencies. Its headquarters on this site adjoin the church. Edgar also began the "Pleasant Sunday Afternoon", where major speakers would speak about important public questions.

Irving Benson [6] was Superintendent of the Mission for over 40 years, from 1926 to 1967. Under his leadership, the Pleasant Sunday Afternoon was broadcast on radio, widely across Victoria. The Central Methodist Mission took many new initiatives in that time, and he was knighted for his services to the community. However his conservative political views placed him increasingly at odds with the leadership of the Methodist Church.

His successor was Arthur Preston, Superintendent from 1968 to 1981. Under his leadership the Mission closed many of its institutions and replaced them by personal services. He was also a strong vocal opponent of the war in Vietnam.

In the 1970s, the Gospel Hall Chinese Church outgrew its building in Little Bourke St, and transferred its main service to Wesley Church.

Wesley Church became a Congregation of the Uniting Church in Australia in 1977, as did all Methodist Churches in Australia.

In 2000, both the Congregation and the Mission Board became polarised over proposals to establish a primary care health facility in the grounds, which would have included the option of supervised drug injection. As a result of this very public dispute, the Synod of Victoria separated the Mission from the Congregation in 2001. They now function as two separate bodies.

Since 2001, Wesley Congregation has become very cross-cultural, including members from many Asian cultures. This tendency has been encouraged by the previous minister, Jason Kioa, and the present minister, Douglas Miller.

Wesley Church's website [7] describes its worship and theological style as "orthodox biblical teaching, classical reformed worship, and a cross-cultural lifestyle".

Architecture

Wesley Church was designed by Joseph Reed, who also designed the Melbourne Town Hall, the Scots' Church and the Independent Church (now St. Michael's in Collins St. The church is in the English Gothic style and takes the shape of a cross.

The church is 50.3 metres long from north to south and 23.5 metres across at the transepts. It has an octagonal spire rising 53.3 meters above ground level.

Wesley's organ was the first pipe organ in Melbourne. It was built in England, and arrived in Melbourne in 1842, being moved to the present church in 1858. It was largely rebuilt in 1957.

Inside the church are two paintings by the noted Australian painter Rupert Bunny (1864–1947): "The Prodigal Son" (Luke 15:11-32) and "Abraham's Sacrifice" (Genesis 22:1-14), which Bunny gave to Wesley Church in 1934.

A statue of John Wesley stands in front of the church. It was sculpted by the British sculptor Paul Raphael Montford in 1935.

The grounds contain other buildings, including the former School House, 1852, the old Parsonage, and Nicholas Hall, an art deco style hall which was a gift of the Nicholas family. Wesley House is the administrative centre of Wesley Mission. The Princess Mary Club, built to provide accommodation for young women starting study or a career in the city, was opened in 1926.

The grounds also contain an olive tree transplanted to the church grounds in 1875, but believed to be from a cutting brought to Melbourne from Jerusalem in 1839. This claim cannot be verified. If true, this tree could be the oldest imported tree in Victoria.

Sources

"A Century of Victorian Methodism", by C Irving Benson, Spectator Publishing Company, Melbourne, 1935.

"In Celebration of Faith: Stories and photos through 150 years at Wesley Church, Melbourne", edited Bill Gillard, 2008, published by Wesley Church Council to mark the 150th anniversary of the Church building.

External links

- Wesley Church Website [7]
- Gospel Hall Website [8]
- Wesley Mission Victoria Website [9]

Bishopscourt, East Melbourne

Bischopscourt is a large colonial mansion, located on Clarendon Street in East Melbourne, Australia.

Designed by Newson & Blackburn using blue stone in a style of gothic architecture, it was completed in 1853. The red brick wing was added in 1903.

Since completion, it has been used as the residence for all of Melbourne's Anglican Bishops and Archbishops since its completion. Between 1874 and 1876, it was used as Victoria's Government House.

The house is on the Victorian Heritage Register.

References

- Grant, James (2010). *A Suitable Residence: A Brief History of Bishopscourt Melbourne.* Australian Scholarly Publishing Pty Ltd. ISBN 978 1 921509 80 3.

Shrine of Remembrance

The **Shrine of Remembrance**, located in Kings Domain on St Kilda Road, Melbourne, Australia was built as a memorial to the men and women of Victoria who served in World War I and is now a memorial to all Australians who have served in war. It is a site of annual observances of ANZAC Day (25 April) and Remembrance Day (11 November) and is one of the largest war memorials in Australia.

Designed by architects Phillip Hudson and James Wardrop who were both World War I veterans, the Shrine is in a classical style, being based on the Tomb of Mausolus at Halicarnassus and the Parthenon in Athens. Built from Tynong granite, the Shrine originally consisted only of the central sanctuary surrounded by the ambulatory. The sanctuary contains the marble Stone of Remembrance, upon which is engraved the words "Greater love hath no man". Once a year, on 11 November at 11 a.m. (Remembrance Day), a ray of sunlight shines through an aperture in the roof to light up the word "Love" in the inscription. Beneath the sanctuary lies the crypt, which contains a bronze statue of a soldier father and son, and panels listing every unit of the Australian Imperial Force. In 2002-2003 a Visitor Centre was built within the foundations of the Shrine. The visitor centre incorporates an education centre (including three classrooms and meeting room), an audio-visual centre, gallery space, a retail shop and an administration office, as well the Hall of Columns (in which the Changi Flag is on display) Gallery of Medals, entry courtyard and Remembrance Garden. The walls of both the entry courtyard and Remembrance Garden have been built to complement the Ray of Light ceremony that takes place on 11 November of every year.

The Shrine went through a prolonged process of development which began in 1918 with the initial proposal to build a Victorian memorial. Two committees were formed, the second of which ran a competition for the memorial's design. The winner was announced in 1922. However, opposition to the proposal (led by Keith Murdoch and *The Herald*) forced the governments of the day to rethink the design, and a number of alternatives were proposed, the most significant of which was the ANZAC Square and cenotaph proposal of 1926. In response, General Sir John Monash used the 1927 ANZAC Day march to garner support for the Shrine, and finally won the support of the Victorian government later that year. The foundation stone was laid on 11 November 1927, and the Shrine was officially dedicated on 11 November 1934.

History

Conception: 1918–1922

A war memorial in Melbourne was proposed as soon as the war ended in November 1918. In the early 1920s the Victorian state government appointed the War Memorials Advisory Committee, chaired by Sir Baldwin Spencer, which recommended an "arch of victory" over St Kilda Road, the major boulevard leading out of the city of Melbourne to the south. In August 1921 an executive committee was formed, with the former commander of the Australian forces in the war, General Sir John Monash, as its

Ceremonial Avenue, looking towards the city of Melbourne from the shrine

driving force. The committee soon abandoned the idea of an arch and proposed a large monumental memorial to the east of St Kilda Road, a position which would make it clearly visible from the centre of the city. A competition was launched in March 1922 to find a design for the new memorial, open both to British subjects residing in Australia and any Australian citizens who were residing overseas. A total of 83 entries were submitted, and in December 1923 the design offered by two Melbourne architects (and war veterans), Phillip Hudson and James Wardrop, was announced as the winner.

Opposition and response: 1922–1927

The winning design had a number of supporters, including publications such as *The Age* and George Taylor's Sydney-based trade journal, *Building*, prominent citizens including artist Norman Lindsay and University of Sydney Dean of Architecture, Leslie Wilkinson, and the Royal Australian Institute of Architects (who had been heavily involved in the competition). Nevertheless, the design was also fiercely criticised in some quarters—especially by Keith Murdoch's *Herald*, Murdoch reportedly describing the Shrine as "too severe, stiff and heavy, that there is no grace or beauty about it and that it is a tomb of gloom"—on the grounds of its grandiosity, its severity of design and its expense. As part of the campaign against the Shrine proposal, the *Herald* searched for alternative concepts, arguing that the funds could be better spent on more practical projects such as a hospital or a war widow's home. Furthermore, some Christian churches also attacked the design as pagan for having no cross or other Christian element.

Sir John Monash (left), one of the leading proponents for the Shrine, and Keith Murdoch (right) editor-in-chief of the Melbourne paper *The Herald*, a leading opponent who described the proposed Shrine as "a tomb of gloom".

The new Victorian Labor government of 1924, under George Prendergast, supported the *Herald's* view, and pushed for a memorial hospital instead of the Shrine. When the Labor government was replaced with John Allan's Country/National coalition, the plan changed once again, leaning towards the earlier suggestion of an arch of victory to be built over St. Kilda Road. As a result of the debate, significant delays postponed the construction of the new memorial, so a temporary wood-and-plaster cenotaph was raised for the 1926 ANZAC day march. The success of the temporary cenotaph led the Victorian government to abandon the earlier project in 1926, and propose instead to build a permanent cenotaph in a large "ANZAC Square" at the top of Bourke St in front of Parliament House. While this would have involved demolishing the Windsor Hotel, one of Melbourne's favourite hotels, the new plan won the support of the *Herald*, the Returned Soldiers League (RSL) and the Melbourne City Council.

Nevertheless, both Monash and Legacy still supported the Shrine. After a vote in favour of the Shrine by their executive council, Legacy started a public relations campaign, gaining the support of much of the media—although the council, state government and the *Herald* continued to oppose. In 1927, with the then Duke of York, Prince Albert, visiting the country, Monash spoke on the eve of ANZAC day at the RSL dinner, arguing for the Shrine. The audience had been seeded with supporters, who provided a standing ovation at the conclusion of his speech, which helped to produce a groundswell of support. When a vote was called for, the majority voted in favour of the Shrine proposal. The next day, with

Monash leading 30,000 veterans in the 1927 ANZAC Day march, and with the new support of the RSL, The *Age*, and the *Argus*, the Shrine proposal had gained "new momentum". Faced with such support, and with Monash's arguments that the ANZAC Square would be prohibitively expensive, Edmond Hogan's new Labor government decided in favour of the Shrine.

Another early point of contention (although not explicitly related to the nature of the memorial) concerned the possibility of incorporating a "Tomb of the Unknown Soldier" into the memorial—an approach that was championed by the St. Kilda RSL, who revealed plans to bury a soldier from either Gallipoli or France on ANZAC day, April 25, 1922. This proposal received considerable debate, and was countered by the argument that the Unknown Warrior in Westminster Abbey represented all of the dead of the British Empire. Monash was on the side of those against such a burial, as while he could see a place for an Unknown Soldier in a national memorial, he did not feel that it would be suitable at the Victorian Shrine. The Stone of Remembrance was later placed in the position where an Unknown Soldier might have been laid. An Australian Unknown Soldier was eventually interred at the Australian War Memorial by Prime Minister Paul Keating on 11 November 1993.

Construction and dedication: 1927–1934

The foundation stone was laid on 11 November 1927, by the Governor of Victoria, Lord Somers. Although both the Victorian and Commonwealth governments made contributions, most of the cost of the Shrine (£160,000 out of a total of £250,000) was raised in less than six months by public contributions, with Monash as chief fundraiser.

The dedication ceremony for the Shrine of Remembrance. Over 300,000 people were in attendance, a figure that was approximately a third of Melbourne's population at the time.

Monash, who was also an engineer, took personal charge of the construction, which began in 1928 and was handled by the contractors Vaughan & Lodge. Monash died in 1931, before the Shrine was finished, but the Shrine was the cause "closest to his heart" in his later years.

Work was finally completed in September 1934, and the Shrine was formally dedicated on 11 November 1934 by the Duke of Gloucester, witnessed by a crowd of over 300,000 people—a "massive turnout" given that Melbourne's population at the time was approximately 1 million, and, according to Carl Bridge, the "largest crowd ever to assemble in Australia to that date".

The Shrine in the 1930s showing the reflecting pool in front of the north face, where the World War II Forecourt is now located

Post World War II: 1945–1985

After World War II it was felt necessary to add to the Shrine an element commemorating the Australian war dead of the second great conflict. Once again a competition was run, with A. S. Fall and E. E. Milston as the joint winners. Milston's design was eventually chosen as the one to go ahead, and the result was the World War II Forecourt, a wide expanse of stone in front of the Shrine's north face; the Eternal Flame, a permanent gas flame set just to the west of the north face; and the World War II Memorial, a 12.5-metre-high (41 ft) cenotaph a little further west. The Forecourt replaced a reflecting pool that had previously stood in front of the Shrine. These enlargements were dedicated by Queen Elizabeth II on 28 February 1954. Australia's involvements in later wars, such as the Korean War, the Malayan Emergency, the Vietnam War and the Gulf War, are commemorated by inscriptions.

In 1951 the body of Field Marshal Sir Thomas Blamey, Australia's military commander during World War II, was held at the Shrine for three days for public viewing followed by a State funeral on site. 20,000 people visited the Shrine as he lay in state.

During the Vietnam War the Shrine became a centre of conflict when anti-war demonstrators protested during ANZAC Day services against Australia's involvement in the war. In 1971 the Shrine was defaced when the word PEACE! was painted in large white letters on the pillars of the north portico. Despite vigorous cleaning, the porous nature of the stone used in the Shrine's construction meant that the slogan remained faintly visible for over 20 years.

In 1985 the Remembrance Garden was added beneath the western face of the Shrine to honour those who served during post-World War II conflicts.

Redevelopment: 2002 – present day

The Shrine after the completion of the 2002-2003 redevelopment.

Restoration work on the terraces surrounding the Shrine during the 1990s raised once again the possibility of taking advantage of the space under the Shrine: as the Shrine had been built on a hollow artificial hill, the undercroft (although at the time filled with rubble from the construction) provided a large space for development. At a planned cost of $5.5 million, the new development was intended to provide a visitor's centre, administration facilities and an improved access to the Shrine's crypt, as many of the remaining veterans and their families found the stairs at the traditional ceremonial entrance difficult to climb. In redeveloping the site, special consideration was given to the positioning of the new entrance. The original plan was to use a tunnel from the east, but this was discarded as it had "no sense of ceremony". Instead it was decided to develop two new courtyards, and place the new gallery under the northern steps. Construction commenced in 2002, with the design by Melbourne architects Ashton Raggatt McDougall, and the new areas were opened in August 2003. The completed project was awarded the Victorian Architecture Medal by the Royal Australian Institute of Architects in 2004.

After this construction was complete, there were still more calls to further develop the site, and especially to provide facilities for education about the wars. A $62 million proposal was presented in 2006, incorporating a museum and an underground carpark. Designed once again by Ashton Raggatt McDougall, the proposal was opposed by local residents and some council members, and ran into significant funding problems when the Federal Government decided not to help with funding.

Architecture and features

Materials for building the Shrine were sourced from within Australia: the chosen building stone was granodiorite quarried from Tynong; the internal walls use sandstone from Redesdale; and the black marble columns used stone from Buchan. This raised some concerns when redeveloping the Shrine, as the Tynong quarry was no longer in use, and it proved to be prohibitively expensive to reopen the site. Fortunately another quarry in the area was available and was able to provide the necessary stone.

Exterior

The design of the Shrine is based on the ancient Mausoleum of Maussollos at Halicarnassus, one of the Seven Wonders of the World, and the Parthenon in Athens. It is a structure of square plan roofed by a stepped pyramid and entered on the north and south through classical porticos, each of eight fluted Doric columns

One of the four groups of statuary which mark the corners of the Shrine.

supporting a pediment containing sculpture in high relief. The porticos are approached by wide flights of steps which rise in stages to the podium on which the Shrines sits. The east and west facing fronts are marked at the corners by four groups of statuary by Paul Raphael Montford, representing Peace, Justice, Patriotism and Sacrifice. The Art Deco style and motifs draw on Greek and Assyrian sculpture. The symbolism is Neo-Classical.

Around the outer stone balustrade that marks the Shrines external boundary are the "battle honours" disks, 16 stone discs. These represent the battle honours granted by King George V and commemorate Australia's contributions to the following battles: Landing at Anzac, (that is, Gallipoli), Sari Bair, Rumani, Gaza-Beersheba, the North Sea, the Cocos Islands, Megiddo, Damascus, Villers Bretonneux, Amiens, Mont St Quentin, the Hindenburg Line, Ypres, Messines, Pozieres and Bullecourt.

The Sanctuary

Interior

Inside the Shrine is the Sanctuary, a high vaulted space entered by four tall portals of Classical design. A simple entabulature is carried on sixteen tall fluted Ionic columns and supports a frieze with twelve relief panels sculptured by Lyndon Dadswell, depicting the armed services at work and in action during World War I. At the centre of the Sanctuary is the Stone of Remembrance. This is a marble stone sunk below the pavement, so that visitors must bow their heads to read the inscription on it:

GREATER LOVE HATH NO MAN

The inscription is part of a verse from the Bible (John 15:13) "Greater love hath no man than this, that a man lay down his life for his friends". The Stone is aligned with an aperture in the roof of the Sanctuary so that a ray of sunlight falls on the word LOVE on the Stone of Remembrance at exactly 11 a.m. on 11 November, marking the hour and day of the Armistice which ended World War I. Since the introduction of daylight saving in Victoria, the ray of sunlight is no longer in the right place at 11 a.m. A mirror has been installed to direct sunlight onto the Stone at 11 a.m. During the rest of the year, a light is used to simulate the effect.

Monash, with the advice of Professor T. G. Tucker and the assistance of Bernard O'Dowd and Felix Meyer, reworded Phillip Hudson's inscription which appears on the western wall of the Shrine:

> LET ALL MEN KNOW THAT THIS IS HOLY GROUND. THIS SHRINE, ESTABLISHED IN THE HEARTS OF MEN AS ON THE SOLID EARTH, COMMEMORATES A PEOPLE'S FORTITUDE AND SACRIFICE. YE THEREFORE THAT COME AFTER, GIVE REMEMBRANCE.

This inscription again aroused criticism, according to Taylor, "for having no Christian, (or, indeed, religious), element", but was considered to fit the Australian tradition of "stoic patriotism".

The inscription on the eastern wall, not written by Monash, reads:

> THIS MONUMENT WAS ERECTED BY A GRATEFUL PEOPLE TO THE HONOURED MEMORY OF THE MEN AND WOMEN WHO SERVED THE EMPIRE IN THE GREAT WAR OF 1914–1918.

A ray of light hits the Stone of Remembrance in the Sanctuary, at 11am on November 11. (photo circa 1940)

The Sanctuary is surrounded by an ambulatory, or passage, along which are forty-two bronze caskets containing hand-written, illuminated Books of Remembrance with the names of every Victorian who enlisted for active service with the Australian Imperial Force (AIF) or Australian Naval and Military Expeditionary Force in World War I or died in camp prior to embarkation.

Crypt

Beneath the Sanctuary is the Crypt containing a bronze statue of a father and son, representing the two generations who served in the two world wars. Around the walls are panels listing every unit of the AIF, down to battalion and regiment, along with the colours of their shoulder patch. The Crypt is hung with the standards of various battalions and regiments, listing their battle honours.

Visitor Centre

Visitors approach the shrine through the Entrance Courtyard, with "Lest We Forget" inscribed on one wall and a quote from former Governor-General Sir William Deane on the other. The Garden Courtyard, on the same alignment, features the Legacy Olive Tree and a seating area. Both courtyards are finished in Tynong Granite.

The gallery of Medals has a 40-metre-long (130 ft) wall displaying around 4000 medals, each symbolically representing 100 Victorians who have served in war and peacekeeping operations, and six who have died. A feature of the gallery is the Victoria Cross awarded to Captain Robert Grieve during the Battle of Messines in 1917. The Cross was lent to the Shrine by Wesley College, Melbourne.

The Cenotaph and Eternal Flame

World War II Forecourt

The cenotaph is a tall pillar constructed of Harcourt Granite. Inscribed on its surface are the names of the defence forces, together with the theatres of war they served in. Atop the cenotaph is a basalt sculpture of six servicemen carrying a bier with a corpse, draped by the Australian flag. The sculpture symbolises "the debt of the living to the dead". The Eternal Flame is placed nearby, representing eternal life. The flame is kept alight at all times and in all weather conditions.

At the other side of the forecourt are three flagpoles. The usual arrangement comprises the Australian flag on the left, the Victorian flag in the middle and one of the flags of the three defence forces on the right. Other flags may be flown on special occasions, arranged according to strict protocols.

Remembrance Garden

The Remembrance Garden features a pool, waterfall and Harcourt granite wall bearing the names of the conflicts and peacekeeping operations in which Australia participated following World War II, such as Kuwait (Gulf War) and East Timor.

Shrine Reserve and environs

Although the original architects had proposed including four statues of war leaders, Monash rejected this plan. Instead there were to be no statues representing individual members of the Australian Defence Force at the shrine itself, although a number of statues were to be added in the surrounding parklands. The first of these was "The Man With The Donkey" representing John Simpson Kirkpatrick, although he was not named on the statue, and officially the work is said to represent the "valour and compassion of the Australian soldier". Nearby is the Lone Pine (*Pinus brutia*). This tree, planted in 1933, is one of four seedlings planted in Victoria from seeds of a cone brought back by Sgt. Keith Mc Dowell from Gallipoli. The statue, by Wallace Anderson, was installed in 1936 on the initiative of women who had founded a "Mother's Tribute". A statue of Monash was also commissioned and was designed by Leslie Bowles. Casting was due to begin in 1938, but the onset of World War II delayed work, and thus it was not installed until 1950, and, as with Simpson and his donkey, was located away from the shrine.

The Shrine is set in a large expanse of parkland officially called Kings Domain. Over the years many other war memorials have been built in this area, including the Australian-Hellenic Memorial to Australian and Greek dead in the Battles of Greece and Crete in 1941, and statues of Monash and Blamey. Most of the trees which line the approaches to the Shrine bear plaques commemorating individual Army units, naval vessels or Air Force squadrons, placed there by veterans' groups. An older memorial to Victorians killed in the Second Boer War of 1899–1902 is also located nearby on the corner of St Kilda and Domain Roads.

The Driver and Wipers Memorial

The Driver and Wipers Memorial, also in the Shrine reserve, commemorates the thousands of Australian lives lost during the fighting at Ypres; "Wipers" is the way servicemen pronounced "Ypres" during World War I. The bronze soldiers are the work of the British sculptor Charles Sargeant Jagger and originally stood outside the Museum and State Library of Victoria in Melbourne. They were transferred to the Shrine in 1998. The Driver is a soldier holding a horse whip and bridles, wearing breeches,a protective legging, spurs, and a steel helmet, and the figure is a recasting of one of the figures from the Royal Artillery Memorial in Hyde Park, London, UK. The other bronze, the "Wipers" figure, is a British infantry soldier standing guard with standard issue .303 rifle, bayonet fixed, a German helmet at his feet. This too is a recasting, taken from the Hoylake and West Kirby War Memorial in Merseyside, UK.

On July 19, 2008 being the 92nd anniversary of the Battle of Fromelles a replica of the 1998 sculpture by Peter Corlett in the *VC Corner Australian Cemetery and Memorial*, Fromelles was unveiled. This depicts Sergeant Simon Fraser, 57th Battalion, (a farmer from Byaduk, Victoria), rescuing a wounded compatriot from *no man's land* after the battle.

Commemorative services

For the past 70 years the Shrine has been the centre of war commemoration in Melbourne. Although Remembrance Day (11 November) is the official day for commemorating the war dead, it has gradually been eclipsed in the public estimation by ANZAC Day (25 April), which unlike Remembrance Day is a specifically Australian (and New Zealand) day of commemoration. ANZAC day at the Shrine is observed through a number of ceremonies. The first of these is the Dawn Service, an event that attracted a record crowd of more than 35,000 in 2007. This is followed by an official wreath-laying service where officials march to

A parade during a ceremony commemorating Operation Pedestal near the Shrine

the Shrine and lay wreaths in the Sanctuary. Later, the ANZAC Day March approaches the Shrine via St Kilda Road and the forecourt, before being dismissed at the steps and is followed by a commemoration service held between 1:00 and 1:30 p.m.

On Remembrance Day, Victorian leaders and community members gather to commemorate "the sacrifices made by Australians in all wars and conflicts". A minutes silence is observed at 11 a.m. as the Ray of Light illuminates the word LOVE on the Stone of Remembrance.

Throughout the rest of the year, ceremonies and wreath laying services are held by Victorian unit associations and battalions in the Sanctuary, around memorials in the Shrine Reserve and near remembrance trees specific to various associations.

Management

The Shrine is managed by the Shrine of Remembrance Trustees, eight individuals appointed by the Governor in Council, on the advice of the Minister for Planning in the Victorian Government. The Trustees are responsible for the care, management, maintenance and preservation of the Shrine and Shrine Reserve.

Traditionally, security for the Shrine has been provided by the Shrine Guard, whose members were men with a military background. All of the original twelve members of the Shrine Guard had won bravery medals during World War I. When the Shrine Guard merged with the Victoria Police Protective Service, some civilians began to serve. During the hours the Shrine is open to the public or in use for any ceremony, they wear a uniform representing an Australian Light Horseman of World War I, with Victoria Police Force insignia.

See also

Other ANZAC articles

- Australian and New Zealand Army Corps, the name used to describe the combination of the Australian and New Zealand Army Corps during wartime
- Anzac Cove, a small, cove on the Gallipoli peninsula in Turkey.
- ANZAC Day, a public holiday in New Zealand and Australia on 25 April every year to commemorate the landing at Gallipoli
- ANZAC spirit, a component of modern Australasian mythology describing the spirit of mateship and cheerful suffering amongst Australians and New Zealanders

References

- Bridge, Carl (2005). "Appeasement and After: Towards a Re-assessment of the Lyons and Menzies Governments' Defence and Foreign Policies, 1931–41". *The Australian Journal of Politics and History* **51**.
- Day, Norman (2003-10-20). "Shrine of Remembrance" [1]. *The Age*.
- Duck, Siobhan (2006-04-05). "Funds call for Shrine". *Malvern Prahran Leader*: p. 7.
- Guerrera, Orietta (2001-06-01). "Pilgrimage easier at reshaped Shrine". *The Age*: p. 8.
- Harrison, Dan (2007-04-25). "'Record crowd' at Melbourne service" [2]. *The Age*. Retrieved 2008-07-14.
- Hetherington, John (1973). *Blamey, controversial soldier : a biography of Field Marshall Sir Thomas Blamey, GBE, KCB, CMG, DSO, ED*. The Australian War Memorial and the Australian Government Publishing service. ISBN 0-642-99382-3.
- Hill, Jeanette (2003-12-09). "Our show of strength". *Herald Sun*.
- Inglis, K. S.; Brazier, Jan (2008). *Sacred Places: War Memorials in the Australian Landscape* (3rd ed.). Victoria, Australia: Melbourne University Press. ISBN 978-052285479-4.
- Isaacson, Peter (1999). "Shrine of Remembrance". *Victorian Historical Journal* **70** (1): 43–53.
- Kleinman, Rachel (2006-03-29). "Shrine plan under fire". *The Age*: p. 9.
- McMullin, Ross (2007-07-16). "After 92 years, cobbers stand tall at the Shrine" [3]. The Age. Retrieved 2008-07-17.
- Minchin, Liz (2005-04-23). "At the going down of the sun, and in the morning, guards watch a sacred site". *The Age*: p. 9.
- Perry, Roland (2004). *Monash: The Outsider Who Won a War*. Random House Australia. ISBN 1-74051-280-4.
- Reed, Dimity (2003-08-09). "New-generation veneration — Shrine of Remembrance". *The Age*: p. 8.
- Royall, Ian (11 December 2007). "Shrine of Remembrance's structure in the wars" [4]. *Herald Sun*. Retrieved 2008-07-12.

- Serle, Geoffrey (1982). *John Monash: A Biography*. Victoria, Australia: Melbourne University Press. ISBN 0-522-84239-9.
- Serle, Geoffrey (1986). "Monash, Sir John (1865 – 1931)" [5]. *Australian Dictionary of Biography*. Melbourne University Press. pp. 543–549. Retrieved 2008-07-13.
- Sheehan, Mark (November 2007). "Australian Public Relations Campaigns: A select historical perspective 1899–1950" [6] (PDF). Australian Media Traditions 2007, Distance and Diversity: Reaching New Audiences. Charles Sturt University, Bathurst, Australia. Retrieved 2008-07-14.
- Silkstone, Dan (2004-07-19). "Medal awarded to St Kilda Road veteran who survived new trenches". *The Age*.
- Taylor, William (2005). "Lest We Forget: the Shrine of Remembrance, its redevelopment and the heritage of dissent" [7] (PDF). *Fabrications* **15** (2): 102. Retrieved 2008-07-12.
- Wilson, Neil (2003-08-09). "Rise & shrine". *Herald Sun*: p. 6.
- Wilson, Neil (2004-11-06). "A special day for a very special place". *Herald Sun*.
- Worthy, Scott (2004). "Communities of Remembrance: Making Auckland's War Memorial Museum". *Journal of Contemporary History* **39** (4, Special Issue: Collective Memory): 599. doi:10.1177/0022009404046756 [8].

External links

- Shrine of Remembrance, Melbourne - Official Site [9]

South Melbourne Town Hall

South Melbourne Town Hall is a civic building located at Bank Place in South Melbourne, a suburb of Melbourne, Australia.

It is of state heritage significance to Victoria being listed on the Victorian Heritage Register (H0217).

The hall was built between 1879-80 to the design of local architect Charles Webb in the Second Empire style, and is considered one of the grandest examples of the style in Australia.

South Melbourne Town Hall. The colours of the Swans Australian Football League club are draped from the tower with respect to the former South Melbourne team competing in the 2006 AFL Grand Final.

South Melbourne Town Hall in 1880

The building is on the Victorian Heritage Register and is part of the important Bank Place precinct, one of the best preserved Victorian era conservation areas in the world.

During the 1950s, the decorative mansard roof elements were removed.

After the amalgamation of the City of South Melbourne with the City of Port Melbourne and the City of St Kilda in 1994 to form the City of Port Phillip, the Town Hall now functions as secondary offices for the new Port Phillip City Council (City of Port Phillip).

The building was restored in 2004 from a government heritage grant, enabling the reinstatement of the decorative roof and iron cresting.

The South Melbourne Town Hall is now home also to the Australian National Academy of Music (ANAM), which is the national centre for performance excellence for the further development of musicians with outstanding talent in Australia.

See also

- List of town halls in Melbourne
- City of Port Phillip
- List of mayors of Yarra

Geographical coordinates: 37°50′03″S 144°57′34″E

Melbourne Town Hall

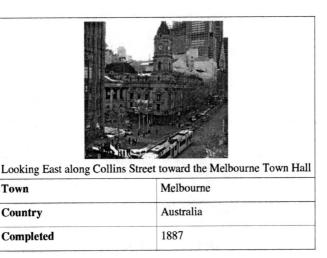

Looking East along Collins Street toward the Melbourne Town Hall	
Town	Melbourne
Country	Australia
Completed	1887

Melbourne Town Hall is the central municipal building of the City of Melbourne, Australia, in the State of Victoria. It is located on the northeast corner of Swanston and Collins Streets, in the central business district. It is the seat of the Local Government Area of the City of Melbourne.

History

Melbourne was officially incorporated as a town on December 13, 1842, with Henry Condell as its first Mayor. However, it wasn't until 1854 that its first Town Hall was completed. Begun in 1851, the work ground to a halt with the beginning of the Victorian gold rush. The foundation stone of a new, grander Town Hall was laid on November 29, 1867 by the visiting Prince Alfred, Duke of Edinburgh, after the demolition of the first. The current Town Hall officially opened on August 9, 1870 with a lavish ball.

The foundation stone of the additional front portico was laid in 1887, and Sir Henry Weedon laid the foundation of the administrative annex building in 1900.

In 1925, a fire destroyed a large part of the town hall, including the main auditorium and pipe organ. It was rebuilt and enlarged, extending east over the site previously occupied by the Victoria Coffee Palace, an early temperance hotel frequented by Melbourne's power brokers. The rebuilt section lost some of Reed's original flourishes including the elaborate mansard roof.

Architecture

The Town Hall was designed by the famous local architect Joseph Reed, in the Second Empire style. Reed's designs also included the State Library of Victoria, the Royal Exhibition Building, and Melbourne Trades Hall.

Melbourne Town Hall, 1910

The building is topped by Prince Alfred's Tower, named after the Duke. The Tower includes a 2.44 m diameter clock, which was started on August 31, 1874, after being presented to the council by the Mayor's son, Vallange Condell. It was built by Smith and Sons of London. The longest of its copper hands measures 1.19 m long, and weighs 8.85 kg.

The Main Auditorium includes a magnificent concert organ, now comprising 147 ranks and 9,568 pipes. The organ was originally built by Hill, Norman & Beard (of England) in 1929 and was recently rebuilt and enlarged by Schantz Organ Company of the United States of America .

Tourism

- List of Town Halls in Melbourne
- List of Mayors and Lord Mayors of Melbourne

External links

- City of Melbourne official website [3]
- Disability information [1]
- [2]

Geographical coordinates: 37°48′55″S 144°58′00″E

Box Hill Town Hall

The **Box Hill Town Hall** is a landmark civic building located (at 37°49′09″S 145°07′36″E) on Whitehorse Road, Box Hill, Victoria, Australia. Designed in the Neo-Grec style by architects JS Gawler and JCA Isbett, the town hall was built between 1934 and 1935. It was the administrative and community headquarters of the City of Box Hill prior to that city's amalgamation with the City of Nunawading to form the new City of Whitehorse in 1994.

Box Hill Town Hall.

The town hall is described as having "regional architectural, historic and social importance" by the National Trust of Australia (Victoria). Its imposing façade has been utilised by the television series *Neighbours* as the external setting for the court house in the fictional town of Erinsborough. The interior includes a main hall and other community and meeting spaces. There are two dates engraved on the town hall's portico – 1927, the year Box Hill was proclaimed a city, and 1994, the year of amalgamation. The crest of the former City of Box Hill is also featured on the portico.

In 2006, the town hall underwent a $6.5 million redevelopment as a hub for community based services and programs and a home for the City of Whitehorse arts and historical collections.

See also

- List of Town Halls in Melbourne

External links

- Box Hill Town Hall [1] (City of Whitehorse)

Brighton Town Hall

Brighton Town Hall	
U.S. National Register of Historic Places	
Brighton Town Hall, April 2008	
Location:	12 Cty Rd. 31, Brighton, New York
Coordinates:	44°26′27″N 74°13′57″W
Area:	0.9 acres (0.36 ha)
Built/Founded:	1914
Architect:	Muncil, Benjamin A.
Architectural style(s):	Bungalow/Craftsman
Governing body:	Local
Added to NRHP:	November 7, 2003
NRHP Reference#:	03001121

Brighton Town Hall is a historic town hall located at Brighton, Franklin County, New York. It was built in 1914 and is a modest, one story American Craftsman style building measuring 35 feet wide and 58 feet deep. It rests on a fieldstone foundation with exposed cobblestone piers at the front. It features three telescoping, graduated gables with exposed rafters and decorative braces. The interior contains a large, 30 feet by 34 feet meeting hall. It was designed by noted architect Benjamin A. Muncil.

It was listed on the National Register of Historic Places in 2003.

Brunswick Town Hall

Brunswick Town Hall is located on the corner of Dawson Street and Sydney Road in the inner northern Melbourne, suburb of Brunswick, Victoria, Australia.

Brunswick was declared a municipality in 1857, after residents petitioned for municipal government. The first municipal chambers were erected in 1859 on Sydney Road at Lobb's Hill, between Stewart and Albion Streets. The present Town Hall is an imposing Victorian building in the Second Empire style, built in 1876.

In 1908 Brunswick became a city.

Diagonally opposite from the Town Hall is the Mechanics' Institute, built in 1868, and used for education and social activities. A monument to the Free Speech fights of the 1930s stands near the corner. The building was acquired by the Brunswick City Council in 1927 and for many years served as the Brunswick Municipal Library.

During 1973 the Brunswick City Council embarked on a plan to demolish the Town Hall and build a modern five story building to house all of council services. The Brunswick Progress Association led a successful public campaign in 1974 against council, to stop the demolition of the town hall.

After the amalgamation of the City of Brunswick with the City of Coburg and the southern portion of the City of Broadmeadows in 1994 to form the City of Moreland, the Town Hall now functions as secondary offices for the new Moreland City Council (City of Moreland).

The Brunswick Town Hall and Atrium is available for hire, and is a venue for the Brunswick Music Festival. The Town Hall building contains the Counihan Gallery and the Brunswick branch of the Moreland City Library.

References

- *It happened in Brunswick 1837-1987* by Les Barnes. Published Brunswick Community History Group
- Moreland City Council Official Website [1]

See also

- List of Town Halls in Melbourne
- City of Brunswick

External links

- http://www.moreland.vic.gov.au/services/brunswicktownhall.htm

Geographical coordinates: 37°46′18″S 144°57′38″E

Camberwell Town Hall

Camberwell Town Hall is located, on Camberwell Road, Camberwell, an inner eastern suburb of Melbourne, Australia.

The Town Hall was built in 1891 in the free classical style and features Second Empire influences in the steep pitch of the clock tower's pyramidal mansard roof.

After the amalgamatian of the City of Camberwell with the Cities of Hawthorn and Kew on 22 June 1994 to form the City of Boroondara, the Town Hall with the Camberwell Civic Centre became the main municipal offices.

See also

• List of Town Halls in Melbourne

Geographical coordinates: 37°50′04″S 145°03′36″E

Camberwell Town Hall.

Coburg City Hall

The **Coburg City Hall**, formerly the Town Hall of the City of Coburg, is located on Bell Street, Coburg, Melbourne, Australia.

The original building, built by Cockram & Cooper Builders and designed by C.R. Heather A.R.V.I.A., consisted of a white dome and two wings (each with a hall), and was officially opened on 1 April 1922, by the Earl of Stradbroke, and Mayor W.E. Cash. The foundation stone reads: "Built in honour of those who served in the Great War 1914-18."

The stone on the Eastern Wing (now near the new office extension) reads: "C.E. Williams for efforts to establishing a free Public Library in Coburg. 30 June 1923".

The Coburg Town Hall had the first installed, Australian-designed and constructed film projection unit (Raycophone) in 1930. At the opening night Mayor Cr. Campbell read letters from the Premier and PM Scullin who wrote: "If similar steps were taken extensively the present depression would be vastly relieved". It is also reported that the dome at the front of the theatre used to show a neon sign saying "Talkies" until the late 1940s.

On the corner of Elm and Urquhart Street is the "Coburg City Band and Truby King Rooms". The foundation stone was laid on 10 October 1925 by Sir Truby King, and completed on 24 July 1926, with a keystone laid by Mayor Cr. J. Robinson. It was designed by D.McC.Dawnson C.E. and now houses the Elm Grove Infant Welfare Centre.

After the amalgamation of the City of Coburg with the City of Brunswick and the southern portion of the City of Broadmeadows in 1994 to form the City of Moreland, the City Hall became the corporate headquarters of the new Moreland City Council (City of Moreland).

Following the amalgamation, the City Hall was extended from Bell Street through to Urquhart Street, and included additional function rooms built in 2000.

External links

- theaterorgans.com [1]

Geographical coordinates: 37°44′27″S 144°58′09″E

Collingwood Town Hall

Collingwood Town Hall is a civic building located on Hoddle Street in Abbotsford, a suburb of Melbourne, Australia.

The hall was built between 1885 and 1890 to the design of local architects George R. Johnson in the Second Empire style, rich in detail and prominent mansard roofs and pyramid domes. It is widely considered one of the finest Town Halls in Australia, and, along with the Sydney Town Hall and South Melbourne Town Hall, one of the best example of the style in Australia.

Fire destroyed the interiors in the 1920s, which were significantly remodelled at the time in an Art Deco style.

After the amalgamatian of the City of Collingwood with the City of Fitzroy and the City of Richmond in 1994 to form the City of Yarra, the Town Hall now functions as secondary offices for the new City.

Collingwood Town Hall is now a used for special functions and as an exhibition space.

Close up of the Collingwood Town Hall

Collingwood Town Hall on Hoddle Street

See also

- List of Town Halls in Melbourne
- City of Yarra
- List of mayors of Yarra
- List of mayors of Collingwood

Geographical coordinates: 37°48′14″S 144°59′33″E

Fitzroy Town Hall

Fitzroy Town Hall is a civic building located in Napier Street in Fitzroy, a suburb of Melbourne, Australia.

It was constructed in two separate stages. The first consisted of a hall and tower which was designed by William J. Ellis and built in 1863. Between 1887 and 1890 a new stage designed by George Johnson was added to this comprising municipal offices, a police station and a courthouse as well as extensions to the hall. The clock tower added at this time replaced the original tower.

The building is an example of the Free Classical style of Victorian architecture and is recorded as a "Heritage place" by Heritage Victoria.

After the amalgamation of the City of Fitzroy with the City of Collingwood and the City of Richmond in 1994 to form the City of Yarra, the Town Hall now functions as secondary offices for the new Yarra City Council (City of Yarra).

Fitzroy Town Hall clock tower

See also

- List of Town Halls in Melbourne
- City of Yarra
- List of Mayors of Yarra
- List of Chairmen and Mayors of Fitzroy

Fitzroy Town Hall

References

Geographical coordinates: 37°48′08″S 144°58′46″E

Footscray Town Hall

Footscray Town Hall, also known as *Maribyrnong Town Hall* since council amalgamations in the 1990s, is a civic building located on Napier Street in Footscray, a suburb of Melbourne, Australia. The hall was built in 1936 to the design of architect Joseph Plottel in the Romanesque style. It replaced the previous town hall on the same site, which was demolished in 1935. The building is now used as the main council chambers of the City of Maribyrnong.

See also

- List of town halls in Melbourne
- City of Maribyrnong

References

Geographical coordinates: 37°48′17″S 144°54′02″E

Heidelberg Town Hall

The civic building in Ivanhoe	
Coordinates	37°45′56″S 145°02′44″E
Alternate names	The Centre Ivanhoe
Town	Ivanhoe
Country	Australia
Completed	1937
Architect	Peck & Kemter

Heidelberg Town Hall is a civic building located on Upper Heidelberg Road in Ivanhoe, a suburb of Melbourne, Australia. It is now more commonly known as **The Centre Ivanhoe**

Opened in April 1937, the building was designed by architectural firm Peck & Kemter in association with A.C. Leith & Bartlett for the Heidelberg City Council (now Banyule City Council) and was influenced by the Hilversum Town Hall in the Netherlands. It is recorded as a "Heritage place" by Heritage Victoria who regard it as "the greatest and most eloquent expression of the interwar brick Moderne style in Victoria."

See also

- List of Town Halls in Melbourne

External links

- Official website [1]

Northcote Town Hall

Northcote Town Hall is a civic building located in High Street in Northcote, a suburb of Melbourne, Australia.

It was designed by George Johnson and built in 1887 as the municipal offices and council chambers for the City of Northcote.

After the amalgamation of the City of Northcote with the City of Preston in 1994 to form the City of Darebin, the Town Hall was redeveloped and renovated into an Arts, Community and Cultural venue.

Northcote Town Hall

The town hall now boasts seven meeting rooms for community meetings, training and passive recreation, two large studios for performances and events, a large main hall for functions and events seating up to 450 people and an outdoor civic square used for outdoor markets and performances.

See also

- List of Town Halls in Melbourne

External links and references

- Northcote Town Hall (official web site) [1]
- Darebin Historical Encyclopedia: Northcote Town Hall (images) [2]
- Northcote Town Hall location map [3]

Geographical coordinates: 37°46′28″S 144°59′51″E

North Melbourne Town Hall

North Melbourne Town Hall is the former town hall of the Town of Hotham (later renamed the Town of North Melbourne) in the state of Victoria. It is listed in the register of the National Trust (file no. B2388)

> *"The building is of noble proportions, exquisite in design, tastefully ornamented, and reflects the greatest credit on the architect, Mr J.R. (sic) Johnson." North Melbourne Advertiser 23 June 1876.*

It has been under the jurisdiction of the City of Melbourne since 1905 and is currently used as an "Arts House".

It is located on the corner of Errol and Queensberry Streets, in North Melbourne.

The Town Hall, built in 1876, was designed by Architect George Raymond Johnson, in the

North Melbourne Town Hall

Classical style of Victorian architecture. He also designed the Collingwood, Daylesford, Fitzroy, Kilmore, Maryborough and Northcote Town Halls.

A cast-iron drinking fountain on the footpath nearby the hall features an ornamental kangaroo and is registered by the National Trust of Victoria.

See also

- List of Town Halls in Melbourne

References

- Hannan, Bill. *The Pride of Hotham: the history of North Melbourne's most prominent landmark* [1], Hotham History Project, 2006.
- Butler, Graeme. *North and West Melbourne Conservation Study*, Melbourne City Council, 1983.
- Johnson, Ken. *People and Property in North Melbourne: development and change in an inner suburb of Melbourne, in the nineteen fifties and sixties*, Australian National University, Urban

Research Unit, 1974.
* Mattingley, Albert. *The Early History of North Melbourne*, The Victorian Historical Magazine, December, 1916, and March, 1917, The Historical Society of Victoria.

External links

* History of North Melbourne [2]
* North Melbourne Town Hall, Walking Melbourne [3]
* Arts House, City of Melbourne [4]
* North Melbourne Town Hall, National Trust [5]

Geographical coordinates: 37°48′12″S 144°56′59″E

Victorian Trades Hall

Victorian Trades Hall is a Trades Hall building located in the suburb of Carlton, Melbourne, Victoria, Australia, and home to the Victorian Trades Hall Council. It is located on the corner of Lygon Street and Victoria Street, just north of the Melbourne central business district.

Victorian Trades Hall entrance on Lygon Street

The original Trades Hall was opened in May 1859 after being built by workers as an organising place for the labour movement in Melbourne. The workers financed the construction of the building themselves. The hall underwent an upgrade from 1874 to 1925 at the hands of architectural firm Reed & Barnes and it remains one of the most historically important sites in Melbourne today, being classified by the National Trust and included in the Register of Historic Buildings (Victoria).

The hall is located across the road from the eight hour day monument which was erected to honour the Victorian workers who won the first 8 hour working day in the world in 1856. It is the birthplace of organisations like the Victorian Labour Party and Australian Council of Trade Unions and home to the Victorian Trades Hall Council.

Four flags fly from the roof of the building: the Australian Flag, the Eureka Flag, the Australian aboriginal flag, and the Red flag. (See Photo)

Trades Hall is home to many of the Victorian trade unions, left-wing political parties and radical organisations. The various rooms of the hall can be hired out for functions, meetings or conferences and it is often used for theatrical productions and to display artwork. The hall has a bar which is patronised by trade union members and political activists and a bookshop which sells radical texts.

In recent times, as well as being the centre for union activity, the Trades Hall Council has opened the Trades Hall building to many cultural events, plays, and concerts including the Melbourne Comedy Festival - concentrating on political and 'on the edge' performances.

Victorian Trades Hall has been incorrectly referred to as Melbourne Trades Hall in several recent references, but the more established and historical references cite "Victorian Trades Hall" or simply "Trades Hall" as the correct name.

References

- *Melbourne Trades Hall Memories* Marcella Pearce (1997) Victorian Trades Hall Council ISBN 0958884668

External links

- Victorian Trades Hall Council [1]
- Trades Hall & Literary Institute [2]
- New International Bookshop [3]
- 8 Hour Day: The battle for civilised working hours [4]

Geographical coordinates: 37°48′23″S 144°57′58″E

Parliament House, Melbourne

Parliament House in Melbourne, located at Spring Street in East Melbourne at the edge of the Melbourne city centre, has been the seat of the Parliament of Victoria, Australia, since 1855 (except for the years 1901 to 1927, when it was occupied by the Parliament of Australia).

Parliament House, Melbourne

History

In 1851, even before the colony of Victoria acquired full parliamentary self-government, Governor Charles La Trobe instructed the colonial surveyor, Robert Hoddle, to select a site for the colony's new parliament to meet. Hoddle selected a site on the eastern hill at the top of Bourke Street, which at that time, when few buildings were more than two storeys high, commanded a view of the whole city. A competition was held for a design for the building, and John Knight's design won the first prize of £500,[citation needed] but was not used. The government architect, Charles Pasley, subsequently came up with a design of his own.

Lithograph of the original plans. The proposed reading room dome and wings were never completed.

Subsequent observers have suggested that he borrowed heavily from Leeds Town Hall, which even today is widely considered to be among the finest civic buildings in the world. The design was later modified by an architect in his office, Peter Kerr. Construction of the project was managed by John Knight who was also on Casley's staff. The building is an example of Greek Revival architecture.

In December 1855 construction began on the site in Spring Street, and the building was completed in stages between 1856 and 1929. The chambers for the Victorian Legislative Assembly and the Victorian Legislative Council were finished in 1856, at which time Bourke Street ran between the two chambers. The library was completed in 1860, and the Great Hall (now Queen's Hall) and the vestibule in 1879. In the 1880s, at the height of the great boom fuelled by the Victorian Gold Rush, it was decided to add a classical colonnade and portico facing Spring St, which today gives the building its monumental character. This was completed in 1892. The north wing was completed in 1893 and refreshment rooms at the back of the building were added in 1929.

Despite its protracted construction and evolution of the design, the building today feels very much a single entity. The flow of the rooms, particularly taken in context with the main facade leading to the Queen's Hall and the parliamentary chambers, is both logical and visually impressive.

Pasley and Kerr's design included plans for a dome, but these were abandoned when a sharp depression began in 1891, and the dome was never built. From time to time governments have expressed interest in completing the building by adding the dome, but have been deterred by the enormous cost. The Kennett government, elected in 1992, set up a committee to examine building the dome. In 1996, Kennett and the then Opposition Leader John Brumby, reached an agreement for the building to be completed by the turn of the century but the idea was abandoned when the trade unions would not guarantee that the project would go ahead without industrial disputes.

From 1901 to 1927 Parliament House was the home of the Commonwealth Parliament, since the new capital city envisaged in the Australian Constitution did not yet exist and there were long delays in finding a site and beginning construction. During these years the Victorian Parliament met in the Royal Exhibition Building in Carlton. Many of the major events of the early federal period took place in this building, including the formation of the Federal Parliamentary Australian Labor Party, the "fusion" of the Free Trade Party and the Protectionist Party into the first Liberal Party in 1909 and the split in the Labor Party over conscription in 1916. The building is also notable in having the first set of electrical bells used to call members to divisions (installed circa 1877).

In 2005-2006, the Parliament celebrated its 150th anniversary.

Gallery

Victoria Parliament

Victoria Parliament House

Victoria
Parliament
Melbourne
(Entrance Gate)

External links

- Parliament of Victoria [1]
- Parliament of Victoria, Virtual Tour [2]
- Disability information [3]

Geographical coordinates: 37°48′40″S 144°58′24″E

Hamer Hall, Melbourne

Hamer Hall, The Arts Centre	
The interior of Hamer Hall as seen from the back of the stage	
Coordinates	37°49′13″S 144°58′6″E
Former names	Melbourne Concert Hall
Type	Concert Hall
Location	Southbank, Victoria
Owner	The Victorian Arts Centre Trust
Started	1973
Completed	1982
Other dimensions	2,661 seat concert hall
Architect	Roy Grounds and Company
Other designers	John Truscott

Hamer Hall (formerly the Melbourne Concert Hall) is a 2,661 seat concert hall, the largest venue in the Arts Centre complex, used for orchestra and contemporary music performances. It was opened in 1982, and was later renamed Hamer Hall in honour of Sir Rupert Hamer (the 39th Premier of Victoria) shortly after his death in 2004.

2010 redevelopment

Construction on the A$128.5 million redevelopment of Hamer Hall is due to begin in 2010. The Hamer Hall redevelopment is the first stage of the Southbank Cultural Precinct Redevelopment and will be delivered through an alliance between Arts Victoria, Major Projects Victoria, the Arts Centre, Ashton Raggatt McDougall and the Baulderstone. The redevelopment of Hamer Hall will include a new outlook to the city and new connections to central Melbourne, St Kilda Road and the Yarra River, new and expanded foyer spaces, better amenities, new stairs, better disability access, escalators and lifts, and improved acoustics, new auditorium seating, cutting-edge staging systems.

Federation Square

Type	Public space
Location	Melbourne, Australia
Coordinates	37°49′04″S 144°58′07″E
Opened	26 October 2002
Operated by	Federation Square Pty Ltd
Status	Open all year

Federation Square (also colloquially known as **Fed Square**) is a cultural precinct in the city of Melbourne, Australia. It comprises a series of buildings containing a public broadcaster, art galleries, a museum, cinemas, exhibition spaces, auditoria, restaurants, bars and shops around two major public spaces, one covered (The Atrium), the other open to the sky, and composed of two spaces that flow into one another (St. Paul's Court and The Square). The majority of the precinct is built on top of a concrete deck over busy railway lines. Construction began in 1998 and the site opened in 2002.

A major addition to the precinct in 2006 was **Federation Wharf**, which extended Federation Square to the Yarra by redeveloping the vaults under the Princes Bridge into cafes and ferry terminals with elevator access to Federation Square.

Location and layout

Federation Square occupies roughly a whole urban block bounded by Swanston, Flinders, and Russell Streets and the Yarra River. The open public square is directly opposite Flinders Street Station and St Paul's Cathedral. The layout of the precinct helps to connect the historical central district of the city with the Yarra River and a new park Birrarung Marr. This refocusing of the city on the Yarra River also partly reinforces links with the Southbank district, whose redevelopment has been ongoing as a key part of central Melbourne since the late 1980s.

Federation Square from Eureka Tower Skydeck.

The site of Federation Square has had a variety of former uses. The Gas and Fuel Buildings, Jolimont Yard and the Princes Bridge railway station were the immediate predecessors, though in the nineteenth century there was a morgue on the site. The result of an international design competition held in 1997 that received 177 entries, Federation Square was designed by Don Bates and Peter Davidson of Lab Architecture Studio.

360° panorama of Federation Square

Design

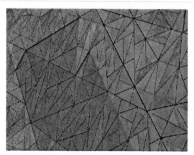

Federation Square's unique sandstone building façade

The Square

A key part of the plaza design is its large, fixed public screen, which has been used to broadcast major sporting events, such as the AFL Grand Final, and still continues to do so. During the 2006 FIFA World Cup, thousands of football fans braved cold nights to watch the matches on the Federation Square screen.

Main square paving

The complex of buildings forms a rough U-shape around the main open-air square, oriented to the west. The eastern end of the square is formed by the glazed walls of The Atrium. While bluestone is used for the majority of the paving in the Atrium and St. Paul's Court, matching footpaths elsewhere in central Melbourne, the main square is paved in 470,000 ochre-coloured sandstone blocks from Western Australia and invokes images of the Outback. The paving is designed as a huge urban artwork called 'Nearamnew', by Paul Carter and gently rises above street level, containing a number of textual pieces inlaid in its undulating surface.

The Atrium

"The Atrium" is one of the major public spaces in the Federation Square cultural precinct in central Melbourne, Australia. It is a street-like space, five-stories high with glazed walls and roof. The exposed metal structure and glazing patterns follow the pinwheel tiling pattern used elsewhere in the precinct's building facades.

The Labyrinth

The "Labyrinth" is a passive cooling system sandwiched above the railway lines and below the middle of the square. The concrete structure consists of 1.2 km of interlocking, honeycombed walls. It covers 160 m^2. The walls have a zig-zag profile to maximize their surface area, and are spaced 60 cm apart.

During summer nights, cold air is pumped in the combed space, cooling down the concrete, while heat absorbed during the day is pumped out. The following day, cold air is pumped from the Labyrinth out into the Atrium through floor vents. This process can keep the Atrium up to 12 °C cooler than outside. This is comparable to conventional air conditioning, but using one-tenth the energy and producing one-tenth the carbon dioxide.

During winter, the process is reversed, whereby warm daytime air stored in the Labyrinth overnight, to be pumped back into the Atrium during the day.

The system can also partly cool the ACMI building when the power is not required by the Atrium.

Night panorama of Federation Square

Cultural Institutions

In addition to a number of shops, bars, cafés and restaurants, Federation Square's cultural facilities include:

- The Australian Centre for the Moving Image (ACMI)
- The Ian Potter Centre: NGV Australia
- The BMW Edge Amphitheatre
- The Melbourne television and radio headquarters of the Special Broadcasting Service (SBS), one of Australia's two publicly-funded national broadcasters
- NGV Kids corner
- Melbourne Visitor Centre

Ian Potter Centre: NGV Australia

The Ian Potter Centre houses the Australian part of the art collection of the National Gallery of Victoria (NGV), and is located at Federation Square (international works are displayed at the NGV International on St Kilda Rd). There are over 20,000 Australian artworks, including paintings, sculpture, photography, fashion and textiles, and the collection is the oldest and most well-known in the country.

Well-known works at the Ian Potter Centre include Frederick McCubbin's *Pioneers* (1904) and Tom Roberts' *Shearing the Rams* (1890). Also featured are works from Sidney Nolan, John Perceval, Margaret Preston and Fred Williams. Indigenous art includes works by William Barak and Emily Kngwarreye.

ACMI – Australian Centre for the Moving Image

The Australian Centre for the Moving Image has two cinemas that are equipped to play every film, video and digital video format, with attention to high quality acoustics. The screen gallery, built along the entire length of what was previously a train station platform, is a subterranean gallery for experimentation with the moving image. Video art, installations, interactives, sound art and net art are all regularly exhibited in this space. Additional venues within ACMI allow computer-based public education, and other interactive presentations.

Australian Centre for the Moving Image

In 2003, ACMI commissioned SelectParks to produce an interactive game-based, site specific installation called AcmiPark. AcmiPark replicates and abstracts the real world architecture of Federation Square. It also houses highly innovative mechanisms for interactive, multi-player sound and musical composition.

NGV Kids corner

The NGV Kids corner is a free space with art installations and activities for children and their families.

Controversies & Criticism

When the winning bid was announced in 1997, the design was a source of great controversy, being widely supported by the design community and causing outrage among heritage advocates. There was a change of government during its construction, and the incoming Labor administration ordered a significant design revision to appease conservative critics. The original design included several five-storey 'shards', two of which were free-standing on the north-western edge of the precinct. These two structures were intended to provide a framed view of St. Paul's Cathedral from the St. Paul's Court part of the new plaza. A report drawn up by Evan Walker proposed that the westernmost shard interfered with a so-called "heritage vista", a view of the cathedral from the middle of the tram tracks on Princes Bridge to the south.

For a while after its opening on 26 October 2002, Federation Square remained controversial among Melburnians due to its unpopular architecture, but also because of its cost – $440 million and entirely publicly funded – and for the delays in construction (as its name suggests, it was to have opened in time for the centenary of Australian Federation on 1 January 2001). The construction manager was Multiplex.

However, the negativity was short-lived[citation needed], with approximately 90% of people surveyed reported liking all, or at least parts, of Federation Square. Despite fears that the plaza would remain empty because of its location on the edge of Melbourne's centre, the open space has proved to be a remarkably popular place for protests, performances, cultural gatherings, celebrations and just 'hanging out'. Federation Square is Victoria's second most popular tourist attraction, and was expected to attract between six and seven million visitors in 2003.

Federation Square won five awards in 2003 at the Victorian Architecture Awards, including the Victorian Architecture Medal.

The designers of Federation square did not get any work for 6 months after the completion of the A$450 million public space. Instead they received hate-mail. [1]

In 2009, it was voted as being the 5th ugliest building in the world by editors and members of the popular website Virtual Tourist. [1]

Photo gallery

Overview of Melbourne Federation Square

Melbourne City skyline from Federation Square

Melbourne Federation Square (SBS Building)

Federation Square Theatre (BMW Edge)

See also

- Australian Landmarks
- Confederation Square, Ottawa, Canada

References

- Brown-May, A and Day, N (2003) Federation Square, South Yarra, Vic: Hardie Grant Books (ISBN 1-74066-002-1)
- "Melbourne gets square" Sydney Morning Herald (Australia), October 19, 2002.

External links

- Federation Square [1]
- Federation Square "FedCam" [2]
- Culture Victoria – images and video of Federation Square and the history of the site [3]

Clocktower Centre

The **Clocktower Centre**, previously known as **Essendon Town Hall** or **Moonee Ponds Town Hall**, is a civic building in Moonee Ponds in Melbourne, Australia. Operated by the City of Moonee Valley, it is a venue for performing arts as well as community and corporate activities. It is located at 750 Mount Alexander Road, at the junction with Pascoe Vale Road.

The Clocktower Centre

Building history

The building has evolved substantially over time. It was originally built as the Essendon Mechanics Institute, opening in September 1880.

In February 1886 it was officially rechristened as the Essendon Town Hall. By 1914 the town hall had been extended and was reopened in July of that year. In 1930, a clock was installed in the clocktower and in 1941 the building was again modified with sections being rebuilt.

After the council chambers were moved to the new civic centre in 1973, the town hall was converted to a community centre. It was renovated and officially opened as the Essendon Community Centre in 1976. A fire in 1978 caused substantial internal damage to the building but by 1979 it has been repaired and reopened.

In February 2000 following substantial renovations, the building was officially reopened as the Clocktower Centre.

See also

- List of Town Halls in Melbourne

External links

- Clocktower Centre [1]
- The City of Moonee Valley History Online: Clocktower Centre History [2]
- Picture Australia: Town Hall, Moonee Ponds ca. 1908. [3]

Geographical coordinates: 37°45′56″S 144°55′28″E

Victoria Barracks, Melbourne

Coordinates	37°49′39″S 144°58′14″E
Architectural style	Renaissance Revival
Town	Melbourne
Country	Australia
Started	1856
Completed	1872

Victoria Barracks in St Kilda Road, Melbourne

Located on St Kilda Road in Melbourne, Australia, **Victoria Barracks Melbourne** is of architectural and historical significance as one of the most impressive 19th century government buildings in Victoria, Australia.

Pre-World War II

Originally built, as accommodation for British Imperial Garrison troops, including the 12th and 40th Regiment of Foot who were involved in putting down the armed Eureka Stockade rebellion in Ballarat Victoria, and later the Colony of Victoria's colonial forces. The Barracks housed the Department of Defence from the creation of the Commonwealth of Australia (Federation) in 1901 until 1958 when the Department of Defence moved to the new Russell Offices in Canberra. The earliest building (G Block) at Victoria Barracks were built by soldiers on the 40th Regiment, under the supervision of a Royal Engineer officer, from 1856 to 1858, while the remaining buildings were built by civil contractors with the original bluestone buildings being constructed between 1856 and 1872. A large extension (A Block New Wing) was added to accommodate HQ Department of Defence in 1917 and while it looked like the original A Block building the construction method and interior was completely modern for the time.

Another modern, for the time, art deco building (M Block) was added in 1939 and the floor was the first continuous concrete pour in Australia. The Barracks were named in honour of Queen Victoria. There are also Victoria Barracks in Sydney and Brisbane.

World War II

During World War II, Victoria Barracks Melbourne housed the Australian War Cabinet. The War Cabinet comprised senior MP's from the Government and Opposition parties. The Defence Secretariat occupied the second floor of 'A Block New Wing' which also contained the office of senior military staff, the Secretary of the Department Defence (Sir Frederick Shedden), visiting Ministers of State and their secretaries and support staff, and the War Cabinet room. The wartime Prime Ministers (Robert Menzies and later John Curtin) also had offices near the War Cabinet Room throughout the War. Eric Nave's Navy cryptographic unit was at Victoria Barracks until it moved to FRUMEL.

Myth has it that the US General Douglas MacArthur had an office at the barracks however this is not true as his HQ was at the Hotel Australia in the Melbourne CBD.[citation needed] It was in fact General Sir Thomas Blamey who had his HQ at the Barracks while serving as Commander-in-Chief, Australian Military Forces, and simultaneously in international command as Commander-in-Chief Allied Land Forces in the South-West Pacific Area under MacArthur.

Post-World War II

Victoria Barracks Melbourne currently accommodates the corporate headquarters and ten Systems Program Offices (business units) of the Defence Materiel Organisation's Land Systems Division, as well as elements of Joint Logistics Command and the Defence Service Group.

A number of facilities within Victoria Barracks are named after notable military events, people or places. These include:

- The Shedden Auditorium (after Sir Frederick Shedden)
- The War Cabinet Room (used as the main conference room for the World War II War Cabinet)
- The Blamey Room (after Field Marshall Sir Thomas Blamey)
- The Tresco Room (after the Tresco Estate, the Royal Australian Navy's premier residence in Sydney){

A ghost supposedly lives there. It has supposedly killed three Japanese tourists.

HM Prison Pentridge

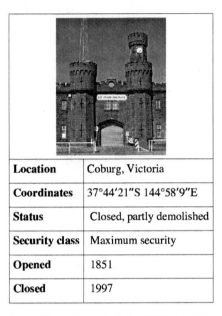

Location	Coburg, Victoria
Coordinates	37°44′21″S 144°58′9″E
Status	Closed, partly demolished
Security class	Maximum security
Opened	1851
Closed	1997

HM Prison Pentridge was an Australian prison built in 1850 in Coburg, Victoria. The first prisoners arrived in 1851. The prison officially closed on 1 May 1997.

Pentridge was often known by the nickname "The Bluestone College", "Coburg College" or the "College of Knowledge". The grounds were originally landscaped by renowned landscape gardiner Hugh Linaker. Since decommissioning, the prison has been partly demolished to make way for a housing development which threatens preservation of the history of the site. Large buildings have been built and a 16 floor modern apartment block is being planned.

The site is split in two with the northern prison being developed by Valad Property Group and the other areas by Pentridge Village. The former have proven to be uninterested in the history of the prison and are hoping to "re-brand" the site in order to make their apartments, wine bars, hotels and cafes more marketable.

The recent removal, without prior permission, of the famous "HM Prison Pentridge" sign from the National Trust Listed front gate of the Prison might be an example of their disregard for the significance of the site. The front gate showing the "HM Prison Pentridge" sign is featured on the cover of Australian band Airbourne's debut album Runnin' Wild.

The 1994 Australian film *Everynight ... Everynight* details prison life inside Pentridge's H Division.. The opening scene of this film is considered to be one of the most accurate portrayals of what was H Division's mandatory "reception bash".

The 2000 Andrew Dominik film "Chopper" was partially filmed in H Division. The early parts of the film feature H Division and provide a powerful insight into the harsh nature of the division.

The 1988 John Hillcoat and Evan English film "Ghosts... of the Civil Dead" was largely based on events that occurred at Pentridge prison's Jika Jika maximum security division.

Divisions

The prison was split into many divisions, named using letters of the alphabet.

- A - short and long-term prisoners of good behavior
- B - long-term prisoners with behavior problems
- C - Vagabonds and short term prisoners, where Ned Kelly was imprisoned (Demolished in 1976)
- D - remand prisoners
- E - similar to "A"
- F - remand and short-term
- G - psychiatric problems
- H - high security, discipline and protection
- J - Young Offenders Group- Later for long-term with record of good behavior
- Jika Jika - maximum security risk and for protection, later renamed to K Division

Jika Jika high security unit

Jika Jika, opened in 1980 at a cost of 7 million Australian dollars, was a 'gaol within a gaol' maximum security section, designed to house Victoria's hardest and longest serving prisoners. It was awarded the 'Excellence in Concrete Award' by the Concrete Institute of Australia before being closed in the middle of controversy after the deaths of five prisoners in 1987.

The design of Jika Jika was based on the idea of six separate units at the end of radiating spines. The unit comprised electronic doors, closed-circuit TV and remote locking, designed to keep staff costs to a minimum and security to a maximum. The furnishings were sparse and prisoners exercised in aviary-like escape proof yards.

In 1983 four prisoners escaped from 'escape proof' Jika Jika. When two prison officers were disciplined in relation to the Jika Jika escape a weeklong strike occurred.

1987 Jika Jika prison fire

In a protest initiated by conditions in Jika Jika, inmates Robert Wright, Jimmy Loughnan, Arthur Gallagher, David McGauley and Ricky Morris - from one side of the unit - and Craig 'Slim' Minogue and three other inmates on the other side sealed off their section doors with a tennis net. Mattresses and other bedding were then stacked against the doors. The windows in the day room were then covered with paper so the prison officers couldn't identify which prisoners caused the ensuing damage.

Plumbing was then torn from the walls in the cells to enable the prisoners to breathe after the fire started, as Jika Jika was a climate controlled division and devoid of any fresh air circulation.

In spite of the men's attempts to avoid the toxic black smoke by breathing through the plumbing, prisoners Robert Wright, Jimmy Loughnan, Arthur Gallagher, David McGauley and Ricky Morris died in the fire. Convicted Russell Street bomber Craig Minogue and 3 other inmates survived as they were evacuated when the fire started.

Victorian Attorney General and Minister for Corrections Jim Kennan ordered the closure of Jika Jika immediately afterwards.

Proposed demolition of H Division Yards

In 2009 Valad Property Group submitted their redevelopment masterplans to the Minister for planning Justin Madden. They contained the demolition of the 100 year old labour yards at the eastern end of A Division in order to make way for a road. These yards are an important example of 19th century attitudes towards prisoner rehabilitation, they measure only around 4m by 5m and were where prisoners broke rocks with hand held hammers until the mid 1970s. After 1958 the yards became part of H Division, the prisons notorious punishment and protection division. The yards were the scene of numerous murders, suicides, stabbings, bashings and riots and during the 1970s were a focal point of what became a broad based drive to "ban the bash" (unofficial beatings from guards) in Victorian prisons. This division is also where Ronald Ryan, the last man executed in Australia, spent his last night alive and where Bill O'Meally became the last man to be flogged in Australia in 1958. These yards are an important part of Australia's penal and social history as well as being an extremely evocative example of what was one of Australia'a most feared and brutal penal divisions. The current plan to demolish the yards is seen by many as a disgraceful, disrespectful and short-sighted proposal for a place which holds national and state significance.Wikipedia:Avoid weasel words

Grave sites

Main article: Ned Kelly

The grave site of bushranger Ned Kelly lies within the former walls of Pentridge Prison while Ronald Ryan's remains have been returned to his family. Kelly was executed by hanging at the Melbourne Gaol in 1880 and his remains moved to Pentridge Prison in 1929, after his skeleton was disturbed on 12 April 1929, by workmen constructing the present Royal Melbourne Institute of Technology (RMIT) building. The gravesite, as of 2005, is covered in many weeds and is largely unkept by the developers, who have fenced off the area until a decision is made on its upkeep. Reverend Peter Norden, former prison chaplain at Pentridge Prison is campaigning for the site's restoration.

Ned Kelly the day before his execution by hanging. His remains are buried at the former **Pentridge Prison** site.

As of 2009, most of the bodies have been exhumed by archaeologists and are either awaiting identification at the Melbourne morgue or have been returned to their families. The developers of the prison continue to push for the sidelining of the site's history in order to make apartments more marketable. Removal and inadequate commemoration of the grave sites is an example of this.

Executions

- David Bennett 26 September 1932
- Arnold Karl Sodeman 1 June 1936
- Edward Cornelius 26 June 1936
- Thomas Johnson 3 January 1939
- George Green 17 April 1939
- Alfred Bye 22 December 1941
- Eddie Leonski (US soldier and serial killer) 9 November 1942
- Jean Lee 19 February 1951
- Norman Andrews 19 February 1951
- Robert David Clayton 19 February 1951
- Ronald Joseph Ryan 3 February 1967

Last execution

Main article: Ronald Ryan

Ronald Ryan was the last man executed at Pentridge Prison and in Australia. Ryan was hanged in "D" Division at 8.00 on February 3, 1967 after being convicted of the shooting death of a prison officer during a botched escape from the same prison. Later that day, Ryan's body was buried in an unmarked grave within the "D" Division prison facility. To this day there's still debate on Ryan's conviction.

Notorious prisoners

- Dennis Allen, oldest member of the Pettingill family. (d. 1987)
- Garry David, (d. 1993), also known as Garry Webb, responsible for the Community Protection Act 1990
- Peter Dupas, Australian serial killer
- Keith Faure, Convicted of murdering Lewis Caine and Lewis Moran with Evangelos Goussis during the Melbourne gangland killings was also the basis for the character of Keithy George in the film Chopper
- Christopher Dale Flannery, aka Mr Rent-a-Kill, hitman
- Kevin Albert Joiner, murderer, shot dead trying to escape in 1952.

Entrance of Pentridge gaol circa 1861.

- Ned Kelly, bushranger
- Julian Knight, murdered 7 people in the Hoddle Street Massacre
- Eddie Leonski, the Brownout Strangler
- John Nicholls, Carlton footballer
- Craig 'Slim' Minogue, Russell Street Bomber
- Kevin Murray, Fitzroy footballer, Brownlow Medal winner
- Clarrie O'Shea, trade unionist
- Frank Penhalluriack
- Victor Peirce, member of the Pettingill family, acquitted of the 1988 Walsh Street police shootings. Killed in 2002.
- Harry Power, bushranger
- Mark "Chopper" Read, Gang leader
- Gregory David Roberts, Author of Shantaram, escapee of Pentridge who fled to India

- Ronald Ryan - The last person to be executed in Australia.
- Maxwell Carl Skinner, constant escapee, infamous for commandeering a Coburg Tram in one of his escapes
- William Stanford, sculptor
- Stan Taylor, actor and convicted Russell Street bomber
- Squizzy Taylor, gangster
- John Zarb, first person to be found guilty of having failed to comply with his call up notice during the Vietnam War

Timeline

- 1850's 'F' Division opened
- 1870's 'G' Division opened as an Industrial Reformatory School
- 1894 Female prison at Pentridge ('D' Division)
- 1951 Last woman executed in Australia, Jean Lee is hanged.
- 1967 Last execution in Australia - Ronald Ryan (between 1842 and 1967, 186 prisoners were executed)
- October 1987 - Five prisoners die in a fire in Jika Jika during riots over prison conditions. Craig Minogue and 3 other inmates survived the fire.
- 1 May 1997 - Pentridge Prison is closed.
- Present day - Development threatens the integrity and preservation of the sites important history

Escapes

- 1899 Pierre Douar - Suicided after recapture
- 1901 Mr Sparks - never heard of again
- 1901 John O'Connor - Caught in Sydney two weeks later
- 1926 J.K. Monson - caught several weeks later in W.A.
- 1939 George Thomas Howard - caught after two days
- 1940 K.R. Jones - Caught in Sydney two weeks later
- 1951 Victor Franz - caught next day.
- 1952 Kevin Joiner - Shot dead escaping
- 1952 Maxwell Skinner - pushed off prison wall broke leg
- 1957 Willam O'Malley - caught after 15 minutes
- 1957 John Henry Taylor - caught after 15 minutes
- 1961 Maurice Watson - caught next day
- 1961 Gordon Hutchinson - caught next day
- 1965 Ronald Ryan - caught in Sydney 19 days later
- 1965 Peter Walker - caught in Sydney 19 days later

- 1972 Dennis Denehy -
- 1972 Gary Smedley -
- 1972 Alan Mansell -
- 1972 Henry Carlson -
- 1973 Harold Peckman - caught next day
- 1974 Edward "Jockey" Smith -
- 1974 Robert Hughes -
- 1974 George Carter -
- 1976 John Charles Walker -
- 1977 David Keys -
- 1980 Gregory David Roberts (at the time known as Gregory Smith) - escaped in broad daylight with Trevor Jolly and subsequently went to India after a brief period in New Zealand
- 1980 Trevor Jolly -
- 1982 Harry Richard Nylander -
- 1987 Dennis Mark Quinn - Recaptured in New Zealand 19 days later

External links

- http://www.forbidden-places.net/urban-exploration-h-m-melbourne-s-pentridge-prison
- http://www.jikamemorial.com/
- http://www.dse.vic.gov.au/DSE/nrenpl.nsf/LinkView/ 65832EB675B1698CCA257306001BFF89164714CEFA29277FCA257359001C9DCD#pentridge

City Baths, Melbourne

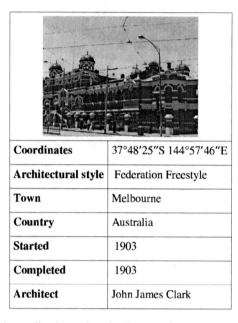

Coordinates	37°48′25″S 144°57′46″E
Architectural style	Federation Freestyle
Town	Melbourne
Country	Australia
Started	1903
Completed	1903
Architect	John James Clark

City Baths, in Melbourne, Australia, is a historically significant building. Located at 420 Swanston Street, it is of architectural significance.

The Melbourne City Council opened the first Melbourne City Baths on 9 January 1860, which housed public baths. The objective was to stop people from bathing in the Yarra River, which by the 1850s had become quite polluted and the cause of an epidemic of typhoid fever which hit the city resulting in many deaths. However, people continued to swim and drink the water. The Baths were leased to a private operator, but lack of maintenance resulted in such deterioration of the building that the Baths was closed in 1899.

New baths designed by John James Clark were opened on 23 March 1904. Strict separation of men and women was maintained, right down to separate street entrances. Two classes of facilities were maintained, with second class baths in the basement and first class baths on the main floor. Mixed bathing was introduced in 1947 and the popularity of the swimming pool began to increase.

The Baths now house a swimming pool, squash courts and a gymnasium. The swimming pool is divided into four lanes, an Aqua Play lane, a Medium Lane, a Fast Lane and a Slow Lane (or Aquatic Education, when swimming lessons are given) to cater for all types of swimmers. There is also a spa and a sauna.

External links

- Official website [1]

hey hey

Old Melbourne Gaol

Location	Melbourne, Victoria, Australia
Status	Museum
Opened	1 Jan 1845
Closed	July 1924
Managed by	National Trust of Australia

The **Old Melbourne Gaol** is a museum and former prison located in Russell Street, Melbourne, Victoria, Australia. It consists of a bluestone building and courtyard, and is located next to the old City Police Watch House and City Courts buildings. It was first constructed starting in 1839, and during its operation as a prison between 1845 and 1924, it held and executed some of Australia's most notorious criminals, including bushranger Ned Kelly and serial killer Frederick Bailey Deeming. In total, 135 people were executed by hanging. Though it was used briefly during World War II, it formally ceased operating as a prison in 1924; with parts of the gaol being incorporated into the RMIT University, and the rest becoming a museum.

The three-storey museum displays information and memorabilia of the prisoners and staff, including death masks of the executed criminals. At one time the museum displayed Ned Kelly's skull, before it was stolen in 1978; as well as the pencil used by wrongly convicted Colin Campbell Ross to protest his innocence in writing, before being executed. Paranormal enthusiasts claim the museum is haunted, with claims of ghostly apparitions and unexplained voices near cells.

History

A land allotment of scrub to the north-east of Melbourne was selected as Port Phillips first permanent gaol. On 1 January 1838, George Wintle was appointed to be gaoler at the prison at £100 a year; with the site becoming colloquially known as *Wintle's Hotel*. Construction of the gaol started in 1839–1840 on Collins Street West, but it was considered too small at the time. A second gaol was then built between 1841 and 1844 at the corner of Russell and La Trobe Streets, adjoining the then Supreme court. The first cell block was opened for prisoners in 1845, but the facilities were considered inadequate; escapes occurring frequently. The gaol was already crowded by 1850.

With the discovery of gold in 1851 (when the Port Phillip District became the new Colony of Victoria), and the resulting influx of population, law and order became more difficult maintain. Subsequently, a new wing, with its own perimeter wall, was constructed between 1852 and 1854; the building using bluestone instead of sandstone. The design was based on that of British prison engineer Joshua Jebb, and especially the designs for the Pentonville Model Prison in London (which suited the current prison reform theories at the time). The new wing was extended in between 1857 and 1859, with the boundary wall also being extended during this time. In 1860, a new north wing was built; which included entrance buildings, a central hall and chapel. Between 1862 and 1864, a cell block was built for female prisoners on the western side — it was basically a replica of the present east block (until this time, female convicts were not kept apart from the male prisoners). In 1864, the perimeter wall, and the gaol overall, was completed; making it a dominant feature of authority on the Melbourne skyline.

At its completion, the prison occupied an entire city block, and included exercise yards, a hospital in one of the yards (1864), a chapel, a bath house and staff accommodation. A house for the chief warders was built on the corner of Franklin and Russell streets, and 17 homes were built for jailers on Swanston street in 1860. Artefacts recovered from the area indicate that even the gaolers and their families lived within the gaol walls in the 1850s and 1860s.

Operation

Much of daily life inside the gaol could be gleaned from sources such as diaries written by John Castieau, governor of the gaol between 1869 and 1884. During its operation, the gaol was used to house short-term prisoners, lunatics and some of the colony's most notorious and hardened criminals. It also housed up to twenty children at a time — including those imprisoned for petty theft or vagrancy, or simply those staying with a convicted parent. Babies under twelve months old were allowed to be with their mothers. The youngest prisoner was recorded as three year old Michael Crimmins, who spent 6 months in the prison in 1857 for being idle and disorderly. In 1851, the 13 and 14 year old O'Dowd sisters were imprisoned because they had nowhere else to go.

Calico hood

Prisoners convicted of serious crime, such as murder, arson, burglary, rape and shooting, would begin their time on the ground floor with a time of solitary confinement. They were also forbidden from communicating with other prisoners, which was strictly enforced by the usage of a silence mask, or calico hood, when outside their cells. They would only be given a single hour of solitary exercise a day, with the remaining 23 hours spent in their cells. Inside the cells, prisoners would be able to lie on a thin mattress over the slate floors. They could only bathe and change clothes once a week, and attend the chapel on Sundays (with a Bible provided to promote good behaviour). Prisoners might only have been allowed to finally socialise with other prisoners towards the end of their sentences.

The routine for prisoners was regulated by a system of bells, and enforced by punishments; prisoners who obeyed the rules would be promoted to the second floor – whereby they would be allowed to work in the yards everyday. Male prisoners would perform hard labour – including breaking rocks, and other duties in the stone quarries, while women would sew, clean and cook. Women would also make shirts and waistcoats for male prisoners, as well as act as domestic servants for the governor and his family. Prisoners who had become trusted, those nearing the completion of their sentence, and debtors, were housed on the third floor communal cells. These top level cells were large, and held up to six prisoners at time; and were mostly reserved to prisoners convicted of minor crimes such as drunkenness, vagrancy, prostitution or petty theft.

Executions

During its operation, the gaol was the setting for 135 hangings. The most infamous was that of bushranger Ned Kelly at the age of 25, on 11 November 1880. After a two day trial, Kelly was convicted of killing a police officer. As stated by law at the time, executed prisoners were buried (without head) in unmarked graves in the gaol burial yard. The head was normally removed from the body as part of the phrenological study of hanged felons. Historian and associate professor of Wollongong University John McQuilton states that the lack of monitoring for burial processes was odd, given Victorian society's normally brilliant attention to detail.

The first hanging of a woman in Victoria, Elizabeth Scott, was performed in the prison on 11 November 1863 – along with her co-accused, Julian Cross and David Gedge. The last person to be executed was Angus Murray in 1924, the same year the gaol was closed.

Ned Kelly

Main article: Ned Kelly

Edward "Ned" Kelly, born sometime between June 1854 and June 1855, was an Irish-Australian bushranger, and was seen by some as merely a cold-blooded killer, while to others he was a folk hero for his defiance of the colonial authorities. As a youth he clashed with the Victoria Police, and after an incident at his home in 1878, police parties searched for him in the bush. He killed three policemen, and subsequently the colony proclaimed Kelly and his gang wanted outlaws. A final violent confrontation with police took place at Glenrowan on 28 June 1880. Kelly, dressed in a home-made plate metal armour and helmet, was captured and sent to jail. He was hanged for murder at the Old Melbourne Gaol in November 1880. His notoriety affirmed his as a polarising iconic figure in Australian history, folk lore, literature, art and film.

Old Melbourne Gaol gallows

Colin Campbell Ross

Main article: Colin Campbell Ross

Colin Campbell Ross, an Australian wine-bar owner, was wrongly convicted of the rape and murder of 12 year old Alma Tirtschke in December 1921. The case, dubbed the *Gun Alley Murder*, was heavily influenced by public hysteria at the time, which ultimately served to condemn him. Despite his pleas of innocence (including an attempt whereby a letter was thrown over the gaol walls), he was executed by hanging in the gaol in April 1922 (only 115 days after the body was found). A new four-strand rope was used for the first time at the execution, and proved to be a failure; Ross slowly strangled for more than forty minutes before his death. A prison report later ruled that such a rope must never be used again. He was posthumously pardoned on 27 May 2008.

Frederick Bailey Deeming

Main article: Frederick Bailey Deeming

Frederick Bailey Deeming was born on 30 July 1853. At 16 years of age he ran away to sea, and thereafter, he began a long career of crime, largely thieving and obtaining money under false pretences. He was responsible for the murder of his first wife Marie, and his four children, at Rainhill, England, on or about 26 July 1891, and a second wife, Emily, at Windsor, Melbourne, on 24 December 1891. Less than three months elapsed between the discovery of Emily Mather's body in Windsor, Melbourne, in March 1892, and Deeming's execution at the Old Melbourne Gaol for her murder in May 1892; a remarkably short time by comparison to modern western legal standards. After his execution, there was public speculation that Deeming was in fact Jack the Ripper.

List of recorded executions			
Name	**Year born**	**Execution date**	**Crime**
Bob (Aboriginal)		20 January 1842 (Age 27)	Murder
Jack (Aboriginal)		20 January 1842 (Age 27)	Murder
Charles Ellis		20 June 1842 (Age 18)	Shooting
Martin Fogarty		20 June 1842 (Age 18)	Shooting
Daniel Jepps		20 June 1842 (Age 27)	Shooting
Jeremiah Connell		27 January 1847 (Age 27)	Murder
Bobby (Aboriginal)		30 April 1847 (Age 25)	Murder
John Healey		29 November 1847 (Age 29)	Murder
Augustus Dancey (or Dauncey)		1 August 1848 (Age 19)	Murder
Patrick Kennedy		1 October 1851 (Age 30)	Murder
James Barlow		22 May 1852 (Age 32)	Murder
Roger (Aboriginal)		5 September 1852 (Age 30)	Murder
John Riches		3 November 1852 (Age 29)	Murder
George Pinkerton		4 April 1853 (Age 19)	Murder
Aaron Durrant		11 July 1853 (Age 38)	Robbery
John Smith		23 August 1853 (Age 25)	Robbery
Henry Turner		23 August 1853 (Age 25)	
William Atkins		3 October 1853 (Age 29)	
George Wilson		3 October 1853	
George Melville		3 October 1853	
Michael Finnessy		25 October 1853	
Alexander Ram		25 October 1853	
John Smith		23 November 1853	
Joseph West		27 December 1853	
William Twiggem	1824	2 March 1857	Murder

Chu-a-Luk	1827	2 March 1857	Murder
Samuel Gibbs		12 November 1858	Murder
George Thompson		12 November 1858	Murder
Thomas McGee		19 February 1863	
Julian Cross		11 November 1863	Murder
David Gedge	1844	11 November 1863	Murder
Elizabeth Scott	1840	11 November 1863	Murder
James Bennett		1 December 1863	
Christopher Harrison	1809	3 August 1864	Murder
William Carver	1824	3 August 1864	Robbery under Arms
Samuel Woods	1823	3 August 1864	Robbery under Arms
John Stacey		5 April 1865	
Joseph Brown		5 May 1865	
Peter Dotsalaere		6 July 1865	
Robert Bourke	1841	29 November 1866	Murder
Bernard Cunningham		31 March 1868	
Joseph Whelan		31 March 1868	
Michael Flannigan	1833	31 March 1869	Murder
James Ritson		3 August 1869	
Patrick Smith		4 August 1870	
James Cusik		30 August 1870	
James Sury		14 November 1870	
Patrick Geary		4 December 1871	Murder
Edward Feeney		14 May 1872	
An Gaa		30 August 1875	Murder
Henry Howard		4 October 1875	
John Taylor (aka Weechurch)	1830	6 December 1875	attempted murder
Basilo Bondietto		11 December 1876	
William Hastings		14 March 1877	
Ned Kelly	1854	11 November 1880	Murder

Name		Date	Crime
James Hawthorn		21 August 1884	Murder
William O'Brien		24 October 1884	Murder
William Barnes		15 May 1885	Murder
Freeland Morell	1847	6 January 1886	Murder
George Symes		8 November 1888	Murder
Filipe Castillo	1869	16 September 1889	Murder
Robert Landells	1837	16 October 1889	Murder
John Thomas Phelan	1861	16 March 1891	Murder
John Wilson	1868	23 March 1891	Murder
Fatta Chand		27 April 1891	Murder
William Coulston		24 August 1891	Murder
Frederick Deeming		23 May 1892	Murder
John Conder		28 August 1893	Murder
Frances Lydia Alice Knorr	1867	15 January 1894	Murder
Ernest Knox	1873	19 March 1894	Murder
Frederick Jordan	1864	20 August 1894	Murder
Martha Needle	1864	22 October 1894	Murder
Arthur Buck	1868	1 July 1895	Murder
Emma Williams		4 November 1895	Murder
Charles Strange	1874	13 January 1896	Murder
Alfred Archer	1866	21 November 1898	Murder
William Robert Jones		February 21, 1900	Murder
Albert McNamara		14 April 1902	Arson
August Tisler		20 October 1902	Murder
James Williams	1885	8 September 1904	Murder
Joseph Victor Pfeiffer		1912 April 1912	Murder
John Jackson		24 January 1916	Murder
Antonio Picone		18 September 1916	Murder
Albert Budd		29 January 1918	Murder
Arthur Geoffrey Oldring		15 April 1918	Murder
Colin Campbell Ross	1892	24 April 1922	Murder – pardoned 86 years later
Angus Murray	1882	14 April 1924	Murder

Closure and re-opening

In 1870, a review of the penal system was conducted, with the recommendation being made to close the gaol and relocate prisoners to more suitable locations. The gaol gradually slowed its operations, and demolished portions of the original site between 1880 and 1924. In 1924, the jail was finally closed. However, in March 1927, the Old Melbourne Gaol was integrated into part of the new Emily McPherson College, and was used for educational purposes. This necessitated changes to the prison; in 1929, despite poor record keeping of prisoner burials, historical evidence suggested the remains of approximately 32 executed prisoners, including Ned Kelly, were exhumed from the Old Melbourne Gaol and buried at mass graves in a quarry at Pentridge. In 1930, the women's cell block, walls and several other buildings were demolished, and a further four coffins were believed to have been moved to Pentridge in 1937.

During World War II, the gaol was used as a military prison for soldiers found to be absent without leave. A new wall was built in the eastern courtyard during this time, so that cell block inmates were separated from the college girls. After the end of the war, the section used for holding prisoners was then used only as a storage facility for the Victoria Police Force, whose headquarters were nearby in Russell Street.

Gates of the gaol, now part of RMIT

In May 1974, the sections used by the school were remodelled by architects Eggleston, McDonald and Secomb, to act as the schools food and fashion departments. The Emily McPherson College was merged into RMIT University in 1979, bringing the gaol entrance gates, and other facilities alongside it. In 1990, RMIT performed work to restore the enclosed balcony to its former 1927 design. In 1994, RMIT performed further work to landscape the inner courtyard, and in 1995, removed the temporary war-time pavilion classrooms. As of 2010, the sections that RMIT owns are collectively known as the "RMIT Building 11. Architect: Colonial Government Architect", and include the entrance block and chapel; with the bath house and chapel serving as art studios.

Museum

In 1957, the National Trust of Australia listed the Old Melbourne Gaol on its heritage register, and a year later marked it as a site that needed to be preserved at all costs. Furthermore, in 1965, the Melbourne Junior Chamber of Commerce floated the idea of converting it into a museum, for the purposes of tourism. In 1972, the gaol was reopened as a public museum, under the management of the National Trust of Australia (Victoria).

As of 2010, the gaol is recognised as Victoria's oldest surviving penal establishment, and attracts approximately 140,000 visitors per year. The cells have been filled with information about individual prisoners, which also serve to illustrate the history of Melbourne itself, which began as a penal settlement.

In addition to historical information, it also includes various memorabilia; including death masks, an iron mask, and a pair of leather gloves designed to prevent inmates from practising self-abuse. Notably, it still includes Ned Kelly's death mask, pistol and replica of his suit of armour, as well as the pencil used by Colin Ross to write a letter protesting his innocence, which he threw over the prison walls.

Operators also run several features, including the candlelit *Hangman's Night Tour* (with actors portraying prolific and brutal hangman Michael Gateley), and the daily *Watch House Experience*; an interactive performance in which visitors are treated as the prisoners would have been during its operation. In 2010, the Old Melbourne Gaol *Crime and Justice Experience* won the heritage and cultural tourism category at the Qantas Australian Tourism Awards in Hobart.

Ned Kelly's skull

A skull, believed to be Ned Kelly's, was on display in the museum until it was stolen in 1978. Efforts have been taken by scientists and the government to determine the location of the skull, and whether it was authentic to begin with; it was reported that members of the public may have the remains of bones and teeth taken as souvenirs when graves were exhumed in 1929. Special interest was directed to finding a photograph of former South Melbourne councillor Alex Talbot holding Ned Kelly's skull, and information on grave exhume contractor Lee of *Lee and Dunn*, or his family, who was tasked with delivering Kelly's skull to the governor. In 2009, West Australian farmer Tom Baxer handed a skull to authorities, arguing that it was the one stolen from the jail. Former Pentridge prison chaplain Father Peter Norden has stated that he believed the skull handed in could not belong to Kelly, and that it probably belonged to a woman.

Haunting

The museum is considered haunted by paranormal enthusiasts, including British parapsychologist Darren Done. Done spent a night at the gaol in 2003, and claimed that he heard unexplained voices, and detected evidence of an electrical interference to suggest paranormal activity. He has since undertaken more research at the jail, and in 2005, he claimed to have recorded a ghostly figure with a grotesque visage standing in a doorway at the gaol. Theories suggest that the voice of a woman, claimed to have been heard, might belong to Elizabeth Scott (the first woman hung at the gaol). Notably, none of the reported hauntings are related to that of Ned Kelly. Local enthusiast group GhostSeekers Australia conducts monthly tours to gather data and statistics for paranormal activity; making use of various monitoring equipment. However, Joe Nickell, a writer for the *Skeptical Inquirer*, argues that evidence of ghostly phenomena at the site is scant.

External links

• Old Melbourne Gaol website [1]

References

Geographical coordinates: 37°48′29″S 144°57′55″E

Newport Workshops

The **Newport Railway Workshops** is a facility in the Melbourne suburb of Newport, Victoria, Australia, that builds, maintains and refurbishes railway rollingstock. It is located between the Williamstown and Werribee railway lines.

Overview of the 'West Block' section of the workshops, with the clocktower and admin block to the left and Steamrail depot to the right.

History

Plans for a workshop at Newport started in the 1860s, to replace the temporary Williamstown Workshops but nothing came of it. It was not until 1880 that work begun, when the Victorian Railways purchased annexes used at the 1880 Melbourne Exhibition and erected one of them at Newport, calling it the Newport Carriage Workshops when it began operation in 1882.

Construction of the permanent workshops commenced in 1884, and was completed in 1889. Although the earlier carriage workshop closed at this time, it reopened in 1895 to manufacture signal equipment. The first carriages built by the workshops were completed in 1889, but locomotives were manufactured by the Phoenix Foundry in Ballarat, the first locomotive being built in 1893. The main elements of the workshops are a central office block and clock tower, the 'East Block' for carriage and wagon works, and 'West Block' for heavy engineering and locomotive building. Expansion followed in 1905–1915, and 1925–1930. During World War II the workshops were turned over to military production, with the rear fuselage, and empennage of Bristol Beaufort bombers being built there.

At the peak of operation it was one of Victoria's largest and best-equipped engineering establishments, with up to 5,000 employees on site. The workshops had its own cricket ground, and in the 1920s the game of Trugo is said to have been invented by workers on their lunch hour. In the 1980s the original segments of the workshops were removed from everyday use, and modern workshops built along the eastern side of the site, which remains in use today.

Tenants

Current revenue operations are carried out in the eastern section of the workshops by EDI Rail, who carry out work including locomotive and carriage maintenance, and diesel engine, bogie and wheelset overhauls; for customers including V/Line. The workshops is also provided with the only broad gauge underfloor wheel lathe in Victoria. A section of the workshops is also leased to Siemens for maintenance of their Siemens suburban trains.

In the EDI Rail section, BL class, G class, and N class diesel locomotives are undergoing overhauls

The original 1880s workshops have been maintained for heritage uses. The 'West Block' area are occupied by a number of railway preservation groups such as Steamrail Victoria and R707 Operations, while the 'East Block' has been retained by the Department of Infrastructure for the storage of disued trams and other rail rollingstock. The ARHS Railway Museum is located south of the workshops, near North Williamstown railway station.

References

External links

- Photos: Newport Workshops [1] - tour of the EDI Rail section of the Workshops

Further reading

- *The Newport Story* Doenau, G Australian Railway Historical Society Bulletin November;December, 1979 pp249-272;274-288

- *Reminiscences of an Apprentice at the Victorian Railways' Newport Workshops 1959-1963* Clark, A.J. Australian Railway Historical Society Bulletin, February, 1996 pp35-55

- *Experience at Newport Workshops 1941-1946* Whalley, S.C. Australian Railway Historical Society Bulletin, November, 2002 pp403-406

Geographical coordinates: 37°51′06″S 144°52′55″E

Queen Victoria Market

The **Queen Victoria Market** (also known as the **Queen Vic Markets** or simply as the **Queen Vic** or "Vic Market") is a major landmark in Melbourne, Australia, and at around seven hectares (17 acres) is the largest open air market in the Southern Hemisphere. The Market is significant to Melbourne's culture and heritage and has been listed on the Victorian Heritage Register. The Market is named after Queen Victoria who ruled the British Empire, from 1837 to 1901.

The Queen Victoria Market is the only surviving 19th century market in the Melbourne central business district. There were once three major markets in the Melbourne CBD, but two of them, the Eastern Market and Western Market, both opened before the Queen Victoria, closed in the 1960s. It also forms part of an important collection of surviving Victorian markets which includes the inner suburban Prahran Market and South Melbourne Market.

A relief on the external façade of the Meat and Fish Hall building

History

Starting as a small market to the east of the city in the 1850s, it gradually expanded into space made available by the closure of the old Melbourne Cemetery west of Queen Street and north of Franklin Street. The reinternment of human remains from the closure of the cemetery caused a great deal of controversy at the time. As there were about 10,000 burials on the site, there still remain approximately 9,000 people buried under the sheds and car park of the Queen Victoria Market. Every time work is carried out at the market, bones are disturbed. A memorial to these people stands on the corner of Queen Street and Therry Street. The Market was originally wholesale and retail fruit and vegetables, but has been retail since the wholesale market in Footscray Road was opened in 1969.

Attempts to close the market in the early 1970s were scuttled by bans conducted by the Builder Labourers' Federation and community groups.

The market was once known as a thriving underground pirated goods centre. A massive crackdown in 1997 has helped to clean up the market's image, but has also resulted in an increase in prices for these types of goods.

In 2003, the roofs of the market were equipped with 1,328 solar photovoltaic panels, covering 2000 square metres and generating 252,000 kilowatt-hours of electricity each year, the largest such renewable energy installation in the City of Melbourne. The grid has been considered as the largest urban grid-connected solar photovoltaic installation in the Southern Hemisphere upon completion.

Today

Today, the Market is a major Melbourne tourist destination, offering a variety of fruit and vegetables, meat, poultry and seafood, gourmet and deli foods as well as specialty delicacies. It also has a large non-food related market, selling a diverse range of clothing, shoes, jewellery and handmade art and crafts.

The market is also known for the hot doughnut van which has operated for over half a century and become part of local tradition, being known for its jam donuts.

The Market is open every day of the week except Mondays and Wednesdays. On Wednesday evenings in the summer months, there is a night market which offers dining, bars, live entertainment and a variety of other stalls.

In January 2010, the *Herald Sun* reported that city planners wanted to transform the market into a "gourmet hub" by introducing upmarket food stalls. Lord Mayor Robert Doyle said he brought up the idea after visiting London's Borough Market, which has a "boutique" feel that could work in Melbourne.

Notes

References

- Fyfe, Melissa (2003-03-11). "Has the sun set on solar power?" [1]. *The Age* (Melbourne): p. 11. Retrieved 2009-07-22.
- Hastie, David (2010-01-03). "Traders attack boutique market plan" [2]. *Sunday Herald Sun*: p. 26. Retrieved 2010-01-03.

External links

- Official site [3]
- Queen Victoria Market photos [4]

Geographical coordinates: 37°48′25″S 144°57′24″E

Hotel Windsor (Melbourne)

Hotel Windsor	
Hotel Windsor behind the Parliament Reserve fountain in 2010	
Location	100-150 Spring Street, Melbourne, Victoria
Coordinates	37°48′43″S 144°58′22″E
Opening date	1884 (Grand Hotel) 1888 (Grand Coffee Palace) 1897 (Grand Hotel) 1920 (Windsor Hotel) 2008 (Hotel Windsor)
Architect	Charles Webb
Management	Halim Group
Owner	Halim Group
Rooms	180
Suites	20
Restaurants	1
Floors	5
Parking	off-site
Website	http://www.thewindsor.com.au

The Hotel Windsor is a 5 Star luxury hotel in Melbourne. The Windsor is Australia's only surviving grand 19th century city hotel and only official "grand" Victorian era hotel.

The hotel has a significant role in the History of Australia as the place where the Constitution of Australia was drafted in 1898.

For much of its 20th Century life the hotel, dubbed the **Duchess of Spring Street**, was one of the most favoured and luxurious hotels in Melbourne. It has hosted many notable national and international guests.

The Windsor is situated on Bourke Hill in the Parliament Precinct and is a Melbourne landmark of high Victorian architecture.

The Windsor is currently planning a major renovation which is expected to begin in late 2011 .

Notable Guests

Notable guests at the Windsor have included Margaret Thatcher, George VI of the United Kingdom and Elizabeth Bowes-Lyon (as Duke and Duchess of York), Meryl Streep, Anthony Hopkins, Gregory Peck, Laurence Olivier, Vivien Leigh, Katharine Hepburn, Basil Rathbone, Lauren Bacall, Douglas Fairbanks, Claudette Colbert, Robert Helpmann, Rudolph Nureyev, Dame Nellie Melba, Dame Joan Sutherland, Dame Margot Fonteyn, Michael Dukakis, Muhammad Ali, Barry Humphries, Don Bradman and the Australia national cricket team as well as Australian prime ministers Sir Robert Menzies, Malcolm Fraser, Bob Hawke, Paul Keating and John Howard.

History

The hotel was built in two stages by shipping magnate George Nipper, both designed by Charles Webb in a broadly Renaissance Revival style. Originally named the Grand Hotel, the first section (the southern half) was completed in 1884.

The northern half, which included the distinctive twin mansard roofed towers in the Second Empire style, was completed in 1888, just in time to host visitors to the Centennial Exhibition in the Royal Exhibition Building. A notable feature is the stone sculpture, attributed to John Simpson Mackennal, over the main entrance with male female figures known as 'Peace and Plenty' reclining over the English and Australian Coat of Arms. The extension was undertaken by a new owner, temperance movement leader James Munro, who burnt the liquor licence in public and operated the hotel as a coffee palace, renamed the "Grand Coffee Palace".

Re-licenced in 1897, it became the Grand Hotel and in 1898 the Constitution of Australia was drafted in the hotel.

The present name dates from 1920, when the hotel was sold and refurbished, and honours the British Royal Family.

For much of its 20th Century life, the hotel dubbed the **Duchess of Spring Street** was one of the most favoured and luxurious hotels in Melbourne, hosting many notable national and international guests.

Decline and demolition proposal

With the construction of modern 'international' hotels, starting with the Southern Cross in 1962, the Windsor declined in popularity. In a bid to regain marketshare, the Windsor expanded, purchasing the four storey White Heart Hotel on the Bourke Street corner. The White Heart was demolished and a new classically inspired extension using elements from the old hotel became the Windsor's north wing. Later in the decade a 25 storey residential tower was developed on the opposite side of Little Collins Street, significantly overshadowing the Windsor.

By the mid 1970s, it was run-down and the other major historic 19th century hotels in Australia, the Federal and the Menzies in Melbourne, and the Australia and Metropole in Sydney, had all been demolished.

Several proposals were put forward which included the demolition of the Windsor. A 1974 proposal for a 38 storey tower on the corner of Spring and Bourke Street was opposed by the state government and the National Trust. The Rupert Hamer led state government purchased the building in 1977 to ensure its preservation and in 1980 leased it to The Oberoi Group.

New Owners and Restoration

Oberoi undertook a major restoration of the hotel in 1983 costing USD$6.6 million, reinstating the decorative 19th century colour schemes to the lobby, stairhall, and especially the Grand Dining Room, where huge brass chandeliers were reproduced from photographs. This was one of the first major private historic restorations in Melbourne, and won a Victorian Architect's Institute award. Its position as a leading five-star hotel and a major Melbourne landmark was then firmly re-established. The cricketer's bar, afternoon tea in the grand dining room, and the top-hatted doorman all resumed

Melbourne Windsor Hotel Lobby after restoration in 2008

their status as Melbourne institutions. The John Cain II state government sold the hotel to the Oberoi Group giving the company freehold possession in 1990. In 2005, Oberoi sold the hotel to the Halim family.

2000s - Redevelopment proposals

The Halim group first proposed to redevelop the Windsor in 2008 shortly after acquiring remaining shares from the Oriental Pacific Group and rebranding as "Hotel Windsor", with a $45 million redevelopment which proposed to modernise many of the interiors although they would not disclose whether the hotel was running at a loss or making a profit. The plan was approved by Heritage Victoria and the government after significant negotiations with the owners which included reducing the heritage impacts of the proposal. However development did not commence due to the Financial crisis of 2007–2010.

In July 2009, the Halim group proposed a new $260 million refurbishment project which would add 152 rooms to the hotel. This would involve demolition of the hotel's 1960s-era North wing, and replacing it with a contemporary building with facilities expected by guests staying in a five star hotel. A thin curtain wall tower designed by Denton Corker Marshall was proposed be built at the rear of

Windsor Place. The architects proposed that the fritted wavy glass of the facade was a solution to minimise the visual impact of the tower. The application submitted to Heritage Victoria included restoration of the 1880s facade facing Spring and Little Collins Streets.

The National Trust of Australia (Victoria), opposed to the development responded with a campaign named 'Save the Windsor'. and claimed that the proposed tower was inappropriate and would breach established height controls for the Bourke Hill precinct initially put in place to protect vistas of the Windsor, Parliament House and St Patrick's Cathedral. These controls do not exist south of the Windsor where there are taller buildings, including 99 Spring Street, an apartment building completed in 1971. At 24 floors and 77 metres it is shorter than the proposed tower, yet it fronts onto the heritage precinct of Spring Street and is located directly next to the Windsor.

In late February 2010 a news leak occurred which erupted in a government scandal surrounding the redevelopment of the Windsor Hotel. A document prepared by a senior media advisor to Planning Minister Justin Madden was sent by email to the ABC Newsdesk. It detailed plans by the Victorian Government to run a sham community consultation process in a bid to reject the plans. In response to public outcry, a probity officer was appointed to oversee the decision making process.

On 18 March 2010 The Hotel Windsor's renovation plans were approved by Planning Minister Justin Madden . This is the final step in the approval process.

A protest on the steps of Parliament House, coordinated by the National Trust was held on Thursday 25 March 2010. Rod Quantock, Bob Brown and Brian Walters gave speeches with Brown claiming in his speech that the Windsor is of national heritage significance and that the matter would be raised in federal parliament. Geoffrey Rush, not able to attend, also strongly opposed the development, comparing its destruction with the Bombing of Dresden in World War II.

Greg Barber, Bob Brown and Brian Walters attending the 2010 protest rally in Melbourne

The Halim Group responded adamant that its intention was to preserve the Windsor's viability into the future rather than destroy it, "never did I imagine that the debate would become so crazy that a hotel development would be compared to the bombing of Dresden," said Mr Adi Halim . On an episode of the ABC's Stateline aired 26 March, The Hotel Windsor's CEO stated that the National Trust had in fact supported the Windsor's renovation plans during the period open for public comment yet the National Trust refused to appear on the program[citation needed].

The Senate of Australia officially recognised the national significance of the Windsor Hotel in a motion led by Bob Brown which was agreed by the senate. The National Trust took an appeal against the development to the Supreme Court of Victoria.

The Windsor's renovations are expected to begin in late 2011 .

External links

- Official Site [1]
- Victorian Heritage Database [2]
- Official site of the renovation plans [3]

Bali Memorial, Melbourne

The **Bali Memorial** in Melbourne is situated in Lincoln Square, Carlton, Victoria, facing Swanston Street. It commemorates the innocent victims of the 2002 Bali bombings. 202 people perished in the bombings, including 88 Australians of whom 22 were Victorians.

The memorial was officially opened on 12 October 2005, the third anniversary of the bombings. The Bali Memorial features a fountain, incorporating 88 individual water jets

Bali Memorial, Carlton

– one for Australian lost in the catastrophe and 202 lights to represent all of the victims. For the 24 hours of 12 October each year, the individual water jets stop and offer a place to reflect on those who died in the bombings.

Geographical coordinates: 37°48′09″S 144°57′47″E

Spencer Street, Melbourne

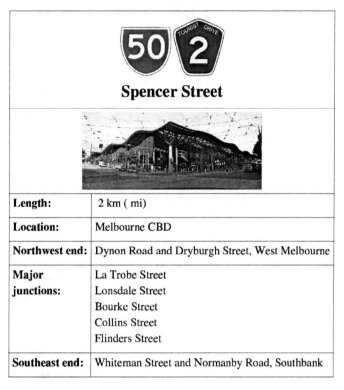

Length:	2 km (mi)
Location:	Melbourne CBD
Northwest end:	Dynon Road and Dryburgh Street, West Melbourne
Major junctions:	La Trobe Street Lonsdale Street Bourke Street Collins Street Flinders Street
Southeast end:	Whiteman Street and Normanby Road, Southbank

Spencer Street is a major street in the central business district of Melbourne, Victoria, Australia. It is named for John Spencer, 3rd Earl Spencer, Chancellor of the Exchequer under Lord Melbourne, the Prime Minister of the United Kingdom.

Spencer Street was the site of the first permanent buildings in the settlement now called Melbourne. The home of John Batman was built on nearby Batman's Hill where he lived until his death and the early camps of Captain William Lonsdale and Charles La Trobe were located along the street.

Important buildings on Spencer Street include Southern Cross Station (formerly Spencer Street Station), the offices of *The Age* newspaper, the former Mail Exchange, Grand Hotel (former Victorian Railways administration offices), the former Sir Charles Hotham Hotel and the HM Melbourne Assessment Prison. For many years, Spencer Street was also the location of Melbourne's General Post Office.

Geography

Running roughly from north to south, Spencer Street forms the western edge of the Hoddle Grid. To the north Spencer Street becomes Dynon Road, and to the south it Clarendon Street after crossing the Spencer Street Bridge over the Yarra River.

History

The street was once considered an unfashionable and unattractive end of town, but with the construction of Melbourne Docklands, Southern Cross Station and a Direct Factory Outlets shopping complex, and demolition of eyesores such as the power station, several high rise apartment buildings have been built since the late 1990s.

The street was also home to the 1890 era Spencer Street Power Station which has been abandoned since 1982. The power station was asbestos-ridden, with demolition beginning in 2006.

Rippon Lea Estate

Rippon Lea Estate is a historic property located in Elsternwick, Victoria, Australia. It is under the care of the National Trust of Australia.

It was built in 1868 for Sir Frederick Sargood, a wealthy Melbourne businessman, politician and philanthropist. Frederick and his wife Marian bought 42 acres (170000 m^2) of land at Elsternwick, about 8 kilometres from the Melbourne central business district, in 1868 and built a two-storey, 15 room house. An extensive pleasure garden was laid out around the house, together with glasshouses, vegetable gardens and orchards. The gardens were designed to be self-sufficient as regards water, and the large man-made lake on the property was designed to store stormwater run-off from the surrounding area.

The front gates of the Rippon Lea estate

The Sargood family lived at Rippon Lea until Frederick's death in 1903, and over the years extended the house on several occasions. The greatest structural changes occurred in 1897 when the house was extended to the north, and a tower was added. The style of the house has been described as "polychromatic romanesque" and the architect, Joseph Reed, was said to have been inspired by the architecture of the Lombardy region of northern Italy. The house also contained many other innovations; it was one of the first in Australia to be lit by electricity, produced by its own generators, and Sargood employed a full-time electrician to maintain the system, and the fittings included an electrically-powered bell system to communicate with the servants quarters and kitchens below stairs.

Rippon Lea today from the front lawn

On Frederick's death in 1903, the property was sold to a consortium of real estate developers who had plans to demolish the house and subdivide the land. Elsternwick at this time was a new suburb on the outskirts of Melbourne; 35 years earlier when the Sargoods bought the land, it had been well outside the built-up area of Melbourne.

The house was empty for six years, while the developers sold off various parcels of land, particularly the orchards and paddocks. Before, however, the final carve-up of the estate could be undertaken, the leader of the consortium, Sir Thomas Bent, died and the property was put on the market in 1910.

It was bought by Ben and Agnes Nathan, who owned the Maples chain of furniture stores in Melbourne. The Nathans lived there until Ben's death in 1935. The property then passed to their eldest daughter, Louisa, along with a legacy of £1 million.

Louisa (married name, Mrs Timothy Jones) was a leading figure in the Melbourne social set in the 1930s. She undertook extensive remodelling and renovation of the house to allow her to entertain on a lavish scale. The interior of the house was redecorated in a restrained classical 1930s style, drawing heavily on Hollywood film style of the 1930s and Syrie Maugham's "all white room" as influences. These renovations substantially altered most of the surviving Victorian features of the house -- for example, the wallpaper in the entrance hall and corridors (originally embossed in gold) was over-painted in white, as were the marble columns around the main entrance.

The ornate iron-framed ballroom built by Frederick Sargood (which was converted from an earlier conservatory) was demolished to make way for a lavish "Hollywood style" swimming pool and ballroom and 14 acres (57000 m^2) of gardens were maintained. Mrs Jones also installed a new modern kitchen on the ground level and the original basement kitchen and service areas were closed up, which fortunately preserved many of the surviving 19th century features of this section of the house, including the cool room, the wine cellar and the large fuel stove.

In preparation for the 1956 Olympic Games in Melbourne, a section of the property was compulsorily acquired by the Victorian government to house a new television studio complex for the Australian Broadcasting Corporation (ABC). The Rippon Lea studio became the ABC's Melbourne studio and in later years were used as the production centre for many renowned ABC programs including *Bellbird*,

Countdown, *The Big Gig* and *The Late Show*.

Another section of the property was compulsorily acquired by the state government a few years later and Mrs Jones fought a long-running legal action against it. She eventually settled with the government, agreeing that, on her death the house and the land still in her possession would be bequeathed to the National Trust. With Mrs Jones death on July 27, 1972, the house and gardens were reunited with the disputed acquisition, saving the estate from the threat of sale and subdivision and allowing the public to enjoy the estate in perpetuity.

Of particular note in the grounds are the lake, the spectacular iron-framed fernery, the swimming pool and associated ballroom (1939, now leased to Peter Rowland Catering for social functions) and the stable complex (1868). The rooms of the basement kitchen complex are also of special interest, having been built in the 1880s and then abandoned in 1938 following the installation of a modern kitchen on the ground floor. Today they are a rare surviving Australian example of a 19th century kitchen suite; comprising kitchen, scullery, pantries, cool rooms, servants' hall and wine cellar.

The front door of Rippon Lea

View of the lawns

View of the house from the lawn

The swimming pool as put in by Louisa, and where the original ballroom once was

The hallway on the 1st floor (note that image is less than perfect due to the restriction of no flash photography and no camera tripods inside the house)

Ground floor doors leading to servants areas. House decorated for Christmas as photograph was taken in mid December

View from the back garden showing the large fernery structure to the right

Inside the fernery as seen in the previous photo

The small boat house on the lake

A wrought iron seat by the lake

External links

- Official Rippon Lea website operated by the National Trust [1]
- Photo galleries of Rippon Lea Estate and function hire details [2]
- Culture Victoria – story and historical images of Rippon Lea and the families who lived there [3]

Geographical coordinates: 37°52′45″S 144°59′58″E

Valentines Mansion

Valentines Mansion is situated in Valentines Park in the London Borough of Redbridge. Built in 1696 for Lady Tillotson, the widow of the Archbishop of Canterbury, it was a family house until Sarah Ingleby, its last inhabitant, died on 3 January 1906. It became the property of Ilford Borough Council and was used as council offices until 1994. It is owned by the London Borough of Redbridge.

It is a Grade II* listed building and it was on the Buildings at Risk Register until 2009. It has undergone an extensive refurbishment financed by the Heritage Lottery Fund and by the London Borough of Redbridge. The Mansion is set in an 18th-century formal garden. The garden itself has a Grade II listing from English Heritage and this has also been extensively restored.

Nearby Tube Stations

• Gants Hill is a five minute walk from the Mansion.

Nearby Mainline Railway Stations

• Ilford mainline station is a five minute bus ride from the Mansion.

External links

• Valentines Mansion Website [1]
• Events and more at Valentines Mansion Website [2]
• Visiting information [3] - London Borough of Redbridge
• Valentine Park Conservationists [4]
• Mansion access details at English Heritage [5]

Geographical coordinates: 51°34′19.40″N 0°3′58.80″E

Rialto Towers

<table>
<tr><td colspan="2" align="center">Rialto Towers</td></tr>
<tr><td colspan="2" align="center">
Rialto Towers as viewed from the base of the towers</td></tr>
<tr><td colspan="2" align="center">General information</td></tr>
<tr><td>Location</td><td>Melbourne, Australia</td></tr>
<tr><td>Status</td><td>Complete</td></tr>
<tr><td>Constructed</td><td>1982-1986</td></tr>
<tr><td>Use</td><td>office</td></tr>
<tr><td colspan="2" align="center">Height</td></tr>
<tr><td>Antenna or spire</td><td>270 m (886 ft)</td></tr>
<tr><td>Roof</td><td>251 m (823 ft)</td></tr>
<tr><td colspan="2" align="center">Technical details</td></tr>
<tr><td>Floor count</td><td>63 (plus 3 underground)</td></tr>
<tr><td>Floor area</td><td>84000 m^2 (904200 sq ft)</td></tr>
<tr><td colspan="2" align="center">Companies involved</td></tr>
<tr><td>Architect(s)</td><td>Gerard de Preu and Partners
Perrott Lyon Mathieson</td></tr>
<tr><td>Contractor</td><td>Grollo Australia</td></tr>
</table>

The **Rialto Towers** (often **The Rialto**) is the second-tallest reinforced concrete building and the tallest office building in the Southern Hemisphere, when measured to its roof (several other skyscrapers in Australia are taller if their spires are included, as are some other structures in Australia such as communications masts and observation towers). Mounted atop the building is a 19 metre antenna, which does not count toward its overall height according to the Council on Tall Buildings and Urban Habitat's *Height to Architectural Top* category. The building is located at 525 Collins Street, in the western side of the central business district of Melbourne, Australia.

The Rialto Towers featured Melbourne's first skyscraper public observation deck which operated between 1994 and December 31, 2009. It was also the location of Melbourne's first Tower running event.

At the time of its completion it was the 23rd tallest building in the world and the 2nd tallest outside of the United States (behind First Canadian Place in Toronto, Canada).

Background

The site of the Rialto Towers (Flinders Lane, Collins Street, Winfield Square and Robbs Lane) was occupied by several buildings including Robb's Buildings (now demolished), a grand classical styled 5 storey Victorian office building designed by Thomas Watts and Sons (and reputedly the tallest in the Melbourne City Centre in 1885), a 1920s building of the same size, the Rialto Building (1889) designed by William Pitt and the Winfield Building (1890) designed by Charles DEbro & Richard Speight all formed a uniform height limited streetscape along Collins Street and around the corner of King Street.

During the 1970s, the large derelict site was owned by the National Mutual Life Association of Australasia and it was around 1979 when the first development proposal was prepared and submitted to the Melbourne City Council.

Little progress was made until 1980 when the site was acquired by Grollo Australia. Despite the structural integrity of Robb's buildings and objections by the National Trust of Victoria, Grocon successfully argued that the retention of Robb's Buildings would spoil the effect of the proposed building and that as it would not integrate well with the new

The old Rialto Building (right) and Winfield Building (left) were retained as part of the development.

structure and that the Rialto should have its own modern concrete and glass podium. During the application process Rialto and Windfield buildings were added to heritage registers and a 10 metres frontage and side facades including Victorian roofscape and turrets and small access laneway were retained to be integrated into the development.

Construction

Robb's buildings were subsequently demolished opening the way for construction to begin on the Rialto.

Designed by architects Gerard de Preu and Partners in association with Perrott Lyon Mathieson, the building was built between 1982 and 1986, opening in October 1986, and takes its name from the much older Rialto Building next door. The massive glass curtain wall façade of reinforced blue tinted mirrored glass is its central feature and changes colour during the day, ranging from a trademark dark blue to a brilliant gold during sunset.

It is 251 m (824 ft) high, with 63 floors and 3 basement floors. It comprises two conjoined towers, the shorter North Tower being 185 m high with 43 floors. In total, there are 84,000 m² of office space.

Early tenants moved into the lower floors while the upper floors were still under construction in 1984.

Observation Deck

The Melbourne Observation Deck opened to the public on July 19, 1994 and is on the 55th floor of the South Tower, at 234 m. Views of up to 60 km can be had on a clear day. It is serviced by two express passenger lifts. However, on December 31, 2009, the observation deck closed to become a restaurant.

Panoramic view from the Rialto at night showing the CBD and Southbank lit up

A ~180 degree panoramic image of Melbourne's Hoddle Grid (CBD) and Southbank on the right side, as viewed from the Rialto Observation Deck

Rialto Run-up

Inspired by the popular Empire State Building Run-Up, a stair race up the 242 metre, 1222-1254 step race to the 53th floor of the Rialto building was first run in the late 1980s and became and annual event with both mens and women's divisions known as the **Rialto Run-up**. Previous winners include Robin Rishworth (1989,1990); Geoff Case (1991). The winner was awarded with a trip to New York to compete in the Empire State Building race.

Statistics

In total there are 36 passenger lifts, 95 km of lift cables, 706 lift door openings and 1,450 staircase steps. The outer surface of the building has 13,000 windows.

See also

• Australian Landmarks

External links

• 🔊 Media related to Rialto Towers at Wikimedia Commons
• Rialto Towers [1]
• Melbourne Observation Deck [2]
• Walking Melbourne profile [3]
• Rialto Run Up [4]

List of tallest buildings in Australia

Next Shortest	Next Tallest
Central Park 249m	Bourke Place 254m

Heights are to highest architectural element.

List of tallest buildings in Melbourne

Next Shortest	Next Tallest
Melbourne Central 246m	Bourke Place 254m

Heights are to highest architectural element.

Geographical coordinates: 37°49′08″S 144°57′30″E

Royal Exhibition Building

Royal Exhibition Building and Carlton Gardens*	
UNESCO World Heritage Site	
State Party	Australia
Type	Cultural
Criteria	ii
Reference	1131 [1]
Region**	Asia-Pacific
Inscription history	
Inscription	2004 (28th Session)
* Name as inscribed on World Heritage List. [2] ** Region as classified by UNESCO. [3]	

The **Royal Exhibition Building** is a World Heritage Site-listed building in Melbourne, Australia, completed in 1880. It is located at 9 Nicholson Street in the Carlton Gardens, flanked by Victoria, Nicholson, Carlton and Rathdowne Streets, at the north-eastern edge of the central business district. It was built to host the Melbourne International Exhibition in 1880-1881 and later hosted the opening of the first Parliament of Australia in 1901. Throughout the 20th century smaller sections and wings of the building were subject to demolition and fire, however the main building, known as the Great Hall, survived.

It received restoration throughout the 1990s and in 2004 became the first building in Australia to be awarded UNESCO World Heritage status, being one of the last remaining major 19th century exhibition buildings in the world. It sits adjacent to the Melbourne Museum and is the largest item in Museum Victoria's collection. Today, the building hosts various exhibitions and other events and is closely tied with events at the Melbourne Museum.

History

The Royal Exhibition Building was designed by the architect Joseph Reed, who also designed the Melbourne Town Hall and the State Library of Victoria. According to Reed, the eclectic design was inspired by many sources. The dome was modeled on the Florence Cathedral, while the main pavilions were influenced by the style of Rundbogenstil and several buildings from Normandy, Caen and Paris.

Lithograph of the building hosting the World's Fair of 1880 showing the rear wings which no longer exist.

The foundation stone was laid by Victorian governor George Bowen on 19 February 1879 and it was completed in 1880, ready for the Melbourne International Exhibition. The building consisted of a Great Hall of over 12,000 square metres and many temporary annexes.

1880–1901

In the 1880s the building hosted two major International Exhibitions; The Melbourne International Exhibition in 1880 and the Melbourne Centennial Exhibition in 1888 to celebrate a century of European settlement in Australia. The most significant event to occur in the Exhibition Building was the opening of the first Parliament of Australia on 9 May 1901, following the inauguration of

The Royal Exhibition Building from the main avenue of the Carlton Gardens

the Commonwealth of Australia on 1 January. After the official opening, the federal government moved to the Victorian State Parliament House, while the Victorian government moved to the Exhibition Building for the next 26 years.

1901–1970s

The period after this time saw the building used for many purposes. It was a venue for the 1956 Summer Olympics, hosting the basketball, weightlifting and wrestling competitions. As it decayed, it became known derogatively by locals as *The White Elephant* in the 1940s and by the 1950s, like many buildings in Melbourne of that time it was earmarked for replacement by office blocks. In 1948, members of the Melbourne City Council put this to the vote and it was narrowly decided not to demolish the building. The wing of the building which once housed Melbourne's aquarium burnt down in 1953. During the 1940s and 1950s, the building remained a venue for regular weekly dances. Over some decades of this period it also held boat shows, car shows and other regular home and building industry shows. It was also used during the 1950s, 60's and 70's for State High School Matriculation and for the Victorian Certificate of Education examinations, among its various other purposes. Nevertheless, the grand ballroom was demolished in 1979, leaving the main structure in place along with annexes constructed in the 1960s and 1970s. Following the demolition of the grand ballroom there was a public outcry, which prevented the main building from also being demolished.

1980s–present

During a visit to Victoria in 1984, Princess Alexandra (Queen Elizabeth II's cousin) bestowed the royal title on the building and it has been referred to as the Royal Exhibition Building ever since. This title, and the first conservation assessment of the building undertaken by Alan Willingham, sparked a restoration of the interiors of the building in the late 1980s and 1990s, and the construction of a mirror glass annexe (which was later demolished). In 1996 the then Premier of Victoria, Jeff Kennett, proposed the location and construction of Melbourne's State Museum on the adjacent site. Temporary annexes built in the 1960s were removed and in 1997 and 1998, the exterior of the building was progressively restored.

Melbourne Royal Exhibition Building (East Side)

The location of the Melbourne Museum close to the Exhibition Building site was strongly opposed by the Victorian State Labor Party, the Melbourne City Council and the local community. It was as a result of the community campaign opposing the museum development that John Brumby, then State opposition leader, with the support of the Melbourne City Council, proposed the nomination of the Royal Exhibition Building for world heritage listing. The world heritage nomination did not progress until the election of the Victorian State Labor Party as the new government in 1999.

On 1 July 2004, the Royal Exhibition Building and Carlton Gardens was granted listing as a World Heritage Site, the first building in Australia to be granted this status. The heritage listing states that *The Royal Exhibition Building is the only major extant nineteenth century exhibition building in Australia. It is one of the few major nineteenth century exhibition buildings to survive worldwide.*

In October 2009, Museum Victoria embarked upon a major project to restore the former German Garden of the Western Forecourt. The area had been covered by asphalt in the 1950s for car parking.

The main hall inside the building

Current use

The Royal Exhibition Building is still in use as a commercial exhibition venue, hosting many events on a regular basis such as the Melbourne International Flower and Garden Show. Regular tours are also offered by Melbourne Museum.

The Royal Exhibition Building is used as an exam hall for the University of Melbourne, Royal Melbourne Institute of Technology, Melbourne High School, Nossal High School and Mac.Robertson Girls' High School

However, it is no longer Melbourne's largest commercial exhibition centre. The modern alternative to the Royal Exhibition Building is the Melbourne Exhibition and Convention Centre, located in Southbank to the south of the central city area.

See also

- Carlton Gardens
- Garden Palace – Sydney's exhibition building.
- Melbourne Museum

External links

- World heritage listing for the Royal Exhibition Building [4]
- Royal Exhibition Building at Museum Victoria [5]
- Virtual tour of the Royal Exhibition Building [6]

- World Heritage, World Futures [7] — A sustainable conservation project at the world heritage listed Royal Exhibition Building, Melbourne

Geographical coordinates: 37°48′17″S 144°58′16″E

La Mama Theatre (Melbourne)

La Mama Theatre	
Address	205 Faraday St, Carlton, Victoria
City	Melbourne
Country	Australia
Opened	1967
www.lamama.com.au [1]	

The **La Mama Theatre** is a theatrical venue located at 205 Faraday St, Carlton, Victoria. It opened in a former factory building on July 30, 1967 and still operates today under the direction of Liz Jones.

The theatre, an initiative of Betty Burstall, was inspired by the "off-off-Broadway" theatre scene in New York City. Betty and her husband, film maker Tim Burstall, had just returned from a trip to New York and wanted to re-create the vibrancy and immediacy of the small theatres there. La Mama was modelled after a similarly named New York venue.

> "I got the idea for La Mama when we went to New York in the sixties. We were poor. It was impossible to go to the theatre - even to see a film was expensive - but there were these places where you paid fifty cents for a cup of coffee and you saw a performance, and if you felt like it you put some money in a hat for the actors. I saw some awful stuff and some good stuff. It was very immediate and exciting and when I came back to Melbourne I wanted to keep going, but there didn't exist such a place. So I talked around a bit, to a few actors and writers and directors, sounding them out about doing their own stuff, Australian stuff, for nothing ... I decided on Carlton because in 1967 it was a lively, tatty area with an Italian atmosphere and plenty of students ... " (Betty Burstall)

At a time when the production of Australian plays was almost non-existent (and financially risky), La Mama's non-profit organisation provided the venue for the performance of new experimental Australian theatre works.

The first play performed at La Mama was a work by a new Australian writer Jack Hibberd, entitled *Three Old Friends* (1967), whose most successful play *Dimboola* opened there in 1969. The production of Australian works at La Mama soon became a staple, and within the first two years of its life twenty-five new Australian plays had premiered there.

La Mama also nurtured new works by composers, poets, and filmmakers. The opening of the alternative theatre provided a home base for many important figures in theatre and film including Hibberd and Alex Buzo. It was also regularly used by underground performance troupe Tribe (who later collaborated with Spectrum). The theatre's house troupe, the La Mama Group, established by actor-director Graeme Blundell evolved into the Australian Performing Group.

La Mama's foundation marked the beginning of the emergence of a distinctly Australian style of theatre. La Mama also fostered a pool of talent that would flow on into many areas of the Australian arts -- playwrights, actors, directors, technicians, musicians, filmmakers, poets and comedians. The theatre regularly screened new works by film-makers such as Bryan Davies, Nigel Buesst, John Carnody, Bert Dehling and John Duigan, and other notable names associated with the theatre include David Williamson, Barry Dickins, Daniel Keene, John Romeril, Tess Lyssiotis, Helen Collins, Lloyd Jones, Judith Lucy and Richard Frankland.

It is located in a building which was built in 1883 for Anthony Reuben Ford, a local printer. The building has also served as a boot factory, electrical engineering workshop, and a silk underwear factory.

Further reading

- Jones, Liz with Betty Burstall and Helen Garner, *La Mama: History of a Theatre* (Penguin Books Australia, 1988)
- Robertson, Tim, *The Pram Factory: The Australian Performing Group Recollected* (Melbourne University Press, 2001)

External links

- La Mama official website [2]

Geographical coordinates: 37°47′57″S 144°58′04″E

State Theatre (Melbourne)

State Theatre	
Address	100 St Kilda Road
City	Melbourne
Country	Australia
Architect	Roy Grounds
Owned by	Victorian Arts Centre Trust
Capacity	2079
Opened	October 1984
Current use	live theatre, opera, ballet, dance
www.theartscentre.net.au/ [1]	

Melbourne's original **State Theatre** was built in 1929 to seat 3,371 patrons and is situated on Flinders Street. It was conceived as an "atmospheric auditorium", a novelty in Melbourne at the time. Another notable feature was the dual-console Wurlitzer organ, the first to be built "west of Chicago", and since relocated to the Moorabbin Town Hall in 1967. The State Theatre was renamed the Forum in 1963.

The current State Theatre opened in 1984 and is part of the The Arts Centre located by the Yarra River and St Kilda Road, the city's main thoroughfare. The State Theatre is a venue for ballet, opera and other productions (but not plays, which are performed elsewhere). Like the other performance venues within the Arts Centre, the State Theatre is underground. The stage is one of the largest in the world.

Companies performing opera in the State Theatre include Opera Australia (which has presented seven or eight operas each season) and Melbourne City Opera. In the future, it is anticipated the Victorian Opera, created in November 2005 after the separation between the Sydney and Melbourne "wings" of Opera Australia, will also be making appearances there.

The theatre is frequently home to The Production Company, a theatre company specialising in short season revivals of classic Broadway musicals.

External links

- State Theatre page at The Arts Centre website [2]

Geographical coordinates: 37°49′13″S 144°58′6″E

Princess Theatre, Melbourne

Princess Theatre	
Spring Street facade	
Address	163 Spring Street
City	Melbourne
Country	Australia
Designation	Victorian Heritage Register
Architect	William Pitt
Owned by	Marriner Theatres
Capacity	1488 seats
Opened	1857
Years active	1857-
Current use	musicals, opera
www.marrinertheatres.com.au/hireprincess.htm [1]	

The **Princess Theatre** is a 1488-seat theatre in Melbourne, Australia.

It is listed by the National Trust of Australia and is on the Victorian Heritage Register.

History

It was first erected in 1854 by actor-manager George Coppin, who would create Melbourne's theatre land. He already owned the Olympic (known as the 'Iron Pot') on the corner of Exhibition and Lonsdale Streets, installed gas lights in November 1855 into Astley's, and then he would go on to take over the Theatre Royal in Bourke Street.

The Princess Theatre is the second building on the present site - the first being Astley's Amphitheatre which opened in 1854 containing a central ring for equestrian entertainment and a stage at one end for dramatic performances. It was named in honour of the Astley Royal Amphitheatre, near Westminster

Bridge, London

In 1857, the amphitheatre was renovated and the facade extended, then re-opening as the Princess Theatre and Opera House.

By 1885, the partnership of J. C. Williamson, George Musgrove and Arthur Garner, had been formed and they became known as 'The Triumvirate', the business becoming known as J. C. Williamson's. The Triumvirate resolved to build a new theatre.

Completed in 1886 to the design of architect William Pitt; George Gordon to design the interior; and Cockram and Comely as the builders; re-development of the Theatre took place at a cost of £50,000. The design is in the exuberant Second Empire style, and the theatre forms part of the Victorian streetscape of Spring Street.

When completed, it featured the world's first sliding or retractable roof and ceiling. It also featured state-of-the-art electrical stage lighting.

The theatre re-opened, again, on 18 December 1886, with a performance of Gilbert and Sullivan's *The Mikado*. The marble staircase and foyer was hailed as equal to that of the Paris Opera, the Frankfurt Stadt and the Grand in Bordeaux.

On 26 December 1922, new owners, Benjamin John Fuller and Hugh J. Ward renovated and reopened the theatre, with a performance of *The O'Brien Girl*.

In 1987, David Marriner purchased the Princess Theatre; he renovated and had the 1922 origins documented, then 9 December 1989, the theatre re-opened with the musical *Les Misérables*, followed by *The Phantom of the Opera*, establishing a new record for the longest running show ever staged in Victoria.

Ghost sightings

The theatre has experienced several reported ghost sightings.

On the evening of 3 March 1888, the baritone Frederick Baker, known as "Federici", was performing the role of Mephistopheles in Gounod's opera *Faust*. This production ended with Mephistopheles sinking dramatically through a trapdoor returning to the fires of hell with his prize, the unfortunate Dr Faustus. The audience was spellbound. As the audience held its collective breath as Federici was lowered down through the stage into this basement, he had a heart attack and died immediately. They laid him on the floor,

Melbourne Princess Theatre in Spring Street

lifeless, in his crimson vestments. He never came back onstage, never took the bows. When the company was gathered together to be told that Federici had died, they asked, "When?". Being told of what had happened at the end of the opera, they said, "He's just been onstage and taken the bows with us." Since then, many people who have never heard of the Federici story have claimed to see a ghostly figure in evening dress at the theatre. For many years, the third-row seat in the dress circle was kept vacant in his honour.

When a documentary was made nearly 80 years later, by Kennedy Miller in the early 1970s, a photograph of the film set revealed an ashen-faced, partly transparent observer. No-one on the set saw the figure on that day; only the photograph revealed 'the ghost'.

Use

Restored in 1989, the theatre is regarded as Melbourne's home for international musical productions, including:

- *Les Misérables* (1989 & 1998)
- *The Phantom of the Opera* (1990)
- *Cats* (1993)
- *West Side Story* (1994)
- *Disney's Beauty and the Beast*
- *Chess*
- *The Boy from Oz*
- *The Importance of Being Earnest*
- *The Sound of Music* (2000)
- *The Witches of Eastwick* 2002
- *Mamma Mia!* (2002)
- *The Producers* (2004)
- *Swan Lake on Ice* (2006)
- *Dirty Dancing* (2006)
- *Kiss Me, Kate* (2006)
- *The Phantom of the Opera* (2007)
- *Guys and Dolls* (2008)
- *Jersey Boys* (2009)
- *Hairspray* (October 2010)

It has also been used as a venue for the Melbourne International Comedy Festival, including the stage show Puppet Up! in 2007.

External links

- Marriner Theatres [2]
- What's on at Princess Theatre - Citysearch Melbourne [3]

Geographical coordinates: 37°48′39″S 144°58′20″E

Regent Theatre, Melbourne

Regent Theatre	
City	Melbourne
Country	Australia
Designation	National Trust of Australia, Victorian Heritage Register
Capacity	2162
Opened	1929
Current use	musicals, opera
www.marrinertheatres.com.au/venue_regent.jsp [1]	

The **Regent Theatre** is a 2162 seat theatre in Melbourne, Australia. It is listed by the National Trust of Australia and is on the Victorian Heritage Register.

History

When first opened on Collins Street in 15 March, 1929 as the flagship Melbourne theatre for Francis W. Thring's Regent franchise (later sold to Hoyts), the theatre had 3250 seats, was equipped with a Wurlitzer organ and was the second largest theatre to the State Theatre. It also had a ballroom, the Plaza, in the basement.

The cinema was gutted by a fire on the 29 April, 1945 which destroyed both the auditorium and organ. The reconstructed Regent opened on 19 December, 1947, including a new organ, making it one of the last Picture Palaces to be built in the country.

By the 1960s, persistent rumours of the theatre's closure (and of the Plaza Theatre in the basement) forced proposals for it to be split into two cinemas. Ultimately, this was not to be, the theatre being replaced by the Hoyt's Cinema Centre in Bourke Street. The Regent Plaza Theatre is cited as one of the few cinemas adapted for Cinerama outside of North America.

The Regent was located on the site reserved for the Melbourne City Council City Square project and the council had announced intentions to acquire and demolish many of the buildings on the block from 1966.

On 1 July, 1970, Hoyts shut the doors of the Regent for the last time. The South Yarra Regent closed the same night and Ballarat location soon followed suit. The Plaza closed in November of that year. In December, 1970, an auction was held at the theatre where everything that was not bolted down was auctioned off, raising a few thousand dollars.

In response to the closure and clouds over the building's future, a "Save the Regent" committee was formed led by president Loris Webster was formed to preserve the unoccupied building and prevent its demolition by the council.

In 1974 the National Trust declined to list the theatre, claiming it was not of significance (somewhat ironically years later after threats to the building had ceased, the Trust successfully nominated the Regent and Plaza Theatres to the Victorian Heritage Register). In response to the National Trust's stance Lord Mayor Alan Douglas Whalley demanded that the Regent be demolished, presenting a report headed by Sir Roy Grounds to quell the conservationists and claiming that the Regent was not worthy of preservation in declaring that it was "not the Colosseum". The council argued that the long blank side wall of the Regent would compromise architects abilities to create grand visions for the site.

Save The Regent presented a petition of 1,800 signatures to the City Council in May 1975.

Lord Mayor Ron Walker supported his predecessor. However Norm Gallagher helped to place green ban and black bans on the building.

In 1977, Victorian premier Rupert Hamer stepped in to prevent demolition of the Regent by publicly declaring it a landmark and throwing official support for the retention of the building by passing legislation for its protection and offering up to $2 million in interest free loans from the state to restore and maintain it.

Over time, Melbourne's Regent had become the last remaining fully intact theatre of the Regent picture palace franchise. The Regent in Sydney was demolished in 1988 and the Regent Theatre in Brisbane had its interiors substantially altered in 1978. The Ballarat Regent Theatre was modified to become a multi-cinema complex developed in the 1990s. The cinema in Melbourne was the only to be used as a performing arts venue.

The building lay derelict for 26 years. Many suggestions were made during this time as to the Regent's future including demolition, redevelopment as a carpark and even as a poker machine venue. Sadly, much of the Plaza theatre's interior was gutted to make way for the City Square project, with only the ceiling remaining as an original item. However, from photos supplied by a member of the Save The Regent Theatre Committee, Ian Williams, the interior was reconstructed to its original glory.

Redevelopment

Entrepreneur David Marinner earmarked the Regent for restoration when he established a revival movement for classical performing arts theatres in Melbourne during 1991 as part of a strategy to create a monopoly and promote the city as a performing arts capital. In a deal with the Melbourne City Council, Marriner proposed to purchase the adjacent City Square site for development of the multi-storey Westin Hotel and apartments on the condition that some of the money go towards restoring the theatre. The redevelopment took 3 years from September 1993, to its final reopening gala on August 17 1996. The Plaza Theatre was also fully and magnificently restored to its original ballroom format.

The exterior of the Regent is near identical to the now-demolished Sydney Regent theatre and is Renaissance Revival in style. The interiors are of a Rococo style.

The Regent Theatre reopened on October 26, 1996 with a production of Andrew Lloyd Webber's *Sunset Boulevard*.

Use

Over the years, the Regent has seen many live shows, including:

- 1996 - Sunset Boulevard (musical)
- 1997 - Fiddler on the Roof (musical)
- 1998 - Show Boat (musical)
- 1999 - Live at the Regent Theatre: July 1, 1999 (John Farnham concert)
- 2001 - Annie (musical)
- 2001 - Singin' in the Rain (musical)
- 2001 - The Wizard of Oz (musical)
- 2002 - Man of La Mancha (musical)
- 2002 - Oliver! (musical)
- 2003 - We Will Rock You (musical)
- 2004 - Melbourne International Comedy Festival Gala; APRA Music Awards; AFI Awards
- 2004 - Gone with the Wind
- 2005 - The Lion King (musical)
- 2007 - The Wizard of Oz (film with live orchestra)
- 2007 - Imperial Russian Dance Company's Flying Tzars
- 2007 - Melbourne International Comedy Festival Gala
- 2007 - Matthew Bourne's Swan Lake (ballet)
- 2007 - Priscilla Queen of the Desert - the Musical
- 2008 - Wicked (musical)
- 2010 - Cats in March

- 2010 - Fame (musical)
- 2010 - West Side Story
- 2011 - Love Never Dies (musical)

External links

- Marriner Theatres: The Regent Theatre [1]
- http://www.donaldbinks.com.au/regent.htm
- Cats the musical returns to Melbourne - Herald Sun [2]

References

Geographical coordinates: 37°48′56″S 144°58′03″E

Forum Theatre

Forum Theatre	
Flinders Street facade	
Address	154 Flinders Street
City	Melbourne
Country	Australia
Designation	Victorian Heritage Register, Historic Buildings Register
Architect	Bohringer, Taylor & Johnson
Owned by	Marriner Theatres
Capacity	3371
Opened	1929
Years active	1929-1985
Current use	live music, comedy, live theatre
www.marrinertheatres.com.au [1]	

The **Forum Theatre** (formerly known as the "State Theatre") is a theatre located on the corner of Flinders Street and Russell Street in the central business district of Melbourne, Australia. The building was designed by American architect John Eberson, who has designed many theatres across the globe, along with a local architectural firm at the time; Bohringer, Taylor & Johnson. It was designed as an "Atmospheric theatre" movie palace. The interior features reproductions of Greco-Roman statuary and a sky-blue ceiling decorated with small stars, mimicking a twilight sky.

When it opened in February 1929, the cinema had the largest seating capacity in Australia, holding 3371 people. A dual-console Wurlitzer organ of style 270 was installed featuring 21 rows of pipes and a grand piano attachment and oboe horn The building features a Moorish Revival exterior, with minarets and a clock tower.

In the 1963 the venue was converted into two cinemas, the Forum and the Rapallo, by cinema chain Greater Union. In 1978 the Forum was listed on the Historic Buildings Register. In 1981 renovations took place, dividing the complex into Forum I and Forum II. Forum I being the larger of the two is located on the ground floor and generally used for concerts and other large-scale performances, whereas the third-floor Forum II is a smaller venue with a total capacity of 540 as opposed to Forum I's 2300.

The theatre is listed on the Victorian Heritage Register.

In 1985 it was purchased and used by the Revival Centres International, a Christian organisation and fell into disrepair. In 1995 it was purchased by Staged Developments Australia, who redeveloped it for use as a film and concert venue.

It was later bought by David Marriner, as part of a project to establish Melbourne as a major centre for theatre in the Southern Hemisphere.

Today, it is used for concerts by many artists, having hosted performances by Oasis, Ozzy Osbourne, Katy Perry, Cat Power, The Grates, Dirty Three, Sufjan Stevens, Blind Guardian & The Yeah Yeah Yeahs, among others.

It is also a venue for the annual Melbourne International Film Festival, having showcased the popular live act Puppetry of the Penis.

In more recent times, the theatre has been used as a venue for numerous acts during the Melbourne International Comedy Festival, including local favourite Akmal Saleh and international acts, such as Mark Watson, Jason Byrne & Arj Barker, among others.

References

• Thorne, Ross, *Picture Palace Architecture in Australia*, Sun Books Pty. Ltd., South Melbourne, Victoria, 1976.

Geographical coordinates: 37°49′00″S 144°58′10″E

Palace Theatre, Melbourne

Former names	Metro Nightclub Palace Theatre Metro Theatre St James Theatre Apollo Theatre Brennan's Amphitheatre
Location	20-30 Bourke Street, Melbourne, Australia
Opened	May, 1860
Capacity	1855

The **Palace Theatre** (also known as **The Palace**), is an entertainment venue located in Melbourne, Australia. Established in 1860, it is one of the entertainment venues located in Melbourne's business and tourism district.

On Wednesday 28 April 2010, the Palace Theatre played host to MTV Classic: The Launch. The event celebrated the launch of MTV Classic Australia and featured a line-up of local and international artists including former Guns N' Roses guitarist Slash, Angry Anderson and Wolfmother rocker Andrew Stockdale.

External links

- Official Palace Theatre Website [1]
- Official MySpace Page [2]
- Official Facebook Page [3]

Comedy Theatre, Melbourne

Comedy Theatre	
Address	240 Exhibition Street, Melbourne
City	Melbourne
Country	Australia
Capacity	997
Opened	1928
www.marrinertheatres.com.au/venue_comedy.jsp [1]	

The **Comedy Theatre** is a 997 seat theatre in Melbourne. It was built in 1928, and was built in the Spanish style, with a Florentine-style exterior and wrought-iron balconies. It is located at 240 Exhibition Street, and diagonally opposite Her Majesty's Theatre, it is a part of the Marriner Theatre group.

Gallery

Fresco

Fresco detail

Fresco detail

Windows

External links

- Official website [2]

Melbourne Athenaeum

Athenaeum	
The Melbourne Athenaeum	
Address	188 Collins Street
City	Melbourne
Country	Australia
Designation	Victorian Heritage Register, Register of Historic Buildings
Architect	Smith & Johnson
Capacity	1000 (theatre one)
Years active	Since 1839
Rebuilt	1885-1886
Current use	live theatre, comedy, library, readings
www.melbourneathenaeum.org.au [1]	

The **Athenaeum** or **Melbourne Athenaeum** is one of the oldest public institutions in Victoria, Australia, founded in 1839. The first President was Captain William Lonsdale, the first Patron was the Superintendent of Port Philip, Charles La Trobe and the first books were donated by Vice-President Henry Fyshe Gisborne. Originally it was called the **Melbourne Mechanics' Institute**. This was expanded in 1846 to the **Melbourne Mechanics' Institution and School of Arts**. The building on Collins Street was completed in 1842. The Athenaeum played a role in the establishment of Mechanics' Institutes in Victoria.

The Melbourne City Council met in the building until 1852 when the Melbourne Town Hall was built.

The Institution changed its name to the **Melbourne Athenaeum** in 1873. At that time, as now, a major activity was a library. In 1877, membership was 1681 and in 1879 there were 30,000 visits to the library. In 1880 it was reported 'that the floor of the large hall was the only one in Melbourne expressly constructed for dancing'. The front of the building was rebuilt in 1885 and 1886.

In October, 1896, the first movie was shown in Australia in the Athanaeum Hall. The Hall became a regular venue for screening films and the premier of The Story of the Kelly Gang by the Tait brothers was at the Athenaeum in 1906. The theatre in its present form was created in 1921. The theatre was the first venue in Australia to screen talking pictures. The Melbourne Theatre Company leased the theatre from 1976 to 1985 when the lease was taken over by various entrepreneurs who formed AT Management in 1997.

The Athenaeum housed a small museum in its early days and then an Art Gallery, which closed in 1971, after which it was converted into a smaller theatre space by the MTC. This space, as of 1997 is now home to the Comedy Club and, in the last few years, Melbourne Opera.

The library continues to exist as a large subscription library with members throughout Victoria, although its membership has declined from a peak of 7,579 in 1950.

The building was added to the Register of Historic Buildings in 1981 and is listed on the Victorian Heritage Register.

It has been used as a venue for the Melbourne International Comedy Festival and since 2006 has been the venue for the Last Laugh Comedy Club since it moved from North Melbourne.

References

- Time-Line History of the Melbourne Athenaeum [2]
- *The Melbourne Athenaeum, a short history*, 2001.

External links

- Melbourne Athenaeum web site [3]
- Melbourne Athenaeum Theatre One Tickets [4]

Geographical coordinates: 37°48′54″S 144°58′02″E

Her Majesty's Theatre, Melbourne

Her Majesty's Theatre	
Her Majesty's Theatre, 2003	
Address	219 Exhibition Street
City	Melbourne
Country	Australia
Designation	Victorian Heritage Register
Architect	Nahum Barnet
Owned by	Mr Mike Walsh, OBE
Capacity	1700
Opened	1886
Previous names	Alexandra Theatre His Majesty's Theatre
Current use	musicals, opera
www.hmt.com.au [1]	

Her Majesty's Theatre is a 1700 seat theatre in Melbourne, Australia. Built in 1886, it is located at 219 Exhibition Street, Melbourne. It is classified by the National Trust of Australia and is listed on the Victorian Heritage Register.

Purchased in 2000 by Mike Walsh, the theatre was restored and refitted to accommodate larger productions.

History

The gold rush of the 1850s brought both increased prosperity and population to the new colony of Victoria. Melbourne thrived and businesses flourished. The first recorded use of the area near the corner of Stephen (later to become Exhibition) Street and Little Bourke Street – land traditionally owned by the people of the Kulim nation – as a venue for entertainment was in 1880, when tiered seating was constructed and an openair venue for circuses and equestrian shows established.

The Hippodrome lasted four years before the French born entrepreneur, Jules François de Sales Joubert, secured a 30 year lease on the site and commissioned architect Nahum Barnet to design a theatre, business and accommodation complex.

In 1886, construction began on the Eiffel Tower in Paris; in New York, the Statue of Liberty was dedicated and in Melbourne, work on Joubert's project was completed. On the 1st of October, The Alexandra Theatre opened. Named after the then Princess of Wales, wife of the future King Edward VII, the theatre was the largest in the Southern Hemisphere, boasting a capacity of 2,800. The very first show staged was the comedy, *Bad Lads*. Also in the first year, the Australian classic, For the Term of His Natural Life, was performed, as was Saturday afternoon wrestling and a season of Italian opera.

The early days of The Alec (as it became known) were problematic. Joubert had spent almost twice his original budget on construction and had been unable to obtain the required operating licences for the hotel, bars and cafes of the complex. By November 1887, he was insolvent.

Early in 1888, the Australian born, internationally renowned actor and playwright, Alfred Dampier, leased the theatre and introduced a successful programming and pricing formula. The Alec prospered.

In 1900, well-known expatriate American theatrical producer, James Cassius Williamson, took over the lease of the theatre and engaged architect William Pitt to supervise renovations. The stage was lowered by 60 centimetres and the stalls and orchestra pit raised by almost 30 centimetres. The Dress Circle was remodelled and new boxes added. Seats were re-upholstered, re-painting carried out and a new stage curtain and new stage lighting installed. The theatre, re-vamped and re-christened Her Majesty's Theatre in honour of Queen Victoria, re-opened with a production of Gilbert and Sullivan's HMS Pinafore on the 19th of May.

In 1909, after a private sound test, Dame Nellie Melba, by then an international star, declared that the theatre's acoustics were "dead" and that she would not perform unless they were altered. Further renovations to the theatre's interior were carried out in time for Dame Nellie to hold her Australian opera debut in November 1911.

On the 6th of July, 1913, J. C. Williamson − the biggest theatrical entrepreneur in the world at the time − died at the age of 68. As a mark of respect, all the Williamson theatres 'were dark' for one night, a rare tribute. The company he'd established with Her Majesty's Theatre as its flagship however, continued to prosper, featuring the operettas of Gilbert and Sullivan as staple fare well into the 1920s.

The name change from The Alexandra to Her Majesty's Theatre occurred eight months before the death of Queen Victoria. The theatre management steadfastly continued the honour, by maintaining the name despite the fact there was now a King on the throne. In 1924, a decision was taken to rename the theatre again. Her Majesty's Theatre became His Majesty's Theatre, this time in honour of King George V, after whose mother, the original theatre had been named.

Despite the changes in identity, the theatre consistently played host to the world's best artists and shows. The legendary Russian ballerina, Anna Pavlova, captivated Australian crowds at performances in 1926 and 1929.

Previous productions at Her Majesty's include

• 1959: *My Fair Lady* (Original Australian Production 1959)

- *Evita*
- *A Chorus Line*
- *Cats*
- *Hot Shoe Shuffle*
- *The Mikado*
- 1993: *42nd Street*
- 1998: *Chicago*
- 2002: *The Hollow Crown*
- 2003: *Cabaret*
- 2003: *Hair*
- 2003: *Nutcracker on Ice*
- 2004: *Eureka*
- 2005: *Mamma Mia!*
- 2005: *Die Fledermaus* (Melbourne Opera Company)
- 2006: *An Inspector Calls*
- 2006: *Così fan tutte* (2006 Victorian Opera Company)
- 2006: *Oklahoma!* (2006 Joining The Chorus - Victorian State Schools)
- 2007: *Madame Butterfly* (Melbourne Opera Company)
- 2007: *Miss Saigon*
- 2007: *The Love of the Nightingale* (2007 Victorian Opera Company)
- 2007: *Orphée et Eurydice* (2007 Victorian Opera Company)
- 2007: *Monty Python's Spamalot*
- 2008: *Fiddler on the Roof*
- 2008: *Billy Elliot the Musical*
- 2009: *Chicago The Musical*
- 2010: *MAMMA MIA!*
- 2010: *Mary Poppins*

Her Majesty's Theatre will host the Melbourne seasons of MAMMA MIA! from 13 February 2010. The theatre is also home to the Australian premiere season of Mary Poppins, from 29 July 2010.

External links

- Official site [1]

Geographical coordinates: 37°48′39″S 144°58′11″E

Capitol Theatre, Melbourne

Capitol Theatre	
Swanston Street facade	
Address	113 Swanston Street
City	Melbourne
Country	Australia
Designation	Victorian Heritage Register
Architect	Walter Burley Griffin
Owned by	RMIT
Opened	1924
Years active	Since 1924
Current use	university lectures, events
www.capitol.rmit.edu.au [1]	

The **Capitol Theatre** is a single screen cinema located in Melbourne, Australia (opposite the Melbourne Town Hall). In 1999, it was purchased by Royal Melbourne Institute of Technology (RMIT University), and is used for both university lectures and events.

History

The Capitol Theatre was commissioned by a group of Melbourne businessmen, including the Greek Consul-General Anthony JJ Lucas, and was designed by the renowned architect Walter Burley Griffin. Lucas had worked previously with Burley Griffin on the development of both the *Vienna Cafe* as well as his own property *Yamala* in Frankston. Construction began in 1921 and was completed in 1924.

The building belongs to the interwar period and the architectural style is Chicagoesque. The interior foyer was remodelled in the 1960s to make way for the Capitol Arcade, although the spectacular theatre has been retained. It was described by the leading architect and academic Robin Boyd as "the best cinema that was ever built or is ever likely to be built".

In 2005, RMIT announced that the theatre would get a AUD$190,000 upgrade, including repairs to the Alhambra-inspired ornamental ceiling. The Theatre is listed on the Victorian Heritage Register.

External links

- RMIT Capitol website [2]
- Heritage listing [3]

Geographical coordinates: 37°48′55″S 144°57′59″E

Malthouse Theatre, Melbourne

Malthouse Theatre	
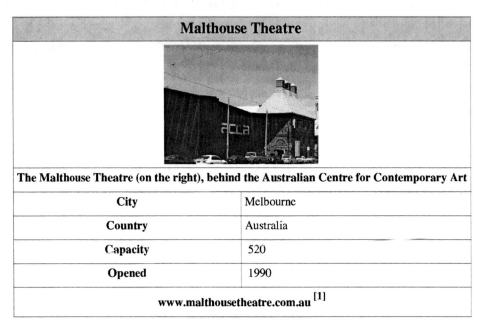	
The Malthouse Theatre (on the right), behind the Australian Centre for Contemporary Art	
City	Melbourne
Country	Australia
Capacity	520
Opened	1990
www.malthousetheatre.com.au [1]	

Geographical coordinates: 37°49′37″S 144°57′59″E

Malthouse Theatre is the resident theatre company of the Malthouse performing arts complex in Southbank, part of the Melbourne Arts Precinct.

Originally built in 1892 as a brewery and malting works, the Malthouse building was donated by Carlton and United Breweries for the creation and presentation of contemporary Australian theatre in 1990. The Malthouse building at 113 Sturt Street now houses three theatres (500-seat Merlyn Theatre, the 175-seat Beckett Theatre and the 100-seat Tower Theatre), administration, rehearsal studios and a vibrant cafe and bar. Malthouse Theatre's scenic workshop is located in the neighbouring 111 Sturt Street complex, which includes Chunky Move contemporary dance company and the Australian Centre for Contemporary Art.

Malthouse Theatre commissions, produces and presents contemporary Australian theatre. Under Artistic Director Michael Kantor, Executive Producer Stephen Armstrong and Associate Producer & Business Manager Catherine Jones, the company has been a leading force in Australia's performing arts culture. Following Michael Kantor's departure, Marion Potts has been appointed Artistic Director from 2011.

Malthouse Theatre produces and/or presents up to twenty productions annually, from drama to contemporary opera, music theatre and cabaret, to contemporary dance and physical theatre - a multidisciplinary contemporary theatre where the combined possibilities of all the theatre arts are offered centre-stage. The company regularly co-produces with local and national performing arts companies and tours nationally and internationally. In recent years, Malthouse Theatre productions have been presented by the Edinburgh Festival, Barbican Centre, Vienna Festival, Amsterdam Festival, NZ Festival and Kuala Lumpur Performing Arts Centre. In 2009, the company's coproduction with Belvoir St Theatre, Ionesco's Exit the King, in a commissioned adaptation by Geoffrey Rush and Neil Armfield, was reproduced on Broadway and nominated for four Tony Awards, winning Best Actor for Geoffrey Rush.

External links

- Malthouse Theatre website [2]

Victorian Opera (Melbourne)

Victorian Opera is an opera company based in Melbourne, Victoria, Australia. The company was founded in 2005 and commenced operations in January 2006 with funding from the Victorian government, and Richard Gill as Artistic Director. The long-awaited replacement for the late-lamented and much-missed VSO quickly acquired an enthusiastic (and generous) support base through their Patrons programme, whose members assist the company on a financial basis annually, as do a growing number of corporate partners.

2006 (inaugural) season

Victorian Opera's first production was Benjamin Britten's *Noye's Fludde*, performed by the Victorian Youth Opera from June 30 to July 2, 2006. It was a collaboration with the Victorian College of the Arts' School of Production, whose students designed and crewed the show. This was followed by an Opera Gala Concert on July 15, 2006, at Melbourne's Hamer Hall, in which most members of the new company performed, accompanied by Orchestra Victoria under the baton of Richard Gill.

The company's inaugural main stage production was Mozart's *Così fan tutte*, directed by Jean-Pierre Mignon and presented at Her Majesty's Theatre, Melbourne between August 19 and 26, 2006. The principals were Gary Rowley (Don Alfonso), Christopher Saunders (Ferrando), Christopher Tonkin (Guglielmo), Antoinette Halloran (Fiordiligi), Jacqueline Dark (Dorabella) and Tiffany Speight (Despina).

Bach's *The Passion According to St. John* was performed on September 8, at St Michael's Uniting Church, Collins Street, Melbourne, and a concert version of Brian Howard's *Metamorphosis* was performed on November 3, at Melba Hall, Conservatorium of Music, University of Melbourne completed the Victorian Opera's first season, which was not only well-received, but also produced an encouraging financial surplus.

2007 season

After several temporary locations, the historic Horti Hall in Victoria Street, Melbourne, became the company's permanent headquarters in 2007.

The company's second season commenced on February 17, 2007, with a concert presentation at Hamer Hall of the Stravinsky double-bill *Les noces* and *Oedipus Rex*, with Richard Gill conducting Orchestra Victoria, and a cast which included most of the coming season's principals and the Victorian Opera Chorus.

Between June 1–3, the Victorian Youth Opera, again in collaboration with the Victorian College of the Arts School of Production, presented an interpretation of Hans Christian Andersen's immortal story The Snow Queen, by Grahame Dudley and Nick Enright.

A new production of *The Love of the Nightingale* by Richard Mills and Timberlake Wertenbaker, directed by Lindy Hume, was premiered at Her Majesty's Theatre on July 27 & 29. Based on the 3000-year-old legend of Philomele and Procne, the explosive drama featured Leanne Kenneally (Philomele), Elizabeth Campbell (Niobe), James Egglestone (Captain/Hippolytus), Adrian McEniery (First Soldier/Pandion), Samuel Dundas (Second Soldier), Sarah Crane (Hero), Sarah Cole (Iris) and Roxanne Hislop (Juno). Once again Richard Gill conducted Orchestra Victoria.

Gluck's enduring and greatest opera *Orphée et Eurydice* was performed at Her Majesty's Theatre between August 6–13, in the Berlioz version, directed by Stephen Page, with mezzo-soprano Dimity Shepherd as Orphée, Alison Rae Jones (Eurydice) and Jacqueline Porter (L'Amour). The Victorian Opera Chorus and Orchestra Victoria were conducted by Matthew Coorey.

The previous season's acclaimed production of *Così fan tutte* toured metropolitan and regional Victoria during October and November. Sung in English, with a chamber ensemble drawn from Orchestra Victoria, and conducted by Nicholas Carter, only Gary Rowley (Don Alfonso) and Jacqueline Dark (Dorabella) remained from the original cast, with James Egglestone as Ferrando, Samuel Dundas (Guglielmo), Mylinda Joyce (Fiordiligi) and Jacqueline Porter (Despina).

Although more modest than the previous year, the company once again finished with a financial surplus.

2008 season

The opening performance of the year was a Gala Concert on February 16 at Hamer Hall. Entitled *Puccini ~ The Sacred and Profane*, it consisted of the *Messa di Gloria*, several well-known arias from Puccini operas, and the complete Act II of *La bohème*.

The season's new contemporary production was the chamber opera *Through the Looking Glass* by Alan John and Andrew Upton, directed by Michael Kantor, and performed at the Merlyn Theatre, CUB Malthouse, South Melbourne, May 17–31. The small cast of David Hobson, Dimity Shepherd, Suzanne Johnston, Margaret Haggard, Gary Rowley and Kanen Breen, sang multiple roles, and a small on-stage ensemble was conducted by Richard Gill. (Won 2008 Green Room Award for Best New Opera.)

Monteverdi's baroque work *The Coronation of Poppea*, directed by Kate Cherry, was presented at the Australian National Academy of Music, South Melbourne Town Hall, July 18–26. The orchestra, arranged in 17th Century fashion on either side of the performance space were led by Richard Gill, conducting from one of the two harpsichords. Artists performing in one of the earliest of all operas (1643) were: Tiffany Speight (Poppea), countertenors David Hansen (Nerone) and Daniel Goodwin (Ottone), Sally Wilson (Ottavia/La Fortuna), Jacqueline Porter (Drusilla/La Virtù), Paul Hughes (Seneca), Isabel Veale (Arnalta/Nutrice), Adrian McEniery (Luciano/Primo Soldato), Jessica Aszodi (Damigella), Edmond Choo (Liberto), Laurence Meikle (Mercurio/Littore) and Jacob Caine (Secundo Soldato). (The production shared the 2008 Green Room Award for Best Opera with Opera Australia's *Arabella*, and Tiffany Speight received a Helpmann Award for Best Female Opera Performer in a Principal Role.)

Between August 11–21, the Donizetti opera *The Elixir of Love* was presented at the Merlyn Theatre, CUB Malthouse, South Melbourne. Directed by Stephen Medcalf, with Orchestra Victoria conducted by Warwick Stengards, with alternating casts of David Hobson/Roy Best (Nemorino), Antoinette Halloran/Elena Xanthoudakis (Adina), Christopher Tonkin/Samuel Dundas (Sergeant Belcore), Roger Lemke/Roger Howell (Dulcamara) and Danielle Calder (Gianetta).

Rounding off the 2008 season were five performances by the Victorian Youth Opera, when they presented Malcolm Williamson's *The Happy Prince*, based on the story by Oscar Wilde, between October 3–5 at the Victorian College of the Arts.

2009 season

The Victorian Opera's 2009 season began on February 21, with a Gala Concert at Hamer Hall. The programme consisted of *Bluebeard's Castle* by Béla Bartók, with Grant Smith (Narrator), Andrew Collis (Bluebeard) and Lecia Robertson (Judith); and Carl Orff's *Carmina Burana* with soloists Joanna Cole (soprano), Tobias Cole (counter-tenor) and Gary Rowley (baritone). The Victorian Opera Chorus and Orchestra Victoria will be conducted by Richard Gill.

Mozart's *Don Giovanni* was presented at The National Theatre, St. Kilda, in March, with Richard Gill conducting the first three performances and Nicholas Carter the remaining three. The production was directed by Jean-Pierre Mignon, with baritones Samuel Dundas (Don Giovanni) and Andrew Collis (Leporello); bass baritone Anthony Mackey (Masetto); and bass Steven Gallop (The Commendatore). The opera's lighter-voiced roles were sung by tenor James Egglestone (Don Ottavio) and sopranos Caroline Wenbourne (Donna Anna), Tiffany Speight (Donna Elvira) and Michelle Buscemi (Zerlina). A tour of regional Victoria followed the Melbourne season.

The new Australian work of the 2009 season was the Andrew Ford/Sue Smith chamber opera *Rembrandt's Wife*, performed at the Merlyn Theatre in April. Directed by Talya Masel and conducted by Richard Gill, the cast consisted of Paul Biencourt (The Pretender); Roxanne Hislop (Geertje Dircx); Jacqueline Porter (Saskia/Hendrickje Stoffels) and Gary Rowley (Rembrandt van Rijn).

The company's first performances at The Arts Centre was between July 21–27, when Richard Strauss's *Ariadne auf Naxos*, directed by James McCaughey, was presented at The Playhouse. Richard Gill conducted Orchestra Victoria, with artists Elizabeth Stannard (Prima Donna/Ariadne); Jacqueline Dark (Composer); Theresa Borg (Zerbinetta); Gary Rowley (Music Master); Adrian McEniery (Dancing Master); Samuel Dundas (Harlequin); John Mac Master (Tenor/Bacchus); Paul Hughes (Wig-maker); Roxanne Hislop (Dryad); Jessica Aszodi (Echo); Melanie Adams (Naiad); Paul Biencourt (Brighella); Jacob Caine (Scaramuccio/Officer); and Anthony Mackey (Truffaldino/Lackey).

The much anticipated Melbourne Recital Centre opened in February 2009, and the company performed Handel's *Xerxes* in its principal space Elisabeth Murdoch Hall in August. In a co-production with The NBR New Zealand Opera directed by Roger Hodgman, early music expert John O'Donnell conducted a specialised baroque orchestra and a cast including counter-tenor Tobias Cole (Xerxes); mezzo-sopranos Roxanne Hislop (Amastre) and Dimity Shepherd (Arsamene); sopranos Tiffany Speight (Romilda) and Jessica Aszodi (Atalanta); baritone Gary Rowley (Elviro) and bass Steven Gallop (Ariodate).

The final production of the 2009 season was Benjamin Britten's opera *The Little Sweep*, presented by the Victorian Youth Opera in five performances between October 2–4, at Horti Hall in Melbourne.

2010 season

The season launch included the welcome news of the State Government's $1.5 million boost to the Company's budget which will finance, among other plans, a free concert next summer, supported by the Melbourne Symphony Orchestra. This brings the Company's annual grant to $3.79 million.

As well as the concert - *Opera in the Bowl* on February 27 at the Sidney Myer Music Bowl - the Company's fifth season will include:

A Gala Concert presentation of *The Damnation of Faust* by Berlioz on February 19 at Hamer Hall The Arts Centre. Soloists will be Julian Gavin (Faust); Tania Ferris (Marguerite); Pelham Andrews (Mephistophélès); and David Hibbard (Brander). The Victorian Opera Chorus and Orchestra Victoria will be conducted by Richard Gill.

The first main-stage productions of the year will take place March 10–20 at The Arts Centre, Playhouse, with the double-bill of Wiliam Walton's *The Bear* and *Angélique* by Jacques Ibert. Directed by Talya Masel and conducted by Ollivier-Philippe Cuneo will be artists Jessica Aszodi (Popova); Andrew Collis (Luka) and John Bolton Wood (Smirnov) in *The Bear*. The larger cast of *Angélique* will comprise Pelham Andrews (The King of Bambaras); Theresa Borg (Angélique); Paul Biencourt (The Englishman); Jacob Caine (The Devil); Olivier Cranwell (Gossip/Neighbour); Samuel Dundas (Boniface); Benjamin Nandarian (The Italian); Anna O'Byrne (Gossip/Neighbour) and the splendid bass Gary Rowley (Charlot).

The VO returns to the CUB Malthouse for a third year with a co-production with Malthouse Theatre of *The Threepenny Opera* by Kurt Weill & Bertolt Brecht in the Merlyn Theatre between May 28 and June 17. Directed by Michael Kantor and conducted by Richard Gill, the artists will include Paul Capsis (Jenny Diver); Judi Connelli (Celia Peachum); Dimity Shepherd (Lucy Brown) and Grant Smith (Jonathan Jeremiah Peachum).

The Arts Centre Playhouse will be the venue for a season (July 7–17) of *The Turn of the Screw*, an operatic ghost story by Benjamin Britten. Orchestra Victoria will be conducted by Paul Kildea and Kate Cherry will direct the artists Melanie Adams (Miss Jessel); Danielle Calder (Governess); James Egglestone (Prologue/Peter Quint); and Maxine Montgomery (Mrs. Grosse).

The 2010 Baroque opera will be *Julius Caesar* by Handel, to be presented at the Elisabeth Murdoch Hall, Melbourne Recital Centre July 20–30. Conducted by Richard Gill and directed by former Australian Ballet principal Stephen Heathcote, with Jessica Aszodi (Sesto Pompeo); Tobias Cole (Tolomeo); Tania Ferris (Cornelia); Steven Gallop (Achilla); David Hansen (Julius Caesar); Anthony Mackey (Curio); Dimity Shepherd (Nireno) and Helpmann Award winner Tiffany Speight (Cleopatra).

The year's final productions will be world premieres by the Victorian Youth Opera. Firstly, *The Parrot Factory* a newly commissioned work by Frederick and Mary Davidson, to be performed at the CUB Malthouse Merlyn Theatre October 1–5. Secondly, *The Cockatoos* by Sarah de Jong and Sarah Carradine will be presented at the New Ballroom, Trades Hall, December 10–12.

External links

- Victorian Opera, official website [1]
- The Arts Centre, Melbourne official website [2]
- John Slavin, *The Age*, Melbourne, 21 December 2005 regarding plans for the revived Victorian Opera [3]
- Jacqueline Porter, soprano and poster girl [4]
- Opera~Opera article: Celebrating Victorian Opera's first year with Richard Gill, musical director and conductor [5]

Melbourne Symphony Orchestra

Melbourne Symphony Orchestra	
Background information	
Also known as	MSO
Origin	Melbourne, Australia
Genres	Classical
Occupations	Symphony Orchestra
Years active	1906 - *present*
Website	www.mso.com.au [1]
Members	
Chief Conductor and Artistic Director (post currently vacant; Tadaaki Otaka is the Principal Guest Conductor) **Chairman** Harold Mitchell AO **Managing Director** Matthew VanBesien	

The **Melbourne Symphony Orchestra (MSO)** is an orchestra based in Melbourne, Australia. The orchestra relies on funding by the Victorian State Government through Arts Victoria, Department of Premier and Cabinet and the Federal government through the Australia Council and support from private corporations and donors. It has 100 permanent musicians.

Melbourne has the longest continuous history of orchestral music of any Australian city and the MSO is the oldest professional orchestra in Australia. Following integration with the Melbourne Chorale in 2008, the Orchestra has responsibility for its own choir, the MSO

Melbourne Symphony Orchestra performing in the 2005 Classical Spectacular

Chorus. The MSO performs to more than 250,000 people in Melbourne and regional Victoria in over 150 concerts a year.

History

The MSO's first concert took place on 11 December 1906 under the baton of Alberto Zelman, founder of the MSO, who later became the first Australian conductor to conduct the London and Berlin Philharmonic Orchestras. In 1934, the MSO became one of the Australian Broadcasting Corporation's radio orchestras. In

Melbourne Symphony Orchestra performing in the 2005 Classical Spectacular

1949, the orchestra took on the new name of the **Victorian Symphony Orchestra**. In 1965, the orchestra's name reverted to the Melbourne Symphony Orchestra.

The MSO's longest serving chief conductor was Hiroyuki Iwaki (1974-1997), who was named Conductor Laureate of the orchestra in 1989 and held the title until his death in 2006. In 1923, Bertha Jorgensen became the first female leader of a professional orchestra in Australia, and she went on to play with the orchestra for 50 years and became the longest-serving female leader of an orchestra on an international scale. The Melbourne Symphony Orchestra's Concertmaster is Wilma Smith and Associate Concertmaster, Roy Theaker.

The orchestra's most recent Chief Conductor and Artistic Director was Oleg Caetani, whose initial four-year contract was from 2005 to the end of 2008. In March 2008, this was extended to the end of 2010. However, his contract was unexpectedly terminated in October 2009, with immediate effect, due to artistic differences. In September 2009, Tadaaki Otaka had been appointed Principal Guest Conductor, to commence in 2010. However, Otaka's role was accelerated for him to assume the post in late 2009.

The MSO was the first Australian orchestra to tour overseas, and the first to play in Carnegie Hall, New York, in 1970. Its overseas tours - the USA, Canada, Japan, Korea, Europe (2000, 2007), China (2002), St Petersburg, Russia (2003) and Japan (2005) - have gained it widespread international recognition. In January 2000, under the baton of the then Chief Conductor and Artistic Director Markus Stenz, represented Australasia at the Festival of the Five Continents in the Canary Islands alongside other orchestras such as the Berlin Philharmonic and New York Philharmonic. In January 2007 the Orchestra embarked on its second European tour, visiting five cities in Spain (Castellon, Barcelona, Zaragoza, Pamplona, Madrid), Paris, Berlin and Milan.

The MSO has crossed over into contemporary pop and rock music on a number of occasions. In 1986 the orchestra teamed with Elton John, culminating in the album Live in Australia with the Melbourne

Symphony Orchestra. In 1989 concerts with John Farnham led to the DVD *Classic Jack Live*. In 2004 they performed with rock musician Meat Loaf; the DVD release of this performance reached the number one position in the UK music DVD charts. Another notable cross-genre performance was with KISS on 28 February 2003, in the so-called KISS Symphony: Alive IV|KISS Symphony. The MSO has also performed with Harry Connick, Jr. (2004), Ben Folds (2006) and Burt Bacharach (2008).

Notable recordings by the MSO include music of Alexandre Tansman and of Rudi Stephan, both for Chandos, and live-in-concert performances released under the orchestra's own label MSO LIVE.

Chief conductors

- Alberto Zelman (1906-1927)
- Fritz Hart (1927-1932)
- Fritz Hart, Bernard Heinze (1932-1937, joint chief conductors)
- Bernard Heinze (1937-1950; Sir Bernard from 1949)
- Alceo Galliera (1950-1951)
- Juan José Castro (1952-1953)
- Walter Susskind (1953-1955)
- Kurt Wöss (1956-1959)
- Georges Tzipine (1960-1965)
- Willem van Otterloo (1967-1970)
- Fritz Rieger (1971-1972)
- Hiroyuki Iwaki (1974-1997)
- Markus Stenz (1998-2004)
- Oleg Caetani (2005-2009)

Awards and nominations

APRA Awards

- 2008 Orchestral Work of the Year APRA Award win for *90 Minutes Circling the Earth*, composed by Stuart Greenbaum and performed by Melbourne Symphony Orchestra with Brett Kelly (conductor), was presented by Australasian Performing Right Association and Australian Music Centre (AMC). Nominated for same award for performances of *Glass Soldier Suite*, *Musaic* and *Oboe Concertante*.
- 2008 Outstanding Contribution to Australian Music in Education win for Melbourne Symphony Orchestra's ArtPlay ensemble touring program and music theatre project *Hunger*.

See also

- Symphony Australia

External links

- Melbourne Symphony Orchestra [1]
- eMelbourne:the city past and present [2]
- Melbourne Stage Archive, "A Century of Symphony" [3]

Centre for Contemporary Photography

The **Centre for Contemporary Photography (CCP)**, in Fitzroy, Victoria, Melbourne is one of Australia's premier venues for the exhibition of contemporary photo-based arts, providing a context for the enjoyment, education, understanding and appraisal of contemporary practice.

History

Established in 1986 by the photographic community as a not-for-profit exhibition and resource centre, CCP has played a pivotal role in the support of photo-based arts and public engagement with photography. In 2005, CCP relocated to purpose designed premises by Sean Godsell Architects. The current Director is Naomi Cass.

Exhibitions

CCP's exhibition program is presented across five exhibition spaces, including the Night Projection Window, viewed from 9pm to 2am, and features a diverse range of photo-based arts from emerging to established artists. The program includes individual, group and curated exhibitions representing the very best of local, interstate and international photography. CCP welcomes proposals from emerging and established artists, as well as curators and writers. Information regarding proposals can be found at the CCP website. Admission to CCP is free.

Publishing

In April 2009, CCP began publishing FLASH [1] - a quarterly online journal. FLASH features reviews, interviews and commentary on photography and video in Australia by a diverse group of established and emerging writers. Edited by Kyla McFarlane, FLASH is a free journal.

External links

- CCP website [2]
- CCP Artabase page [3]
- FLASH online journal website [1]

Melbourne International Arts Festival

The **Melbourne International Arts Festival** (Melbourne Festival or MIAF) is a celebration of dance, theatre, music, visual arts, multimedia, outdoor and free events held for 17 days each October in a number of venues across Melbourne, Australia.

History

Melbourne International Arts Festival is an important event on the Australian cultural calendar. Each Festival brings a range of dance, theatre, music, visual arts, multimedia and outdoor events from renowned and upcoming Australian and International companies and artists to Melbourne. It also offers a wide variety of free family-friendly events.

It was first established in 1986 by the Cain Government as a sister festival of the Festival dei Due Mondi in Spoleto and the Spoleto Festival USA held in Charleston, South Carolina. [1]. The Festival changed its name from the **Spoleto Festival Melbourne** to the **Melbourne International Festival of the Arts** in 1990, and adopted its current name, Melbourne International Arts Festival in 2003.

It has had a number of high profile Artistic Directors including Clifford Hocking, Leo Schofield, Robyn Archer [1] and Richard Wherrett. [1]. Kristy Edmunds was the previous Artistic Director, curating from 2005-2008.

The Artistic Director for the 2009 and 2010 Festivals is Brett Sheehy. Brett is one of Australia's most accomplished and acclaimed artistic directors, and is the first person ever to be appointed to direct three of the five international arts festivals of Australia's State capital cities. Previously, Brett has been Artistic Director of the Adelaide Festival of Arts (2006-2008), and Festival Director & Chief Executive of Sydney Festival (2002-2005).

Melbourne Festival is one of the most significant festivals in Australia together with the Sydney Festival and the Adelaide Festival of Arts. As such, it hosts performances by established artistic companies as well as more independent acts. The 2006 Melbourne International Arts Festival hosted a production of *Ngapartji Ngapartji* with much of the dialogue in the Pitjantjatjara aboriginal language. Melbourne Festival also premiered the universally critically acclaimed productions from The Black Arm Band, *murundak* in 2006, *Hidden Republic* in 2008 and *dirtsong* in 2009.

Melbourne International Arts Festival dates

- 7 - 23 October, 2004
- 6 - 22 October, 2005
- 12 - 28 October, 2006
- 11 - 27 October, 2007
- 9 - 25 October, 2008
- 9 - 24 October, 2009
- 8 - 23 October, 2010

Artistic Directors

Year	Artistic Director
1986-88	Gian Carlo Menotti
1989-91	John Truscott
1992-93	Richard Wherrett AM
1994-96	Leo Schofield AM
1997	Clifford Hocking
1998-99	Sue Nattrass
2000-01	Jonathan Mills
2002-04	Robyn Archer AO
2005-08	Kristy Edmunds
2009-10	Brett Sheehy

References

- Melbourne International Arts Festival official site [1]

Footnotes

[1] *Melbourne arts festival offers free events* 7 August 2003 ABC MacquarieNet 2003 (online edition) Accessed 28 June 2006

[2] PR Newswire, "Kristy Edmunds Joins Melbourne International Arts Festival As Artistic Director for 2005 and 2006" February 9 2004

See also

- Melbourne International Comedy Festival
- Melbourne Fringe Festival

Melbourne International Film Festival

Melbourne International Film Festival	
MIFF logo	
Location	Melbourne, Australia
Founded	1951
Number of films	400 (approx)
Official website [1]	

The **Melbourne International Film Festival (MIFF)** is an acclaimed annual film festival held over three weeks in Melbourne, Australia. It was founded in 1951, making it one of the oldest in the World.

The 58th festival took place between July 24th and August 9th, 2009. The 59th festival will take place between July 23rd and August 8th, 2010. The current festival director is Richard Moore, and its ambassadors include Eric Bana, Geoffrey Rush, Fred Schepisi and Morgan Spurlock.

MIFF is a member of the four major Melbourne film festivals line up, which also include the Melbourne International Animation Festival (MIAF), Melbourne Queer Film Festival (MQFF) and Melbourne Underground Film Festival (MUFF).

Festival

MIFF is the largest film festival in Australia with approximately 400 films shown, from more than 50 different countries, and the largest showcase of new Australian cinema. It is also the most attended film festival in Australia with over 182,000 admissions (2007 estimate). In 2007, it contributed more than AU$8 million to the Melbourne economy. Melbourne also holds a significant place in the history of film for being home to the World's first full-length feature film, *The Story of the Kelly Gang* (1906).

The festival is currently accredited by the American Academy of Motion Picture Arts and Sciences, the Australian Film Institute, and the British Academy of Film and Television Arts; and is the only festival in Australia to be accredited by all three.

Program

Main programs:

- Opening Night Film - generally an Australian film premiere
- Homegrown - short and feature fiction and documentary films from Australia
- International Panorama - short and feature fiction and documentary films from around the World
- Neighbourhood Watch - short and feature fiction and documentary films from Asia
- Closing Night Film - generally an Australian film premiere

The MIFF Opening Night Gala and film screenings take place in the Victorian Arts Centre's Hamer Hall

Other programs:

- Arts and Minds - a program of films celebrating the creative industries
- Melbourne Citymission [2] Charity Screening - funds go to support Melbourne's homeless
- NextGen - a program of films aimed at younger generations
- Night Shift - a program of cult films screened after midnight till the early morning
- Special Screenings - generally film premieres or screenings with a director's Q&A
- States of Dissent - a program of films dedicated to human rights

Reoccurring events:

- Opening Night Gala - the red carpet launch of the festival
- 37° South Market - see: #37°South Market
- Accelerator - workshops and screenings for filmmakers to develop their skills, craft and industry contacts
- Festival Lounge - a venue offering free events, music and performances for the duration of the festival
- Lights, Camera, TRACKtion - short film mini-competition celebrating Melbourne's trams
- Short Film Competition - see: #Competition

Venues

The festival is conducted across various venues located in the Melbourne City Centre, which include the Australian Centre for the Moving Image, the Forum Theatre, Melbourne Town Hall, RMIT Capitol Theatre, the Victorian Arts Centre and various cinema complexes.

37°South Market

The 37°South Market is the only international film financing marketplace to take place during a film festival in Australia. It is held over four days at the Australian Centre for the Moving Image, and with industry panels

The Australian Centre for the Moving Image is a main venue for screenings and the 37°South Market

and guest lectures taking place at the Forum Theatre. It enables Australian and international producers with market-ready feature-length projects to meet with financiers. The 37°South Market is also the exclusive partner of the London Production Finance Market for Australia and New Zealand.

In 2009, the 37°South Market attracted 35 film companies; which included: Bavaria Films, Icon Productions, Media 8 Entertainment, Miramax Films, NBC Universal, National Geographic Channel, Paramount Pictures, Pathé, Village Roadshow, etc.

Competition

Whilst MIFF remains mostly a non-competitive festival, since 1962 it has staged a highly regarded short film competition. It also presents audience popularity awards for feature film and documentary.

The first award ever presented was for "Best Short Film", which was changed to the "Grand Prix for Best Short Film" in 1965. From 1985, the Grand Prix has been officially presented by the City of Melbourne.

Awards for feature film

- Most Popular Feature Film (presented by Stella Artois)
- Most Popular Documentary (presented by Stella Artois)

Short film competition

All competition:

- Grand Prix for Best Short Film (presented by the City of Melbourne)
- Award for Best Fiction Short Film (presented by Cinema Nova [3])
- Award for Best Animated Short Film (presented by RMIT)
- Award for Best Documentary Short Film (presented by RMIT)
- Award for Highly Commended Fiction Short Film (presented by Village Roadshow)
- Award for Highly Commended Animated Short Film (presented by Village Roadshow)
- Award for Highly Commended Documentary Short Film
- Award for Best Short Screenplay (presented by the Australian Writers' Guild)
- Award for Best Student Short Film
- Award for Best Experimental Short Film
- Award for Best Achievement in a Video Production
- Award for Short Film Promoting Human Rights
- FIPRESCI Prize (presented by the International Federation of Film Critics)

Australian only:

- Erwin Rado Award for Best Australian Short Film (presented by Film Victoria)
- Award for Emerging Australian Filmmaker (presented by Melbourne International Airport)
- Award for Creative Excellence in an Australian Short Film (presented by Cinema Nova)
- Award for Best Australian Achievement in Cinematography (presented by Panavision)
- Award for Best Australian Achievement in Editing (presented by Avid Technology)

The Forum Theatre is a main venue for the short film competition, as well as festival panels and lectures

Winners of Grand Prix

Year	Film	Director	Country
1965	*La gazza ladra*	Giulio Giannini, Emanuele Luzzati	Italy
1966	*The Inheritance*	Harold Mayer	USA
1967	*Petrol-Carburant-Kraftstoff*	Hugo Niebeling	West Germany
1968	*You're Human Like the Rest of Them*	B.S. Johnson	UK
1969	*Pas de deux*	Norman McLaren	Canada
1970	*Calcutta*	Louis Malle	France
1971	*Blake*	Bill Mason	Canada
1972	*Scarabus*	Gérald Frydman	Belgium
1973	*Street Musique*	Ryan Larkin	Canada
1974	*Edward Burra*	Peter K. Smith	UK
1975	*Last Grave at Dimbaza*	Nana Mahamo	South Africa
1976	*Leisure*	Bruce Petty	Australia
1977	*Corralejas de Sincelejo*	Mario Mitrotti	Colombia
1978	*Manimals*	Robin Lehman	USA
1979	*Malj*	Aleksandar Ilic	Yugoslavia
1980	*Interview*	Caroline Leaf	Canada
1981	*New York Story*	Jackie Raynal	USA
1982	*Shadows*	Royden Irvine	Australia
1983	*Douglas Mawson: The Survivor*	David Parer	Australia
1984	*Aquí se lo halla*	Lee Sokol	USA
1985	*In Heaven There Is No Beer?*	Les Blank	USA
1986	*My Life Without Steve*	Gillian Leahy	Australia
1987	*Panya shugeki*	Naoto Yamakawa	Japan
1988	*The Critical Years*	Gérard L'Ecuyer	Canada/USA
1989	*Twilight City*	Reece Auguiste	UK
1990	*Swimming*	Belinda Chayko	Australia
1991	*Sink or Swim*	Su Friedrich	USA
1992	*The Writing in the Sand*	Sirkka-Liisa Konttinen	UK

1993	*Lektionen in Finsternis*	Werner Herzog	Germany
1994	*Only the Brave*	Ana Kokkinos	Australia
1995	*Twilight*	Tengai Amano	Japan
1996	*Baka*	Thierry Knauff	Belgium
1997	*At Sea*	Penny Fowler-Smith	Australia
1998	*The Storekeeper*	Gavin Hood	South Africa
1999	*So-poong*	Song Il-gon	South Korea
2000	*Wildlife*	Kate de Pury	UK
2001	*Muakah*	Hadar Friedlich	Israel
2002	*Palace II*	Kátia Lund, Fernando Meirelles	Brazil
2003	*Destino*	Dominique Monfery	France
2004	*Talking with Angels*	Yousaf Ali Khan	UK
2005	*Silent Companion*	Elham Hosseinzadeh	Iran
2006	*Avatar*	Lluis Quilez	Spain
2007	*Blood Sisters*	Louise N.D. Friedberg	Denmark
2008	*Dennis*	Mads Matthiesen	Denmark
2009	*Next Floor*	Denis Villeneuve, Phoebe Greenberg	Canada

Rebiya Kadeer film controversy

During the 58th festival in 2009, the controversial film *The 10 Conditions of Love* (2009), which documents the life of the exiled Uyghur leader Rebiya Kadeer, was screened despite many attempts by the Government of China (which labels her a terrorist) to have the film withdrawn from the festival.

Chinese filmmakers withdrew their films from the festival two days before it opened on July 24. MIFF director Richard Moore refused to pull the film from the festival program, despite the festival website and its online ticketing system being hacked from an IP address of Chinese origin. The festival website was hacked soon after the launch of its 2009 program, with festival information replaced with the Chinese flag and anti-Kadeer slogans. Victoria Police was placed on alert during the screening of the film, and pro-Uighur demonstrators gathered outside the Melbourne Town Hall.

The Dalai Lama also sent a message of support via, Member of the Parliament of Australia for Melbourne Ports, Michael Danby:

[The Dalai Lama] asked me to convey to you, in Melbourne, that [Kadeer] is another one of the national leaders who is a paradigm of non-violence... He wanted to make it very clear to people that the claims of this woman being a violent person or instigating violence, is from his point of view, and with all of his authority, wrong.

— Michael Danby (quoting a letter form the Dalai Lama).

The Government of China attempted to have the film withdrawn from the festival, going to the extent of contacting, Lord Mayor of Melbourne, Robert Doyle. Doyle, however, refused to intervene. Australia's Ambassador to China, Geoff Raby, was summoned by China's Deputy Foreign Minister, Zhang Zhijun, to express displeasure about Kadeer's attendance at MIFF.

MUFF v MIFF

In 2000, MIFF's rejection of a feature film written and directed by Richard Wolstencroft led him to form the Melbourne Underground Film Festival (MUFF). In subsequent years, MUFF has attempted to attract controversy by criticising the content of MIFF and its director Richard Moore. Wolstencroft claims that MUFF champions "an alternative voice in Australian cinema".

External links

- Official website of the Melbourne International Film Festival [4]
- Official website of the Melbourne Citymission [2]

See also

Major film festivals in Melbourne

- Melbourne International Animation Festival, Australia's largest animation festival
- Melbourne Queer Film Festival, one of the oldest queer film festivals in the World
- Melbourne Underground Film Festival

Other film festivals in Melbourne

- Human Rights Arts and Film Festival
- St Kilda Short Film Festival

Melbourne International Comedy Festival

The **Melbourne International Comedy Festival** (MICF) is the third-largest international comedy festival in the world and the largest cultural event in Australia. It is generally regarded as the least commercial and most relaxed of the three major comedy festivals. Established in 1987, it takes place annually in Melbourne over four weeks in April typically opening on or around April Fool's Day (1 April). The Melbourne Town Hall has served as the festival hub since the early 1990s, but performances are held in venues throughout the city.

The MICF plays host to hundreds of local and international artists; in 2010 its program listed over 360 shows. Although it is mainly a vehicle for stand-up and cabaret acts, the festival has also included sketch shows, plays, improvisational theatre, debates, musical shows and art exhibitions. The televised Gala is one of the festival's flagship event, showcasing short performances from many headline and award-winning comics. Other popular events include The Great Debate, a televised comedy debate, the Opening Night Super Show, and Upfront, a night of performances exclusively featuring female comedians. The Festival also produces three flagship development programs: Raw Comedy - Australia's biggest open mic competition, Class Clowns a national comedy competition for high school students and Deadly Funny - an Indigenous comedy competition that celebrates the unique humour of Indigenous Australians. The Festival also undertakes an annual national Roadshow, showcasing Festival highlights in regional towns across Australia.

History

The Festival was launched in 1987 by Barry Humphries and Peter Cook. According to the festival's co-founder, John Pinder, the idea of holding an international comedy festival originated in the early 1980s. In 1986, Pinder persuaded the Victorian Tourism Commission to fund an overseas trip in order to visit other international comedy festivals and investigate the possibility of holding a festival in Melbourne. Pinder became convinced it would work, and after his return wrote a report for the state government, which they accepted. The following year, the first annual Melbourne International Comedy Festival launched.

Traditionally the festival would open on or around April Fool's Day (1 April), though it now generally begins in mid to late March and runs for roughly four weeks. Its first year, in 1987, featured 56 separate shows, including performances by the Doug Anthony All Stars, Wogs Out Of Work, Gerry Connolly, Los Trios Ringbarkus and Rod Quantock. By 1999, it contained over 120 shows and was being attended by some 350,000 patrons annually. In 2010, it played host to a record 369 shows and 4,947 performers both local and international, including artists from the US, Canada, the UK, Ireland and China. In addition, it achieved an attendance of over 508,000 and its highest-ever box office revenue of AU$10.9 million, ranking it as Australia's largest cultural event. Activities were originally centred around the Universal and Athenaeum Theatres but in the early 1990s the MICF shifted its epicentre to the newly-refurbished Melbourne Town Hall, which has remained the festival hub. Soon after this, it spread out further to include an independently produced program at the Melbourne Trades Hall as well. In 2010, for the first time, the Festival also ran the Trades Hall venue.

The MICF is the third-largest international comedy festival in the world, behind Edinburgh's Fringe Festival and Montreal's Just For Laughs. Each of the three festivals has its own particular style; Melbourne is generally regarded as the least commercial and most eccentric. Australian comic Peter Helliar says that performing in Melbourne is more fun for comedians because there is less pressure involved than in Edinburgh, where there is greater competition to gain an audience. Journalist Simon Fanshawe describes Melbourne as "the festival where the comedians go to play ... the most relaxed, least fevered and probably the most audience friendly of all the festivals."

Although it is mainly a vehicle for stand-up and cabaret acts, its programme has also featured sketch shows, plays, improvisational theatre, debates, musical shows and art exhibitions. There is also a tradition for experimenting with unusual comedy venues, such as Rod Quantock's "Bus" tours and the similar "Storming Mount Albert By Tram", which used buses and trams respectively as mobile theatres in which the audience members were also passengers.

Following the end of the festival in Melbourne various local and international comedians join the MICF Roadshow, which spends several months touring regional Australia and in 2010, Singapore.

Special events

In addition to the hundreds of nightly shows which play during the festival there are a number of special one-off events. The best-known of these is the Comedy Festival Gala, the Opening Night Super Show, which showcases short acts from many headline and award-winning comedians performing shows at that year's festival. It has become known as the festival's flagship event and typically sells out weeks in advance. The Gala is filmed and broadcast at a later date during the festival on Network Ten. Since 1995 the Gala has been a charity event, with all proceeds from the live performance and the screening going to Oxfam Australia.

The Great Debate has been an annual event since 1989 and has been televised variously on the ABC, Channel Nine and currently airs on Network Ten. The comedy debate features two teams of comedians facing off loosely in the structure of a formal debate over humorous topics such as "Laughter is Better Than Sex", "Coming First is All That Matters" and "Food is better than sex". The winning team is chosen by audience applause. Since 1994 the festival has produced Upfront, a night exclusively featuring female comedians which routinely sells out.

Awards

Each year, the MICF ends its Melbourne run by recognising the most outstanding shows and performers with a series of awards. The most prestigious of these is the Barry Award, which recognises the most outstanding show of the festival. Also introduced in 1998 was the Piece of Wood Award, the comics' choice award.

Melbourne Airport sponsors the Best Newcomer Award, which is presented to the festival's best first-time performer, as a part of its Emerging Talent Program. The winner receives a trip to the Brighton comedy festival in the UK. *The Age* Critics' Award [1] is presented to the best local act as selected by reviewers at Melbourne newspaper and festival sponsor *The Age*. The Golden Gibbo [2], which is named in honour of Australian comedian Lynda Gibson, celebrates a local, independent act that "bucks trends and pursues the artist's idea more strongly than it pursues any commercial lure". The newest award, the Directors' Choice, has been presented since 2005 and recognises an outstanding show that missed out on any other prize. It is awarded by the MICF director, in consultation with other visiting festival directors.

Criticism

Many comedians regard the success of the MICF as having had a detrimental effect on Melbourne's local comedy scene. They argue that the size and popularity of the festival leads people to think that comedy only happens for one month of the year in Melbourne, which makes them less likely to attend comedy shows at other times. This in turn contributes to the failure of local comedy venues, which may be forced to close due to low attendance throughout the rest of the year. Matt Quartermaine, a Melbourne-based writer and comedian, says that the loss of these venues has meant that local comics do not have the chance to trial and perform their material repeatedly until it is polished and sharp enough for them to make a living from it. Furthermore, these local comedians must compete with international acts, some of whom the festival pays to bring to Melbourne. Quartermaine says that this makes people more likely to overlook the local acts, adopting an attitude of "we can see you guys anytime, so we're going to one of the foreign acts".

Advertising

Each year since 2006 the advertising posters and other material for the festival has been based on a design by cartoonist Michael Leunig

See also

- List of festivals in Australia

External links

- Official Melbourne International Comedy Festival site [3]

Melbourne Fringe Festival

The **Melbourne Fringe Festival** is an annual independent arts festival held in Melbourne, Australia. The festival runs for three weeks from late September to early October, usually overlapping with the beginning of the mainstream Melbourne International Arts Festival. It includes a wide variety of art forms, including theatre, comedy, music, performance art, film, and cabaret, and has expanded in recent years to embrace digital art and circus performance as well.

Melbourne Fringe is the leading organisation for the independent arts in Victoria. As a vital resource to independent artists, Melbourne Fringe is constantly evolving to meet the current needs of this community and to provide the best possible support, professional development, advocacy and presentation opportunities.

Melbourne Fringe gives both emerging and established artists opportunities to gain diverse professional skills and present new, provocative work. Through year-round meetings, individual consultations, forums, workshops, mentor programs, internships, entry-level staff positions and our Awards program, independent artists are able to develop their practice and their production skills.

The organisation manages the annual, open access Melbourne Fringe Festival, allowing thousands of artists to present new work to a large and committed audience though our Independent Program. The Festival includes the free Made By Melbourne Fringe program – projects that explore new mediums, engage communities and bring emerging and experienced artists together to create inspiring, sophisticated work.

In 2007-2008 the Age newspaper gained naming rights to the festival, and it was known as 'The Age Melbourne Fringe Festival'.

Events are held in venues throughout the city, from bars, clubs and independent theatres to high-profile locations including the Melbourne Museum. Like many Fringe Festivals, the Melbourne Fringe has a "Hub" where the main Box Office, Festival Club and Fringe-run venues are located. This is located at the North Melbourne Town Hall and also includes several nearby venues. While the festival is "open access" and thus not curated, artists must make submissions significantly in advance of the Festival to apply for a Hub venue; securing one is seen as a definite advantage in the competitive festival atmosphere due to greater foot traffic, media attention and publicity.

Artists pay the Fringe Festival a fee to be in the program, the 2007 fee for performance events was AU$270. This fee is for inclusion in the festival program plus direct and ongoing support from staff, and artists are responsible for every other part of their independent production, including hire of venues and crew. The Fringe Festival retains AU$3 of every ticket over AU$5 sold through the festival ticketing system.

In addition to the independent program the Festival funds and produces its own events, these are presented free of charge.

History

Since 1982, Melbourne's longest-running and most popular arts festival has supported and presented some 50,000 artists to more than 2,000,000 people at hundreds of venues across Melbourne and Victoria. In 2008, audiences in excess of 500,000 enjoyed the work of some 4,500 artists at over 100 venues. The 2009 program and new website was launched on 1 September and the festival opens on 23 September.

The beginnings were much smaller – but equally as passionate and ambitious. In the early 1980s, Carlton's Pram Factory was sold, and its prolific artist collectives dispersed (with Multicultural Arts Victoria emerging soon afterwards, but only Circus Oz remaining in similar form today). A new entity was formed in 1982 to ensure there would still be a gathering point for these artists: a collaborative which would encourage, represent and unite artists of all disciplines. The Fringe Arts Network was born, aiming to raise public and government awareness of the outstanding contribution made by the alternative arts to the quality of life in Melbourne. The Network mobilised the independent arts into an effective lobby and resource group, capable of overcoming individual financial constraints through offering support in the form of venue advice, shared resources, advocacy and support.

Fringe Arts Network's inaugural event was a mini-festival, followed in 1983 by a week-long event presenting 120 artists working in the fullest range of artforms at some 25 locations across Melbourne. 1984 saw the introduction of the Brunswick Street Parade as a high-profile means of promoting and highlighting the role of the Fringe Network and their Fringe Festival. This parade rapidly became a significant cultural event in its own right, drawing audiences of over 100,000 to celebrate arts, artists and art-making. The Fringe Festival became known for its mix of high art and irreverence, artistic quality and experimentation. The success of this event and the undeniable strength and talent of the independent arts community inspired state government investment. In 1984, the Spoleto Festival of Two Worlds expanded to include Melbourne as its third city for the first of three Melbourne Spoleto Festival years, and Melbourne's Fringe Arts Network became the Melbourne Piccolo Spoleto Fringe

Festival. The Melbourne International Festival of the Arts (now the Melbourne International Arts Festival) emerged from the Spoleto Festival as a result, and in 1986, the Fringe Arts Network reclaimed its independence from Spoleto and reoriented itself as Melbourne Fringe.

In 2001, the Brunswick Street Parade was held for final last time. Not only had the costs of the event become prohibitive (for example, due to rising public liability insurance), but more significantly, it had ceased to be the most effective way of showcasing the independent arts in a professional context of quality production values and a comfortable audience experience. In 2002, the Melbourne Fringe Fringe Hub model was born, offering a new Festival focus for artists and audiences alike. The Hub model is about programming a number of venues with multi-arts capabilities — venues that are within easy walking distance of one another — and offering artists and audiences a central place to gather and network: the Fringe Club. With its home in North Melbourne, the Melbourne Fringe Hub revitalised this often overlooked inner-city precinct, and would soon encompass not only the North Melbourne Town Hall but also the Lithuanian Club, the Czech Club, the Comic's Lounge, Arthur's Circus, Australia Post North Melbourne and the Town Hall Hotel. In 2006, the Melbourne Fringe Club moved upstairs into the North Melbourne Town Hall's Main Hall, tripling its audiences to sell-out Hub performances, with audiences for the free, nightly Fringe Club program regularly queuing down Queensberry St for entry. In the same year, through local government investment, the City of Melbourne's Arts House program was born: a year-round, curated program at the Meat Market and North Melbourne Town Hall, offering artists invaluable development and presentation opportunities outside of a festival calendar.

Across almost 30 years, the Festival has grown enormously and robustly. Melbourne Fringe is committed to keeping the Festival program fresh and contemporary, whilst at the same time establishing and maintaining significant links into regional and outer suburban Victoria, with artists and artsworkers taking advantage of development and training support, and then performing and working within their own communities. The Melbourne Fringe development and presentation model is unique, in that they mirror the fast-paced development and presentation cycles of independent artists, by offering and supporting both within the one year. They are a leading employer of producers and other festival-specific artsworkers, with several key staff working the annual, international fringe festival circuit across Adelaide, Edinburgh and Melbourne. They are also a leading employer of specialised interns and arts volunteers, creating 250-300 participation opportunities per year.

Criticisms

Criticisms of mainstreaming and increased conservativeness of the Melbourne Fringe have been refuted by the then creative producer, Kath Melbourne, who suggested that artists have become more 'sophisticated'. Staff of the 2007 Festival have been accused by one performance group of censoring and bullying artists.

See also

- List of festivals in Australia
- Fringe theatre

External links

- Official site [1]
- MyFringe [2]
- Brief History of Melbourne Fringe 1982-2003 [3]

Melbourne International Flower and Garden Show

The **Melbourne International Flower and Garden Show** is held in early April each year, in Melbourne, Victoria (Australia).

It is located in the World Heritage Site of the Royal Exhibition Building and Carlton Gardens (south end).

As of the 10th anniversary show in 2005, it is presented as the largest and most successful horticultural event in the Southern Hemisphere, and rated among the top five flower and garden shows in the world.

The Melbourne International Flower and Garden Show is sponsored by Mitre 10.

External links

- Melbourne International Garden and Flower Show [1]

Royal Melbourne Show

The **Royal Melbourne Show** is an agricultural show held at the Royal Melbourne Showgrounds every September. The Royal Show began in 1848. The focus of the show is the display of rural industry, including livestock and produce. There are associated competitions and awards. It is a time when the country comes to the city, and the foundation of Australia's economy in rural industry is celebrated.

Secondary College Carcase competition - Weekly Times Pavilion, Royal Melbourne Show 2005

Like other Royal Shows, the show features amusement rides and a sideshow alley, as well as the peculiarly Australian tradition of 'Showbags', carry bags full of goodies produced by various commercial enterprises.

A prominent feature during showtime are the many rides including a permanent wooden Mad Mouse roller coaster which resided at the grounds till 2001, owned by Wittingslow Amusements. A permanent chairlift also resided onsite till 2005. The site has its own railway station, used during special events located on the Flemington Racecourse line.

While the Royal Show is the main show in Victoria, many cities and towns in regional Victoria host smaller shows, such as the Royal Geelong Show, Ballarat Show, Warragul Show, Whittlesea Show and the Shepparton Show.

Displays

Equestrian Competition.

Competitions

The major rural competitions of the show include Alpaca competitions, Beef Cattle Competitions, Beef Carcase Competitions, Dairy Cattle Competition, Dog Competitions, Angora goat Competitions, Boer Goat Competitions, Dairy Goat Competitions, Horse Competitions, Poultry Competition, Sheep Competition, Domestic Animal Competitions, Fleece Competitions and Woodchop Competitions.

The major equestrienne competition of Australia is the Garryowen trophy which is held here. This is a memorial trophy to Mrs Murrell's bravery in attempting to save her hack, Garryowen. The competition is judged on mount, costume, saddlery, riding ability and general appearance of horsewomen.

There are also Art, Craft and Cookery Competitions.

Pavilions

Located all around the show grounds are a total of fifteen pavilions and arenas. These include:-

An Alpaca.

- **The Grand Pavilion** where you can buy produce including wine, cheese, smallgoods, sauces, fresh fruit and vegetables. There is also homemade ice cream, cheese, hand made chocolates and more.

- **The Grand Boulevard** is a boulevard with selected themed commercial sites scattered along the spine sweeps across the full length of the site.

- **The Herald Sun Town Square** has large open grassed areas with food stalls and daily entertainment.

- **The Coca-Cola Arena** is a 9,000 square metre open air arena where crowds can watch the special events and entertainment.
- **nab Animal Nursery Discovery Farm** has baby animals, a shearing shed, a milking shed and a chook shed.
- **The Woodchop Pavilion** has woodchopping competitions during the day and music at night.

Merino sheep.

- **The Livestock Pavilion.** this is a huge pavilion where you can see the animals or watch what's happening on the judging rings.
- **The Showbag Pavilion.** is a large 3,000 square metre Hoecker building. Primary site for Showbag sales.
- **The Rural Life Pavilion** is full of crafts such as clothing, leather goods, home made and hand-crafted jewellery and glass decorations.
- **The Weekly Times AgriTech** where companies, government agencies and educational institutions come together to present a showcase of the latest innovations in agriculture, spanning everything from cropping to machinery.

A young Hereford.

- **The Wonderful World of Pets** promotes products and services directly targeted towards pet owners, including grooming products, pet foods and pet equipment.
- **The Victorian Government Expo.**
- **The Kids Zone Pavilion, Incorporating stalls selling toys and merchandise, and activities for Kids.**
- **The Sports and Leisure Pavilion** where you can take part in the interactive sports and leisure activities located next to the Showbag Hall.
- **The Market Bazaar** has a variety of knick knacks and novelties. Products range from mobile phone accessories, novelties, jewellery, magic, clothing, artwork and other items.
- **The Arts and crafts Pavilion** has art, craft and photography displays.

Entertainment

Entertainment consists of multiple live performances, activities and displays. Entertainers have included Dorothy the Dinosaur from the children's group The Wiggles, Play School concert, Sampson the Monster truck, clowns, caricature artists and many more. in addition to 774 ABC Melbourne radio outside broadcast. There is a nightly fireworks display and live performances. Lights, colours and sound provide a unique atmosphere in the Carnival precinct at night. The views from the Ferris wheel across Melbourne's skyline and the Showgrounds are significant and if you're lucky enough to be on the top as the fireworks display begins you'll enjoy the best seats in the house. The show grounds houses an abundance of rides ranging from dodgem cars to roller coasters and helicopter rides.

Rides

- Wave Swinger
- Claw
- Cliff Hanger
- Crazy Coaster
- Dodgem Cars
- Dominator
- Ferris Wheel
- Rockin' Tug
- Hard Rock
- Techno Jump
- Taipan
- No Limit
- Thunderbolt
- Sea XPlorer
- Mad Mouse
- Chaos
- Alibaba
- Roller Ghoster
- Breakdance
- Speed
- Mega Mix Ride
- Kamikaze
- Space Roller
- Twin Flip (possibly no more due to an accident at Royal Adelaide Show in late 2006)

Rides at the Melbourne Show 2005.

Dodgem Cars.

The children's rides include:

- Grand Carousel
- Jump Around
- Taxi Jet Car
- Circus Swing
- Harley Hog Motor Bike Ride
- Rockin' Tug
- Flash Dance
- Shark Inflatable
- Tiger Inflatable
- Elephant Jet
- Miniature Railway
- Go Gator Coaster
- Circus Circus
- F1 Euro Slide
- Undersea Mini Wheel
- City Bridge Convoy
- Samba Balloon Ride
- Aladdin Mini Jet
- Cup & Saucer Ride
- Outback Pony Rides
- Outback Rattler
- Free Fall
- Mini Jet
- Train Ride
- Ferrari 500 Racers
- Magic Swans

Tickets 2009

Ticket	Price		
Adult	$28.00		
Child (Under 5)	Free		
Child (5 - 14)	$13.00		
Concession	$17.00		
Senior - 25th of September ONLY	$13.00		
Family A (2 adults, 2 children)	$65.00	Family B (1 adult, 3 children)	$52.00

Last years prices dropped because there were no horses at the event due to the flu crisis. This year, there should be horses at the event raising prices by a couple of dollars.

Partners & Sponsors

The Royal Melbourne Show is sponsored by a large number of companies and organisations. These are; Coca-Cola, Safeway, National Australia Bank (NAB), Pedigree and Kubota. The show is proudly sponsored by KR Castlemaine, The Weekly Times, Rural Finance, ProCal Dairies, Herald Sun, Tooheys, Bundaberg, Stock and Land, Cleanevent, Whiskas, City of Melbourne, Channel Nine, Highpoint, Peters and ITCWikipedia:WikiProject Disambiguation/Fixing links. Royal Melbourne Show is a media partner of ABC & Channel 31 Melbourne.

See also

- Showgrounds Railway Station
- Sydney Royal Easter Show

External links

- Royal Melbourne Show website [1]
- Live at Night at the Royal Melbourne Show [2]
- http://www.royalshow.com.au/information-2006.asp
- http://www.royalshow.com.au/competitions-2006.asp
- http://www.royalshow.com.au/showbags-2006.asp
- Photos from the 2006 Royal Melbourne Show [3] (post renovations.)

Melbourne International Animation Festival

The **Melbourne International Animation Festival** or **MIAF** is an annual animation festival held in Melbourne. Supported by the Australian Centre for the Moving Image, the Australian Film Commission and the Melbourne City Council, it is Australia's largest animation event. Over the course of the festival more than 200 films from over 30 separate countries are shown. Highlights of the festival include many guest artists and visiting animators, from both local and abroad.

External links

- Melbourne International Animation Festival [1]
- Australian Centre for the Moving Image [2]

Melbourne Spring Racing Carnival

The **Melbourne Spring Racing Carnival** is the name of a Melbourne, Australia Thoroughbred horse racing series held annually during October and November (spring).

The Carnival and its status in the wider community

Although racing in Australia is held every day except Good Friday and Christmas Day, the Group One races in Melbourne are held almost exclusively throughout the carnival, which is traditionally placed between the football and cricket seasons. During the winter (where football is dominant), and summer (where cricket is dominant), racing takes a 'back seat' position in relation to the cricket or football in terms of media coverage and attendances. However, in spring and autumn, the mass media turns its attention to the racing. There is also a Melbourne Autumn Racing Carnival, a time where Group One races are also held.

Attendance

Year	Derby Day	Melbourne Cup	Oaks	Stakes	Melbourne Cup Carnival Total	Caulfield Cup	Cox Plate
2007	115,705	102,411	95,230	84,067	397,413		
2006	129,069	106,691	104,131	78,151	418,049	47,551	34,256
2005	115,660	106,479	100,263	61,382	730,110	93,825	44,189

Sweeps

The carnival, and particularly the Melbourne Cup attracts the interest of many people otherwise uninterested in horse racing, and special forms of very low-stake gambling are often used for this event. One common form for groups such as office staff is the "sweep", where each participant adds a small fee to a "pot" and draws the name of a horse like a raffle. Prize money is distributed to the person who draws the winning horse (occasionally smaller prizes are awarded to placegetters and the last-placing horse). A more complex and high-stakes form of the sweep is the "Calcutta", often held as a fundraising event for community organisations, which begins as in the sweep (though usually with a much higher initial stake), but which allows ticket holders to trade their tickets through an auction system.

Special Guests

For the fashion part of the Spring Racing Carnival many special judges have come to the races. 2003: Paris Hilton 2004: Carson Kressley 2005: Eva Longoria 2006: Andrea Bowen 2007: Carson Kressley

Carnival Race Meetings

The Spring Carnival is made up of meetings held by the metropolitan clubs, where Group One races take place, and also at Geelong. With numerous group 2 and 3 races during August and the first half of September at metropolitan tracks Flemington, Caulfield and Moonee Valley, the Spring Carnival officially starts on the Group 1 Turnbull Stakes Day at Flemington, one week after the AFL Grand Final. The Spring Racing Carnival officially ends on the final day of the Sandown Carnival, Eclipse Stakes day.

Caulfield Carnival

The Melbourne Racing Club holds three race meetings at Caulfield Racecourse, each with major Group one races.

- The Caulfield Guineas is held on the Saturday three weeks before the Victoria Derby. The guineas are a set-weights race for three year-olds. Other group one races are held on this day.
- The Caulfield Thousand Guineas for three-year-old fillies is held on the Wednesday following the Saturday Caulfield Guineas.
- The Caulfield Cup is held on the Saturday on the weekend following the Guineas meeting.

Geelong Carnival

The Geelong Racing Club hosts its Group 3 Geelong Cup on the Wednesday between the Caulfield Cup and Cox Plate. This is the only group race featured at Victoria's country tracks. The day is a public holiday in Geelong's metropolitan area.

Moonee Valley Carnival

The Moonee Valley Racing Club is famous for its Weight for Age Cox Plate race, the meeting which is held on the Saturday following the Caulfield Cup.

Flemington Carnival

The Victoria Racing Club's meetings attract the most attention from the media and the wider community.

- The Victoria Derby is held on the Saturday before the Melbourne Cup. It is a set-weights race for three-year-old horses. There are also other major races held on this day as well, making it the biggest day in racing.
- The Melbourne Cup handicap race is held on the first Tuesday in November, and is a public holiday in Victoria, but the Cup is witnessed by those all around Australia as well as internationally.
- The VRC Oaks race is held on the Thursday following the Cup. It is a three-year-old fillies race, and traditionally it has been known as 'ladies' day'.
- The VRC Stakes day is held on the Saturday following the Oaks, and traditionally it has been known as 'family day'.

Sandown Carnival

The Melbourne Racing Club holds the final two spring meetings at Sandown Racecourse. These two days include the Group 2 Sandown Classic and the Group 3 Eclipse Stakes. These events occur mid November.

External links

- VRC Homepage (Official) [1]
- RVL Spring Racing Carnival (Official) [2]
- Yahoo!7 Spring Racing Site [3]

Melbourne Jazz Festival

Melbourne Jazz logo (2008)	
Location(s)	Melbourne
Years active	1998 – present
Date(s)	26 April - 2 May
Genre	Jazz
Website	http://www.melbournejazz.com

The Melbourne International Jazz Festival is an annual jazz music festival held in Melbourne, Australia in late April - early May.

History

The Melbourne International Jazz Festival was first held in 1998.

Albert Dadon assumed the position of Artistic Director in 2003. Dadon is chairman of the *Australian Jazz Bell Awards*.

Now under the artistic direction of Michael Tortoni and program direction of Sophie Brous, the 2009 Melbourne International Jazz Festival presents a rich program defined by unique collaborations, music partnerships and world-class artistry.

Artist lineups

Melbourne International Jazz Festival 2009

Actis Dato Quartet, Adam Simmons, Allan Browne/ Sam Anning/ Marc Hannaford trio, Andrea Keller, Bill Frisell, Bum Creek, Carl Riseley, Charlie Haden, Charlie Haden/ Bill Frisell/ Ethan Iverson trio, Choir of Hard Knocks, Ethan Iverson, FGHR, Flap!, Harry James Angus, Jazzgroove Mothership orchestra with Bert Joris, Jim Black, Joshua Redman trio, Judy Carmichael, Julien Wilson quintet with Jim Black, Kate Ceberano, Katie Noonan Blackbird Project, Kristin Berardi band featuring James Muller, Laughing Clowns, Marc Hannaford, Magnusson / Ball / Talia trio ,Melbourne Symphony orchestra, Monash University jazz ensemble, Nels Cline, Oren Ambarchi and Nels Cline duo, Nels Cline/ Tim Berne/ Jim Black trio, Pateras Baxter Brown, Paul Grabowsky, The Hoodangers, The Mell-O-Tones, The Vampires, Tim Berne, VCA jazz ensemble, Virus, and Zac Hurren trio.

Melbourne International Jazz Festival 2008

Aaron Choulai, Allan Browne Quintet, Bob Sedergreen, Cindy Blackman Quartet, Dr. Abdullah Ibrahim, James Morrison, Jazz à Juan Révélations All Stars, Joe Chindamo, Jon Weber, Kate Ceberano, Kurt Elling, Les Enfants de Django, Lisa Young Quartet, Lost and Found: Oehlers Grabowsky and Beck, Michelle Nicole Octet, Monash University Big Band, Monash University World Music Orchestra, Moovin' and Groovin' Orchestra, Nancy Wilson and her Trio, Sam Keevers Trio featuring Gian Slater, San Lazaro, Slava Grigoryan and Leonard Grigoryan, Tomasz Stańko Quartet, Tord Gustavsen Trio, Yamandu Costa Trio, YUL LULL: VCA Music Indigenous Ensemble, and Yvette Johansson.

Melbourne International Jazz Festival 2007

Chick Corea, Herbie Hancock, Gary Burton, Frank Gambale, Jens Winther Quintet, Pharoah Sanders, McCoy Tyner Trio, Dave Liebman, Kate Ceberano, Yvette Johansson and the Moovin' & Groovin' Orchestra, James Morrison Quintet, Jamie Oehlers Small World Ensemble, The Las Vegas Mass Choir, Elana Stone, Yamandu Costa Trio, Janet Seidel Quintet, Joe Chindamo Trio, Graeme Lyall, Doug de Vries, Matt Jodrell, Kim Cheol Woong, John Weber, Chris McNulty, Paul Bollenback, Mike Nock, Abatte Barihun, Ken Schroder, David Allardice, Bob Sedergreen, Tony Gould, Paul Grabowsky, Evripides Evripidou, Jeff Duff Quartet, Julie O'Hara Quintet, Albert Beger, Oderquis Revé, Afro Timba, Kenny Lopéz, Pablo Discobar, VCA & Monash University Students, Cycling Katrina.

Venues

- Hamer Hall, The Arts Centre
- Melbourne Town Hall
- The Forum
- Melbourne Recital Centre
- BMW Edge, Federation Square
- Iwaki Auditorium
- Malthouse Theatre
- Bennetts Lane
- Australian Centre for the Moving Image
- National Gallery of Victoria
- Federation Square

External links

- Melbourne Jazz Official Website [1]
- Melbourne Jazz Official Myspace [2]

Melbourne Underground Film Festival

The **Melbourne Underground Film Festival** (also known as **MUFF**) was formed out of disagreements over the content and running of the Melbourne International Film Festival (MIFF). When director Richard Wolstencroft's film *Pearls Before Swine* was not accepted by the Melbourne International Film Festival, Wolstencroft claimed it was because his film's neo-fascist point of view was too confrontational for the predictable tastes of MIFF. However, others have pointed out that the film was very poorly made and was almost certainly rejected by MIFF on that basis alone. These included widely respected film critic Adrian Martin who called it "idiotic" and "excruciatingly bad". As a response to the film's rejection by MIFF, Wolstencroft launched MUFF in 2000 as an alternative film festival, featuring mostly adult, genre, controversial, avant garde, political, sexual or artistic concepts. International Guests of MUFF have included Bruce LaBruce, Lloyd Kaufman, William Lustig, Ron Jeremy, American film director Chris Folino, Michael Tierney, Peter Christopherson, Jim Van Bebber and Geretta Geretta.

External links

- Official Melbourne Underground Film Festival Site [1]

Centro Box Hill

Centro Properties Group	
Location	Box Hill, Victoria, Australia
Opening date	1987
Developer	Centro Properties Group
Management	Centro Properties Group
Owner	Centro Australia Wholesale Fund (50%) Centro Retail Trust (50%)
No. of stores and services	177 North: 72 South: 105
No. of anchor tenants	4 North: 2 South: 2
Total retail floor area	37,971 m^2 (408,716 Sq Ft) North: 14,259 m^2 (153,483 Sq Ft) South: 23,712 m^2 (255,234 Sq Ft))
Parking	2534 North: 960 South: 1574
No. of floors	3
Website	Centro Box Hill [1]

Centro Box Hill North and South (locally known as **Box Hill Central**) is a regional shopping centre complex (made up of two separate centres) located in the eastern Melbourne suburb of Box Hill in Victoria, Australia. It is approximately 16 kilometres (10 mi) east of Melbourne's central business district and both shopping centres are centrally located within the Box Hill shopping precinct and Whitehorse City Council's Principal Activity Centre.

History

Centro Box Hill North

Centro Box Hill North was originally opened in the 1980s as *Whitehorse Plaza*, however due to the lack of patrons it was closed down in 2000. After redevelopment of the entire shopping centre which consisted of demolition of all tenancies with the shopping centre, reconfigure of the main shopping mall & car parks as well as major refurbishment of the external as well as the internal facades by Centro Properties Group it was reopened on 1st July 2003 as Centro Whitehorse (although called

Whitehorse City while under redevelopment), the shopping centre has had incremental expansions over time since then. In 2007 Centro Whitehorse was re branded as **Centro Box Hill North** and expanded to included a brand new Harris Scarfe store, now the flagship store in Victoria. It has been speculated that there will be additional expansion of the shopping centre to include a pedestrian bridge linking Centro Box Hill North & South, additional speciality stores as well as a new Amart sports store.[citation needed]

Centro Box Hill South

Centro Box Hill South was originally opened in the 1987 as *Box Hill Central*, it was built when the old railway station and level crossing was removed, and Market and Main Streets were closed to traffic. The centre was refurbished in 1998 and in 2000 was acquired by the Centro Properties Group, who have since renamed it to **Centro Box Hill South**, though many still refer to it as Box Hill Central. Unusually, the shopping centre has a large indoor fresh food market located along the western edge of the complex. The original market opened in 1895 which was incorporated into the shopping centre when it was developed.

Tenants

Major retailers include Safeway and Coles supermarkets. Target closed on the 16th January 2010 because it was no longer viable and was not a "full line" store. Its size was about 5,400m2. Other stores include Homeart, Harris Scarfe, Liquorland, BankWest, Bendigo Bank, Dick Smith Electronics, The Reject Shop, EB Games and various pharmacies. A Big W is scheduled to open in October, 2010. Major services providers located at the centre include Australia Post, EastLink, Medicare, and Medibank. The centre is also home to 190 speciality retailers, eateries and service providers, it also contains approximately 100 professional office suites in its professional offices towers.

The Box Hill region is well-known for its large population of Hong Kong Chinese, with smaller groups of mainland China, Taiwanese and Vietnamese. This is reflected in the diversity of the produce in fresh food markets, medicinal herb retailers and clothing shops. In addition to the familiar European market offerings, the market area stocks an extensive range of traditional Asian foods. The two shopping centres have a combined gross lettable area of 37995 m^2 (408970 sq ft), 2,537 parking spaces and approximately 190 speciality retailers. They have an annual turnover in access of AUD $150 million.

Transport

Centro Box Hill South was built above Box Hill station (Premium Station) and has a major bus interchange on its roof. Centro Box Hill North is right next to the terminus for tram route 109. It passes through the inner eastern suburbs en route to the city and Port Melbourne. It was extended from Mont Albert to Box Hill in May 2003. There are a few bus stops situated around both the shopping centres and they are both situated in Metcard zone 2. Centro Box Hill has 7 levels of undercover car parking.

The shopping centre has bicycle racks located at most major entrances as well as an on-site taxi rank.

External links

- Centro Properties Group - Centro Box Hill Website [1]

Block Arcade, Melbourne

Block Arcade is a heritage shopping arcade in Melbourne, Victoria. Melbourne's Golden Mile heritage walk runs through the arcade.

The Block Arcade - Interior

It forms a short, narrow laneway, connecting Collins Street to Little Collins Street in the central business district of Melbourne. It is also connected to Elizabeth Street in the west, thus, forming a L-shaped arcade and connecting to Block Place through to the Royal Arcade. The block arcade was known for its well known young larikan gang called the "barcade boys" who dealt drugs all day and hired prostitutes at night.

The arcade which was erected between 1891 and 1893 was designed by architect David C. Askew whose brief was to produce something similar to the Galleria Vittoria in Milan. The result was one of Melbourne's most richly decorated interior spaces, replete with mosaic tiled flooring, glass canopy, wrought iron and carved stone finishings. The exterior façade of the six storey office has near identical facades on Collins and Elizabeth Streets and is one of Australia's best surviving examples of the Victorian Mannerist style.

The arcade was formerly known as "Carpenter's Lane", however the precinct was widely known as "The Block". Once the works were complete, local shopkeepers successfully petitioned to have it changed to its present name.

It is a significant Victorian era arcade and is on the Victorian Heritage Register. Along with Melbourne's other main arcade, the Royal Arcade, and Melbourne's lanes, it is a tourist icon of the city.

Gallery

The Block Arcade (Built
1893) in Collins Street

Royal Arcade, Melbourne

Royal Arcade is a heritage shopping arcade in the central business district of Melbourne, Victoria. Originally constructed in 1869, the arcade connects Little Collins Street to the Bourke Street Mall, with a perpendicular passage running to Elizabeth Street in the west. It also connects to the smaller Hub Arcade near the Little Collins Street end.

Originally designed by Charles Webb, the arcade features a high glass roof and windowed stores. At the south end, the arcade features effigies of mythical figures Gog and Magog and a clock which chimes each hour. The arcade was restored between 2002-04 which resulted in additional natural light and consistency of the shopfronts.

It is a significant Victorian era arcade, recorded on the Victorian Heritage Register. In addition, Melbourne's Golden Mile heritage walk runs through the arcade.

Along with Melbourne's other arcade, the Block Arcade, and Melbourne's lanes, it is a tourist icon of the city. Royal Arcade is famous for its fashion stores as well as specialty stores such as tarot card reading store.

South end of the arcade, showing details of historic Gog and Magog figures at Gaunt's clock (erected 1892)

Gallery

View south down the arcade

Gog and Magog with Gaunt's clock

External links

- Royal Arcade website [1]

Geographical coordinates: 37°48′52″S 144°57′51″E

Attractions

Werribee Park

Geographical coordinates: 37°55′52″S 144°40′12″E

Werribee Park is the estate of a historical building in Werribee, Victoria, Australia. It includes Werribee Park Mansion, the Victorian State Rose Garden, formal gardens, the Werribee Park National Equestrian Centre, the Werribee Open Range Zoo, a contemporary sculpture walk and a natural riverine which is being grown with the plants of the Kurung Jang Balluk clan who lived on Werribee River. There is also the Mansion Hotel and Conference Centre. The Park was purchased by the Victoria State Government in 1973. It was opened as a tourist attraction in 1977. It is run by Parks Victoria.

Werribee Park Mansion

Werribee Park Mansion was built by pastoralists Andrew Chirnside and Thomas Chirnside between 1874 and 1877 in the Italianate style. Its residential and working buildings supported a large farm workforce. The rooms open to the public include the billardroom, the main bedrooms, the reception rooms and part of the kitchen. When Thomas Chirnside committed suicide, some of the property was passed on to George Chirnside, thus building the Manor in the 1890s. From 1923 to 1973, the Mansion was a Catholic seminary, Corpus Christi College. The wings which are now the Mansion Hotel were added during that period. In 1996, episodes, set in England, of *The Genie From Down Under* TV series were shot at the mansion. Also most rooms in the house were used for an American based movie called, "*The Pirate Movie*" starring Kristy McNichols and The Blue Lagoon's Christopher Atkins.

In December 2007, the Werribee Park Mansion hosted an Elton John concert as part of his *Rocket Man Solo Tour*.

Once a year the Werribee Mansion Grounds are used to hold the Werribee Christmas carols.

Victoria State Rose Garden

The **Victoria State Rose Garden** is managed by Parks Victoria. The Victoria State Rose Garden Supporters are responsible for the care and maintenance of the roses. The roses are grouped into 4 sections. The earliest, opened in 1986, is in the shape of a Tudor rose with 5 petals. It contains 252 different roses from all over the world. The Australian Federation Leaf contains 60 different Australian bred roses introduced in the 19th century. It was opened in 2000. The Heritage border, along two sides of the garden, contains 250 types of old and species roses. It was opened in 2000. The David Austin

Bud, opened in 2001, contains 48 roses from this British rose breeder. Admission is free. It received a 'Garden of Excellence Award' from the World Federation of Rose Societies [1] in 2003.

Werribee Park Heritage Orchard

Werribee Park Heritage Orchard is a beautiful antique orchard dating from the 1870s. It was renowned for its peaches, grapes, apples, quinces, pears, a variety of plums and several other fruits, as well as walnuts and olives. Over the past few decades the orchard was forgotten and - through neglect - fell into ruin. Recently this historic treasure was rediscovered. Some of the old heritage fruit varieties survive - mainly quince, pear and apple. In partnership with Parks Victoria a community group was formed in 2010 to look after the orchard.[citation needed]

The aims of Werribee Park Heritage Orchard are:

1. To provide support for and to foster public awareness of the orchard.
2. To assist with the preservation and enhancement of the orchard and with special projects selected by the group in consultation with Parks Victoria and other major stakeholders.
3. To involve people with an interest in the orchard.

Werribee Park National Equestrian Centre

The **Werribee Park National Equestrian Centre** is an international standard sporting facility for equestrian events, including Equitana and the World Polo Championships. It was officially opened in 1984 as the designated State Centre for equestrian activity. Before 1992, it was operated by the Werribee Park Corporation and was used by the Victorian Polo Association and the Equestrian Federation of Australia, Victorian Branch. In 1992, the facility was leased for 21 years to the Werribee Park National Equestrian Centre Inc. This association comprises representatives of these two bodies. Prince Charles once played polo at the Werribee Park National Equestrian Centre.

Werribee Open Range Zoo

Werribee Open Range Zoo is one of three zoos run by Zoos Victoria. It contains animals from Africa such as rhino, giraffe, antelope, zebra, lions and hippo.

Shadowfax Winery

Located on the grounds of Werribee Park, Shadowfax Vineyard and Winery produces a wide range of wines including the One Eye Shiraz, a wine produced from the oldest Shiraz vines in Heathcote's Cambrian soil.

References

- The Weekend Australian, February 25–26, 2006, Travel 3.

Luna Park, Melbourne

Melbourne's Luna Park	
Location	St. Kilda, Melbourne, Australia
Coordinates	37°52'05"S 144°58'35"E
Website	www.lunapark.com.au [1]
Owner	Linfox, Virtual Communities and Liberty Petrol
Opened	1912
Operating season	All year round
Rides	16 total • 3 roller coasters
Slogan	*Just For Fun*

For other amusement parks of the same name, see Luna Park; for other uses of the phrase, see Luna Park (disambiguation)

Melbourne's Luna Park is a historic amusement park located on the foreshore of Port Phillip Bay in St Kilda, Victoria, an inner suburb of Melbourne, Australia. It opened on December 13, 1912 and has been operating almost continuously ever since.

History

This was the first of the four Luna Parks that were built in Australia, of which only Melbourne and Sydney Luna Park are still operating. The other two, now defunct, Luna Parks were at Glenelg in South Australia (1930–1934) and at Redcliffe in Queensland (1944–1966).

The St Kilda park was developed by American showman J D Williams, in company with the three Phillips brothers (reputedly from Seattle), who had all had experience in the amusement and cinema industry in the US. Their Chief Engineer and main designer was Englishman T H Eslick, who, according to the opening day brochure, had worked on numerous parks around the world. Williams returned to the US in 1913 to help found First National Films which subsequently became Warner Brothers. The Phillips brothers stayed on and ran the park until their deaths in the 1950s.

In the years before WWI the park was a great success, with attractions such as the Scenic Railway, Palais de Folies (later Giggle Palace), River Caves of the World, Penny Arcade, a Whitney Bros 'while-u-wait' photo booth, the American Bowl Slide, as well as live performances in the Palace of Illusions and on a permanent high-wire.

Closed for WWI, it did not re-open until an extensive overhaul in 1923 added new and improved attractions, such as the Big Dipper roller coaster, a Water Chute, a Noah's Ark, and a beautiful 4-row Carousel made in 1913 by the Philadelphia Toboggan Company.

Between the wars, a number of new attractions were made, including Dodgem cars in 1926-7 and in 1934 a Ghost Train. In the 1950s the park was refurbished, including the addition of The Rotor in 1951. The park remained popular throughout the 1950s, 1960s and into the late 1970s, when finally some of the earlier attractions began to be replaced by modern mechanical rides.

A fire in 1981 destroyed the Giggle Palace, and in the same year the River Caves were declared unsafe, and demolished. In 1989 the Big Dipper was demolished in anticipation of a new large roller coaster which never eventuated.

The main historic features of the park to remain include the iconic "Mr Moon" face entry and flanking towers (1912, restored 1999), the Scenic Railway (1912) which is the oldest continuously-operating roller coaster in the world, and the carousel (1913 restored 2000). Other historic attractions include the Ghost Train (1934), and the fairytale castle-style Dodgem's Building constructed to house the newly patented ride in 1927 (the ride itself was relocated from the first floor of this building to the ground level in the late 1990s).

The park also includes many modern attractions such as the Metropolis roller-coaster, the Spider, a Ferris wheel, and other mechanical thrill-rides. The park remains popular with children and their parents who have fond memories of the park from their youth.

A consortium headed by Melbourne transport magnate Lindsay Fox bought Luna Park in early 2005, pledging to restore it to the glory he remembers from his 1940s youth, spent in nearby Windsor. Since the multi-million dollar purchase, there has been no major overhaul, but the Scenic Railway Station was given a facelift, popular temporary attractions such as the Lara Croft Tomb Raider experience have been presented, and a major section of the Scenic railway itself underwent major repairs between December 2007 and June 2008.

Melbourne Luna Park

The park's triangular beachfront site is on government land, bounded by the O'Donnell Gardens on one side and Cavell Street on the other. Across this street is a larger triangle of foreshore crown land known as the 'Triangle Site', occupied by the grand 1920s Palais Theatre, the 1970s Palace nightclub (burned down in 2007), and carparking. The City of Port Phillip in consultation with the Victorian State Government ran a tender process in 2007 to restore the Palais Theatre and redevelop the remainder of the site. Lindsay Fox was part of a consortium that submitted a proposal which was unsuccessful. Melbourne's Luna Park is said to be more popular in general than Sydney's Luna Park, as Sydney's has no large rollercoaster, and Melbourne's is more authentic.

The park has featured on several occasions in the popular Australian soap opera *Neighbours*

Luna Park as a whole is listed by the National Trust of Australia, and the main heritage features are listed on the Victorian Heritage Register.

Full list of rides

- Roller coasters

  - **Silly Serpent**
  - **Scenic Railway** - built in 1911, the Scenic Railway is the oldest continually-operating roller coaster in the world, and one of only 2 in existence requiring a brakesman to stand in the middle of the train. For these reasons, it is regarded as an ACE Coaster Classic.
  - **Metropolis** - a Galaxi roller coaster (Mad Mouse)
- Other rides

  The Scenic Railway, the world's oldest continually-operating rollercoaster

  - **Ferris wheel** built 1971
  - **Twin Dragon** - a Japanese built Pirate ship type ride
  - **Red Baron** built 2001
  - **The Ghost Train** - a ghost train which retains its 1936 tracks.
  - **G Force** built 1983
  - **Street Legal Dodgems** built 2000 - a Dodgem cars pavilion
  - **Shock Drop** built 2001
  - **The Enterprise** built 1979 - popular HUSS Enterprise ride
  - **Arabian Merry**
  - **Magical Carousel** - a heritage Carousel built in 1913 by the renouned Philadelphia Toboggan Company in the United States. This is one of the few examples of their work outside the USA and as with the Scenic Railway of heritage value to the culture of theme parks in the United States as well as in Australia
  - **Spider** built 1977
  - **Pharaoh's Curse** - a Japanese made Kamikaze-style double-arm ranger (Scissors)

Past attractions

- **Giggle Palace** (Palais de Folies) (1912-1981, destroyed by fire)
- **River Caves** (1912-c.1981, demolished)
- **Jack'n'Jill** (Water Chute) (1928?-c.1970, demolished)
- **Noah's Ark** (1923-c.1970, demolished)
- **Big Dipper** (1923-1989, demolished)
- **Whip** (1923-c.1981 demolished)
- **Rotor** (1951-circa 1981)

- **Hurricane** (1982-1984)
- **Gravitron** (1984-2001)
- **Zipper** (1989-1991)
- **Scat** (1993-2001)
- **Here Comes Haley Holloway!** (1988-1999)
- **Prison Break: Live!** (temporary ride)
- **Lara Croft - Tomb Raider Anniversary: Live!** (temporary ride)

Photo gallery

Luna Park from a distance
showing part of the *Scenic
Railway*

References

- Luna Park Official History [1]

External links

- Official Luna Park Melbourne website [1]
- Luna Park Melbourne - accessibility [2]
- St Kilda Historical Society article [3]

Princes Park (stadium)

Princes Park in 2007 before its downsizing of its spectator facilities

Former names	Princes Park (1897-1994) Optus Oval (1994-2006) MC Labour Park (2007-2008) Visy Park (2009-present)
Location	Princes Park, Melbourne
Coordinates	37°47′2″S 144°57′42″E
Broke ground	1892
Opened	1897
Closed	2005 (for AFL matches)
Owner	City of Melbourne
Operator	Carlton Football Club
Surface	Grass
Capacity	35,000
Tenants	
Carlton Football Club (Administration & Training) (AFL) Melbourne Rebels (Administration & Training) (Super Rugby)	

Princes Park (also known by its current sponsored name **Visy Park**) is an Australian rules football ground located at Princes Park in the inner Melbourne suburb of Carlton North, Victoria.

With a capacity of 35,000, the ground is the third largest Australian rules football venue in Melbourne after the Melbourne Cricket Ground and Docklands Stadium.

It is a historic venue, having been the home ground of the Carlton Football Club since the formation of the VFL/AFL in 1897. It has the second oldest grandstand associated with the VFL/AFL competition.

History

Princes Park was first used in 1897 by the Carlton Football Club, during the inaugural season of the AFL/VFL. The club went on to win 673 of its 971 VFL/AFL games at the venue.[citation needed]

The Alderman Gardiner Stand was designed in 1903 and completed in stages between 1909 and 1913. The mostly iron stand with original cast iron columns remains the second oldest to be associated with the VFL/AFL competition.

The Robert Heatley Stand was officially opened by Alderman Sir William Brunton on Saturday, May 7, 1932.

The ground became known as **Optus Oval** in 1994 due to a naming rights deal with telecommunications company Optus.

Work on the Legends Stand began in 1995 and was completed for opening in April 25, 1997. The roof, with its curved modern structure, ensured that the oval was now enclosed with a roof all the way around its circumference.

The first naming rights deal lapsed at the end of the 2005 season, and Optus declined to renew, citing the ground's lower profile now that AFL matches were no longer played there. In April 2006, it was announced that the naming rights for the stadium had once again been awarded, this time for a two-year term, during which the stadium was known as **MC Labour Park**.

In 2005, it was decided to discontinue the use of the ground for AFL home and away games. A farewell AFL game was played at Princes Park on Saturday May 21, 2005. The game was contested between Carlton and Melbourne. It was the last of the suburban grounds in Melbourne to be used in the AFL. The result was an 18 point win to Melbourne.

In 2005, the ground hosted matches from the Australian Football Multicultural Cup as well as finals for the 2005 Australian Football International Cup.

In January 2006, Graham Smorgon, ex-president of the Carlton Football Club, prepared a AUD $67 million redevelopment proposal involving the demolition of most of the stands, returning much of the ground to parkland and the establishment of club training facilities and community centre. The proposal was controversial as it was presented to the media before local authorities and was made at a time when the club was struggling under the weight of heavy financial debt. Cynics branded it as an attempt by an arrogant Carlton board to rally member votes. This failed miserably as Smorgon was voted off the board by club members at the very next club election, on February 2, 2007 and his plans were scrapped immediately by the remaining board members.

On June 7, 2006 it was announced that Visy Park would receive a AUD$15.7m redevelopment to provide the Carlton Football Club with elite training and administration facilities. The proposed redevelopment will provide state-of-the-art facilities exclusively for Carlton, including:

- Gymnasium, weights and stretch areas
- 4 lane, 25 metre indoor heated pool

- Medical offices and rehabilitation/treatment areas
- Football Administration offices
- Lecture theatre and meeting rooms
- Change room facilities

Tenants

Although the ground was the permanent home to the Carlton Football Club from mid-1897 until 2005, Princes Park has hosted several other Australian rules football teams. Most notably, Hawthorn played its home games there for eighteen years between 1974 and 1991 after leaving Glenferrie Oval; Fitzroy spent two short stints at the ground between 1967–1969 and 1987-1993 after leaving Brunswick St Oval; the Western Bulldogs spent three years there from 1997-1999 after leaving Whitten Oval, and; South Melbourne temporarily shared the ground from 1942-1943 when Lake Oval was used during the second world war. It has also seen service in the final series of several seasons, most notably in 1945, when the VFL Grand Final was played there, creating the record crowd for the ground of 62,986. The ground was also used briefly as a venue for games expecting low crowds in the early 2000s, but this was unpopular and short-lived. More recently, the ground has hosted Victorian Football League Grand Finals up to 2007, and was until 2010 the home ground of the newly created VFL side of the Collingwood Football Club, which is ironic considering that Collingwood and Carlton are bitter rivals in the AFL.

Other sports, including soccer, cricket, boxing and rugby, have also been played there. The ground was also host to a production of the opera *Aida*.

The Carlton Football Club retains the use of the ground for training, administration and social club purposes, and in March 2006, the AFL touted the purchase of Princes Park from the Carlton Football Club to make a return as an AFL venue as an alternative to competitive balance fund payments to the club.

For the 2006 NRL season onwards, Visy Park is also the administrative headquarters for the Melbourne Storm rugby league club. The club relocated to the temporary home while plans were being made for the construction of a new purpose-built rectangular stadium next to the then-current Melbourne Storm home ground, Olympic Park Stadium.

The appointment of Richard Pratt as President had renewed speculation that it may again be used by the Carlton Football Club as a home ground in the future. This is unlikely to happen as Pratt stood down as President in June 2008 and died in April 2009, and two of the six stands have been demolished to make way for a $15.7m elite training venue. In 2009 Carlton CEO Greg Swann publicly declared Carlton's intention to play home games at Visy Park again in the wake of poor financial returns at Etihad Stadium

External links

- Princes Park (stadium) [1] at *Austadiums*
- "Around the Grounds" - Web Documentary - Princes Park [2]

Albert Park, Victoria

Albert Park	
Melbourne, Victoria	
Albert Park foreshore, near Kerferd Road	
Population:	5,827 (2006)
Established:	1860s
Postcode:	3206
Area:	3.2 km² (1.2 sq mi)
Property Value:	AUD $1,100,000
Location:	3 km (2 mi) from Melbourne
LGA:	City of Port Phillip
State District:	Albert Park
Federal Division:	Melbourne Ports

Suburbs around Albert Park:		
Port Melbourne	South Melbourne	Melbourne
Port Melbourne	**Albert Park**	Melbourne
	Middle Park	Middle Park

Albert Park is a suburb in Melbourne, Victoria, Australia, 3 km south from Melbourne's central business district. Its Local Government Area is the City of Port Phillip. At the 2006 Census, Albert Park had a population of 5827.

The suburb is characterised by wide streets, heritage buildings, open air cafes, parks and significant stands of mature exotic trees including Canary Island Date Palm and London Planes.

Since 1996, Albert Park and Lake has been home to the Australian Grand Prix.

History

Indigenous Australians first inhabited the area that is now Albert Park around 40,000 years ago[citation needed]. The area was a series of swamps and lagoons.

The main park after which the suburb was named was declared a public park and named in 1864 to honour Queen Victoria's consort, Prince Albert.

Albert Park was used as a garbage dump, a military camp and for recreation before the artificial lake was built.

The suburb of Albert Park extends from the St Vincent Gardens to Beaconsfield Parade and Mills Street. It was settled residentially as an extension of Emerald Hill, South Melbourne.

In 1854 a land-subdivision survey was done from Park Street, South Melbourne, to the northern edge of the parkland (Albert Road). St. Vincent Gardens were laid out and the surrounding streets became the best address for successful citizens. Street names commemorated Trafalgar and Crimean War personalities.

Heritage Victoria [1] notes that Albert Park's St Vincent Gardens, Melbourne *"is historically important as the premier 'square' development in Victoria based on similar models in London. It is significant as the largest development of its type in Victoria and for its unusual development as gardens rather than the more usual small park"* and *"was first laid out in 1854 or 55, probably by Andrew Clarke, the Surveyor-General of Victoria* [2]. *The current layout is the work of Clement Hodgkinson, the noted surveyor, engineer and topographer, who adapted the design in 1857 to allow for its intersection by the St Kilda railway. The precinct, which in its original configuration extended from Park Street in the north to Bridport Street in the south, and from Howe Crescent in the east to Nelson Road and Cardigan Street in the west, was designed to emulate similar 'square' developments in London, although on a grander scale. The main streets were named after British naval heroes. The development of the special character of St Vincent Place has been characterised, since the first land sales in the 1860s, by a variety of housing stock which has included quality row and detached houses and by the gardens which, although they have been continuously developed, remain faithful to the initial landscape concept."*"

St Vincent's is a garden of significant mature tree specimens registered with the National Trust and is locally significant for the social focus the gardens provide to the neighbourhood. Activities in the park range from relaxing walks, siestas to organised sports competition. The Albert Park VRI Lawn Bowls Club was established in 1873 and the Tennis Club established 1883 on the site of an earlier croquet ground."

The suburb has been home to the Formula One Australian Grand Prix since 1996. The choice of Albert Park as a Grand prix venue was controversial, with protests by the Save Albert Park group. In preparing the Reserve for the race existing trees were cut down and replaced during landscaping, roads were upgraded, and facilities were replaced, most notably the Melbourne Sports and Aquatic Centre. Today, the lake circuit is popular with strollers, runners and cyclists. Dozens of small yachts sail around the lake on sunny days. In December 2006 Polo returned to Albert Park reserve after an absence of 100 years.

Nick Heidfeld and Nico Rosberg racing at the 2008 Australian Grand Prix

Sport

Bob Jane Stadium is located in Albert Park. It was the former home of the South Melbourne football club and is home to Victorian Premier League team South Melbourne FC. The purpose built football (soccer) stadium was built on the site of the old Lakeside Oval which was an historic Australian rules football venue. Albert Park is also where NBL's basketball team, Melbourne Tigers's administration is based, although they play their games at State Netball and Hockey Centre in Royal Park.

Local landmarks

- **Albert Park** - the massive Albert Park Reserve, (formerly South Park in the 19th century until it was also renamed after Prince Albert) is nearby. It is a significant state park managed by Parks Victoria. It is also known as the site of the Melbourne Grand Prix Circuit, home to the Formula One Australian Grand Prix each March; usually on the Labour Day weekend.
- **Bridport Street** - centre of affluent living
- **Victoria Avenue** - known for its cafes, delicatessens and boutiques
- **Kerferd Road** - Kerferd Road is a royal boulevard of elm trees with a giant reserve between flanked on either side by an unusual array of eclectic semi-detached Edwardian homes
- **Kerferd Kiosk** - an iconic Edwardian pavilion
- **Kerferd Pier** - terminates Kerferd Road and is a jetty out onto Port Phillip Bay. Many use it for fishing. Sharks have occasionally been found around the pier.
- **Beaconsfield Parade** - a main thoroughfare between St Kilda and Port Melbourne which runs along the Port Phillip Bay foreshore and is flanked by grand buildings and Victorian terrace homes

- **Victoria Hotel** - a grand hotel (formerly a Coffee Palace) built in 1887 on Beaconsfield Parade - now apartments and cafe bar.
- **St Vincent Gardens** - the most important 'square' development in Victoria, if not Australia, based on similar models in London
- **Melbourne Sports and Aquatic Centre** - large swimming centre which hosted the 2006 Commonwealth Games squash, swimming and diving events. MSAC has basketball and table tennis courts too.

Famous former citizens

- Roy Cazaly - Australian rules football legend (birthplace).

Gallery

View over Albert Park Lake

See also

- City of South Melbourne - the former local government area of which Albert Park was a part.

Reference list

- Barnard, Jill and Keating, Jenny, "People's Playground: A History of the Albert Park", Chandos Publishing, 1996.
- Melway, 29th Edition, Ausway Publishing, 2001.

External links

- Albert Park Yacht Club [1]
- Albert Park (The Park) [2]
- St Vincent Gardens [3]
- Albert Park Primary School [4]

Geographical coordinates: 37°50′31″S 144°57′00″E

Footscray Park

Footscray Park is one of the largest and most intact examples of an Edwardian park in Australia. The 15 hectare park is located on the south bank of the Maribyrnong River in Footscray in Victoria. It is classified as a heritage place on the Victorian Heritage Register for its aesthetic, horticultural and social significance to the State of Victoria and was the first gardens to be placed on the register. The park is noted for its botanical collection, ornamental ponds and garden structures.

Entry path in Footscray Park

History

The park was established following lobbying by local citizens to establish parkland on the site. The original layout of the park was designed by architect Rodney Alsop, who won a design competition for the park in 1911. The Footscray Park Beautification Committee was formed by the residents and supported by local businesses and individuals . Much of the work was carried out by volunteers, including local Boy Scouts. By 1914 the park already had a large collection of Australian native species, predominantly Eucalyptus and Acacias. Many of the gardens structures including arbours, bridges and ponds were constructed by unemployed Victorians during the Depression. The majority of the layout and installation of features was carried out under the direction of David Mathews who was Superintendent of Parks and Gardens for the City of Footscray between 1916 and 1964. William Nicholls, an orchid specialist, also assisted in the task.

Detail from original plan

The slopes of the park were a vantage point for a crowd of 40,000 to see Bert Hinkler land his plane at Flemington Racecourse in 1928 as part of an Australian tour following his successful completion of the first solo flight from England to Australia.

Park layout and features

The entrance to the park on Ballarat Road features stone walls and wrought iron grates which incorporate the wording "Footscray Park". A World War I memorial which was unveiled in 1922 stands at the entranceway. It features an Italian-sculpted marble statue of *Victory* on a granite base.

A rustic stone columned lookout shelter and pergola which was designed and built by students from Footscray Technical School in 1928 has a view toward the Maribyrnong River and Flemington Racecourse. Nearby a mounted

Entrance

bust of Henry Lawson honours the Australian poet and writer and the inaugural Henry Lawson Literary Society commemorative event held in the park.

The park has two (originally three) major paths running east-west along the embankment which are bisected by a north-south path (the T.B. Drew Memorial Walk) which descends the embankment through a wisteria-covered arbour to Thomson Water Garden.

The Alfred Green Memorial Fountain (locally known as the "platypus fountain") is an unusual granite fountain that is supported at its base by two sculpted platypus.

The park also has open playing fields on the flat area near the river.

Trees

The park has a diverse collection of mature trees, including palms, elms, ash, oaks, cypress, various Australian species as well as a number of species which are rare in cultivation in Australia. The following trees are cited in its heritage listing:

- *Angophora hispida* (Dwarf Apple)
- *Brahea armata* (Blue Hesper Palm)
- *Cupressus macrocarpa* 'Hodginsii'
- *Ficus microcarpa* var. hillii (Hill's Fig)
- *Ulmus glabra 'Exoniensis' (Exeter Elm – in poor condition)*

Events

Footscray Park is the venue for two large Melbourne events - The Saltwater Festival and the Vietnamese Festival.

External links

- Heritage Council Victoria: Footscray Park [1]
- The Footscray Historical Society: The Citizens' Memorial Statue – Victory [2]

Geographical coordinates: 37°47′39″S 144°54′16″E

Fawkner Park, Melbourne

Fawkner Park is a popular park in Melbourne's South Yarra and part of the City of Melbourne. It provides recreational areas for teams playing Cricket, Softball, Soccer, Australian Rules Football, Tennis and Rugby.

History and Layout

The park was created in 1862, named after Melbourne co-founder John Pascoe Fawkner. It is trapezoidal in shape with an area of 41 hectares (101

Fawkner Park with Melbourne central business district in the background

acres), gently sloping towards a flat area, and was originally used for over seven different activities at one time, in sections specified for the purpose. It was also commonly used for walks and promenading. The layout of today remains similar to that of over 100 years ago, with pathways cutting through the park, edged with elm, oak and Moreton Bay Figs.

External links

• Draft Master Plan [1]

Geographical coordinates: 37°50′28″S 144°58′55″E

Edinburgh Gardens, Melbourne

Edinburgh Gardens is a large park located in North Fitzroy. It is bounded by Brunswick Street and St Georges Road to the west, the curve of Alfred Crescent to the north and east, and Freeman Street to the south. It was created from a grant of land in March 1862 by Queen Victoria and laid out by Clement Hodgkinson, who designed many of Melbourne's parks and gardens,. At approximately 24 hectares (59 acres) in size, the park is large by inner urban standards.

Fitzroy Memorial Rotunda, erected in 1925

History

Statement of Significance 1978

Edinburgh Gardens were nominated for inclusion on the Register of the National Estate in 1978.

"The Edinburgh Gardens are significant in terms of the large number of established trees and garden beds and the associated garden furniture - cast iron bollards, drinking fountain, fixed seats and bandstand. The tennis club house, train track and fixed train engine and the Bowling Club house and lawns are integral to this significance, while the adjacent cricket ground, with its two gatehouses and historic grandstand, is of complementary significance. They are also notable for the open space they provide and the manner in which they complement and close the vistas observable while passing along Alfred Crescent. The significance of the precinct is seen to lie in the marriage of the built environment with a sylvan landscape. It is enhanced by the quality of individual elements, both built and floral, in terms of their historical, architectural, recreational and visual amenity".

Statement of Significance 2004

The area later known as the Edinburgh Gardens was set aside as a temporary public reserve in 1862. Soon after the reservation was gazetted, the first of the sporting organizations to become associated with the place, the Collingwood Commercial Cricket Club was given occupancy, establishing a tradition of organised sport within the Gardens which continues today. Around 1872 the reserve acquired its name, commemorating Prince Alfred, the Duke of Edinburgh. The balance of the Gardens was not immediately laid out or cultivated, and grazing of the land continued until the early 1880s. While the various sporting clubs had already made improvements to their respective areas, the Fitzroy Council was not appointed as managers of the Gardens until 1878. In 1882 the Gardens were permanently reserved and in 1883 a formal layout, trenching and tree planting commenced to the straightforward design of Joseph Martin Reed, Victorian Lands Department district surveyor. In 1888 the Gardens were divided by an excision of land through the centre for construction of the Fitzroy spur line of the Inner Circle Railway. The Gardens continued to be redeveloped to various degrees throughout the twentieth century with the addition of further sporting, ornamental and memorial structures and plantings. The Edinburgh Gardens retains most of its earliest path system as well as a number of subsequent additions. It also retains avenues of mature elms, together with other specimen trees and significant twentieth century examples of rare perimeter planting. A substantial number of significant nineteenth and early twentieth century structures and buildings survive within the Gardens.

Description

The Edinburgh Gardens precinct is defined by the escargot shaped reserve originally set aside for Public Gardens, the Fitzroy and the North Fitzroy Cricket Grounds and a [former] railway station and line. The unique shape of the gardens stems from the resolution between different street grids and the desire to create a circus along Georgian lines. The scheme for a grand crescent with central gardens, playing grounds and rail facilities was developed as the most logical answer to this dilemma.

The park is unique due not only to the size, but also the strange features, and unusual history of the reserve. For example, the centrepiece of the park is a pedestal designed to hold a large statue of Queen Victoria. However, this statue only stood watch over the gardens for three years before mysteriously going missing more than a century ago. It was never replaced, and the bare plinth remains as a strange reminder[citation needed].

Former Railway in Edinburgh Gardens

A spur of the former Inner Circle Railway once bisected the gardens. The Fitzroy spur diverged from the line along Park Street, followed Mark Street across Alfred Crescent and finished at the former Fitzroy Station, located behind Brunswick Street Oval. This passenger service was never viable, and was closed only a few years after being built. The area was then used as a freight yard until the 1980s.

Some sections of the old track are still visible through the park. Level crossings were retained when the tracks were removed. The old line has been replaced with a shared path that joins the Linear Park Reserve and leads to the nearby Capital City Trail.

Factories associated with the line have been demolished and the land either returned to the Edinburgh Gardens or sold.

A timber pedestrian bridge remained in the south-west of the gardens until about 2003. it was sold and removed to make way for a low-rise development for the Office of housing.

W.T. Peterson Community Oval

An Australian rules football oval located at the south-western corner of the gardens, the W.T. Peterson Community Oval (named after a 21-year veteran of the Fitzroy City Council) (GC: 37°47′20.54″S 144°58′51.26″E) is better known to generations of Fitzroy Football Club supporters as the Brunswick Street Oval. The ground has a capacity of approximately 15,000 spectators. It served as the club's home ground in the VFA competition, and later the VFL competition from 1883 until 1966. The last game played there was

The grandstand at the W. T. Peterson Community Oval, built 1888

in August 1966 when Fitzroy played St Kilda. Fitzroy lost that match by 84 points. Even though the ground is silent and hardly used, (except by the Yarra Junior Football League), it is considered the spiritual home ground of Fitzroy. The playing ground is now framed by the remaining original features of the oval: the visiting members gate structure at the corner Freeman and Brunswick Streets, and late nineteenth century grandstand, gates and ticket box on the opposite side of the oval. The main grandstand is on the Victorian Heritage Register.

Fire gatherings

Activity in the park in the last few years has been occasioned by a weekly fire-twirling night, traditionally held on Wednesdays near the rotunda. This runs all year round, usually quietening down in the Winter and then peaking in attendance during the summer months when the nights are warmer and the energy is high. The gatherings are mostly attended by Melbourne fire-twirlers and members of the local hippie and psychedelic trance scenes. Usually beginning at 8:30-9pm and running until midnight, it has provided a wonderful opportunity for pros and newcomers alike to learn new tricks, demonstrate skills and share stories and advice about all things fire-twirling.

UPDATE: The fire gatherings don't happen anymore.

External links

- "Around the Grounds" - Web Documentary - Brunswick Street [1]
- "Edinburgh Gardens Conservation Management Plan" - Allom Lovell & Associates and John Patrick Pty Ltd, January 2004 [2]
- "Edinburgh Gardens Master Plan" - John Patrick Pty Ltd, 2003 [2]

Geographical coordinates: 37°47′21″S 144°58′51″E

Carlton Gardens, Melbourne

Carlton Gardens is also the name of a small street in London, England which has had some prominent residents. It is covered in the Carlton House Terrace article.

Royal Exhibition Building and Carlton Gardens*	
UNESCO World Heritage Site	
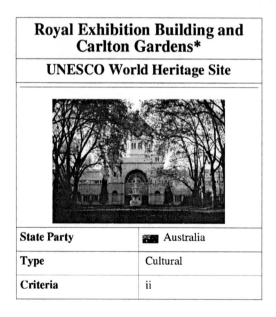	
State Party	🇦🇺 Australia
Type	Cultural
Criteria	ii

Reference	1131 [1]
Region**	Asia-Pacific
Inscription history	
Inscription	2004 (28th Session)
* Name as inscribed on World Heritage List. [2] ** Region as classified by UNESCO. [3]	

The **Carlton Gardens** is a World Heritage Site located on the northeastern edge of the Central Business District in the suburb of Carlton, in Melbourne, Victoria, Australia.

The 26 hectare (64 acre) site contains the Royal Exhibition Building, Melbourne Museum and Imax Cinema, tennis courts and an award winning children's playground. The rectangular site is bound by Victoria Street, Rathdowne Street, Carlton Street, and Nicholson Street. From the Exhibition building the gardens gently slope down to the southwest and northeast. According to the World Heritage listing the **Royal Exhibition Buildings and Carlton Gardens** are "*of historical, architectural, aesthetic, social and scientific (botanical) significance to the State of Victoria.*"

The gardens are an outstanding example of Victorian era landscape design with sweeping lawns and varied European and Australian tree plantings consisting of deciduous English oaks, White Poplar, Plane trees, Elms, Conifers, Cedars, Turkey Oaks, Araucarias and evergreens such as Moreton Bay Figs, combined with flower beds of annuals and shrubs. A network of tree lined paths provide formal avenues for highlighting the fountains and architecture of the Exhibition building. This includes the *grand allee* of plane trees that lead to the exhibition building. Two small ornamental lakes adorn the southern section of the park. The northern section contains the Museum, tennis courts, maintenance depot and curator's cottage, and the children's playground designed as a Victorian maze.

The listing in the Victorian Heritage Register says in part:

> "*The Carlton Gardens are of scientific (botanical) significance for their outstanding collection of plants, including conifers, palms, evergreen and deciduous trees, many of which have grown to an outstanding size and form. The elm avenues of Ulmus procera and Ulmus × hollandica are significant as few examples remain world wide due to Dutch elm disease. The Garden contains a rare specimen of Acmena ingens, only five other specimens are known, an uncommon Harpephyllum caffrum and the largest recorded in Victoria, Taxodium distichum, and outstanding specimens of Chamaecyparis funebris and Ficus macrophylla, south west of the Royal Exhibition Building.*"

Wildlife includes possums, ducks and ducklings in spring, Tawny Frogmouths, Kookaburras and other urban environment birds.

The gardens contain three important fountains: the Exhibition Fountain, designed for the 1880 Exhibition by sculptor Joseph Hochgurtel; the French Fountain; and the Westgarth Drinking Fountain.

Carlton Gardens south

History

- 1839 - Large tracts of land surrounding the original town grid of Melbourne were reserved from sale by Superintendent Charles La Trobe. Most of this land was later sold and subdivided or used for the development of various public institutions, but a number of substantial sites were permanently reserved as public parks, including the Carlton Gardens as well as Flagstaff Gardens, Fitzroy Gardens, Treasury Gardens and Kings Domain.

- Circa 1856 - The City of Melbourne obtained control of the Carlton Gardens, and engaged Edward La Trobe Bateman to prepare a design for the site. The path layout and other features of the design were built although limitations on funding for maintenance etc. resulted in frequent criticism.

- 1870s - The colonial Victorian Government resumed control of the Gardens and minor changes and were made under the direction of Clement Hodgkinson. The site was soon afterwards drastically redesigned for the 1880 Melbourne International Exhibition by the architect Joseph Reed. The prominent local horticulturist William Sangster was engaged as a contractor to redevelop the gardens.

- 1880 - Exhibition Building completed for the Melbourne International Exhibition that year. Temporary annexes to house some of the exhibition in the northern section were demolished after the exhibition closed on 30 April 1881.

- 1888 - Melbourne Centennial Exhibition to celebrate a century of European settlement in Australia.

- 1891 - The curator's Lodge was completed and lived in by John Guilfoyle.

- 1901 - First Parliament of Australia opens in the Exhibition Building. The west annex of the Building becomes the site of the Victorian Parliament for the next 27 years.

- 1919 - buildings became an emergency hospital for influenza epidemic victims
- 1928 - Perimeter fence removed leaving the bluestone footings.
- Second World War the buildings were used by the RAAF.
- 1948 to 1961 - part of the complex was used as a migrant reception centre.
- 2001 - Taylor Cullity Lethlean with Mary Jeavons wins a landscape award for design and building a new children's playground *of elegant yet robust resolution.* The Jury described the design as *a distinctive and unified design that respects its historic setting and addresses the demands of creative play for spatial and visual variety.*
- July 2004 - After several years of lobbying by the Melbourne City Council, The **Royal Exhibition Building** and **Carlton Gardens**, Melbourne, were inscribed on the World Heritage List at the 28th session of the World Heritage Committee held in Suzhou, China.

The Exhibition Building is still used for exhibitions, including for the annual Melbourne International Flower and Garden Show. The Melbourne Exhibition and Convention Centre, opened in 1996 at Southbank, provides more modern facilities and has become Melbourn'e prime location for exhibitions and conventions. It also hosts the exams for University of Melbourne in recent years.

External links

- World heritage listing for Carlton Gardens [4]
- Melbourne City Council - Carlton Gardens [1]
- World Heritage Listing [2]
- Melbourne International Flower Show [1]
- Open Space and Recreation - Merit Carlton Gardens Playground [3]
- Heritage Register Online: Royal Exhibition Building and Carlton Gardens [4]
- World Heritage, World Futures [7] — Restoration of the Western Forecourt of the Royal Exhibition Building, Melbourne

Geographical coordinates: 37°48′22″S 144°58′13″E

St Vincent Gardens, Melbourne

St Vincent Gardens in the Melbourne suburb of Albert Park, is an Australian park of national significance.

It is an example of nineteenth century residential development around a large landscaped square. Development occurred as a result of a boom following the Victorian gold rush. It was influenced by similar, urban design in London, but such design on such a scale is unparalleled in Australia.

In the shape of a large rectangular area with semi-circular crescents at either

The picturesque Victorian era gardens at the centre of the square

end, the heritage area includes the St Vincent Place precinct bounded by Park Street, Cecil Street, Bridport Street, Cardigan Place and Nelson Road. The park is bisected by Montague Street, allowing the passage of trams on route 1. Several of the streets are lined with the original cobbled blue stone and gutters. It is registered with the National Trust of Australia and on the Victorian Heritage register for its *aesthetic, historical, architectural and social significance to the State of Victoria.*

Significance

The gardens are particularly important according to the Victorian Heritage Register:

> *as a reflection of the aspirations of middle class residents in South Melbourne. Because of the shared outlook on and use of the gardens, the precinct has developed a sense of community cohesion unusual in the Melbourne context. The gardens are also socially important as a focus of community life for the surrounding district with the maintenance of their amenity a priority of municipal government since their inception. The existence of the tennis and bowls clubs [1] in the gardens for over a century is a further manifestation of this social importance.*

The Australian Demographer Bernard Salt [2] included the precinct as first among his "favourite places that have been designed by planners" :

> "St Vincent Place, Albert Park: Where would such a list start but in my home city of Melbourne? Surely this residential precinct known only to Melburnians must be one of this nation's town planning treasures. Here are two extended but connecting crescents laid out around gardens

which are overlooked by double-storey Victorian terrace houses. Designed in the early 1850s, St Vincent Place was virtually a gated community: the well-to-do would promenade around ``their *public gardens; smaller wooden houses for servants and the working classes were relegated to the lesser enveloping crescents."*

History

First design was probably by Andrew Clarke, the Surveyor-General of Victoria, in 1854 or 1855. Clement Hodgkinson adapted the design in 1857 to allow for its intersection by the St Kilda railway line, Melbourne.

Development of the gardens occurred during 1864-1870 with plans by Clement Hodgkinson in 1869 showing an overall plan of the reserve, including the older tree plantings, the path system at the western end and the circular theme of the paths design at the eastern end.

The Albert Park Bowls Club [1] was established in the park in 1873.

The gardens were rejuvenated during 1903-1910 with much of the original landscaping being retained.

In 2004, a Canary Island Palm was removed suffering from fusarium wilt otherwise known as Panama Disease. In 2005 six significant trees were lost after a wild storm.

The improved appearance of the gardens over recent years has been due to local government projects required as part of a Conservation Management Plan (CMP). The creation of mulched beds around significant trees has improved their condition and large herbaceous beds have been restored using heritage plant stock. The most obvious works include the reconstruction of the western half of the path network along accurately plotted heritage alignments using the original orange-coloured, granitic, sand surface and steel edging. This included the installation of an on-site stormwater dissipation system, which now uses surface runoff to help irrigate lawn areas and minimise water usage. The perimeter hedge around the gardens uses original Lonicera heritage plant stock sourced from Dame Elisabeth Murdoch's 'Cruden Farm [3].' This hedge will grow to a height of approximately 700mm. The CMP and further detailed historical investigations have led to the design of entry treatments for each of the entrances to the Gardens. Composed of bluestone walls and timber posts, the new entrances have been accurately designed to closely resemble the original appearance and layout of the old entrances. Reconstruction of the entry treatments in the western half of the Gardens commenced earlier this year. The northern and southern border beds have been planted with heritage plant stock in accordance with planting designs prepared by Jill Orr-Young.

Plantings & Monuments

Plantings include lines of Algerian Oak (*Quercus canariensis*) and Canary Island Palms (*Phoenix canariensis*).

There are specimen plantings of:

- Brush Cherry
- Coral Tree
- Lilly Pilly
- Moreton Bay Fig
- Norfolk Island Pine
- Peony
- Southern magnolia *(Magnolia grandiflora)*
- Whitewillow

There is a monumental garden dedicated to the Australian entertainer Maurie Fields, a former resident of the area.

The Charles Moore Memorial Drinking Fountain [4] commemorates Charlie Moore, a Boer War soldier and Essendon Football Club full forward. Moore was born 24 Sep 1875 in Fiji, married Rose Walters on 9 May 1898 at Fitzroy, Victoria (Vic reg 3227) and died 13 May 1901 at Doornbosch, South Africa.

The Alexander Rose Garden commemorates the contribution of Harold Alexander, Clerk of the City of South Melbourne from 1936-1964, who fostered munciipal welfare services.[5] Under his administration, Australia's first 'community chest' for social welfare was set up. After the war, be bought Nissen huts to provide hot meals to returned servicemen. They were the forerunners of today's senior citizens clubs. Alexander appointed the council's first social worker and oversaw Australia's first meals on wheels service in 1953. He helped set up 'Claremont' aged care hostel. From 1927 he also fought to have Wirth's Circus site on Southbank reserved for the state's art gallery and cultural centre. He played for South Melbourne Football Club for five years.[6]

Gallery

The picturesque gardens at
the centre of the square

References

- City of Port Phillip - St Vincent Gardens [3]
- Albert Park Bowls Club [1]
- Citation [1] in the National Trust of Australia and Victorian Heritage Register.
- Bernard Salt, "It's a gift when beauty goes according to plan", The Australian , Page 026 , Thursday 6 July 2006
- State Library Postcard [2] (undated)
- State Library Postcard of the Bowling Green [3] (undated)
- View of St. Vincent Gardens with St. Vincent Place, South Melbourne in background [4] (1904-1932)

Geographical coordinates: 37°50′20″S 144°57′20″E

Royal Botanic Gardens, Melbourne

Royal Botanic Gardens Melbourne	
 *A section of the Fern Gully in the Royal Botanic Gardens*	
Type	Public Park
Location	Melbourne, Australia
Size	36 hectares
Opened	1846
Operated by	Board of the Royal Botanic Gardens
Annual visitors	1 million (aprox)
Status	Open (7:30-9am to sunset)
Terrain	Low undulating hills
Vegetation	Australian Native, Lawns, Non-native traditional gardens
Water	Yarra River, Ornamental Lake, Nymphaea Lake
Paths	Sealed
Facilities	Information centre, Gift shop, Toilets, Barbecues, Shelter, Cafe and Tea rooms
Landmarks	Yarra River, Ornamental Lake, National Herbarium
Connecting Transport	Train, Tram, Bus, Car

The **Royal Botanic Gardens Melbourne** are internationally renowned botanical gardens located near the centre of Melbourne, Victoria, Australia, on the south bank of the Yarra River. They are 38 hectares of landscaped gardens consisting of a mix of native and non-native vegetation including over 10,000 individual species. They are widely regarded as the finest botanical gardens in Australia, and among the best in the world. However, the gardens are also noted for their historical contribution to the introduction of invasive species.

The Royal Botanic Gardens have a second division in the outer Melbourne suburb of Cranbourne, some 45km south-east of the city. The 363 hectare Royal Botanic Gardens, Cranbourne have a focus solely on Australian native plants, and feature an award-winning special section called the *Australian Garden*, which was opened in May 2006.

The Royal Botanic Gardens Melbourne are adjacent to a larger group of parklands directly south-east of the city, between St. Kilda Road and the Yarra River known as the **Domain Parklands**, which includes;

- Kings Domain
- Alexandra Gardens
- Queen Victoria Gardens

Governance and history

The gardens are governed under the *Royal Botanic Gardens Act 1991* by the Royal Botanic Gardens Board, who are responsible to the Minister for Environment.

In 1846 Charles La Trobe selected the site for the Royal Botanic Gardens from marshland and swamp.

In 1857 the first director was Ferdinand von Mueller, who created the National Herbarium of Victoria and brought in many plants.

In 1873 William Guilfoyle became Director and changed the style of the Gardens to something more like the picturesque gardens that were around at that time. He added tropical and temperate plants.

In 1877 Sir Edmund Barton, Australia's first Prime Minister and Jane Ross were married at the Royal Botanic Gardens.

In 1924 a shooting massacre occurred at the Gardens resulting in the death of four people.

Horticulture

Living collections at the Botanic Gardens include Australian Forest Walk, California Garden, Cacti and Succulents, Camellia Collection, Cycad Collection, Eucalypts, Fern Gully, Grey Garden, Herb Garden, Long Island, New Caledonia Collection, New Zealand Collection, Oak Lawn, Perennial Border, Roses, Southern China Collection, Tropical Display-Glasshouse, Viburnum Collection and Water Conservation Garden.

These plant groups have been chosen for their value, rarity, diversity and interest.

Ecology

The gardens include a mixture of native and non-native vegetation which invariably hosts a diverse range of both native and non-native fauna. The gardens host over 10,000 floral species, the majority being non-native species. The gardens were the origin from which many introduced species spread throughout south-eastern Australia as seeds were traded between early European botanists in the mid-1800s, studying the Australian flora.

Native vegetation

From the gardens establishment in 1846, much of the native vegetation was removed as botanists such as Baron Von Mueller planted a range of species from around the world. While initially much of the native wetlands and swamplands in the gardens were left, around the turn of the century these were re-landscaped to create the Ornamental Lake. Despite this however, there are some large eucalypts remaining including the prominent *Separation Tree*, a 300-year-old River Red Gum, under which Victoria was declared a separate colony. In August 2010 the Separation Tree was attacked by vandals and it is not clear if it will survive. The Royal Botanic Gardens, Cranbourne focus solely on Australian native plants.

Non-native traditional gardens

The Royal Botanic Gardens Melbourne were initially intended to be a horticultural exhibition for the public to enjoy, many seeds were traded between early European botanists such as Arthur and Von Mueller, who planted non-native species. The Queen and her grandfather, Dame Nellie Melba and Paderewski contributed plantings on occasions throughout the gardens history. Much of the gardens have been separated into themed sections such as:

- Herb Garden
- Arid Garden
- Fern Gully
- Bulbs
- Rose Garden

Lawns

The gardens host areas of non-native tough-wearing lawns of various sizes that are carefully maintained;

- Huntingford Lawn
- Hopetoun Lawn
- Northern Lawn
- Tennyson Lawn
- Princes Lawn
- Central Lawn
- Western Lawn
- Eastern Lawn
- Oak Lawn
- Southern Lawn
- Australian Lawn

Plant science

Since its earliest days, the Royal Botanic Gardens is involved in plant research and identification. This is done primarily through the National Herbarium of Victoria, which is based at the Gardens. The Herbarium is also home to the State Botanical Collection, which includes over 1.2 million dried plant specimens, and an extensive collection of books, journals and artworks. Research findings are published in the journal Mulleria, which is a scientific representation of the work done in the Gardens in any one year. More recently, the Australian Research Centre for Urban Ecology has been established to look at plants which grow in urban environments specifically.

Education and visitor information

Opening hours

The Gardens are open every day of the year at 7.30am and close at dusk.

The Gardens Visitor Centre is open seven days a week:

- Weekdays 9.00am – 5.00pm
- Weekends 9.30am – 5.00pm

Transport The Gardens are a 15-minute walk or 5-minute tram ride from Flinders Street Station to the Domain Road Interchange on tram routes 3, 5, 8, 16, 64, 67. Street parking is available for 2- to 4-hour periods.

The Ian Potter Foundation Children's Garden

The 5,000 square metre *Ian Potter Foundation Children's Garden* is designed as a discovery area for children of all ages and abilities. The Ian Potter Children's Garden is based in South Yarra, off the main site. This area is closed for two months of the year from the end of Victorian July school holidays for rest and maintenance.

The Tan

There is a 3.8-km running track parallel to the perimeter fence of the Botanic Gardens. Officially termed *The Tan Track* as it has a surface of tan-coloured stone aggregate, it is more commonly and affectionately known as *The Tan*.

Royal Botanic Gardens: The National Herbarium of Victoria - founded in 1853

The Tan originally served as a horse track for Melbourne's well-heeled, and is now one of Melbourne's most frequented locations for joggers. Locals, visitors and famous alike now share the space as its international reputation has grown. *The Tan* is often used in training by professional athletes, such as AFL footballers, particularly during pre-season time-trials. Running greats such as Hicham El Guerrouj, Steve Ovett, Cathy Freeman, and Sonia O'Sullivan have all rubbed shoulders with the general public on *The Tan*.

The quickest lap of the Tan has been held by such notable Australian runners as Robert de Castella and Steve Moneghetti (10:41, 2003). The current record is 10 minutes and 12 seconds, run by Craig Mottram in 2004. On the 21st of December, 2006, Craig Mottram unofficially broke his personal best time around the tan, running a scorching 10 minutes and 8 seconds while running with the Richmond Football Club during their pre-season training. He gave the footballers a two-and-a-half minute head start and still managed to beat them comprehensively.

The inaugural *Go the Tan* run was held in early February 2006, and provides the opportunity for participants to run, jog or walk around *The Tan* and receive an official time.

Problems at the Botanic Gardens

Important problems for the Botanic Gardens have included unwanted plant and animal life which interferes significantly with the management of the gardens. There are also problems with water conservation.

Beginning in 2002, the Royal Botanic Gardens had significant problems managing an increasing population of Grey-headed Flying Foxes. It culminated in damaged trees and habitat. The Royal Botanic Gardens managed this by moving the flying foxes to Horseshoe Bend in Ivanhoe, and by disturbing the flying foxes and providing a familiar environment.

In regard to weeds (always a problem with a botanic gardens of this size) the Botanic Gardens developed a strategic plan in 2004 to minimise weed infestations by educating the public and management, and to help conserve the indigenous and other species.

Large numbers of eels in a pond at the
Melbourne Botanical Gardens

Gallery

Ornamental
Lake

A section of the gardens in
winter

Nympheas
Lake

The Herb Garden

The main entrance gate

External links

- RBG website [1]
- Disability information [2]

Geographical coordinates: 37°50'00"S 144°58'49"E

Queen Victoria Gardens, Melbourne

Queen Victoria Gardens	
 *The view from the Queen Victoria statue towards the Victorian Arts Centre*	
Type	Public Park
Location	Melbourne, Australia
Coordinates	37°49′18″S 144°58′18″E
Opened	1905
Status	Open
Terrain	Flat, Riverbank
Vegetation	Australian Native, Lawns, Non-native traditional gardens
Water	Ponds
Paths	Sealed
Facilities	Toilets, Seating
Landmarks	Floral Clock
Connecting Transport	Tram, Bus, Car

The **Queen Victoria Gardens** are Melbourne's memorial to Queen Victoria. Located on 4.8 hectares (12 acres) opposite the Victorian Arts Centre and National Gallery of Victoria, bounded by St Kilda Road, Alexandra Avenue and Linlithgow Avenue.

Queen Victoria's reign started in 1837, two years after the initial European settlement of Melbourne, and upon her death in 1901 it was thought appropriate to declare an enduring monument to her reign. A memorial statue was commissioned from sculptor James White showing the Queen in ceremonial gowns casting her regal gaze across ornamental lakes, sweeping lawns and rose gardens to the Melbourne Arts Centre Spire and the city skyscrapers.

Queen Victoria Gardens are part of a larger group of parklands directly south-east of the city, between St. Kilda Road and the Yarra River known as the **Domain Parklands**, which includes;

- The Royal Botanic Gardens
- Kings Domain
- Alexandra Gardens
- *Queen Victoria Gardens*

Features

The Queen Victoria Gardens' Floral Clock

A huge floral clock is positioned opposite the National Gallery of Victoria, containing over 7,000 flowering plants which are changed twice yearly. The clock was donated in 1966 to the City of Melbourne by a group of Swiss watchmakers. Behind the clock stands a bronze equestrian statue, a memorial to Queen Victoria's successor, King Edward VII. The statue, by Melbourne born sculptor Bertram Mackennal, was unveiled on July 21, 1920.

Queen Victoria Memorial

A granite and marble memorial, commissioned by public subscription from sculptor James White and positioned at the highest point of the gardens, commemorates five aspects of Queen Victoria. The memorial is of white Carrara marble, Harcourt granite and NSW marble, and was unveiled by Sir John Madden on Empire Day, 24 May 1907.

Originally home to native grasses, she-oaks, wattles, paperbarks, and river red gums, the area now consists of ornamental lakes, sweeping lawns, flowerbeds of annuals, and mature European and Australian trees and shrubs in a landscaped garden.

As well as the monuments to *Queen Victoria* and *King Edward VII*, the gardens are notable for their array of sculptures. These include an exploratory play sculpture for children, *The Genie*, by Tom Bass in 1973. *The Pathfinder* was manufactured in 1974 by John Robinson and details a bronze Olympic Hammer thrower in action. *The Phoenix* was sculptored from cast bronze and welded copper sheet by Baroness Yrsa Von Heistner in 1973 to commemorate the 40th International Eucharistic Congress. *The Bronze Water Children* is an installation by John Robinson, made in 1973, which shows playing children at the top of a stream. *The Water Nymph* is a kneeling bronze figure sculptored in 1925 by Paul Montford.

A classic rotunda was built in 1913 and named after Janet Lady Clarke, a philanthropist who worked for the welfare of women in Melbourne.

External links

- Melbourne City Council - Queen Victoria Gardens [1]
- Queen Victoria Memorial [2] (including photographs)

Alexandra Gardens, Melbourne

Alexandra Gardens

Boathouses in Alexandra Gardens from across the Yarra River.

Type	Public Park
Location	Melbourne, Australia
Coordinates	37°49′13″S 144°58′19″E
Size	5.2 hectares
Opened	1901
Status	Open
Terrain	Flat, Riverbank
Vegetation	Australian Native, Lawns, Non-native traditional gardens
Water	Yarra River, Historic Boatsheds
Paths	Sealed
Facilities	Barbecues, Toilets, Shelters, Bicycle hire, Seating
Landmarks	Yarra River
Connecting Transport	Tram, Bus, Car

The **Alexandra Gardens** are located on the south bank of the Yarra River, opposite Federation Square and the Melbourne Central Business District, in Victoria, Australia. The Gardens are bounded by the Yarra River to the north, Princes and Swan street bridges, with Queen Victoria Gardens and Kings Domain across Alexandra Avenue to the south. The gardens are part of the Domain parklands which stretch to the Royal Botanic Gardens and were first laid out in 1901, under the direction of Carlo

Catani, Chief Engineer of the Public Works Department. They are listed on the Victorian Heritage Register due to their historical and archaeological significance.

Alexandra Gardens are part of a larger group of parklands directly south-east of the city, between St. Kilda Road and the Yarra River known as the **Domain Parklands**, which includes;

- The Royal Botanic Gardens
- Kings Domain
- *Alexandra Gardens*
- Queen Victoria Gardens

History

From the time of European settlement of Melbourne in 1835, the area of the gardens were used for timber cutting, cattle grazing and as a brickmakers' field. Regular flooding occurred, until a new channel for the Yarra River was dug from 1896 to 1900 to straighten and widen the river. The spoil was used to fill the swampy lagoons and brickmakers pits and raise the height of the river bank where Alexandra Gardens now stands. Landscaping occurred immediately, and the gardens were planned and laid out for the visit of the Duke of York in May 1901.

Cycling and skating

Pedestrian and cycle access to the gardens is via steps or a ramp from Princes Bridge, or along the promenade from Southbank under Princes bridge. Vehicular access is provided by Boathouse drive from Alexandra avenue. Next to Princes bridge bicycles are available for hire to explore the Capital City Trail along the river. Also the prominent, The Around the Bay in a Day cycling event has its finish line at the Gardens.

Finish area of the 2009 "Around The Bay In A Day" event, in Alexandra Gardens, Melbourne.

A skate park opened in 2001 in the gardens, with a cafe and first aid station, close to some distinctive Canary Island Palms which were planted in 1911.

Rowing clubs

Alongside the Yarra River numerous Rowing Club boathouses nestle in the gardens, including the Mercantile Rowing Club. You will often see rowing coaches cycling along the bike path megaphone in hand, giving instructions to their rowing crew. The Olympic champions, the Oarsome Foursome, were known to train along the Yarra river.

The annual *Henley-on-Yarra regatta* was held from 1904, every spring just before Melbourne Cup day. For a day and a night Melburnians flocked to the Yarra to watch this sporting event, with attendances peaking at 300,000 in 1925. After World War II, the event declined in significance, however the annual *Australian Henley Rowing Regatta* still occurs as an amateur event in December, with recent attempts to increase its popularity.

Past the boathouses are lawns with electric barbecues, which are popular spots for picnics and office parties around Christmas time. As well as lawns fronting the Yarra river, the gardens contain: a star shaped garden bed representing the Federation of Australia; many mature trees including elms and an avenue of planes and oak trees along Boathouse Drive; ornamental flower beds.

External links

- Melbourne City Council - Alexandra Gardens [1]
- Australian Henley Rowing Regatta [2]

Treasury Gardens

The **Treasury Gardens** consist of 5.8 hectares (14.4 acres) on the south-eastern side of the Melbourne Central Business District, East Melbourne, Victoria, Australia. The gardens are bounded by Wellington Parade, Spring Street, Treasury Place, and by the Fitzroy Gardens across Lansdowne street to the west. They form part of a network of city gardens including Fitzroy Gardens, Carlton Gardens, Flagstaff Gardens and Kings Domain. The gardens are listed on the Victorian Heritage list for their historical, archaeological, social, *aesthetic and scientific (horticultural) importance for its outstanding nineteenth century design, path layout and planting.*

Treasury Gardens during winter

Treasury Gardens is a popular destination for lunch

The Gardens are a short walk from Victoria's Parliament House and are overlooked by the old Treasury buildings, and State Offices. They create a landscaped setting for office workers to enjoy during lunch with large areas of lawn and walking paths lined with mature trees. Due to their central location close to the city, they are a popular spot as the starting or ending point for political rallies, demonstrations and festivals. The gardens are also enjoyed by business people and tourists staying at the Hilton Hotel on Wellington Parade, who are able to wander through on their way to the city.

The Victorian heritage listing says "*Fitzroy is unique in comparison for it's scale and uninterrupted landscape. There are some horticultural similarities between Fitzroy and the Treasury Garden, attributed to the initial work of Clement Hodgkinson, however Fitzroy Gardens is unique due to the layering of history and mosaic of different landscaping styles. The avenues of mature Elms and Moreton Bay fig are some of the best tree lined avenues in Victoria."*

Mature tree species include Moreton Bay Fig (Ficus macrophylla), Deodar Cedar (Cedrus deodara), English Elm (Ulmus procera), White Poplar (Populus alba), Dutch Elm (Ulmus x hollandica), Dutch Elm (small-leaved form), Port Jackson Fig (Ficus rubiginosa), Platanus x acerifolia]], Pedunculate oak (Quercus robur), Agonis flexuosa, Phoenix canariensis, Washingtonia robusta, Butia capitata, Chamaerops humilis, River Red Gum (Eucalyptus camaldulensis), Norfolk Island Pine (Araucaria heterophylla), Brachychiton x roseus, and Grevillea (Grevillea hilliana). Along the embankment of Treasury Place there are hydrangeas, ivy and flax. The gardens are

Treasury Gardens during summer

A tame possum in the Treasury Gardens

highly populated with the native common brushtail possums many of which are tame and accustomed to people petting them.

The gardens contain an ornamental pond and a number of memorials:

- Sir William John Clarke Memorial. Marble bust, circa 1902, located by the Treasury building. Erected by public subscription and unveiled by the Governor of Victoria on 22 July 1902.

- Robert Burns Memorial. Bronze replica sculpture by G.A. Lawson of an original erected in the poet's birthplace of Alloway in Scotland. Commissioned by the Caledonian Society in Melbourne, and first erected in St Kilda Road in 1904, and moved to the Treasury Gardens in 1970 due to roadworks.

- President John F. Kennedy Memorial. Bronze bas-relief by sculptor Raymond B. Ewers. Erected in 1965 and located beside the specially landscaped pond and water fountain.

History

- 1850s - The area of the gardens was left as open space after failure to sell allotments due to the swampy nature of the land.

- 1867 - Clement Hodgkinson designed the Gardens as a pattern of diagonally crossing paths lined with trees. Willow trees were planted around an ornamental pond.

- 1902 - William Guilfoyle, director of the Royal Botanic Gardens, Melbourne transforms the ornamental pond into a Japanese Garden. This garden is demolished after the Second World War.

- 1929 - management of the Gardens was transferred to the City of Melbourne

- 1934 - Treasury Gardens was used by the community to celebrate Victoria's centenary

- 1939 - Toilet block built for the Spring Carnival and floral festival. Acknowledged as being of *architectural importance for its uncommon art deco design, decorative pattern brick and tile construction and extensive use of wrought iron detailing, including grills, gates, lamps, signs and brick planter, exhibiting outstanding craftsmanship.*

- 1965 - Monument was erected to the American President, John F Kennedy

- 1996 - Fitzroy and Treasury Gardens Master Plan was adopted by Council

External links

- Melbourne City Council - Treasury Gardens [1]
- Disability information [2]

Geographical coordinates: 37°48′51″S 144°58′34″E

Fitzroy Gardens, Melbourne

The **Fitzroy Gardens** are 26 hectares (64 acres) located on the southeastern edge of the Melbourne Central Business District in East Melbourne, Victoria, Australia. The gardens are bounded by Clarendon Street, Albert Street, Lansdowne Street, and Wellington Parade with the Treasury Gardens across Lansdowne street to the west.

The gardens are one of the major Victorian era landscaped gardens in Australia and add to Melbourne's claim to being the *garden city* of Australia. Set within the gardens are:

- an ornamental lake
- kiosk and cafe
- Conservatory
- Cooks' Cottage - a house where James Cook reputedly spent some years of his childhood (the cottage was in England at that time).
- Sinclair's Cottage (Visitor information)
- Model Tudor village
- Fountains and sculptures
- Band Pavilion
- the Rotunda
- the fairy tree

Cooks' Cottage in the Fitzroy Gardens.

Fairies Tree in the Fitzroy Gardens.

Horticulture

The most notable feature of the Gardens is the wonderful trees that have been used to line many of the pathways.

The gardens were initially designed by Clement Hodgkinson and planted by park gardener, James Sinclair, as a dense woodland with meandering avenues. The land originally had been swampy with a creek draining into the Yarra River. The creek was landscaped with ferns and 130 willows, but that did not stop it smelling foul from the sewage from the houses of East Melbourne. The creek was used for irrigation of the western side of the gardens for fifty years. In the early 1900s the creek water substantially improved when sewerage mains were installed to the residences of East Melbourne.

In the early years quick growing blue gums and wattles were planted to provide wind breaks. Elm Trees were planted to create avenues along pathways, which created a pattern in resemblance to the Union Flag.

An avenue of English Elms in the Gardens.

Clement Hodgkinson described the landscaping design:

> *...the chief desiderata were shade along the numerous paths therein forming important lines of traffic, and such dense and continuous masses of foliage as would tend to check the inroad of dust from the adjacent streets.*

> *Consequently, in such reserves, strict adherence to the rules of landscape gardening, with regard to the grouping of trees, etc., had to be abandoned in favour of the formal lining of the paths with rows of umbrageous trees, and the planting in the background of dense masses of conifers, evergreen shrubs, fern trees, etc., small flowering shrubs and bedding flowers being merely introduced to mask the unsightly aspect of the grass in such reserves during summer*

During the 1880s and 1890s many of the blue gums and elms were removed to create more room for existing trees, as well as sweeping lawns and ornamental flowerbeds.

Heritage Listing

The listing on the Victorian Heritage Register states in part:

Late afternoon sunlight on the Gardens

The Fitzroy Gardens are of historical, aesthetic, architectural, scientific (horticultural) and social significance to the State of Victoria.

Why is it significant? The Fitzroy Gardens are of historical significance as one of a ring of public reserves around Melbourne established in the nineteenth century to provide respite and relaxation for the city's residents. The Fitzroy Gardens have been viewed as the flagship of this group of city gardens, which includes the Flagstaff, Treasury, Carlton and Alexandra Gardens and the Kings Domain. In a statewide context, while not as intact as the Royal Botanic Gardens or the Ballarat Botanical Gardens, the Fitzroy Gardens are an important remnant of the city's nineteenth century garden heritage. They are also a reminder of the city's relatively large investment in public gardens, a reflection of 19th century beliefs about the moral and health benefits of green spaces in often dirty, smelly and overcrowded cities.

The Fitzroy Gardens are of social significance because, from their establishment in the early 1860s, the Gardens have been a place of relaxation,

Scarred Tree - a sign of the original habitation of Melbourne by the Wurundjeri people

passive recreation and entertainment; the Gardens have been the people's park in the city.

Scarred tree

A scarred tree in the gardens has been preserved. The plaque at the bottom of the tree reads:

> *The scar on this tree was created when Aboriginal people removed bark to make canoes, shields, food and water containers, string, baby carriers and other items.*

> *Please respect this site. It is important to the Wurundjeri people as traditional custodians of the land and is part of the heritage of all Australians.*

> *All Aboriginal cultural sites are protected by law.*

History

- 1848 the Fitzroy Gardens were permanently reserved as public gardens, with title shared by the State Government and City of Melbourne. The gardens were known as Fitzroy Square until 1862, named after Sir Charles Augustus FitzRoy, a governor of New South Wales.
- 1857 James Sinclair appointed head gardener, and worked in the gardens until his death in 1882.
- 1860 responsibility for Fitzroy Gardens taken over by the Lands Department. Clement Hodgkinson, the head of the Lands Department, takes a detailed interest in the planning and development of the city parks, including Fitroy Gardens.
- 1862 Path network established and band pavilion built
- 1864 Sinclair's Cottage and Small Tudor style gate keepers lodge built
- 1873 Neo-classical rotunda "Temple of Winds" built
- 1880 Removal of many Blue Gums
- 1890 Every alternate Elm tree on Avenues removed
- 1901 Nursery and stable yard transferred from centre of gardens to present site
- 1908 timber style Kiosk opened
- 1915 External picket fence replaced by stone edging
- 1917 Control of gardens passed onto City of Melbourne
- 1927 Plant Managers house built
- 1930 Conservatory for displaying glass-house plants opened
- 1934 Cook's Cottage erected after being bought, shipped to Australia, and donated by the Grimwade family. Artist Ola Cohn completes carving the Fairies Tree and donates it to the children of Melbourne.
- 1960 Kiosk damaged by fire
- 1960s Central section of creek piped underground
- 1964 New kiosk opened
- 1970s Eighteenth Century Cottage garden added to Cook's Cottage

External links

- Fitzroy Gardens [1]
- City of Melbourne - Fitzroy Gardens [2]
- Disability information [3]

Geographical coordinates: 37°48′45″S 144°58′49″E

Flagstaff Gardens

Flagstaff Gardens is the oldest park in Melbourne, Victoria, Australia, first established in 1862. In 2005 it is one of the most visited and widely used parks in the city by nearby office workers and tourists. The gardens are notable for their archeological, horticultural, historical and social significance to the history of Melbourne.

The gardens are 7.2 hectares (18 acres) of Crown Land bounded by William, La Trobe, King and Dudley streets, managed by the City of Melbourne. On the southeast corner opposite is the entrance to Flagstaff railway station.

Facing north east in the Flagstaff Gardens

Diagonally opposite stands the Victorian branch of the Royal Mint, established 7 August 1869. The former Royal Mint building is a well-preserved example of Victorian Gold Rush boom-period classical styled architecture. The facade features paired columns with scrolled capitals and the Royal Mint coat-of-arms.

On the northeast corner over William Street, is the Queen Victoria Market.

The park contains extensive lawns with a variety of mature trees, flowerbeds and wild animals including possums. The southern end is characterised by deciduous trees, while the northern end contains mature eucalypts. Avenues of elms shade pathways along with several large Moreton Bay Fig trees. The north corner contains a bowling lawn, rose beds, flower and shrub beds. Along William Street there are tennis courts, which also double as volleyball, handball and netball courts. Electric barbecues nearby provides a popular site for office parties in December. Scattered about the lawns and gardens are memorials and sculptures that illuminate some of the social significance of the area.

Flagstaff Gardens have been classified by the National Trust of Australia (Victoria) and is listed by the Australian Heritage Commission and the the Victorian Heritage Register. At the listing ceremony by the Victorian Heritage Council in April 2004, Council Chair Chris Gallagher said "*This listing ensures the much loved trees, landscaping and other individual features are conserved and protected. But it also means the whole site is recognised as an important place for gaining an insight into our historical, archaeological, aesthetic, horticultural and social heritage."*

History

With the establishment of Melbourne in 1835, the first deaths in the colony were buried on high ground between William and King Streets, in what was colloquially called *Burial Hill*. The hill had panoramic views of the small colony, the Yarra River and Port Phillip.

- 1838 - Melbourne cemetery was marked out in what is now the Queen Victoria market, and burials continued at that location.
- 1839 - Superintendent Charles La Trobe first included the site as part of the green belt encircling Melbourne which included Batman's Hill, Carlton Gardens, Fitzroy Gardens, Treasury Gardens and the Kings Domain.
- 1840 - a flagstaff was erected on the hill as part of a signalling system between the town and ships in the Port of Melbourne. The flagstaff proved too small and the following year a fifty foot (15 m) flagstaff was erected.
- 11 November 1850: site of announcement of Victoria's Separation from the Colony of New South Wales, resulting in celebrations with a huge bonfire with about 5,000 townspeople in attendance.
- 1857 - cutting excavated to ease the gradient of King Street. This created the bluestone retaining wall of the high bank along the western boundary.
- 1857-1863 - A Magnetic Observatory and Weather Station was established by Georg von Neumayer on the hilltop. William John Wills worked here as an assistant before being appointed to the Burke and Wills expedition. The observatory moved to the Kings Domain when the Melbourne Observatory was established, as iron in the buildings surrounding Flagstaff Hill were affecting Neumayer's magnetic observations.
- 1860s - the telegraph supersedes signalling by flags.
- 1862 - West Melbourne residents petition the government to turn the hill into public gardens or recreation reserve. Clement Hodgkinson, the Deputy Surveyor-General in charge of city parks, prepared a plan for the gardens and directed its implementation.The Fitzroy and Treasury Gardens were also designed by him.
- 1871 - Memorial to Melbourne's pioneers erected.
- 1873 - Gardens permanently reserved
- 1880 - establishment of path network, lawns, trees and flowerbeds.
- October 9, 1917 - the City of Melbourne was appointed responsible for the Flagstaff Gardens.
- 1918 - children's playground established, one of the first in Melbourne.
- 23 March 2004 - gardens formally added to the Victorian Heritage Register.

References

- City of Melbourne - Flagstaff Gardens [1]
- Flagstaff gardens heritage listing [2]

Geographical coordinates: 37°48′38″S 144°57′16″E

Hedgeley Dene Gardens

Hedgeley Dene Gardens is a public open space in the suburb of Malvern East in Melbourne, Australia. It is one of the most popular parks in the Malvern East locality. It is also significant as an example of public open space design that recreates the qualities of an informal, picturesque English garden or northern European landscape in an Australian suburb. It forms part of a network of linear open spaces in Melbourne's eastern suburbs in the Local Government areas of Stonnington and Boroondara, formed along drainage easements and watercourses such as the Gardiners Creek. However, Hedgeley Dene Gardens is unique due to its particular landscape character.

References

- Cooper, JB (1935) The History of Malvern: From its First Settlement to a City, Melbourne: The Specialty Press
- Strahan, L (1989) Public and Private Memory: A History of the City of Malvern, North Melbourne: Hargreen
- http://www.stonnington.vic.gov.au/www/html/1481-hedgeley-dene-gardens.asp

Geographical coordinates: 37°52′08″S 145°03′14″E

Melbourne Zoo

The main entrance to Melbourne Zoo, 1940.

Date opened	6 October 1862
Location	Parkville, Melbourne, Victoria, Australia
Land area	55 acres (22 ha)
Coordinates	37°47′05″S 144°57′08″E
Number of animals	5,120
Number of species	320
Memberships	ARAZPA
Major exhibits	Elephants, Lions, Tigers, Orang-Utans, Gorillas.
Website	http://www.zoo.org.au

The **Royal Melbourne Zoological Gardens**, commonly known as the **Melbourne Zoo**, contains more than 320 animal species from Australia and around the world. The zoo is 4 kilometres (2.5 mi) north of the centre of Melbourne. It is accessible via Royal Park station on the Upfield railway line, and is also accessible via tram routes 55 and 19, as well as by bicycle on the Capital City Trail. Bicycles are not allowed inside the zoo itself.

Sumatran tiger at the Melbourne Zoo

History

Melbourne Zoo is Australia's oldest zoo and was modeled on London Zoo. The zoo was opened on 6 October 1862 at the Royal Park site of 55-acre (22 ha) on land donated by the City of Melbourne. Before this, animals were housed at the botanical gardens in Melbourne.

Initially the zoo was important for the acclimatisation of domestic animals recovering from their long trip to Australia. It was only with the appointment of Albert Alexander Cochrane Le Souef in 1870 that more exotic animals were procured for public display, and the gardens and picnic areas were developed.

Visitors can see historical cages including the heritage listed *Elephant House* a, which has been renovated and adapted for use for customers paying to sleep overnight in tents at the zoo in popular *Roar and Snore* evenings. These evenings allow the public to see some of the nocturnal animals at the zoo in evening guided tours by keepers. One of the most famous exhibits was Queenie the elephant.

The zoo is set among flower gardens and picnic areas. Many of the animals are now organised in bioclimatic zones: African rainforest featuring gorillas, mandrills, pigmy hippos and parrots; Asian Rainforest with tigers and otters; and the Australian Bush with koala, kangaroos, emu, echidnas and endangered hairy nose wombats. Popular exhibits also include the Butterfly house, the great flight aviary and the Trail of the Elephants. Melbourne Zoo recently obtained three new Asian Elephants from Thailand amidst much controversy regarding their safety and well-being.

The zoo includes a large schools section and caters to many school visitors annually, its immensely popular education program encourages young minds to conserve animals.

The Zoological Board of Victoria administers the Melbourne Zoo, as well as the Werribee Open Range Zoo which features herbivorous creatures in an open range setting; and Healesville Sanctuary on 175 hectares (430 acres) of bushland exhibiting Australian fauna.

On the 15th January 2010 Melbourne Zoo welcomed its first Elephant calf. This is the second elephant calf born in Australia, the first being in Sydney in July 2009.

Melbourne Zoo new seal enclosure has been completed and was opened in December 2009.

Exhibits

- Trails of the Elephants: 5 Asian elephants - male Bong Su and females Mek Kapah, Dokkoon, Kulab and Num-oi - share 3 paddocks. There are 2 baby elephants. One, Mali (born 2010) and her half brother (born 2010) who is unnamed.
- Butterfly House: a greenhouse-style walk-through exhibit for tropical butterflies.
- Orangutan Sanctuary: a rotation exhibit for two families of orangutans (one consisting of pure Sumatran orangutans and the other of Sumatran-Bornean hybrids) and a family of siamangs. The three enclosures are designed to represent an orangatun rehabilitation sanctuary in Sumatra.

- Asian rainforest: the original portion of the Asian rainforest adjoins Trail of the Elephants and includes enclosures for Sumatran Tigers, Asian Small-clawed Otters and two small aviaries for Asian birds.
- Australian Outback: features kangaroos, emus, wombats, koalas, echidnas, lace monitors and a variety of small bird aviaries.
- Great Flight Aviary: a large free-flight aviary dating from the 1930s. Visitors walk along a boardwalk through three different bioregions representing an Australian rainforest, wetlands and bushland. Significant species include Southern Cassowary, Brolga, Royal Spoonbill, Eclectus Parrot and Red-tailed Black Cockatoo
- Savannah: Giraffes, zebras, ostrich and helmeted guineafowl.
- Lion Park: Four male lions (brothers born in 2000) currently live in this exhibit. Adjoining the lion enclosure is an exhibit for African Hunting Dogs.
- Wild Sea: This $20 million development will provide new exhibits for seals, little penguins, Australian pelicans and Fiddler Rays. With underwater sounds and a projector screen coupled with the beautiful lighting effects it has a calming touch of realism.
- Reptile house: contains a variety of Australian and exotic reptiles.
- African rainforest: the major exhibit at the centre of this area is for Western Lowland Gorillas. Five of the zoo's eight gorillas - silverback Rigo and females G-Ann, Yuska, Julia and Jumanto - live in the exhibit. Three batchelor males - Motaba and his sons Yakini and Ganyeka - currently live off-display. Also in the African rainforest is an exhibit for Mandrills. Recently, the African rainforest has seen non-African species - pygmy marmosets, Asian small-clawed otters and European carp - displayed in this area.
- Treetop apes and monkeys: A series of netted enclosures viewed through glass windows from an elevated boardwalk. Species currently include white-cheeked gibbon, ebony langur, lion-tailed macaque, black-handed spider monkey, black-capped capuchin, black-and-white colobus, black-and-white ruffed lemur and common tree shrew.
- Small Cat alley: a series of relatively small enclosures for small carnivores. Species currently include serval, caracal, fishing cat and binturong.

Other exhibits at the zoo include enclosures for collared peccary, maned wolf, snow leopard, Persian leopard, puma, Syrian brown bear, white-nosed coati, ring-tailed lemur, blue-and-yellow macaw, red panda, little penguin, hamadryas baboon, several species of tamarin, Brazilian agouti, Goodfellow's tree kangaroo, meerkat, platypus, De Brazza's monkey, Aldabra giant tortoise and bongo.

Controversy

On 19 January 2008, *The Age* newspaper published allegations of animal cruelty at the zoo.

RSPCA Australia President Hugh Wirth accused the zoo of cover-ups of past involvement with the RSPCA and of putting "the dollar before animal welfare".

> There's a climate of fear with people employed there, who've got to sign confidentiality agreements to keep them quiet even after they've resigned from the zoo.
>
> —Hugh Wirth

The acting chief executive of Melbourne Zoo, Matt Vincent, claimed the zoo's own investigations into the incidents had found no mistreatment of animals, and that the staff had been "devastated" by the allegations.

External links

- Zoos Victoria [1]
- Disability information [2]

Batman's Hill

Batman's Hill in Melbourne, Australia was named for the Vandemonian adventurer and grazier John Batman. Now removed, the 18 metre high hill was located to the south of today's Collins Street and Southern Cross railway station, and is the site of a steel marker the same height as the original hill.

The hill was settled by Batman and his family, who built a house at the base in April 1836, where he lived until his death in 1839. His widow and family then moved from the house and the government requisitioned the house for government offices.

Looking south-west from the Collins Street Bridge towards the site of **Batman's Hill** in 2007. The blue post marking the hill can be seen to the left

In 1837, the Hoddle Grid, the first town plan was designed with Batman's Hill as its western boundary.

The hill had many other uses, in February 1839 it acted as a grandstand for Melbourne's first horse race, with the site later the site of navigation beacons, and a hospital. The western slope of Batman's Hill was sold to the government in 1847 and a powder magazine was built. At the foot of the slopes were tanning pits and melting works.

In 1853 the Victorian Government offered a concession to the Melbourne, Mount Alexander and Murray River Railway Company to build a railway from Melbourne to Echuca, including land to the east of Batman's Hill for the terminus. In 1856 the company failed, and was taken over by the government who formed the Victorian Railways to complete the works, the railway station being erected at Spencer Street in 1858. Growing traffic lead to an expansion of the freight sheds in 1863, with a contract being signed in November that year for the removal of the hill. Demolition was completed by the middle of 1866.

The site now forms the eastern border of the Melbourne Docklands (a precinct of the Docklands development is also named Batman's Hill) and is dominated by Southern Cross Station and the Collins Street bridge built in 2002 to replicate the original curve and shape of the hill. The new headquarters of *The Age* newspaper are located to the southern side of the bridge.

A 1920s hotel, the Batman's Hill Hotel was named after Batman's Hill.

Survey datum

Robert Hoddle used Batman's Hill as the datum for the cadastral survey of the land around Melbourne from 1837. A grid of orthogonal Section lines at one mile spacing, aligned with magnetic north, divided the land into one square mile (640 acre) sections for subdivision and land sales. The section boundaries were adjusted for watercourses. The linear property boundaries, in the absence of pre-existing tracks, were natural locations for major roads. For example:

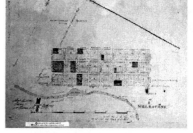

Robert Hoddle's survey of the town of Melbourne in 1837. Batman's Hill–bottom left–is the datum

- Swan Street, Riversdale Road and Somerville Road are on the east-west section line that passes through the datum.
- Victoria Street and Barkers Road run east-west one mile to the north
- Alexandra Parade and Racecourse Road run east-west two miles to the north
- Royal Parade and Sydney Road run north-south along the section line passing through the datum.
- Hoddle Street runs north-south two miles to the east
- Springvale Road runs north-south twelve miles to the east

See also

- Melbourne Docklands

References

Geographical coordinates: 37°49′12″S 144°57′11″E

Melbourne Aquarium

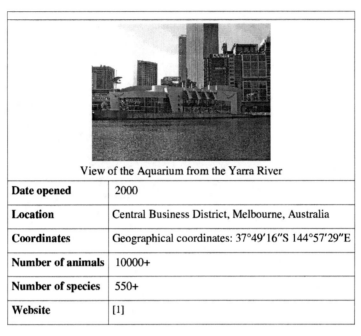

View of the Aquarium from the Yarra River

Date opened	2000
Location	Central Business District, Melbourne, Australia
Coordinates	Geographical coordinates: 37°49′16″S 144°57′29″E
Number of animals	10000+
Number of species	550+
Website	[1]

Melbourne Aquarium is a Southern Ocean and Antarctic aquarium in central Melbourne, Australia. It is located on the banks of the Yarra River beside and under the Flinders Street Viaduct and the King Street Bridge.

History

Built between February 1998 and December 1999, the building was designed by Peddle Thorp architects to resemble a ship moored to the river, and opened in January 2000. The depth of the building however was designed not to be imposing at street level, and extends 7 metres below the surface. At its centre is a world first, 2.2 million litre 'oceanarium in the round' where the spectators become the spectacle to the marine life swimming around them.

Soon after opening, the building had a legionnaires disease outbreak that resulted in 2 deaths and another 60 people being affected. Those affected had visited the aquarium between April 11 and 27, 2000. A damages action was brought in May 2000, ending in February 2004.

The Melbourne Aquarium recently underwent a significant expansion and extends all the way from the Yarra River to Flinders Street. A new entrance has been built on the corner of Flinders and King Streets. The new expansion features exhibits with king penguins and gentoo Penguins, as well as many other Antarctic fish, a first for Australia. The exhibits also feature real ice and snow to simulate Antarctic conditions, and take visitors on an expedition to Antarctica. The penguins are sourced from

Kelly Tarlton's Underwater World in New Zealand.

Features

The Aquarium has a one way self guided tour, spread over four levels:

Level One

- River to Reef, including the giant Murray cod
- Billabong
- Rock Pools
- Mangrove
- Upper Deck Cafe

A staff encounter at an exhibit on Level One of the aquarium.

Ground Floor

- Antarctica, featuring king and gentoo penguins

- Weird & Wonderful, featuring giant crabs and sea dragons
- Coral Atoll
- Sea jellies
- Octopus Cove, featuring Giant Pacific Octopus
- Coral Cafe
- Aquarium Shop

Level B1

- Octopus display
- Kids Play area

Level B2

- Sharks Alive
- BHP Billiton Shark Conservation Project & Animal Nursery
- Oceanarium
- Ocean Theatre

While visiting these features visitors come across horseshoe crabs, scorpions and tarantulas in the 'two creepy caves' and a diverse collection of Australian sea jellies.

While the theme is that of "Southern Oceans" there are a few exceptions including, a floor to ceiling coral atoll, the mangrove exhibit, the billabong exhibit and the rockpool exhibit.

Melbourne Aquarium view from the Queens Bridge

The aquarium is known for its main exhibit, which features huge grey nurse and sandbar whaler sharks, in a large oceanarium containing many diverse species of marine life.

Temporary exhibitions also frequently come to the aquarium.

Research and conservation

- **Grey Nurse Sharks**. The Melbourne Aquarium is involved in a grey nurse shark breeding program aimed at conserving this endangered species, which is already extinct in Victoria. The Aquarium currently has three grey nurse sharks and are looking at intra vitro fertilization (IVF) as a method of breeding. On November 11th, Melbourne Aquarium celebrated Georgie, the grey nurse shark's 10th birthday with a celebratory party.

- **Sea Turtles**. The aquarium is also involved in the rehabilitation of turtles washed down to the cold Victorian waters where they cannot survive. The sea turtles are housed at the aquarium to gain strength whereby they are taken to Queensland to be released.

- **Sea Snakes**. Melbourne Aquarium is home to the worlds first captive pregnant sea snake, it was on display in the coral atoll with two other snakes but has since been moved to a holding tank in the back-of-house area of the aquarium. It is under constant 24-hour video surveillance in the hope the first captive sea snake birth can be caught on film.

Current and past attractions

The current exhibition at the aquarium is of various kinds of creepy creatures, including angler fish, the Japanese spider crab, jellyfish, blood sucking leeches, horseshoe crabs, poisonous scorpions and tarantulas.

The frozen giant squid.

Melbourne Aquarium formerly had a giant squid exhibit (frozen, not alive). This has been moved to the

UnderWaterWorld, Queensland. A quote from their website: "The 7 metre squid is frozen in time in the world's largest man-made block of ice and is on display as part of the Monsters of the Deep exhibit.

The exhibit also features live cuttlefish, bioluminescent fish and octopus hidden in dark, eerie caves and rare footage of a live Humboldt Squid, filmed off the coast of Mexico."[citation needed]

Ownership

The aquarium is owned and operated by MFS Living & Leisure Group (a stapled security listed on both the Australian Securities Exchange and New Zealand Stock Exchange).

MFS Living & Leisure Group's main shareholders are ANZ Nominees Limited, National Nominees Limited, HSBC Custody Nominees (Australia) Limited, Grollo International Pty Ltd and MFS Financial Services Limited.

External links

- Melbourne Aquarium website [1]
- Peddle Thorp Melbourne [4]
- Melbourne Aquarium Photos [2]

Morell Bridge

Morell Bridge	
Official name	Morell Bridge
Carries	Pedestrians and cyclists
Crosses	Yarra River
Locale	Melbourne, Australia
Design	Arch bridge
Opened	1899

The **Morell Bridge** is a bridge over the Yarra River in South Yarra, Melbourne, Australia. Completed in 1899 by General Sir John Monash prior to his involvement in World War I, it is notable for being the first bridge in Victoria to be built using reinforced concrete.

It features decorations on the three arch spans, including large dragon motifs and ornamental Victorian lights. The gutters on the bridge are cobbled bluestone, with a single lane bitumen strip running down the middle. The Bridge is listed on the Victorian Heritage Register.

On June 7, 1998 the bridge was closed to motor vehicles as part of the CityLink project. It is currently used by cyclist and pedestrian traffic, connecting the Royal Botanic Gardens to the Olympic Park precinct.

References

- Morell Bridge [1] at *Structurae*
- "Victorian Heritage Register entry (listing VICH1440)" [2]. *Australia Heritage Places Inventory* [3]. Department of Sustainability, Environment, Water, Population and Communities.
- "Register of the National Estate entry (listing RNE5231)" [4]. *Australia Heritage Places Inventory* [3]. Department of Sustainability, Environment, Water, Population and Communities.

Geographical coordinates: 37°49′39.6″S 144°59′6.0″E

Princes Bridge

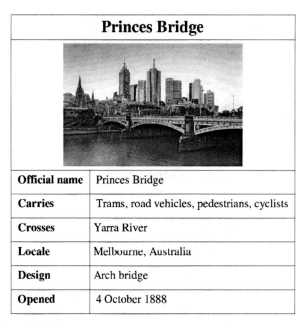

Princes Bridge	
Official name	Princes Bridge
Carries	Trams, road vehicles, pedestrians, cyclists
Crosses	Yarra River
Locale	Melbourne, Australia
Design	Arch bridge
Opened	4 October 1888

Princes Bridge is a historic bridge that crosses the Yarra River in Central Melbourne, Australia. It is built on the site of one of the oldest river crossings in Australia, being the third bridge on the same location, the first was built in 1844 and the current bridge was built in 1888, making it over 120 years old. The bridge connects Swanston Street on the Yarra River's northern bank to St Kilda Road on the southern bank, and carries, road, tram and pedestrian traffic. The bridge is listed on the Victorian Heritage Register.

Because of its position, Princes Bridge is often a focal point for celebratory events in Melbourne such as the Moomba Festival, New Years Eve and many celebrations taking place on the Yarra River where it flows through the city.

History

Prior to the bridge being built, several punts operated on the site.

This bridge is the third to have existed on this site;

- **1844** - a wooden trestle bridge was built
- **1850** - a single span sandstone bridge designed by David Lennox. At the time this was the longest single span bridge in the world, and stood for 35 years.
- **1888** - the current bridge was built to replace the sandstone bridge to cope with increases in traffic and the need to widen the river requiring a longer bridge.

When the first European settlers settled the Central Melbourne area in 1835 there was no permanent crossing point of the Yarra River. Over time various punt and ferry operators set up business in the absence of a bridge. The government in Sydney was unreliable in providing funds for the construction of a bridge, thus most of Melbourne's early infrastructure was provided by private enterprise. On 22 April 1840 a private company was set up with the intention of constructing a bridge across the Yarra. Traders in Elizabeth Street vied with those in Swanston Street to have the through traffic that would be generated by a bridge.

Lieutenant-Governor La Trobe favoured an Elizabeth Street crossing, but despite such official pressure the private company favoured the construction conditions at Swanston Street and it was there in 1840 that they opened their wooden toll bridge. Swanston Street quickly became regarded as the main street until the construction of inner city bypasses directed through-traffic away from the city. By 1850, the government provided funds to build a single span sandstone bridge, which opened on 15 November without tolls. This bridge was the first to bear the 'Princes Bridge' name.

However, within a year, gold was discovered in country Victoria and Melbourne saw a massive increase in population. In addition to the increase in traffic crossing the bridge, there was also a need to handle increased shipping traffic on the Yarra River and the river was widened to cope with this. Construction on the new bridge began in 1886 and was completed in 1888 in time for the second International Exhibition to be held in Melbourne. By that time the Yarra River had been heavily modified both upstream and downstream and the major floods of the early years were becoming less common. As with many historic Melburnian buildings and bridges, the bridge is built on solid bluestone bulwarks, unlike the sandstone popular in Sydney, with plenty of cast iron.

The present bridge was named after Edward, Prince of Wales, and was built between 1886 and 1888 by David Munro. It was designed by John Grainger (1855–1917), the father of the Australian composer Percy Grainger, and was opened on 4 October 1888.

Transport

Pedestrians account for the majority of traffic volumes, as most people crossing the bridge do so on foot or bicycle, however there are many other forms of transport that utilise the bridge:

- **Pedestrian**
- **Tram**
- **Bicycle**
- **Road**

Princes Bridge was also the name of a railway station located on the northern side of the river, to the east of the bridge, on the current site of Federation Square. It was linked to Flinders Street Station by the railway tracks that run underneath the northern approach to the bridge.

Design

Princes Bridge is 30 metres (99 ft) wide and 120 metres (400 ft) long, with bluestone squat half columns resting on piers supporting the three iron girder arches. The coat of arms on the bridge belong to the municipal councils who contributed towards the cost of construction. Other design features include an elaborate balustrade along the top of the bridge, and lamp standards crowning each pier.

The bridge bears a close resemblance to Blackfriars Bridge in London, built around the same time, both excellent surviving examples of Arch Bridge design in the late 19th century.

The bridge underwent a restoration before the 2006 Commonwealth Games.

Gallery

Princes Bridge and Melbourne CBD from the Yarra river

Underside of the iron girder arches

A lamp on the bridge

Melbourne Southbank with Princes Bridge in the foreground

See also

- Crossings of the Yarra River

External links

- Federation Square web site [1] History of the Federation Square site, including a PDF file documenting some of the history of Princes Bridge.
- Panoramic virtual tour from Princes Bridge [2]

Geographical coordinates: 37°49′09″S 144°58′06″E

Sandridge Bridge

Sandridge Bridge	
Carries	Pedestrians, cyclists
Crosses	Yarra River
Locale	Melbourne, Australia
Design	Steel girder
Total length	178.4 m (585 ft)
Width	17 m (55.8 ft)
Longest span	36.9 m (121.1 ft)
Opened	1888

The **Sandridge Bridge** is a historic former railway bridge over the Yarra River in Melbourne, Victoria, Australia, which has been redeveloped in 2006 as a new pedestrian and cycle path featuring public art. It is the third bridge on the site and is listed on the Victorian Heritage Register.

The bridge is 178.4 metres (585 ft) long and is made up of five spans, measuring in length, from the south bank to the north bank: 36.9 metres (121.1 ft), 36.6 metres (120.1 ft), 36.3 metres (119.1 ft), 36.9 metres (121.1 ft) and 31.7 metres (104 ft). The bridge is 17 metres (55.8 ft) wide and the girders are 2.74 metres (8.98 ft) high from the top to the bottom of the flange.

History

The first bridge on the site was built in 1853 for the original Melbourne and Hobson's Bay Railway Company line to Sandridge from Flinders Street Station to Port Melbourne at Hobsons Bay on Port Phillip, the first passenger railway line in Australia. In 1857 the St Kilda railway line had opened parallel to part of the line to Sandridge, and the original bridge was replaced in 1858 by a timber trestle bridge carrying two lines of rail traffic, with the tight curve of the original railway removed by rebuilding the bridge on a more oblique angle as seen today.

The bridge in 1928, with the Flinders Street Viaduct to the left hand side

The current bridge was designed by the Victorian Railways Department and the contract let to David Munro & Co in 1886, the four track bridge opening for traffic in 1888. The actual junction of the Port Melbourne and St Kilda lines was at Flinders Street, with the two pairs of tracks running parallel until Clarendon Street, where the St Kilda line diverged south. Constructed at a 33 degree angle to the river bank, it was one of the first railway structures in Melbourne to use steel girders rather than iron, and the workforce included a young

Train crossing the bridge in 1959

engineering student, John Monash. On either side of the river the steel girders were supported by bluestone and brick buttresses, and on the south side the structure continued as a brickwork viaduct. In the 1920 overhead electrical masts were added as part of the electrification of the line, and the original timber deck was replaced with rail and concrete slabs.

The bridge was last used in 1987 with the conversion of the St Kilda and Port Melbourne railway lines to light rail. Some proposals were made for the light rail to continue over the Sandridge Bridge into Flinders Street station, but instead they were diverted from the railway reserve at Clarendon Street and sent into the city via Spencer Street. The light rail operates today as the route 96 tram to St Kilda, and route 109 tram to Port Melbourne.

The viaduct over Queensbridge Street and the embankment across the South Bank were listed by the National Trust and were noted as being historically significant, but were still removed. Only the segment over the river itself was retained, with a number of different redevelopment plans proposed during the 1990s.

Redevelopment

In 2001 the State Government held an expressions of interest process for refurbishment of the bridge, seeking commercial ventures, but the process was not successful and in 2003 Melbourne City Council and the Department of Sustainability and Environment took over. They committed $15.5 million to restore the bridge, create a plaza on the Southbank side and make connections to walkways on the Yarra north bank. In 2005 it was announced that artist Nadim Karam had been commissioned to create ten abstract sculptures in a piece titled

The bridge after redevelopment

The Travellers, which represents the different types of immigrants who traditionally arrived by train over the bridge from Station Pier. Nine of the sculptures move across the bridge in a 15-minute sequence, moving on bogies running between the two bridge spans.

The bridge was unveiled three days before the 2006 Commonwealth Games in Melbourne, at a final cost of $18.5 million. It included a new pedestrian and cycle path and public space, connecting a new Queensbridge Square at Southbank to Flinders Walk on the north bank. However, only the eastern half of the bridge was reopened, the western half being stabilised and fenced off from public access.

On June 11, 2007, the bridge was vandalised when persons unknown used a sledgehammer to smash 46 of the 128 glass panels of the *Travellers* exhibit. Each glass panel offers information about Australian indigenous peoples or the countries of immigrants to Australia, from Afghanistan to Zimbabwe. It was expected to cost between A$200,000 and A$300,000 to repair and city councillors are considering using more durable materials to replace the glass.

Gallery

Sculptures on the Sandridge Bridge

The glass panels contain information about each country from which immigrants came to Melbourne.

The bridge as viewed from Southbank.

Vandalised glass panels have been sectioned off behind temporary fencing.

Sandridge Bridge Towards
Flinders Street Station

Sandridge
Bridge
(Built 1888)
Redeveloped
in South
Bank End

Melbourne South
Bank &
Sandridge Bridge

Sandridge Bridge
with South &
North Banks

References

Geographical coordinates: 37°49′13″S 144°57′45″E

Melbourne Victory FC

Full name	Melbourne Victory Football Club
Nickname(s)	Victory, The Big V, Melbourne
Founded	2004
Ground	AAMI Park (Capacity: 30,050) Etihad Stadium (Capacity: 56,347)
Chairman	Geoff Lord
Manager	Ernie Merrick
League	A-League
2010–11	2nd (league) 2nd (finals)

Home colours	Away colours

Current season

Melbourne Victory FC is a professional football (soccer) club in the Australian A-League. Based in Melbourne, Victoria, Australia since the 2006-07 season, Melbourne Victory have led the A-League in attendances and is also considered the most successful club domestically in the A-League, having won two A-League Championships and two Premiers Plates.

Melbourne Victory are the only club to complete the Premiership-Championship double twice, winning both during the 2006–07 and 2008–09 seasons. They are also the first and only club to complete the domestic treble, winning the Challenge Cup, Premiership and Championship, all in the 2008–09 season.

History

Beginning

Melbourne Victory was founded in 2003 after the announcement of a revamped domestic league in Australia, which saw the National Soccer League disbanded in 2003 and replaced by the A-League.

Football Federation Australia (FFA) approved the Melbourne Victory consortium as Melbourne's representative in the league, with Belgravia Leisure Pty Ltd backing the club. The chairman and CEO of Belgravia Leisure, Geoff Lord, was installed as the inaugural chairman of Melbourne Victory FC. Melbourne Victory's major sponsor was Samsung.

Gary Cole (an ex-Socceroo) was hired to become Football Operations manager, and was soon joined by Ernie Merrick, appointed as head coach from the Victorian Institute of Sport (VIS). Archie Thompson, a then fringe player for the Socceroos had been playing in Belgium with Lierse S.K., was the club's first player signing. The club soon signed three more internationals for the inaugural squad — then Socceroo Kevin Muscat, Austrian Richard Kitzbichler and Belgian Geoffrey Claeys.

- Trial match #1 MV vs Oakleigh Cannons 30 April 2005 (Melbourne 2-0, Allsopp x2)
- Trial match #2 MV vs Bulleen Zebras 4 May 2005
- FIFA Club World Championship Adelaide vs MV 7 May 2005

The remainder of the squad was quickly assembled, although room was left for signings before Melbourne played its first competitive match against Adelaide United in a World Club Championship qualifier. Unfortunately, this resulted in an inconsistent first season. Although highlights included a 5–0 win over major rivals Sydney FC, Melbourne Victory finished as the worst Australian team (ahead of the New Zealand Knights), whilst Sydney, their major rivals went on to win the first A-League Championship.

The Victory continued the sister-city relationship between Melbourne and Tianjin by playing against Chinese Super League Club Tianjin Teda FC annually during the off-season just like its previous NSL predecessors, for the Lord Mayor's Cup.

Melbourne Victory are consideredWikipedia:Avoid weasel words a broad-based club, appealing to all nationalities. The team colours — navy blue and white — are traditionally Victorian state colours.

Early years 2005—2010

It was widely believed that Melbourne Victory would be contenders for the A-League championship but their inaugural season in the Hyundai A-League was anything but — the team only managed seven wins out of twenty-one matches, finishing second last.

The season saw Melbourne Victory sign two returning Socceroos, (Archie Thompson and Kevin Muscat). The highlight of the season was the 5–0 thrashing of eventual champions Sydney FC (with 2 goals from Archie Thompson and Kevin Muscat, and one from Richard Kitzbichler). At the end of the season the Melbourne Victory player of the year award was handed to Kevin Muscat, and the club top goal scorer going to Archie Thompson.

Melbourne began the 2006–2007 Hyundai A-League season hoping to vastly improve on their 7th place in the inaugural 2005–2006 season. Coach Ernie Merrick had made a number of off-season signings to bolster the squad with skill and experience including 3 Brazilians Alessandro, Claudinho, Fred along with Scottish Premier League player Grant Brebner. After a hugely successful round 2 fixture against Sydney FC at Etihad Stadium which attached the largest home and away crowd for regular club match, Melbourne Victory announced that they would move all but one match from Olympic Park to the new venue Melbourne would become the first team to complete the A-League double in the history of the competition; clinching the premiership against the New Zealand Knights 4–0 at Olympic Park with 4 rounds of competition remaining, then beating Adelaide United 6–0 in the grand final at a sold out Etihad Stadium to take the championship. Melbourne also qualified for the 2008 Asian Champions League as A-League Champions.

Looking to capitalise on their successful 2006–07 campaign, Melbourne made some strong off-season signs including former Socceroo Ljubo Milicevic and Costa Rican international Carlos Hernández to cover the hole left by the departure of Fred to MLS club D.C. United. Again with the league largest crowds and a record membership of over 20,000, Melbourne were undefeated after 7 rounds but the season would slip away with some poor home performances and a mounting injury list. A late season rally gave Melbourne a hope of making the finals up to the second last round but they would finish 5th, 4 points out of the finals. Melbourne became the first side in A-League history to score 100 goals, reaching the mark after 65 games, with their first goal against Wellington Phoenix at Etihad Stadium on 11 January 2008. The 2008 Asian Champions League campaign started with a 2–0 home victory of Korean side Chunnam Dragons but inexperience was to show with the team not able to adapt to the East Asian style and long away trips.

The 2008–09 season brought the start of the A-League Youth League and the introduction of the W-League. Melbourne fielded teams in both competitions. Melbourne actively recruited, bringing in Socceroo Michael Thwaite, Costa Rican World Cup player José Luis López as well as Ney Fabiano from Asian Champions League rivals Chonburi FC.

Melbourne's season got off to an optimal start, winning the Pre-Season Challenge Cup. A 0–0 draw resulted in a penalty shoot-out, Victory winning 8–7 against the Wellington Phoenix.

After grabbing the Pre-Season Cup, the Victory were held to a 0–0 draw away against Sydney FC. They reinforced their premiership favouritism by coasting to 4–2 and 5–0 victories against Wellington Phoenix and the Newcastle Jets. Despite this, they succumbed 0–2 to an undermanned Sydney side at Etihad Stadium in front of 32,000 fans.

On the 6th of December, they became the 1st A-League club to amass total crowd figures of 1,000,000.

On the 24th of January, Melbourne Victory won its final game of the season against Wellington Phoenix . The 2–0 win in front of 29,904 fans placed Victory ahead of Adelaide United on goals scored for the premiership title, a margin United failed to achieve in its 1–0 win over the Central Coast Mariners.

The Victory kicked off their finals campaign on 7 February 2009 in the major semi-final first leg against bitter rival Adelaide United at Hindmarsh Stadium, a game which was won courtesy of goals from Costa Rican Carlos Hernández and Danny Allsopp. The second leg would see Melbourne demolish Adelaide United 4–0 with goals from Thompson, Hernandez, Allsopp and Pondlejak, granting Melbourne passage to the Grand Final on a 6–0 aggregate. Adelaide then defeated Queensland to set up a rematch with Melbourne in the Grand Final, which the Victory won 1–0 with Tom Pondeljak scoring in the 59th minute to regain the A-League Championship and becoming the fist A-League team to win their 2nd Championship.

In, 2009–2010, Greek gambling giant Intralot became the Melbourne Victory's new major sponsor to replace Samsung. Their logo now features on the front of Melbourne Victory's new strip.

The Victory made some off-season changes by releasing Steve Pantelidis and Michael Thwaite to Gold Coast United, Sebastian Ryall to Sydney FC & Veteran goalkeeper Michael Theoklitos ended his contract and later joined Norwich City F.C.. Moreover, José Luis López Ramírez had been terminated from his loan from Deportivo Saprissa & Daniel Allsopp moved to Al Rayyan.

Several new signing were made, bringing goalkeeper Glen Moss from Wellington Phoenix, Thai midfielder Surat Sukha from Chonburi FC, the promotion of Mathew Theodore and Matthew Foschini from the youth squad and the permanent signing of veteran Carlos Hernández from L.D. Alajuelense for three years (after his two year loan). Meanwhile Mate Dugandzic was signed from Melbourne Knights, Robbie Kruse from Brisbane Roar, Marvin Angulo from Club Sport Herediano& Sutee Suksomkit as nine match guest player. On December 1, 2009 it was revealed that Ney Fabiano was leaving Melbourne had signed a contract with Thai Premier League team Bangkok Glass FC for the 2010 season.

Melbourne Victory was drawn into group E in 2010 AFC Champions League along with Seongnam Ilhwa Chunma, Beijing Guoan & Kawasaki Frontale.

Corporate

Geoff Lord and his partners have become the sole owners of Melbourne after buying out the shares held by Football Federation Australia.

Victory struggled to raise the initial $5 million equity capital to join the A-League three years ago and the FFA helped the club over the line by contributing franchise and set-up fees of about $500,000.

The FFA took a ten per cent holding in the club in return, as well as having a representative on the Victory board.

The shareholding was offered back to the club in 2007 and Lord and his partners — including Ron Peck, Richard Wilson and John Harris — raised the money to buy the shares.

Supporters

Melbourne Victory has the largest supporter base in the A-League, and has consistently set membership and attendance records since its establishment.

Sponsors

On 27 October 2005, South Korean electronics giant Samsung became the club's major sponsor in a two year deal. This would ensure that Samsung would have their logo feature on the front and the back of Victory's home and away kits. Prior to the 2006–07 season KFC announced they would also be one of Victory's shirt sponsor's, with their logo appearing on the sleeve of Victory's home and away kits. On 28 January 2009 Samsung said that they would not be renewing their sponsorship for the 2009–10 Hyundai A-League season.

Intralot became the Melbourne Victory's new major sponsor when they signed a two season $2 million dollar contract on 4 May 2009. Their logo now features on the front of Melbourne Victory's new playing strip.

On Friday August 6, it was announced that law firm Florin Burhala Lawyers became Melbourne Victory's official shorts sponsor for the 2010-11 season.

Affiliated clubs

* Tianjin Teda FC
* Chonburi F.C.

Colours and badge

Melbourne's kit colours are navy blue, silver and white (hence the alternate nickname of the Blues/Navy Blues), which encompass the traditional state sporting colours of Victoria. In the first A-League season, only the club badge displayed a chevron, known colloquially as the "Big V", a symbol traditionally used by the Victoria Australian rules football team. In the 2006–07 season the away strip was changed to a grey jersey with a white chevron on the front. This was an immediate hit with the club's supporters, and from the 2007–08 season onwards the Melbourne's home jersey also sported the white chevron on the front. A new kit was introduced for the 2008 AFC Champions League due to AFC rules requiring kits to have player numbers on the front of the uniform as well as the back, which would not fit well with the 'V' on the Victory's regular kit. For the 2009–10 season, Melbourne changed their away jersey to be a reverse of their home jersey; a white shirt with a blue chevron.

A-League

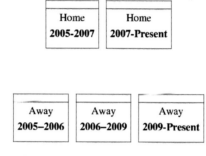

Home	Home
2005-2007	**2007-Present**

Away	Away	Away
2005–2006	**2006–2009**	**2009-Present**

AFC

Home
2008

Away
2008

Stadium

Further information: Etihad Stadium, Olympic Park Stadium, and Melbourne Rectangular Stadium

Melbourne were originally based at the 50 year old Olympic Park stadium, where they played all home matches during the 2005–06 A-League season. This stadium has seated areas only on the wings, with standing-room sandy terraces on the north and south ends. The average crowd during the first year was a healthy 14,158.

Melbourne Victory v Gamba Osaka at the Etihad Stadium in April 2008

On September 2, 2006, Melbourne Victory played Sydney FC at the 56,000 capacity Telstra Dome. The match was a runaway success in terms of crowds, with 39,730 in attendance. Due to this the club moved all home games to 'the Dome' bar one against the New Zealand Knights due to a Robbie Williams concert at the Dome.

This move to such a large stadium was viewed with scepticism by many, but proved to be an outstanding success, with the Grand Final held there. The average attendance rose to 27,728 for the 2006/07 season, 10,000 above the next highest in the A-League. However, some of the Victory's active supporter groups have little affection for "The Dome", citing over-zealous security restrictions for hampering their efforts on match day.

Prior to the 2006–07 season the club had planned to move to a new stadium being built to the east of the current Olympic Park complex. The AAMI Park was originally expected to sit approximately 20,000 spectators (expandable to 25,000) and was to be completed in time for the start of the 2008–09 campaign.

These plans have since been revised after the Victory refused to commit to playing at such a small capacity stadium. On May 23, 2007, the club announced it had signed as a founding co-tenant of the new stadium, which would now be built to accommodate a maximum of 30,050 spectators with further renovations to 50,000 possible.

Etihad Stadium continued to serve as the club's only home ground until the completion of AAMI Park. The club will split its home games between the new stadium and Etihad Stadium from the 2010-2011 A-League campaign onwards; the games of less importance or potential drawing power at the new stadium and the 'blockbusters' and finals matches at Etihad Stadium.

Rivalry

Rivalry exists with Sydney FC, Melbourne Heart and Adelaide United. Victory have recorded big wins against Adelaide (6–0 in the 2006–07 Grand Final) and Sydney (5–0 during the 2005–06 Season).

Sydney is considered Melbourne's major rival, due to Melbourne and Sydney being Australia's two largest cities (see Melbourne-Sydney rivalry). Matches between the two teams are regularly controversial and bitter encounters. Strong tensions are also emerging between the supporters from opposing teams, evident in the sell-out crowds, and Sydney's regular large travelling group of away supporters. The rivalry between the two teams was escalated further after Sydney beat Melbourne in the final match of the 2009/2010 season to win the A-League Premiership, and again beat Melbourne in the 2010 A-League Grand Final.

Adelaide is Melbourne's geographical rival as it is the closest team to Melbourne in Australia (see Melbourne-Adelaide Rivalry). This rivalry also stems from the other football codes, where the interstate rivalry is big between Victorians and South Australians.

Rivalry has also built up from previous encounters, when an incident between the then Adelaide United manager, John Kosmina, and Victory skipper Kevin Muscat took place during a sideline altercation during a match in the 2006–07 season, and when Victory striker Ney Fabiano allegedly spat in the direction of Adelaide defender Robert Cornthwaite during Round 4 in the 2008–09 season. Ney Fabiano was banned for 6 matches. Victory and Adelaide contested both the 2006–07 and 2008–09 Grand Finals, with Melbourne winning both.

Melbourne Heart entered the competition in the 2010-11 season. This is anticipated to create a city rivalry more fierce than those with Sydney FC and Adelaide United.

Current squads

Senior squad

Note: Flags indicate national team as has been defined under FIFA eligibility rules. Players may hold more than one non-FIFA nationality.

No.		Position	Player
1		GK	Michael Petkovic
2		DF	Kevin Muscat *(Captain)*
3		MF	Mate Dugandžić *(Youth)*
4		DF	Petar Franjic *(Youth)*
5		DF	Surat Sukha
6		MF	Leigh Broxham

No.		Position	Player
7		DF	Matthew Kemp
8		MF	Grant Brebner
9		FW	Ricardinho *(Marquee)*
10		FW	Archie Thompson *(Australian Marquee)*
11		MF	Marvin Angulo *(on loan from CS Herediano)*

No.		Position	Player
12		DF	Rodrigo Vargas
13		MF	Diogo Ferreira *(Youth)*
14		MF	Billy Celeski
15		MF	Tom Pondeljak
16		MF	Carlos Hernández
17		DF	Matthew Foschini *(Youth)*
19		DF	Evan Berger
20		GK	Sebastian Mattei *(Youth)*
21		FW	Robbie Kruse
23		DF	Adrian Leijer *(Vice Captain)*
27		MF	Geoff Kellaway *(Injury replacement player)*

Youth squad

Note: Flags indicate national team as has been defined under FIFA eligibility rules. Players may hold more than one non-FIFA nationality.

No.		Position	Player
1		GK	Rani Dowisha
2		DF	Luke Pilkington
3		MF	Jason Ricciuti
4		DF	Nicholas Ansell
6		MF	Paulo Retre
7		FW	James Jeggo
8		MF	Jake Nakic
9		FW	Tedros Yabio

No.		Position	Player
10		MF	Damir Lokvancic

No.		Position	Player
11		FW	David Stirton
12		DF	James Kalafatidis
13		FW	Luke O'Dea
14		MF	Andrew Mullet
15		MF	Chris Windsor
16		MF	Stephen Hatzikostas
17		MF	Anthony Selemidis
18		MF	Daniel Chaabani
20		GK	Alastair Bray

Women's squad

Note: Flags indicate national team as has been defined under FIFA eligibility rules. Players may hold more than one non-FIFA nationality.

No.		Position	Player
1		GK	Melissa Barbieri *(Co-Captain)*
2		DF	Vedrana Popovic
3		DF	Marlies Oostdam
4		MF	Tal Karp *(Co-Captain)*
5		DF	Laura Alleway
6		DF	Maika Ruyter-Hooley
7		MF	Sarah Groenewald
8		FW	Katie Thorlakson
9		MF	Stephanie Catley
10		FW	Deanna Niceski

No.		Position	Player
11		MF	Julianne Sitch
12		MF	Monnique Hansen Kofoed
13		MF	Katrina Gorry
14		MF	Selin Kuralay
15		DF	Jessica Humble
16		MF	Gulcan Koca
17		FW	Caitlin Friend
18		MF	Ursula Hughson
19		MF	Enza Barilla
20		GK	Nicole Paul

Notable former players

See also: List of Melbourne Victory FC players

Below is a **list of notable footballers who have previously played for the Melbourne Victory**. Generally, this means players that have played 50 or more first-class matches for the club. However, some players who have played fewer matches are also included, as are the club's integral founding members, where integral members of a championship winning team, have at least one senior international cap or made significant contributions to the club's history.

Australia
- Daniel Allsopp
- Adrian Caceres
- Eugene Galekovic
- Mitchell Langerak
- Steve Pantelidis
- Daniel Piorkowski
- Michael Theoklitos
- Michael Thwaite

Austria
- Richard Kitzbichler

Belgium
- Geoffrey Claeys

Brazil
- Alessandro
- Fred
- Ney Fabiano
- Leandro Love

Costa Rica
- José Luis López

England
- Joe Keenan
- James Robinson

Thailand
- Sutee Suksomkit

Personnel

Senior Club Officials
- **Chairman:** Geoff Lord
- **Director:** Ron Peck
- **Director:** Richard Wilson
- **Director:** Anthony Di Pietro
- **Director:** Mario Biasin
- **Director:** Ian McLeod
- **Director:** John Harris
- **CEO:** Geoff Miles

Senior Squad Coaching and Medical staff
- **Football Operations Manager:** Gary Cole
- **Manager:** Ernie Merrick
- **Assistant Manager:** Aaron Healey
- **Assistant Manager:** Kevin Muscat
- **Goalkeeping Coach:** Steve Mautone
- **Strength & Conditioning Coach:** Adam Basil
- **Sports Scientist:** Anita Pedrana
- **Physiotherapist:** Sam Bugeja
- **Physiotherapist:** Daniel Jones
- **Personal Trainer:** Andrew Brown
- **Doctor:** Dr Anik Shawdon

Youth Squad Coaching Staff
- **Manager:** Mehmet Durakovic
- **Assistant Manager:** Steve Mautone
- **Team Manager:** Anthony Grima

W-League Team Coaching Staff
- **Manager:** N/A

Coaches
- **2005–Present** Ernie Merrick

Honours

Club
- **A-League Premiership:**
  - **Premiers** (2): 2006-07, 2008–09
  - **Runners-Up** (1): 2009-10
- **A-League Championship:**
  - **Champions** (2): 2006-07, 2008–09
  - **Runners-Up** (1): 2009-10
- **A-League Pre-Season Challenge Cup**
  - **Champions** (1): 2008-09
- **QNI North Queensland Trophy**
  - **Winners** (1) 2006
- **Lord Mayors Cup**
  - **Winners** (1) 2007

Individual

List of Individual award winners who won awards while playing for Melbourne Victory FC.

- A-League Golden Boot Winners
    - 2005/06: Archie Thompson *
    - 2006/07: Daniel Allsopp
- Joe Marston Medal Winners
    - 2006/07: Archie Thompson
    - 2008/09: Tom Pondeljak
- A-League Rising Star
    - 2006/07: Adrian Leijer
- A-League Goalkeeper of the Year
    - 2006/07: Michael Theoklitos
    - 2007/08: Michael Theoklitos
- A-League Coach of the Year
    - 2006/07: Ernie Merrick
    - 2009/10: Ernie Merrick
- A-League Johnny Warren Medallist
    - 2009/10: Carlos Hernandez

(*) Indicates co-winner

Year-by-year history

Melbourne League history

Season	Teams	Pre-Season	Premiership Ladder Position	Finals Qualification	Final Ladder Position	ACL Qualification	ACL Placing
2005–06	8	Semi-Final	7th	DNQ	7th	DNQ	n/a
2006–07	8	5th	**Premiers**	Qualified	**Champions**	Qualified for 2008	DNQ
2007–08	8	8th	5th	DNQ	5th	DNQ	Group Stages (2nd)
2008–09	8	**Winners**	**Premiers**	Qualified	**Champions**	Qualified for 2010	DNQ

| 2009–10 | 10 | - | 2nd | Qualified | 2nd | Qualified for 2011 | Group Stages (4th) |
| 2010–11 | 11 | - | - | - | - | - | Group Stages |

Records and statistics

For detailed records and statistics see Records and Statistics

Records

- **Record Victory**: 6–0 vs Adelaide United, A-League Grand Final, February 18, 2007
- **Record Defeat**: 0–4 (twice): vs Newcastle Jets, January 19, 2007 and vs Central Coast Mariners, November 7, 2009
- **Record Home Defeat**: 0–4 vs Central Coast Mariners, November 7, 2009
- **Record High Attendance**: 55,436 vs Adelaide United, Etihad Stadium, Melbourne, February 18, 2007
- **Record High Attendance (Season)**: 50,333 vs Sydney FC, Etihad Stadium, Melbourne, December 8, 2006
- **Most Goals by a Player in a Game**: 5 - Archie Thompson, A-League Grand Final, February 18, 2007
- **Most Wins in a Row**: 8 - February 4, 2006 – October 8, 2006
- **Highest Season Average Attendance**: 27,728 - A-League 2006–07
- **All-time Leading Goal Scorer**: Archie Thompson - 50 goals (as of May 15, 2010)
- **A-League Leading Goal Scorer**: Archie Thompson - 49 goals (as of May 15, 2010)
- **Most Goals In a Regular season**: Carlos Hernández - 12 goals, A-League 2009–10
- **All-time Leading Appearances**: Kevin Muscat - 111 appearances (as of May 15, 2010)
- **A-League Leading Appearances**: Archie Thompson - 102 appearances (as of May 15, 2010)
- **Longest Period Without Conceding a Goal**: 475 minutes - January 11, 2009 – August 6, 2009 Goalkeeper Michael Theoklitos

Leading scorers

Last updated April 28, 2010,

Competitive, professional matches only, appearances including substitutes appear in brackets.

	Name	Years	A-League	Finals	ACL	Total	Games per goal
1	Archie Thompson	2005/06 -	42 (94)	7 (8)	1 (4)	**50** (106)	2.12
2	Danny Allsopp	2005/06 - 2009	33 (83)	3 (6)	3 (6)	**39** (95)	2.45
3	Kevin Muscat	2005/06 -	26 (92)	0 (9)	3 (10)	**29** (111)	3.83
4	Carlos Hernández	2007/08 -	18 (63)	3 (6)	1 (8)	**22** (77)	3.50
5	Tom Pondeljak	2008/09 -	4 (40)	1 (5)	1 (5)	**7** (50)	7.14
6=	Ney Fabiano	2008/09 - 2009/10	6 (29)	1 (1)	0 (0)	**6** (30)	5.00
6=	Adrian Caceres	2006/07 - 2007/08	6 (40)	0 (2)	0 (5)	**6** (47)	7.83
6=	Rodrigo Vargas	2006/07 -	4 (87)	0 (9)	2 (11)	**6** (107)	17.83
9=	Richard Kitzbichler	2005/06	5 (18)	0 (0)	0 (0)	**5** (18)	3.60
9=	Robbie Kruse	2009/10 -	4 (18)	1 (2)	0 (4)	**5** (24)	4.80
9=	Nick Ward	2007/08 -	5 (39)	0 (5)	0 (12)	**5** (56)	11.20
12=	Fred	2006/07	4 (14)	0 (3)	0 (0)	**4** (17)	4.25
12=	Grant Brebner	2006/07 -	4 (73)	0 (9)	0 (4)	**4** (86)	21.50
12=	Adrian Leijer	2005/06 - 2006/07, 2009/10 -	3 (63)	1 (6)	0 (5)	**4** (74)	18.50

Most number of appearances

Competitive, professional matches only including substitution, number of appearances as a substitute appears in brackets.

Last updated April 28, 2010

	Name	Years	A-League	Finals	ACL	Total
1=	Kevin Muscat	2005/06 -	92 (0)	9 (0)	10 (0)	**111** (0)
2	Rodrigo Vargas	2006/07 -	87 (0)	9 (0)	11 (0)	**107** (0)
3	Archie Thompson	2005/06 -	94 (2)	8 (1)	4 (2)	**106** (5)
4	Danny Allsopp	2005/06 - 2009	83 (1)	6 (0)	6 (0)	**95** (1)
5	Grant Brebner	2006/07 -	73 (18)	9 (3)	4 (0)	**86** (21)
6	Michael Theoklitos	2005/06 - 2008/09	67 (2)	6 (0)	5 (0)	**78** (2)
7	Carlos Hernández	2007/08 -	63 (8)	6 (0)	8 (3)	**77** (11)
8	Adrian Leijer	2006/07 - 2007/08, 2009/10 -	63 (1)	6 (0)	5 (0)	**74** (1)
9	Matthew Kemp	2006/07 -	62 (7)	3 (0)	6 (0)	**71** (7)
10	Leigh Broxham	2005/06 -	55 (16)	4 (1)	10 (0)	**69** (17)

See also

- Sport in Australia
- Sport in Victoria

External links

- Melbourne [1] - Official website
- New Stadium [2] - Melbourne Rectangular Stadium
- MVFC Videos [3] Melbourne Victory Videos

Melbourne Storm

Melbourne Storm

Club information	
Full name	Melbourne Storm Rugby League Club
Nickname(s)	Storm, Stormers storms
Founded	1997 (first season 1998)
Current details	
Ground(s)	AAMI Park – 30,050
Coach(s)	Craig Bellamy
Captain(s)	Cameron Smith
Competition	National Rugby League
2010	16th

Home colours   Away colours

Records	
Premierships	3 (1999, 2007, 2009)
Runners-up	2 (2006, 2008)
Minor premiership	3 (2006, 2007, 2008)

The **Melbourne Storm** are an Australian professional rugby league football club based in the city of Melbourne. The first fully professional rugby league team based in the Australian rules football-dominated state of Victoria, the Storm have played in the last four National Rugby League (NRL) grand finals, making them one of the league's top teams. In October 2009, they were ranked the most popular sports team in Melbourne by a national Roy Morgan Poll.

The club won the minor premiership three times in a row from 2006–2008 and contested each grand final from 2006 to 2009, winning in 2007 and 2009, although these titles were later stripped for salary cap breaches. They were named the NRL Team of the Decade for the 2000s. Their coach, Craig Bellamy, is the incumbent New South Wales State of Origin coach.

From their inception and until the end of 2009, the Storm played their home games at Olympic Park Stadium. As of Round 9 in the 2010 NRL season, the Storm will play home games at AAMI Park, the first being against the Brisbane Broncos. Prior to this, they will play their first three fixtures of 2010 at nearby Docklands Stadium.

Originally a Super League initiative and one of six NRL teams which are privately owned, the Melbourne club is currently 100% owned and operated by News Limited.

As a result of an NRL investigation, it was announced on 22 April 2010 that the Storm had been stripped of its 2007 and 2009 premierships and its 2006-2008 minor premierships, fined a record $1,689,000, deducted all eight premiership points and barred from receiving further premiership points for the rest of the 2010 season after being found guilty of gross long-term salary cap breaches. Several sponsors, most notably ME Bank, Hostplus and Skins withdrew support from the club while Harvey Norman, Jayco, Suzuki and KooGa continued their support, with their logos featuring prominently in a hastily reconfigured jersey. In contrast to those sponsors who distanced themselves, Jayco and Suzuki increased their existing support to compensate for the losses of other sponsors .

History

See also: Rugby League in Victoria

1990s

By 1994, due to the high attendances at recent State of Origin matches (including a then Australian rugby league record crowd of 87,161 in 1994 at the MCG) the Australian Rugby League (ARL) had planned to establish a Melbourne-based team to the premiership by 1998. However, the disruption caused by the Super League war caused great change to the game in Australia. By May 1997, Super League boss John Ribot pushed for a Melbourne based club for his competition, which was the rival against the ARL. Former Brisbane Broncos centre Chris Johns became the CEO of the club and Ribot stepped down from the head of Super League to set up the club. In September 1997, Melbourne announced that Chris Anderson would be their foundation coach, and then Super League announced that the new team would be named the Melbourne Storm.

The Melbourne club then went forward with signing players, mainly from former Super League clubs Perth Reds and Hunter Mariners. Some of these players included Robbie Ross, Glenn Lazarus, Brett Kimmorley and Scott Hill. With the Super League and ARL joining into one competition for the 1998 season, the Melbourne team became part of the National Rugby League (NRL). The Melbourne Storm club was unveiled at a function in the Hyatt in February, 1998.

"In 1997, there were 21 rugby league teams running around Australia (and one in New Zealand), but none in the country's second-largest city. In 1998, with the game reunited, three clubs had been jettisoned and the Melbourne Storm had bobbed up as an unexpected and initially curious addition to the landscape."

The Sunday Age, 1999

In their first ever game, they defeated Illawarra, with Glenn Lazarus as their inaugural captain. Melbourne, in a complete shock to the rest of the competition, won their first four games, before losing to Auckland. They went on to make the finals, but were defeated by the eventual premiers, the Brisbane Broncos.

In January 1999, CEO John Ribot negotiated a deal that saw Melbourne Storm games televised in China every weekend. The club won eight of their first eleven games of the 1999 NRL season, and went on to make the finals in third position on the premiership ladder. The team was beaten convincingly 34–10 in the quarter final by St. George Illawarra. After narrow victories against the Canterbury Bulldogs and the Parramatta Eels however Melbourne once more faced St. George Illawarra, this time winning 20–18 and securing their first (and to date, only) premiership.

2000s

Season 2000 saw Melbourne consistently win after initially losing their first four games of the season. They made the finals (finishing 6th), but were eventually knocked out by Newcastle in the quarter-finals. Between 2001 and 2002, the Melbourne club performed poorly. Cracks were starting to appear between Johns, Ribot and Anderson throughout the period, with Anderson quitting as coach after round 7, 2001. He was replaced by Mark Murray. The Melbourne club failed to make the finals in 2001. Johns left the club as CEO at the end of 2002 and coach Murray was sacked due to Melbourne's poor form, with the club missing the finals for the second year in a row. Wayne Bennett's assistant coach at the Brisbane Broncos, Craig Bellamy was announced as the new coach of Melbourne for 2003. In addition to a new captain in Kiwi international skipper Stephen Kearney, the strict coaching of Craig "Bellyache" Bellamy would see the Melbourne Storm get back on track from the previous lean years.

"Now, the Melbourne Storm are here to stay. They are not moving and News Limited is apparently committed to keeping them financially. I am OK with that. I hated Melbourne when they were in place of traditional teams that were expelled, but that's all over now. If they want to persevere in Melbourne, I have no argument."

Phil Gould, 21 December 2003

Between 2003 and 2005, Melbourne consistently made the finals, but lost games in the semi finals that prevented them from reaching the grand final. On 17 July 2004, during round 19 of the 2004 NRL season, Danny Williams king-hit Wests Tigers' player Mark O'Neill.

Williams defended the incident, using four medical experts to argue on his behalf that he was suffering post-traumatic amnesia when the incident occurred, which he claims was the result of a high tackle by O'Neill just prior to the incident. Despite Williams' claim, he was suspended for 18 weeks by the NRL judiciary. After the decision, Williams stated that he was "obviously disappointed with the outcome". It was the longest suspension in Australian rugby league since Steve Linnane was suspended for twenty weeks for eye-gouging in 1987.

In 2005, Storm coach Craig Bellamy, in his third season as an NRL coach, gained representative honours when he was selected to start coaching the Country Origin.[citation needed]

Season 2006 saw a new-look Storm, with the retirement of captain Robbie Kearns, the emergence of talented rookie halfback Cooper Cronk taking the reigns from longtime number 7 Matt Orford, and the recruitment of hard-man Michael Crocker. Contrary to expectation, 2006 was a standout year for the Melbourne team, winning their first minor premiership following a resoundingly dominant Home and Away Season, including a club record 11 game streak. Melbourne only lost four games in the season, making them outright leaders by four wins. They went on to win their two finals matches, and were subsequently favourites in the 2006 NRL Grand Final. The Storm however lost 15–8 the to the Brisbane Broncos, in a match where controversial refereeing decisions against Melbourne caused much media coverage. Melbourne's television audience for the Storm's NRL grand final appearance was greater than Sydney's was for the Swans AFL grand final appearance'.

In 2007 the Storm avenged for their heartbreaking end to the 2006 campaign by playing as they did in 2006: once again dominating the competition, and finishing on top after 25 rounds. In the first week of the NRL finals, Melbourne played Brisbane, in which Melbourne won 40–0, securing a spot in a preliminary final. In the preliminary final, Melbourne played Parramatta in a game that was tied 10–10 at half time, before a superb second half by Melbourne resulted in the final score of 26–10. The win was particularly satisfying for Melbourne fans, coming soon after Parramatta CEO Denis Fitzgerald said that rugby league should not be promoted in Melbourne. This game drew a larger crowd than chief rival Manly's preliminary final. Melbourne comprehensively defeated Manly 34–8 in the 2007 NRL Grand Final with Greg Inglis winning the coveted Clive Churchill Medal.

Melbourne Storm warming up before a match in 2008

In Season 2008, Melbourne won their third minor premiership after the 26 rounds of regular competition. Despite becoming the first minor premiers since the McIntyre Final Eight System was introduced to lose their opening finals game 15–18 to the New Zealand Warriors, they then defeated the Brisbane Broncos 16–14, scoring in the last minute of their semi final. Bellamy was fined $50,000 for making scathing remarks regarding the NRL's decision to suspend Cameron Smith over a controversial "grapple tackle" on Brisbane's Sam Thaiday. Bellamy wrongly claimed that the administration was corrupt and that bookkeepers already knew that Smith would be denied the opportunity to play for the rest of the season. Along with Melbourne's CEO, Bellamy questioned the NRL's integrity in their opting to sideline Smith and not others who were guilty of committing similar tackles. In their qualifying final, Melbourne convincingly beat the Cronulla Sharks 28–0. But in their second successive grand final appearance against the Manly Sea Eagles, Manly demolished Melbourne 40–0.

At the Dally M Awards for season 2008, Melbourne picked up 6 awards, with 3 to Greg Inglis, and 1 for each of Billy Slater, Cameron Smith and Israel Folau. Billy Slater and Cameron Smith finished 2 points behind Manly's Matt Orford for the Dally M Medal with 22 points each. Billy Slater was awarded the international player of the year Golden Boot award for 2008, following on from Cameron Smith in 2007.

Following the 40–0 defeat, season 2009 was generally an average year on the field by the Storm's lofty standards, Melbourne finished 4th on the ladder after the home and away season, entering the finals clear underdogs. In Week One of the finals, the Storm romped 2008 Premiers Manly 40–12 in the qualifying final, ending their hopes of back-to-back premierships, and laying to bed some of the demons of the 2008 Grand Final. This was followed a fortnight later by a 40–10 thrashing of fierce rivals and 2006 Premiers Brisbane in the preliminary final, ensuring the Storm qualified for their fourth straight grand final (the first since Parramatta from 1981–1984). The Preliminary Final was also a monumental game for the Storm as it saw favourite son Billy Slater score his 100th career try and Cameron Smith became Storm's highest ever point scorer, surpassing Matt Orford's record of 877. The Melbourne Storm then capped off a truly brilliant late-season resurgence to end a rampaging Parramatta side in front of a parochial strong crowd at ANZ Stadium. Parramatta, coming off 10 wins from 11 games, led by the in-form young superstar Jarryd Hayne proved to be no match for the Storm's typical gameplan of grinding football, ensuring a defeat of the razzle-dazzle offload fuelled football of Parramatta. Despite the Storm leading Parramatta at one stage by 16 points, the Eels fought back in a late charge to bring the margin back to 7, with the Storm sealing a 23–16 win with a late Greg Inglis field goal. For his fantastic efforts, Fullback Billy Slater was awarded the 2009 Clive Churchill Medal for Man of the Match. Following the victory in 2009, the Melbourne Storm have been earned the title the NRL Team of the Decade for the 2000s.

However, due to poor negotiation of NRL TV broadcast rights, Channel 9 does not show regular Storm games at prime time in Melbourne.

In the late 2000s the Melbourne Storm were still running at a loss of up to $6M per season.

2010

On 11 January 2010, it was announced that Brian Waldron resigned his position as CEO to take up the same position at the Melbourne Rebels Super 15 team. He was replaced by Matt Hanson who was the Chief Operating Officer, however following the Salary cap revelations Matt Hanson was then stood down and Ron Gauci appointed.

The Storm's first match of the season was the 2010 World Club Challenge against equally dominant English side, the Leeds Rhinos, in very cold and wet conditions the Storm prevailed 18 – 10. For the 2010 NRL season, they will play their first three home games at Etihad Stadium before moving to their new purpose built permanent home ground, AAMI Park.

Salary cap breach

Following claims by a whistleblower that the club was keeping a second set of books, the NRL conducted an investigation in late 2009 and early 2010. After initially denying the claims, Storm officials confessed on 22 April 2010 that the club had committed serious and systematic breaches of the salary cap for the last five years by running a well-organized dual contract and bookkeeping system which left the NRL ignorant of $3.17 million in payments made to players outside of the salary cap, including $550,000 in 2007, $965,000 in 2009 and $1.03 million in 2010.

As a club's compliance with the NRL salary cap is supported by statutory declarations, the club's owners have requested that fraud and perjury charges be laid against those responsible, and has stated that any person who knew of the breach would be expelled from the club. The Victorian Fraud Squad began preliminary investigations on 23 April, and the Australian Securities and Investments Commission also made preliminary investigations and indicated an interest in investigating breaches of the Corporations Act. Storm executives had arranged for inflated invoices to be submitted to hide the payments to players. This involved submitting invoices of up to $20,000 above the real value of the services rendered with this amount paid directly to players by the third party suppliers although there is no suggestion that the suppliers were involved in submitting the inflated invoices.

As a result, NRL Chief Executive David Gallop stripped the Melbourne Storm of their 2007 and 2009 premierships and their 2006, 2007 and 2008 minor premierships (which have been withheld), fined them an Australian sporting record $1,689,000 ($1.1 million in NRL prize money which will be re-distributed equally between the remaining 15 clubs, $89,000 in prize money from the World Club Challenge which will be re-distributed to the Leeds Rhinos, and the maximum of $500,000 for breaching the salary cap), deducted all eight premiership points they had already received in the 2010 season, and barred them from receiving premiership points for the rest of the season.

The Storm initially accepted this decision without question but have since indicated they may appeal the loss of their two premierships and premiership points for the 2010 season, however the court action was later dropped with the Storm paying the NRL's legal costs. The Storm were also ordered to cut their payroll by $1,012,500 to meet the 2011 salary cap by December 31; failure to do so will result in the club being suspended for the 2011 NRL season.

Former CEO Brian Waldron, suspended chief executive officer and former chief financial officer Matt Hanson, and current chief financial officer Paul Gregory are alleged to have been the main culprits behind the breaches. Former chief financial officer Cameron Vale, who is now with the AFL's North Melbourne Football Club, was said to have been the whistleblower on the situation, but he has denied the allegations against him.

On 23 April 2010, Brian Waldron resigned from his position of chief executive of the Melbourne Rebels rugby union club after just six weeks of taking over the expansion team entering the new Super 15 competition. The AFL investigated (and later cleared) St Kilda Football Club's players' payments during Waldron's three-year time at the club alongside now-former Storm CEO Matt Hanson.

On April 23, the NRL seized a secret dossier hidden in the home of acting chief executive Matt Hanson. The dossier contains letters of offer to three of the Storm's star players (Greg Inglis, Billy Slater, and Cameron Smith) and another as yet unnamed player guaranteeing illegal payments in the form of goods from third parties. For one player with a $400,000 contract lodged with the NRL, the letter of offer was valued at $950,000, and contained a $20,000 gift voucher for a national retailer and a $30,000 boat. Other offers included a new car for a player's partner and $30,000 in home renovations. The offers together amounted to $700,000 of which the four players had already received $400,000. While Waldron had signed all the letters of offer only Inglis and Slater had signed theirs, albeit the letters were written in a way that the players may not have realised the extra payments were outside the cap.

The news was referred to by *The Age* newspaper as "The biggest scandal in Australian sports history". The Storm's scandal has also been likened to that of golfing great Tiger Woods and disgraced AFL player Ben Cousins.

Club supporters had mixed reactions and feelings towards the situation as the club was left with "dishonour and shame", as no club had ever been stripped of a competition title in 102 years of professional rugby league in Australia. Many fans dumped their jerseys and other memorabilia at the team's Carlton headquarters on hearing about the incident, and many others simply broke into tears; there was a feeling that former CEO Brian Waldron was to blame and not the players.

Prime Minister Julia Gillard, who is the club's number one female ticket holder, said that supporters would be shocked and saddened, but hoped that they would stand by the club as it rebuilt. Storm chairman Dr Rob Moodie apologised to the fans, many of whom publicly removed their Storm colours and dumped them in disgust.

> We are devastated. This is the lowest day for our club. We have betrayed the trust of the Australian people. We haven't played by the rules.
>
> —Dr Rob Moodie, The Courier Mail

Betting agencies received an "old fashioned betting sting" as some punters found out about the salary cap allegations before they became common knowledge, as the Storm were at $4.20 favourites to win the title at the time and $251 to win the wooden spoon. TAB Sportsbet has claimed it will be due to pay out at least $500,000 before betting was suspended.

Melbourne sports industry experts John Poulakakis (Chief commercial officer, Melbourne F.C.) and Martin Hirons (Melbourne sport business consultant) were reported in The Age, saying it could take little more than four weeks to two months to recover the $2 million it is believed to have already lost in sponsorship.

By April 30 the Age was reporting a surge in club membership of 700 over the five days since the scandal erupted, with members who had previously revoked their memberships contacting the club to have them reinstated.

The matter was referred to ASIC and the Victoria Police on July 15. The matter was also referred to the Australian Tax Office and the Victorian State Revenue Office the next day.

> We had some rats in our ranks. A small group of senior managers at the club orchestrated and concealed the extra payments. They are Brian Waldron, Matt Hanson, Paul Gregory, Peter O'Sullivan and Cameron Vale.
>
> —John Hartigan, chairman and CEO of News Limited, the owner of the Melbourne Storm, The Courier Mail

2011

On the 8th October the NRL draw was released showing that the Storm will play 9 of its first 13 games at home.

Season summaries

P=Premier, R=Runner-Up, M=Minor Premier, F=Finals Appearance, W=Wooden Spoon, S=Stripped of title

(Brackets represent Finals games)

Competition	Games Played	Games Won	Games Drawn	Games Lost	Ladder Position	P	R	M	F	W	Coach	Captain	Details
1998 NRL Season	24 (3)	17 (1)	1	6 (2)	3 / 20				X		Chris Anderson	Glenn Lazarus	Melbourne Storm 1998
1999 NRL Season	24 (4)	16 (3)	0	8 (1)	3 / 17	X			X				Melbourne Storm 1999
2000 NRL Season	26 (1)	14	1	11 (1)	6 / 14				X			Robbie Kearns	Melbourne Storm 2000
2001 NRL Season	26	11	1	14	9 / 14						Chris Anderson Mark Murray	Robbie Kearns Rodney Howe	Melbourne Storm 2001
2002 NRL Season	24	9	1	14	10 / 15						Mark Murray	Rodney Howe	Melbourne Storm 2002

Season											Coach	Captain	Team
2003 NRL Season	24 (2)	15 (1)	0	9 (1)	5 / 15				X		Craig Bellamy	Stephen Kearney	Melbourne Storm 2003
2004 NRL Season	24 (2)	13 (1)	0	11 (1)	6 / 15				X				Melbourne Storm 2004
2005 NRL Season	24 (2)	13 (1)	0	11 (1)	6 / 15				X			Robbie Kearns	Melbourne Storm 2005
2006 NRL Season	24 (3)	20 (2)	0	4 (1)	1 / 15		X	S	X			*Rotating Captains*	Melbourne Storm 2006
2007 NRL Season	24 (3)	21 (3)	0	3	1 / 16	S		S	X				Melbourne Storm 2007
2008 NRL Season	24 (4)	17 (2)	0	7 (2)	1 / 16		X	S	X			Cameron Smith	Melbourne Storm 2008
2009 NRL Season	24 (3)	14 (3)	1	9	4 / 16	S			X				Melbourne Storm 2009
2010 NRL Season	24	14	0	10	16 / 16					X			Melbourne Storm 2010
2011 NRL Season	0	0	0	0	0 / 16								Melbourne Storm 2011

Emblem and colours

Originally, the club favoured the name Melbourne Mavericks with a gunslinger logo holding a fistful of dollars. The club officials were all set to go with this until News Limited's Lachlan Murdoch told them to go with something else because the Mavericks sounded too American. Trams and Flying Foxes were also some ideas that came up. However co-CEOs Chris Johns and John Ribot decided to go with the themes lightning, power and storm. The club then became known as the Melbourne Storm.

The Storm was always going to go with the colours of their state, Victoria. These were navy blue with a white 'V'. But club consultant Peter McWhirter, from JAG fashion house, suggested that they should also have purple and gold to make their merchandise more attractive. These colours appear in the logo, however, on the home jersey they have varied. Between 1998 and 2004 these four colours also appeared but between 2005 and 2009, gold was completely removed and silver introduced. For 2010, gold has returned and silver omitted, also purple has now become the dominant colour in the jersey for the first time.

The home jerseys used by the Melbourne Storm.

1998   1999–2002   2003–2004   2005–2009   2010 – present

The away jerseys used by the Melbourne Storm.

1999–2000   2001–2002   2003–2004   2005–2007   2008–2009   2010–present

Rivalries

St George Illawarra Dragons: The Storm narrowly beat them in their first grand final in 1999, with a late penalty try putting the Storm in front. The following year Anthony Mundine declared that the Storm were not "worthy premiers" in the run up to their round 5 rematch. The Storm responded by beating the Dragons 70-10. In Round 18 the Dragons added to the rivalry by defeating the Storm 50-4. In 2006 the Storm defeated St. George Illawarra in the Preliminary Final. On 21 July 2008, Storm won a match at Olympic Park 26-0, that was highlighted by several ugly brawls. In 2009, the Storm beat them in the Round 1 home game 17-16 with a field goal in Golden Point (the second[citation needed] time the two teams were drawn at fulltime).

Brisbane Broncos. The Melbourne Storm has a strong rivalry with Brisbane, built in large part on the large number of finals games played between the teams, including one final in each year from 2004 to 2009. The move of Brisbane assistant coach Craig Bellamy to Melbourne has also been attributed to fueling the rivalry.

> "When Bellamy left here and went to Melbourne, the rivalry with them went up a notch then... their record is good against us."

Every year since Brisbane's victory over Melbourne in the 2006 Grand Final, Melbourne have ended the Broncos' season by knocking them out of the finals. Melbourne captain Cameron Smith commented on the rivalry prior to their 2009 Preliminary Final at Etihad Stadium.

> "A lot of people talk about us and Manly, but I think all the boys for whatever reason would say we take more satisfaction out of beating the Broncos...we love playing them...there is always plenty of feeling and intensity in the games...it probably wouldn't feel like September if we weren't playing them at some stage."

> – Cameron Smith, 26 September 2009

The Brisbane Broncos defeated the Storm 15–8, under controversial circumstances, in the 2006 NRL Grand Final. The Storm sought revenge through a 40–0 thrashing in the 2007 Qualifying Final at Olympic Park Stadium. The 2008 Semi-Final at Suncorp Stadium ended with Melbourne dramatically winning 16–14 with a try on the final play of the game. In 2009 Brisbane were again beaten by eventual premiers Melbourne, this time 40–10 at Etihad Stadium, catapulting the Storm to their 4th consecutive Grand Final Appearance.

The Broncos and Storm have also traded players recently, including Israel Folau, Scott Anderson and Greg Inglis (Storm to Broncos).

Manly Sea Eagles, whom the Storm defeated 34–8 in the 2007 Grand Final but lost to in the 2008 re-match in a history-making 0–40 loss. To add the rivalry, Melbourne beat Manly 40–12 in the opening final of the 2009 finals series, ending their bid to be back-to-back premiers.

> I haven't been a part of the matches previous to this year which built that rivalry but you certainly get a sense that interest in the game and the level of excitement and enthusiasm from the players goes up,"

> – Brett Finch, 8 September 2009

Stadium and attendances

Melbourne have played the vast majority of their home matches at the city's Olympic Park Stadium, affectionately coined "The Graveyard" by fans due to the incredible 77.2% winning percentage there. It was here that the club played their inaugural home match in the fourth round of the 1998 season on 3 April 1998, having come off the back of three successive away victories. In front of what remains the club's record Olympic Park attendance of 20,522, the team recorded a 26–16 victory over the North Sydney Bears.

The team remained at the ground until the end of the 2000 season. In the 2000 season they attracted an average home attendance of 14,622 still their highest season average. They played at Melbourne Cricket Ground for two games in 2000, and they won both times including the 70–10 thrashing of St George Illawarra Dragons in the Grand Final rematch from the previous year. Following steady attendance increases over the three years, it was decided to move home games to the much larger Docklands Stadium for the following year However, with the team ending

Olympic Park Stadium during a Toyota cup match.

up missing the finals, crowd numbers declined and it was decided to move the team back to Olympic Park. Attendances bottomed out to an average of 8,886 per home game in 2004, but they have steadily risen each year back to an average of 12,474 per home game for the 2008 season. A home attendance record of 33,427 was set in 2007 for the Preliminary Final against Parramatta, at Telstra Dome.

The Storm played their last game at Olympic Park in round 25, 29 August 2009, with a 36–4 thrashing of the Sydney Roosters. For the 2010 Telstra NRL Premiership season, the Storm's first three home games (rounds four, six and seven) were played at Etihad Stadium, before moving into their new home ground, AAMI Park in round nine (9 May 2010) against the Brisbane Broncos. The club had anticipated playing its first game at the new ground in round four against the St George Illawarra Dragons, however, a delay in construction required the opening to be pushed back several weeks.

Stadium records

Home Grounds used by the Storm

Top 5 Home Attendances

From	To	Stadium
1998	2000	Olympic Park Stadium
2001	2001	Docklands Stadium
2002	2009	Olympic Park Stadium
2010	present	AAMI Park

Crowd	Stadium	Opponent	Game Status	Date
33,427	Etihad Stadium	Parramatta Eels	Preliminary final	23/09/2007
27,687	Etihad Stadium	Brisbane Broncos	Preliminary final	26/09/2009
25,480	Etihad Stadium	St George-Illawarra Dragons	Regular Season – 1st home game following premiership (Good Friday)	02/04/2010
23,906	Etihad Stadium	New Zealand Warriors	Regular Season – Anzac Day also 1st game following Salary Cap revelations	25/04/2010
23,239	MCG	St George-Illawarra Dragons	Regular Season – Grand Final Rematch	03/03/2000

Statistics and records summary

For more details on this topic, see List of Melbourne Storm records.

Statistics and Records current as of end of 2010 NRL season

Individual honours

- Top 3 Highest point scorers:
  - Cameron Smith 1004 points (29 tries, 444 goals)
  - Matt Orford 877 points (52 tries, 333 goals, 3 field goals)
  - Matt Geyer 662 points (113 tries, 105 goals)
- Top 5 Try scorers:
  - Matt Geyer 113 tries
  - Billy Slater 112
  - Greg Inglis 78
  - Marcus Bai 70
  - Steven Bell 63
- Most points scored in a season: 242
  - Matt Geyer, 20 tries and 81 goals in the 1999 premiership season.
- Most tries in a season: 21
  - Israel Folau 2007 season.
- Dally M medalists: 1
  - 2006 – Cameron Smith
- Golden Boot Award (World's best player) winners: 3
  - 2007 – Cameron Smith
  - 2008 – Billy Slater
  - 2009 – Greg Inglis

Club honours

- National Rugby League Premierships: 1

1999

- National Rugby League runners up: 2

2006, 2008

- National Youth Competition premierships: 1

2009

- World Club Challenge wins: 2

2000, 2010

- Greatest winning margin: 64 points
  - Vs Wests Tigers, on 5 July 2001, Final score 64 – 0.
- Worst defeat: 46 points
  - Vs Bulldogs (50–4 on 10 August 2003)
  - Vs St. George Illawarra (50–4 on 4 June 2000)
- Most consecutive wins: 11
  - 28 May 2006 (Round 12) – 13 August 2006 (Round 23)
- All time head to head record
  - Since 1998, The Melbourne Storm have the following Win-Loss record.
  - Their wins percentage is currently the second best in the league only second to the Broncos.

Games	Wins	Drawn	Loss	Points for	Points against	Win %
343	211	5	127	8370	6235	62.20%

Coaches and captains

Coaches

- 1998-R7 2001: Chris Anderson
- R8 2001–2002: Mark Murray
- 2003–present: Craig Bellamy

Captains

- 1998–1999: Glenn Lazarus
- 2000: Robbie Kearns
- 2001: Robbie Kearns, Rodney Howe
- 2002: Rodney Howe
- 2003–2004: Stephen Kearney
- 2005: Robbie Kearns
- 2006: Cameron Smith, David Kidwell, Scott Hill, Matt Geyer, Michael Crocker
- 2007 R1-R16: Cameron Smith, Matt Geyer, Michael Crocker, Cooper Cronk, Matt King, Dallas Johnson
- 2007 R17-present: Cameron Smith

The rotating captaincy policy was in place from 2006 until Cameron Smith was made sole captain after the State of Origin series (Round 17) in 2007.

Players

For more details on this topic, see List of Melbourne Storm players.

Representative players

Main article: List of Melbourne Storm representatives

2010 squad

Although other players may play for the Melbourne Storm during the year, all NRL clubs are required to select a top 25 First Grade squad at the beginning of the season.

No.		Position	Player
		SR	Adam Blair
		PR	Jesse Bromwich
		LK	Hep Cahill
		FE	Dane Chisholm
73		HB	Cooper Cronk
		WG	Matt Duffie
		SR	Louis Fanene
		FE	Brett Finch

		HK	Ryan Hinchcliffe
62		SR	Ryan Hoffman
79		CE	Greg Inglis
		CE	William Isa
107		CE	Sam Joe
109		PR	Sinbad Kali
		HB	Luke Kelly
		PR	John Kite
		HK	Rory Kostjasyn
90		PR	Jeff Lima

No.		Position	Player
		LK	Todd Lowrie
		WG	Luke MacDougall
99		SR	Sika Manu
105		WG	Dane Nielsen
		PR	Bryan Norrie
		CE	Justin O'Neill
106		SR	Kevin Proctor
94		WG	Anthony Quinn
		LK	Billy Rogers
60		FB	Billy Slater
55		HK	Cameron Smith (C)
		CE	Chase Stanley
102		PR	Aiden Tolman
		SR	Atelea Vea
76		PR	Brett White
		FB	Gareth Widdop
		HK	James Woolford
		SR	Feleti Mahoni

Source: Storm 2010 Squad [1]

Team of the decade

As part of their 10 year celebrations in 2007, Melbourne Storm released a team of the decade. The 17 man team was selected by former assistant coach Greg Brentnall, foundation CEO John Ribot, Daily Telegraph journalist Steve Mascord and board member Frank Stanton.

No.		Position	Player
1		FB	Billy Slater
2		WG	Matt Geyer
3		CE	Matt King
4		CE	Greg Inglis
5		WG	Marcus Bai
6		FE	Scott Hill
7		HB	Brett Kimmorley
8		PR	Glenn Lazarus (captain)
9		HK	Cameron Smith

No.		Position	Player
10		PR	Robbie Kearns
11		SR	Dallas Johnson
12		SR	Stephen Kearney
13		LK	Tawera Nikau
14		RE	Rodney Howe
15		RE	David Kidwell
16		RE	Ryan Hoffman
17		RE	Cooper Cronk

Supporters

The Melbourne Storm's supporter base grew from almost 500,000 in 2004 to almost 800,000 in 2009, making them the fourth most popular rugby team. The club's supporter group, the "Graveyard Crew", make an Aussie-rules-style banner for the team to run through in important matches.

See also

- Rugby league in Victoria
- Sport in Australia
- Sport in Victoria

External links

Official sites
- Melbourne Storm official website [2]

News sites
- Storm at foxsports.com.au/league [3]

Statistics and information sites
- Melbourne Sttorm statistics tables [4]

- RL1908 Melbourne Storm history [5]

Clubs in the National Rugby League, 2010

Brisbane Broncos · Canterbury-Bankstown Bulldogs · Canberra Raiders · Cronulla-Sutherland Sharks
Gold Coast Titans · Manly-Warringah Sea Eagles · Melbourne Storm · Newcastle Knights
New Zealand Warriors · North Queensland Cowboys · Parramatta Eels · Penrith Panthers
St. George Illawarra Dragons · South Sydney Rabbitohs · Sydney Roosters · Wests Tigers

Former NSWRL / ARL / SL / NRL clubs

Adelaide Rams · Annandale · Balmain Tigers · Cumberland · Glebe
Gold Coast Chargers · Hunter Mariners · Illawarra Steelers · Newcastle · Newtown Jets
North Sydney Bears · Northern Eagles · Perth Reds · South Queensland Crushers
St. George Dragons · University · Western Suburbs Magpies

Melbourne Cricket Club

The **Melbourne Cricket Club** (**MCC**) is a sporting club based in Melbourne, Australia. It was founded in 1838 and is regarded as the oldest sporting club in Australia.

The MCC is responsible for management and development of the Melbourne Cricket Ground, a power given to it by the government-appointed MCG Trust and an Act of Parliament. This also guarantees the club's occupation of about 20 per cent of the stadium for its Members Reserve.

In 1859, the MCC was involved in the drafting of the first set of rules for Australian rules football, and in 1877 hosted the first game of Test cricket in history - played between Australia and England. In 1971, the ground hosted the first One Day International cricket match.

As well as cricket, the MCC is also an umbrella organisation for other sports - golf, lacrosse, baseball, tennis, lawn bowls, real tennis, shooting, field hockey, and squash.

Membership

The Melbourne Cricket Club is the largest sporting club in Australia. As of August 2009 there were 100,280 members of the club, of which 60,286 were full members, and 39,994 were "restricted" members, with 194,097 people registered on the waiting list. After the July 2010 member intake the waiting list for restricted membership consists of people nominated after 31st January 1995.

Full membership entitles members to entry to the Members' Reserve at the MCG for all cricket and football matches and most special sporting events.

Full members also enjoy a range of value-added benefits, which include reciprocal rights at clubs/stadiums around Australia and overseas as well as the opportunity to attend numerous club functions exclusive to MCC members. Restricted members also have access to events, with the exception of the AFL Grand Final. Full members, but not restricted members, are also permitted to nominate candidates for the waiting list, and to vote on club affairs.

Reciprocal Clubs

Members of the MCC are able to access the Members' Area of reciprocal clubs, typically whilst on a short visit to the area. These benefits, with the exclusion of the VRC and Etihad Stadium, are reserved for Full Members. These clubs include:

Etihad Stadium Axcess One, Melbourne Victoria Racing Club (VRC), Melbourne Sydney Cricket Ground, Sydney Brisbane Cricket Ground Trust (GABBA), Brisbane South Australian Cricket Association (Adelaide Oval), Adelaide West Australian Cricket Association (WACA Ground), Perth Tasmanian Cricket Association (Bellerive Oval), Hobart

And other overseas grounds including the Singapore and Hong Kong Cricket Clubs, the Cricket Club of India and the Marylebone Cricket Club (Lord's).

Cricket "Team of the Century"

On December 1, 1999, the MCC announced its cricket team of the century, with all players who had played at least one season for the club since 1906-07 being eligible for selection. The team as selected was:

1. Bill Ponsford
2. Colin McDonald
3. Dean Jones
4. Hunter Hendry
5. Paul Sheahan
6. Warwick Armstrong (Captain)
7. Hugh Trumble
8. Robert Templeton
9. Max Walker
10. Hans Ebeling
11. Bert Ironmonger
12. Vernon Ransford (12th Man)

All members of the team of the century except Robert Templeton had played at least one Test match for the Australian cricket team.

External links

* Melbourne Cricket Club official site [1]

Melbourne Football Club

Melbourne Football Club

Names	
Full name	Melbourne Football Club
Nickname(s)	The Demons, The Dees, Redlegs, Fuchsias (previously)
Season 2010	
Leading Goalkicker	Brad Green (55)
Best & Fairest	Brad Green
Club Details	
Founded	1859
Colours	Navy Blue and Red
Competition	Australian Football League
Chairman	Jim Stynes
Coach	Dean Bailey
Captain(s)	James McDonald
Premierships	12 (1900, 1926, 1939, 1940, 1941, 1948, 1955, 1956, 1957, 1959, 1960, 1964)
Ground(s)	Melbourne Cricket Ground (Capacity: 100,018 incl. standing room)
Other information	
Official website	www.melbournefc.com.au [1]

Guernsey:

Current season:
2010 Melbourne Football Club season

The **Melbourne Football Club**, nicknamed **The Demons,** is an Australian rules football club playing in the Australian Football League (AFL), based in Melbourne, Victoria.

In 1859, a few days after it was founded, some of its members created the code of football that it still plays. In 1862 it competed in what may be the earliest challenge trophy competition, was a foundation member of the Victorian Football Association (VFA) (1877), one of two associations and governing bodies formed in the same year and in 1897 it became a foundation member of the Victorian Football League (VFL) competition which later became the national Australian Football League (AFL).

In 2008 the club celebrated what was the 150th anniversary of the first meeting of its founding members, published "Melbourne FC — Since 1858 — An Illustrated History" and commemorated its formation by naming "150 Heroes" as well as a birthday logo which appears on its official jersey.

History

Origins

See also: Origins of Australian football

The seeds of the Melbourne Football Club were sown in 1858 with matches and early meetings involving influential cricketer Tom Wills, Scotch College headmaster Thomas H. Smith and Melbourne Cricket Club member and publican Jerry Bryant, a personal friend of Wills. Wills was instrumental in the push to establish senior football teams and in the same year wrote a letter pushing for a football club with a "code of laws" to be established. Melbourne's early team had a strong link to the Melbourne Cricket Club through its players playing both football and also for the cricket club and playing under the name of Melbourne, with Wills as its inaugural captain. The first mention of a game played is between Melbourne and South Yarra in September 1858.

The team was formally acknowledged and established as a separate sporting entity by the Melbourne Cricket Club on 14 May 1859.

Foundation

On 17 May in 1859, the Melbourne Football Club was incorporated at Bryant's Parade Hotel in East Melbourne. In attendance were Tom Wills, William Hammersley and J.B. Thompson (some sources also include Thomas H. Smith and/or H.C.A. Harrison). During the meeting, the first set of rules for the game of Australian rules football were written.

In 1861, Melbourne participated in the Caledonian Society's Games, but lost the trophy to the Melbourne University Football Club. The club pushed for its rules to be the accepted rules, however many of the early suburban matches were played under compromised rules decided between the captains of the competing clubs.

Although Melbourne was associated with the cricket club, it was not initially allowed to use the Melbourne Cricket Ground, so the club used a nearby field at Yarra Park as its home ground instead.

By 1866 several other clubs had also adopted an updated version of Melbourne's rules (which were drafted by H.C.A. Harrison).

During the 1870s, Melbourne fielded teams in the Seven Twenties and South Yarra Cup competitions.

After a visit to England by one of the club's officials, the colours of red and green were officially adopted by the club. Shortly following, the club began wearing a predominately red strip and became informally known by supporters as the "Redlegs".

The name "Redlegs" was coined after a Melbourne official returned from a trip to England with one set of red and another of blue woollen socks. Melbourne wore the red set while the blue set were, allegedly, given to the Carlton Football Club. This may be the source of Carlton's nickname, 'The Blueboys'.

Founders of the VFA

In 1877, the club became a foundation member of the Victorian Football Association (VFA). During this time, the club was known as the "Fuchsias". Melbourne never won a VFA premiership, although they were consistently one of the stronger teams in the competition, finishing runner-up four times, to Carlton in 1877 (the inaugural year of the VFA), to Geelong in 1878 and twice to Essendon in 1893 and 1894.

In 1889 the MFC was reincorporated into the MCC, and for many years the two organisations remained unhappily linked. The MFC's close association with the MCC allowed it to claim the MCG as its home ground and gave it access to a wealthy membership base, but Melbourne's reputation as an "establishment" club was not always an advantage. MCC members have the automatic right to attend all events at the ground, including MFC football games. This meant many potential members had a reduced incentive to join the football club, and Melbourne's membership remained one of the lowest in the competition.

Entry to the VFL

In 1897 the MFC was part of the breakaway Victorian Football League, and has been a part of the competition ever since. The team became known as the "Redlegs". This nickname is still used by some members and supporter groups within the club.

In 1900 Melbourne won its first VFL premiership, by defeating Fitzroy. Melbourne's greatest player of these early years of the VFL was Ivor Warne-Smith, who in 1926 won the club's first Brownlow Medal, the League's annual award for the fairest and best player. In that year Melbourne won its second flag. Warne-Smith went on to win a second Brownlow in 1928.

Age of greatness

Demons great Norm Smith (during his playing time at Fitzroy), whom many argue as being a catalyst for the club's early success as a player, then later as a coach of six premierships.

In 1933, the club changed its moniker to the "Demons".

F.V. "Checker" Hughes became Melbourne's coach in 1933, and under his leadership the club entered a golden age. In 1939, 1940 and 1941 Melbourne won its third, fourth and fifth flags. In 1946 Don Cordner became the second Demon to win the Brownlow. In 1947 Fred Fanning kicked a record 18 goals in the last game of the season. The following season Melbourne played the first ever drawn Grand Final, against Essendon, and went on to win the premiership the following week.

Norm Smith became Melbourne's coach in 1952, and the following season Ron Barassi played his first game. These two were to take Melbourne to new heights in the coming years. The Demons made the Grand Final in 1954, losing to Footscray, won the flag in 1955, 1956 and 1957, lost to Collingwood in 1958, and then won again in 1959 and 1960 with Smith as Coach and Barassi as Captain.

1964 Melbourne won its 12th flag, defeating Collingwood, at the end of the season, Barassi left the club to become captain-coach of Carlton. The following season Norm Smith was sacked after a dispute with the club. Although he was soon reinstated, things were never the same again for the Demons. The club appeared in Grand Finals from 1954–1960 and every Finals' Series from 1954–1964.

After the 1954 Grand Final loss to Footscray, no team was able to score 100 points against the club until Collingwood in round 5 1963. The next team was Geelong with 110 in round 1 1964. The 1965 season started with eight wins but only two wins from the next 10 games saw the end of the era. They would have to wait until 1987 for Melbourne to make the finals again.

Decades of disappointment

Poor recruiting zones and management meant that Melbourne, under coaches John Beckwith (1968–70), Ian Ridley (1971–73), Bob Skilton (1974–77), Dennis Jones (1978) and Carl Ditterich (1979–80), languished at the bottom of the League ladder throughout the 1970s. However, in 1971 the club started the season at the top and maintained that position until it lost to Collingwood in round 6. Melbourne was still in second place at the start of the second half of the season but within five weeks was out of the top four and finished with only two more wins and a draw.

In 1976 Melbourne missed what looked to be an almost certain finals appearance. In the final round they only needed to beat bottom side Collingwood and Footscray one place ahead needed to beat top side Carlton. They beat Collingwood at Victoria Park but an unexpected drawn game between Footscray and Carlton saw them miss fifth position. Had Footscray lost the game, Melbourne's superior percentage would have led them to a fifth spot finish.

Melbourne collected Wooden spoons in 1974 and 1978.

In 1980 the MFC finally legally separated from the MCC, becoming a public company, in an effort to attract more members and improve the club's finances. The season produced one less win than 1979 (five) but the club finished higher – 9th. It became evident that drastic action was needed for a club that had missed 16 finals series in a row the return of former star Ron Barassi was seen as the cure. When Barassi had left in 1965 it was felt that he would eventually return and his arrival caused much excitement and an expectation of immediate success.

In 1981, under the chairmanship of Sir Billy Snedden, Barassi returned to Melbourne as coach and immediately appointed Robert Flower as captain. In Barassi's first year the team finished last, but this was attributed to working out who the willing players were and the club won some powerful victories in the next three seasons. But although Brian Wilson won the Brownlow in 1982, and Peter Moore won it in 1984, Barassi was unable to get the club back into premiership contention.

In 1986 Barassi was replaced by John Northey. Under Northey, Melbourne made the finals in 1987, for the first time since 1964, losing the Preliminary Final to Hawthorn on the last kick of the game after the final siren. It was also the last game played by the team captain Robert Flower. In 1988 the Demons did even better, reaching the Grand Final, only to be defeated, again, by Hawthorn.

From 1987 to 1991 Melbourne had five positive win-loss differentials in successive seasons which the club had not been able to achieve since the 1954–65 era. Thereafter things went downhill for Northey, although Jim Stynes won the Brownlow in 1991. In 1992 the club finished 11th, and Northey was replaced by Neil Balme as coach. Balme coached Melbourne into the finals in 1994, but a last game loss to Brisbane saw them drop out of the top eight in 1995, and the club lingered at or near the bottom of the ladder for most of the 1996 season.

Facing oblivion

See also: Melbourne Football Club/Hawthorn Football Club planned merger

By 1996 the club was also in dire financial straits. The board, headed by past player Ian Ridley decided on the desperate step of a merger with Hawthorn. In the ensuing weeks, a passionate debate was fought between pro and anti-merger supporters. In the first few days of this debate, life-long supporters Mark and Anthony Jenkins met with coterie member George Zagon to form the Demon Alternative – an anti-merger group that was to significantly impact on the plans of the incumbent board.

The Demon Alternative recruited members from a wide range of areas but the two most recognised were former player and politician Brian Dixon and Rabbi Joseph Gutnick. The group quickly organised itself into a credible option for Melbourne supporters; however given the support of the AFL and other factors, when the merger issue was put to a vote, a majority of Melbourne members supported the board. In a meeting on the opposite side of town, Hawthorn members rejected their board's proposal and eventually the merger was defeated.

In the aftermath of the merger meetings, Ridley focused on a compromise with the Demons Alternative to ensure that Melbourne could continue as a viable business. His board co-opted Gutnick and Mark Jenkins onto the board and a truce of sorts was struck between all parties.

In the months following the 1996 merger vote, the businessman and Joseph Gutnick became president. He put $3 million of his own money into the club, and sacked Balme as coach midway through the 1997 season. In 1998, under new coach Neale Daniher, the club spent most of the season in the top eight and beat the eventual premiers Adelaide in the Qualifying Final. Melbourne also eliminated St Kilda, but lost to North Melbourne in the Preliminary Final. In 1999 Melbourne finished in the bottom three.

Partial revival

In 2000 Daniher took Melbourne to the Grand Final, but the Demons were convincingly beaten by a rampaging Essendon. The members had expected a new era of success, but in 2001 it was same old story: Melbourne finished 11th. In 2002, although Melbourne again made the finals, Gutnick was voted out by the members.

In 2003 Melbourne plunged into a new crisis, winning only five games for the year and posting a $1 million loss. President Gabriel Szondy resigned and it seemed that Daniher's tenure as coach was under threat. But, continuing the recent trend, in 2004, Melbourne climbed the ladder again, winning 14 games and leading the competition, albeit for one round only, in Round 18. And although the team lost its remaining four games, the club still made the finals, only to lose narrowly to Essendon.

During the 2004 post-season the Demons tragically lost defender Troy Broadbridge in the Asian tsunami, when he was swept off Phi Phi island in Thailand. He was walking along the beach with his wife Trisha when the tsunami struck. His body was found on 3 January 2005, and brought home. A funeral was held on 20 January 2005 in recognition to the No. 20 guernsey he wore during his playing days. During the 2005 off-season, the whole team travelled to the island in which Broadbridge was killed to build a new school for those struck by the tsunami. The No.20 jumper was then rested for two years.

Melbourne started 2005 strongly, being second after Round 12, however losing momentum by Round 19 appeared unlikely to play finals, then wins against Western Bulldogs, Geelong at Geelong (where Melbourne had not won since the late 1980s), and Essendon in Round 22, placed the club seventh and a finals berth,only to lose the Elimination Final to Geelong by 55 points.

In 2006, after a slow start, Melbourne again finished the season in seventh position. After defeating St Kilda in the first Elimination Final by 18 points the season ended the following week when Fremantle beat the Demons by 28 points. Melbourne's coach Neale Daniher had become the second longest-serving coach of Melbourne, and the longest-surviving in the entire history of the VFL/AFL not to have coached a premiership side.

Daniher's departure and rebuilding

Season 2007 was a poor one for Melbourne. After losing their first nine games through a combination of injury and poor form, they finally broke through with wins against Adelaide and Collingwood. But, following a loss to Richmond the next week, Daniher was sacked by the club, and Mark Riley was appointed as caretaker coach. The sacking of Daniher caused significant tension at the club. It was an unpopular move with the leadership group, and captain David Neitz expressed his dissatisfaction over the decision. Winning three of their remaining nine games, Melbourne avoided the wooden spoon and finished 14th.

Dean Bailey was appointed as coach for the 2008 season, but success did not follow, as Melbourne lost their first six matches, before breaking through with a record comeback win in round 7 against Fremantle. They showed signs of improvement, putting up a good fight in round 9 against top-of-the-ladder team Hawthorn, who were undefeated at the time. Melbourne had to wait until Round 14 for the second win. After good performances against Collingwood, Richmond, and Sydney in the preceding weeks, the Demons defeated Brisbane by a solitary point in the two team's first encounter at the MCG in nine years.

2008–Birthday celebrations and financial crisis

Off field, the club remained in serious turmoil. In the first sign of troubles in February 2008, CEO Steve Harris resigned. Paul Gardner addressed the media in response to comments from the club's auditors spelling disaster for the club. Gardner reiterated that the club had posted a $97,000 profit at the end of 2007. Harris was replaced by the high profile former Wimbledon tennis champion Paul McNamee. Despite celebrating the club's birthday with an official mid-season function at Crown Casino, shortly afterward chairman Paul Gardner resigned, handing the presidency to former club champion Jim Stynes who inherited a $4.5 million debt, which media pundits suggested would cripple the club. Hawthorn's president Jeff Kennett caused controversy with remarks about relocating the Demons to the Gold Coast, something which Stynes spoke against. AFL CEO Andrew Demetriou dispelled the notion that the club's future was in doubt, but admitted that Stynes' board faced a huge challenge. Demons legend, games and goalkicking record holder, David Neitz, announced his immediate retirement due to injury on 9 May.

Stynes wasted no time attempting to change the club's direction and eliminate debt, introducing a drive called "Debt Demolition", beginning with a call for members to sign-up. Under Stynes' direction, the new board sacked Paul McNamee after just four months. During McNamee's tenure, he had drawn criticisms for holidaying in Wimbledon to compete in a legends match and after his sacking an attempt to lure Brisbane Lions star Jonathan Brown was also revealed. A 5 August fundraiser raised $1.3

million AUD. The club raised well over $3 million AUD. Despite the reduced debt, in November new club CEO Cameron Schwab declared that it required urgent AFL assistance to continue, requesting additional funding to its special annual distribution. In December, a fallout in negotiations between the Melbourne Cricket Club resulted in the MCC not committing an expected $2 million to the club and Schwab declared that the club's immediate future was in doubt.

This doubt was quickly put to bed when the AFL and MCC finalised negotioations. The AFL committed $1million to the club in 2009, with the MCC matching the AFL contribution.

2009–Improvement

By the mid-point of the 2009 season, things had improved both on and off field for Melbourne. They had secured a record number of members, remerged with the MCC, knocked-off more debt and were starting to show some fight on field. Players such as Liam Jurrah had begun to emerge as top young talents and were catching the eye of the footballing public. However, on the eve of the Round 14 clash against West Coast, influential president Jim Stynes announced that he had cancer, this evoked a very emotional response from the footballing public and the club lifted from three embarrassing defeats the weeks before to convincingly beat West Coast in front of a passionate MCG crowd. At the end of the season, Melbourne finished 16th on the ladder and for a second year in a row won no more than four games which granted them a Priority Pick in the National Draft. Melbourne therefore had picks 1 and 2 in the draft to build on their young talent. At the end of the season fan favourites Russell Robertson, Matthew Whelan and Paul Wheatley announced that they would no longer be playing for Melbourne in 2010 and beyond. During September 2009, midfielder Brock McLean asked to be a traded and a deal involving Carlton's pick 11 in the National Draft was agreed to.

2010–Debt-free

After losing their first game against Hawthorn by 50 points and a narrow defeat to Collingwood, Melbourne strung together three consecutive wins against Adelaide, Richmond and Brisbane, making it the first time they have won three games in a row since 2006. Their 50-point win over the previously undefeated Brisbane Lions, was the upset of the round, along with Port Adelaide's shock win against St Kilda. However, losses to North Melbourne, Western Bulldogs and the poorly performing West Coast seemed to end the Dees finals dream. However, the Demons made a comeback when they narrowly defeated Port Adelaide by one point, at a home game in Darwin. Though subsequent losses to Geelong and Carlton lowered the Demons spirits, they fought a hard battle against arch-enemy Collingwood and came out with a draw. Despite showing great resilience against Collingwood, the Dees were handed two further blows with losses to Adelaide and St Kilda. The following round saw a match-up with Essendon that would decide either team's fate. Though both teams fought hard, the Demons came out on top by 19 points, keeping their finals dreams alive and moving above Essendon on the ladder. The Demons then travelled to Perth, where after a poor start, they fought back, but fell away to lose by 11 points to finals aspirant Fremantle. The next week they faced Sydney at the MCG, for the first time since 2006. Melbourne defeated Sydney by 73 points, thereby inflicting the worst loss Sydney has ever had, under premiership winning coach, Paul Roos. This was followed up with a 10-point win over the Brisbane Lions at the Gabba where the Demons had not won since 2006. The Demons finished the 2010 season in 12th position with eight and a half wins (more than double their win tallies from 2008 and 2009 combined); that could have easily been eleven if not for close results against 2010 Grand Finalists Collingwood during the course of the year (a loss in round 2 and a draw in round 12) and the Western Bulldogs (a four-point loss in round seven).

On 5 August the club announced that Jim Stynes' goal of wiping out the club's debt that had plaugued them for so long had finally been achieved. The event also saw Melbourne enveiled its new logo, which incorporates a trident, the Southern Cross, as well as the inaugural rules of Australian rules football.

Club symbols

Club mascot

Main article: AFL Mascot Manor

The current club mascot is Ronald Deeman, or also known as Ruckle. He carries a trident, has devil horns and has a pointed devil tail.

Club jumper

The current Melbourne club jumper consists of a red V-neck on a navy blue background, with the AFL logo on the front as well as the Hankook Tyres logo, their main sponsor. Kaspersky Lab, Melbourne's other sponsor, has a logo on the back beneath the player's number.

The Melbourne clash strip, new in 2009, consists of a red backing with a traditional blue Demon on the chest. This replaced the much derided grey and red jumper of 2008.

Melbourne also have a third jumper which acts as both a pre-season and a clash jumper. This jumper is white with a blue vee below the chest and the same demon that appears on the red clash jumper but in red instead of blue. On 19 September 2009, CEO Cameron Schwab announced that the club would return to the colours the Demons wore during their era of success in the 1960s. Schwab advised that the current tomato red V would be replaced by one closer to the colour of blood and that the Blue/Purple body would be replaced by Dark Navy. It was not stated whether they would wear the changed jumper for the 2010 season.

Club song

The official Melbourne Club song is called "It's A Grand Old Flag" (sung to the tune of "You're a Grand Old Flag"). The current version of the song played at the ground was recorded in 1972 by the Fable Singers.

It's a grand old flag,

It's a high flying flag,

It's the emblem for me and for you.

It's the emblem of the team we love,

The team of the Red and the Blue.

Ev'ry heart beats true,

For the Red and the Blue,

And we sing this song to you (What do we sing!).

Should old acquaintance be forgot,

Keep your eye on the Red and the Blue,

Support

Membership base

Year	Members	Finishing position
1998	17,870	4th
1999	19,713	14th
2000	18,227	2nd
2001	22,940	11th
2002	20,152	6th
2003	20,844	14th
2004	25,252	7th
2005	24,220	8th
2006	24,698	5th
2007	28,077	14th
2008	29,619	16th
2009	31,506	16th

2010	33,358[1]	12th

[1] Numbers from afl.com.au as of June 30, 2010

[2] Season in progress

Prominent fans

- John So, former Lord Mayor of Melbourne (former number one male ticket holder)
- Terry Bracks, wife of Steve Bracks (number one female ticket holder)
- Hamish Blake, radio presenter on FOX FM
- Max Walker, former Australian cricketer and TV presenter (who played for MFC from 1967–1972)
- Derryn Hinch, radio journalist
- Mal Walden, journalist
- Matt Damon, hollywood actor
- Wilbur Wilde, saxophonist
- Beverley O'Connor, journalist and former club vice-chairman
- Alan Stockdale, President of the Liberal Party and former Treasurer of Victoria
- Ian Henderson, Victorian news reporter

Club honours

Premiership Record	Premiership Record		
Competition	Level	Wins	Year Won
VFL/AFL	Premiers	12	1900, 1926, 1939, 1940, 1941, 1948, 1955, 1956, 1957, 1959, 1960, 1964
VFL/AFL	Runners Up	5	1946, 1954, 1958, 1988, 2000
VFL/AFL	Night/Pre-Season Premierships	3	1971, 1987, 1989
VFL/AFL	Reserves	12	1931, 1932, 1933, 1934, 1935, 1939, 1949, 1956, 1969, 1970, 1984, 1993
VFL/AFL	Under 19s	6	1947, 1953, 1964, 1971, 1981, 1983
VFL/AFL	McClelland Trophy	4	1955, 1956, 1958, 1990
VFL/AFL	Minor Premiers	9	1939, 1940, 1955, 1956, 1957, 1958, 1959, 1960, 1964
VFL/AFL	Wooden Spoons	14	1925, 1927, 1928, 1932, 1942, 1946, 1949, 1950, 1953, 1965, 1997, 2008, 2009
VFA/VFL	Runners Up	4	1877, 1878, 1893, 1894

| Challenge Cup | Premiers | 5 | 1864, 1868, 1870, 1872, 1876 |
| Challenge Cup | Runners Up | 8 | 1862, 1863, 1865, 1866, 1871, 1873, 1874, 1875 |

Melbourne Team of the Century

The Melbourne Football Club Team of the Century was announced on June 24, 2000 at Crown Casino. The selectors were Percy Beames (former player and journalist), Lynda Carroll (club historian), Bill Guest (MFC Director), Greg Hobbs (journalist), John Mitchell (former MFC and MCC President), Linda Pearce (journalist), Dudley Phillips (supporter), Stephen Phillips (media consultant) and Mike Sheahan (journalist), with CEO John Anderson as non-voting chairman.

Melbourne Team of the Century			
B:	John Beckwith	Tassie Johnson	Don Cordner
HB:	Noel McMahen	Gary Hardeman	Don Williams
C:	Brian Dixon	Allan La Fontaine	Robert Flower
HF:	Hassa Mann	Ivor Warne-Smith	Garry Lyon
F:	Jack Mueller	Norm Smith	Percy Beames
Foll:	Denis Cordner	Ron Barassi (Captain)	Stuart Spencer
Int:	Frank Adams	Albert Chadwick	Wally Lock
	Laurie Mithen	Jim Stynes	Todd Viney
Coach:	Norm Smith		

Stan Alves, Ian Ridley, Bob B. Johnson and Greg Wells were all named as emergencies.

150 Heroes

Melbourne FC announced its "150 Heroes" to celebrate its 150th birthday at Crown Casino on 7 June 2008. Each player, or their closest relative, were presented with an official 150 heroes medallion. The criteria for inclusion was games played (minimum of 100), best-and-fairest awards, premierships, Brownlow Medals, contribution to the club and State representation. Those who died in the war were judged based on their achievements before their passing. The heroes named were:

Jim Abernethy, Frank Adams, Bill Allen, Stan Alves, Syd Anderson, Tony Anderson, Lance Arnold, Ron Baggott, Garry Baker, Harold Ball, Ron Barassi, Percy Beames, John Beckwith, George Rickford, Ray Biffin, Barry Bourke, Harry Brereton, Cameron Bruce, Keith Carroll, Geoff Case, Albert Chadwick, Noel Clarke, Geoff Collins, Jack Collins, Chris Connolly, Bob Corbett, Denis Cordner, Don Cordner, Ted Cordner, Vin Coutie, Harry Coy, Jim Davidson, Frank Davis, Ross Dillon, Carl Ditterich, Brian Dixon, Len Dockett, Adrian Dullard, Hugh Dunbar, Richie Emselle, Fred Fanning, Jeff Farmer,

Matthew Febey, Steven Febey, Dick Fenton-Smith, Rolie Fischer, Robert Flower, Laurie Fowler, Maurice Gibb, Peter Giles, Terry Gleeson, Brad Green, Rod Grinter, George Haines, Gary Hardeman, Henry Harrison, Gerard Healy, Greg Healy, Dick Hingston, Paul Hopgood, Danny Hughes, Anthony Ingerson, Eddie Jackson, Alan Johnson, Bob B. Johnson, Tassie Johnson, Trevor Johnson, Travis Johnstone, Gordon Jones, Les Jones, Bryan Kenneally, Allan La Fontaine, Clyde Laidlaw, Frank Langley, Jack Leith, Andrew Leoncelli, Chalie Liley, Wally Lock, Harry Long, John Lord, Andy Lovell, Brett Lovett, Glenn Lovett, Garry Lyon, Hassa Mann, George Margitich, Peter Marquis, Bernie Massey, Anthony McDonald, James McDonald, Fred McGinis, Shane McGrath, Bob McKenzie, Col McLean, Ian McLean, Noel McMahen, Ken Melville, Laurie Mithen, Peter Moore, Jack Mueller, David Neitz, Stephen Newport, Jack O'Keefe, Andrew Obst, Gordon Ogden, Greg Parke, Joe Pearce, Jack Purse, Ian Ridley, Guy Rigoni, Frank Roberts, Russell Robertson, Alby Rodda, Brian Roet, Peter Rohde, Alan Rowarth, David Schwarz, Norm Smith, Steven Smith, Earl Spalding, Stuart Spencer, Charlie Streeter, Steven Stretch, Jim Stynes, Tony Sullivan, Dick Taylor, Ted Thomas, Ian Thorogood, Stephen Tingay, John Townsend, Keith Truscott, Geoff Tunbridge, Bill Tymms, Barrie Vagg, Frank Vine, Todd Viney, Ivor Warne-Smith, Ray Wartman, Athol Webb, Greg Wells, Jeff White, Sean Wight, Don Williams, Brian Wilson, Stan Wittman, Shane Woewodin, Graeme Yeats, Charlie Young, Adem Yze

SomeWikipedia:Avoid weasel words controversy surrounded the inclusion of current football manager and assistant coach Chris Connolly (who had played less than 100 games) and several current players and the non-inclusion of players such as Tom Wills (founder), Allen Jakovich and Troy Broadbridge (who died but not during wartime).[citation needed]

Current squad

As of 12 February 2010:

1 Matthew Warnock	19 Addam Maric	37 Max Gawn
2 Nathan Jones	20 Colin Garland	39 Neville Jetta
3 Clint Bartram	21 Daniel Bell	40 Mark Jamar
4 Jack Watts	22 Brent Moloney	44 Rohan Bail
5 Jordan Gysberts	23 James McDonald	43 Jamie Bennell
6 Matthew Bate	(captain)	46 Sam Blease
7 Brad Miller	24 Liam Jurrah	47 James Strauss
8 James Frawley	25 Kyle Cheney	48 Jack Fitzpatrick
9 Jack Trengove	27 Jared Rivers	**Rookies:**
10 Cale Morton	28 Joel Macdonald	13 Jordie McKenzie
11 Paul Johnson	30 Tom McNamara	26 John Meesen
12 Colin Sylvia	31 Tom Scully	29 Michael Newton
14 Lynden Dunn	32 Cameron Bruce	38 Danny Hughes
15 Ricky Petterd	33 Austin Wonaeamirri	42 Jake Spencer
16 Jack Grimes	34 Stefan Martin	50 Rhys Healey
18 Brad Green	35 Luke Tapscott	
	36 Aaron Davey	

Honour board

The honour board is listed from the first VFL/AFL season and includes the following individual awards:

- **Keith 'Bluey' Truscott Medal** – awarded to Melbourne Football Club's Best & Fairest. Named after Keith Truscott who died in World War II.
- Leading goalkicker award
- **Harold Ball Memorial Trophy** – awarded to the Best First Year Player. Named in honour of Harold Ball who died in World War II.

Season	Position	President	Secretary/General Manager/CEO	Coach	Captain	Best and Fairest	Leading Goalkicker (Total)	Best First Year Player
1897	4th	H. C. A. Harrison	R. C. McLeod		Ned Sutton		Jack Leith (22)	
1898	6th	H. C. A. Harrison	Amos Norcott		Ned Sutton		Charlie Young (21)	
1899	6th	H. C. A. Harrison	Amos Norcott		Eddie Sholl		Jack Leith (21)	
1900	1st	H. C. A. Harrison	Amos Norcott		Dick Wardill		Tommy Ryan (24)	

1901	5th	H. C. A. Harrison	Amos Norcott		William C. McClelland		Frank Langley (17)	
1902	4th	H. C. A. Harrison	Amos Norcott		William C. McClelland		Jack Leith (26)	
1903	7th	H. C. A. Harrison	Amos Norcott		William C. McClelland		Vince Coutie (19)	
1904	6th	H. C. A. Harrison	Amos Norcott		William C. McClelland		Vince Coutie (39)	
1905	8th	H. C. A. Harrison	Amos Norcott		Frank Langley		Harry Cordner (16)	
1906	8th	H. C. A. Harrison	Amos Norcott		Arthur Sowden		Basil Onyons (16)	
1907	7th	T. F. Morkham	George Beachcroft	Alex Hall	Vince Coutie		Jack Leith (21)	
1908	8th	T. F. Morkham	Amos Norcott	Alex Hall	Hugh Purse		Vince Coutie (37)	
1909	5th	T. F. Morkham	J. A. Harper	Alex Hall	Bernie Nolan		Harry Brereton (34)	
1910	9th	T. F. Morkham	G. W. Lamb	Eddie Drohan	Vince Coutie		Stan Fairbarn (24)	
1911	7th	A. A. Aitken	G. W. Lamb		Vince Coutie		Harry Brereton (46)	
1912	6th	William C. McClelland	Andrew Manzie	Alex Hall	Alf George		Harry Brereton (56)	
1913	9th	William C. McClelland	Andrew Manzie	Alex Hall	Alf George		Mick Maguire (13)	
1914	9th	William C. McClelland	Andrew Manzie	Alex Hall	Len Incigneri		Arthur Best (30)	
1915	4th	William C. McClelland	Andrew Manzie	Jack McKenzie	Jack McKenzie		Roy Park (35)	
1916–1918[1]	—	William C. McClelland	Andrew Manzie	George Heinz	George Heinz			

1919	9th	William C. McClelland	Andrew Manzie	George Heinz	George Heinz		George Heinz (15)	
1920	8th	William C. McClelland	Andrew Manzie	Gerald Brosnan	George Heinz		Harry Harker (23)	
1921	6th	William C. McClelland	Andrew Manzie	Percy Wilson	Percy Wilson		Harry Harker (47)	
1922	6th	William C. McClelland	Andrew Manzie	Percy Wilson	Percy Wilson		Harry Harker (47)	
1923	9th	William C. McClelland	Andrew Manzie	Percy Wilson	Percy Wilson		Percy Tulloh (31)	
1924	8th	William C. McClelland	Andrew Manzie	Gordon Rattray	Albert Chadwick		Percy Tulloh (24)	
1925	3rd	William C. McClelland	Andrew Manzie	Albert Chadwick	Albert Chadwick		Harry Davie (56)	
1926	1st	William C. McClelland	Andrew Manzie	Albert Chadwick	Albert Chadwick		Harry Moyes (55)	
1927	5th	Vernon Ransford	Andrew Manzie	Albert Chadwick	Albert Chadwick		Harry Davie (40)	
1928	3rd	Vernon Ransford	Andrew Manzie	Ivor Warne-Smith	Ivor Warne-Smith		Bob C. Johnson (55)	
1929	5th	Joe Blair	Andrew Manzie	Ivor Warne-Smith	Ivor Warne-Smith		Dick Taylor (30)	
1930	5th	Joe Blair	Andrew Manzie	Ivor Warne-Smith	Ivor Warne-Smith		George Margitich (73)	
1931	8th	Joe Blair	Andrew Manzie	Ivor Warne-Smith	Ivor Warne-Smith		George Margitich (66)	
1932	9th	Joe Blair	Charlie Streeter	Ivor Warne-Smith	Ivor Warne-Smith		George Margitich (60)	
1933	10th	Joe Blair	Percy Page	Frank 'Checker' Hughes	Ivor Warne-Smith		Bob C. Johnson (62)	
1934	6th	Joe Blair	Percy Page	Frank 'Checker' Hughes	Colin Niven		Jack Mueller (52)	

1935	6th	Joe Blair	Percy Page	Frank 'Checker' Hughes	Colin Niven	Allan La Fontaine	Maurie Gibb (59)	
1936	3rd	Joe Blair	Percy Page	Frank 'Checker' Hughes	Allan La Fontaine	Allan La Fontaine	Eric Glass (56)	
1937	3rd	Joe Blair	Percy Page	Frank 'Checker' Hughes	Allan La Fontaine	Jack Mueller	Ron Baggott (51)	
1938	5th	Joe Blair	Percy Page	Frank 'Checker' Hughes	Allan La Fontaine	Norm Smith	Norm Smith (80)	
1939	1st	Joe Blair	Percy Page	Frank 'Checker' Hughes	Allan La Fontaine	Jack Mueller	Norm Smith (54)	
1940	1st	Joe Blair	Percy Page	Frank 'Checker' Hughes	Allan La Fontaine	Ron Baggott	Norm Smith (86)	
1941	1st	Joe Blair	Percy Page	Frank 'Checker' Hughes	Allan La Fontaine	Allan La Fontaine	Norm Smith (89)	
1942	8th	Joe Blair	Jack Chessell	Percy Beames	Percy Beames	Allan La Fontaine	Fred Fanning (37)	
1943	7th	Joe Blair	Jack Chessell	Percy Beames	Percy Beames	Don Cordner	Fred Fanning (62)	
1944	8th	Joe Blair	Jack Chessell	Percy Beames	Percy Beames	Norm Smith	Fred Fanning (87)	
1945	9th	Joe Blair	Jack Chessell	Frank 'Checker' Hughes	Norm Smith	Fred Fanning	Fred Fanning (67)	
1946	2nd	Joe Blair	Jack Chessell	Frank 'Checker' Hughes	Norm Smith	Jack Mueller	Jack Mueller (58)	
1947	6th	William Flintoft	Jack Chessell	Frank 'Checker' Hughes	Norm Smith	Wally Lock	Fred Fanning (97)	

1948	1st	William Flintoft	Alex Gray	Frank 'Checker' Hughes	Don Cordner	Alby Rodda	Lance Arnold (41)	
1949	5th	William Flintoft	Alex Gray	Allan La Fontaine	Don Cordner	Len Dockett	Robert McKenzie (40)	
1950	4th	Albert Chadwick	A. S. Thompson	Allan La Fontaine	Shane McGrath	Denis Cordner	Denis Cordner (36)	
1951	12th	Albert Chadwick	Jim Cardwell	Allan La Fontaine	Denis Cordner	Noel McMahen	Robert McKenzie (40)	
1952	6th	Albert Chadwick	Jim Cardwell	Norm Smith	Denis Cordner	Geoff McGivern	Noel Clarke (49)	
1953	11th	Albert Chadwick	Jim Cardwell	Norm Smith	Denis Cordner	Ken Melville	Robert McKenzie (38)	
1954	2nd	Albert Chadwick	Jim Cardwell	Norm Smith	Geoff Collins	Denis Cordner	Noel Clarke (51)	
1955	1st	Albert Chadwick	Jim Cardwell	Norm Smith	Noel McMahen	Stuart Spencer	Stuart Spencer (34)	
1956	1st	Albert Chadwick	Jim Cardwell	Norm Smith	Noel McMahen	Stuart Spencer	Bob B. Johnson (43)	
1957	1st	Albert Chadwick	Jim Cardwell	Norm Smith	John Beckwith	John Beckwith	Athol Webb (56)	
1958	2nd	Albert Chadwick	Jim Cardwell	Norm Smith	John Beckwith	Laurie Mithen	Ron Barassi, Jr. (44), Athol Webb (44)	
1959	1st	Albert Chadwick	Jim Cardwell	Norm Smith	John Beckwith	Laurie Mithen	Ron Barassi, Jr. (46)	
1960	1st	Albert Chadwick	Jim Cardwell	Norm Smith	Ron Barassi	Brian Dixon	Ian Ridley (38)	
1961	3rd	Albert Chadwick	Jim Cardwell	Norm Smith	Ron Barassi	Ron Barassi	Bob B. Johnson (36)	
1962	4th	Albert Chadwick	Jim Cardwell	Norm Smith	Ron Barassi	Hassa Mann	Laurie Mithen (37)	

1963	3rd	Donald Duffy	Jim Cardwell	Norm Smith	Ron Barassi	Hassa Mann	Barry Bourke (48)	
1964	1st	Donald Duffy	Jim Cardwell	Norm Smith	Ron Barassi	Ron Barassi	John Townsend (35)	
1965	7th	Donald Duffy	Jim Cardwell	Norm Smith	Hassa Mann	John Townsend	John Townsend (34)	
1966	11th	Donald Duffy	Jim Cardwell	Norm Smith	Hassa Mann	Terry Leahy	Barrie Vagg (20)	
1967	7th	Donald Duffy	Jim Cardwell	Norm Smith	Hassa Mann	Hassa Mann	Hassa Mann (38)	
1968	8th	Donald Duffy	Jim Cardwell	John Beckwith	Hassa Mann	Ray Groom	Hassa Mann (29)	
1969	12th	Donald Duffy	Jim Cardwell	John Beckwith	Hassa Mann	John Townsend	Ross Dillon (48)	
1970	10th	Donald Duffy	Jim Cardwell	John Beckwith	Tassie Johnson	Frank Davis	Ross Dillon (41)	
1971	7th	Donald Duffy	Jim Cardwell	Ian Ridley	Frank Davis	Greg Wells	Paul Callery (38)	
1972	8th	Donald Duffy	Jim Cardwell	Ian Ridley	Frank Davis	Stan Alves	Greg Parke (63)	
1973	10th	Donald Duffy	Jim Cardwell	Ian Ridley	Stan Alves	Carl Ditterich	Ross Brewer (32)	
1974	12th	Donald Duffy	Jim Cardwell	Bob Skilton	Stan Alves	Stan Alves	Ross Brewer (40)	
1975	10th	John Mitchell	Jim Cardwell	Bob Skilton	Stan Alves	Laurie Fowler	Greg Wells (32)	
1976	6th	John Mitchell	Ivan Moore	Bob Skilton	Stan Alves	Greg Wells	Ray Biffin (47)	
1977	11th	John Mitchell	Ray Manley	Bob Skilton	Greg Wells	Robert Flower	Ross Brewer (26)	
1978	12th	John Mitchell	Ray Manley	Dennis Jones	Greg Wells	Garry Baker	Henry Coles (33)	
1979	11th	Wayne Reid	Ray Manley	Carl Ditterich	Carl Ditterich	Laurie Fowler	Robert Flower (33)	
1980	9th	Wayne Reid	Richard Seddon	Carl Ditterich	Carl Ditterich	Laurie Fowler	Brent Crosswell (31)	

1981	12th	Billy Snedden	Richard Seddon	Ron Barassi	Robert Flower	Steven Smith	Mark Jackson (76)	
1982	8th	Billy Snedden	Richard Seddon	Ron Barassi	Robert Flower	Steven Icke	Gerard Healy (77)	
1983	8th	Billy Snedden	Richard Seddon	Ron Barassi	Robert Flower	Alan Johnson	Robert Flower (40)	
1984	9th	Billy Snedden	Richard Seddon	Ron Barassi	Robert Flower	Gerard Healy	Kelvin Templeton (51)	
1985	11th	Billy Snedden	Ray Manley	Ron Barassi	Robert Flower	Danny Hughes	Brian Wilson (40)	
1986	11th	Billy Snedden, Stuart Spencer	Ray Manley	John Northey	Robert Flower	Greg Healy	Greg Healy (35)	
1987	3rd	Stuart Spencer	Tony King	John Northey	Robert Flower	Steven Stretch	Robert Flower (47)	
1988	2nd	Stuart Spencer	Tony King	John Northey	Greg Healy	Steven O'Dwyer	Ricky Jackson (43)	
1989	4th	Stuart Spencer	Tony King	John Northey	Greg Healy	Alan Johnson	Darren Bennett (34)	
1990	4th	Stuart Spencer	Tony King	John Northey	Greg Healy	Garry Lyon	Darren Bennett (87)	Rod Keogh
1991	4th	Stuart Spencer, Ian Ridley	Tony King	John Northey	Garry Lyon	Jim Stynes	Allen Jakovich (71)	Allen Jakovich
1992	11th	Ian Ridley	Tony King, Hassa Mann	John Northey	Garry Lyon	Glenn Lovett	Allen Jakovich (40)	Chris Sullivan
1993	10th	Ian Ridley	Hassa Mann	Neil Balme	Garry Lyon	Todd Viney	Allen Jakovich (39)	David Neitz
1994	4th	Ian Ridley	Hassa Mann	Neil Balme	Garry Lyon	Garry Lyon	Garry Lyon (79)	Paul Prymke
1995	9th	Ian Ridley	Hassa Mann	Neil Balme	Garry Lyon	Jim Stynes	Garry Lyon (77)	Adem Yze
1996	14th	Ian Ridley, Joseph Gutnick	Hassa Mann	Neil Balme	Garry Lyon	Jim Stynes	David Neitz (56)	Darren O'Brien

1997	16th	Joseph Gutnick	Hassa Mann, Cameron Schwab	Neil Balme,[2] Greg Hutchison[3]	Garry Lyon	Jim Stynes	David Neitz (30), Jeff Farmer (30)	Anthony McDonald
1998	4th	Joseph Gutnick	Cameron Schwab	Neale Daniher	Todd Viney	Todd Viney	Jeff Farmer (47)	Guy Rigoni
1999	14th	Joseph Gutnick	Cameron Schwab, John Anderson	Neale Daniher	Todd Viney	David Schwarz	David Neitz (46)	Peter Walsh
2000	2nd	Joseph Gutnick	John Anderson	Neale Daniher	David Neitz	Shane Woewodin	Jeff Farmer (76)	Matthew Whelan
2001	11th	Joseph Gutnick, Gabriel Szondy	John Anderson	Neale Daniher	David Neitz	Adem Yze	Russell Robertson (42)	Scott Thompson
2002	6th	Gabriel Szondy	John Anderson	Neale Daniher	David Neitz	David Neitz	David Neitz (82)	Steven Armstrong
2003	14th	Gabriel Szondy, Paul Gardner	Ray Ellis	Neale Daniher	David Neitz	Russell Robertson	David Neitz (65)	Ryan Ferguson
2004	7th	Paul Gardner	Steve Harris	Neale Daniher	David Neitz	Jeff White	David Neitz (69)	Aaron Davey
2005	8th	Paul Gardner	Steve Harris	Neale Daniher	David Neitz	Travis Johnstone	Russell Robertson (73)	Chris Johnson
2006	5th	Paul Gardner	Steve Harris	Neale Daniher	David Neitz	James McDonald	David Neitz (68)	Clint Bartram
2007	14th	Paul Gardner	Steve Harris	Neale Daniher,[4] Mark Riley[3]	David Neitz	James McDonald	Russell Robertson (42)	Ricky Petterd
2008	16th	Paul Gardner,[5] Jim Stynes	Paul McNamee	Dean Bailey	David Neitz	Cameron Bruce	Brad Miller (26)	Cale Morton
2009	16th	Jim Stynes	Cameron Schwab	Dean Bailey	James McDonald	Aaron Davey	Russell Robertson (29)	Liam Jurrah
2010	12th	Jim Stynes	Cameron Schwab	Dean Bailey	James McDonald	Brad Green	Brad Green (55)	Tom Scully

Individual awards

Best and Fairest

See Keith 'Bluey' Truscott Medal

Brownlow Medal winners

- Ivor Warne-Smith (1926, 1928)
- Don Cordner (1946)
- Brian Wilson (1982)
- Peter Moore (1984)
- Jim Stynes (1991)
- Shane Woewodin (2000)

Leigh Matthews Trophy

- Jim Stynes (1991)

VFL Leading Goalkicker Medal winners (1897–1955)

- Jack Leith (1897)
- Vince Coutie (1904)
- Harry Brereton (1911, 1912)
- Fred Fanning (1943, 1944, 1945, 1947)

Coleman Medal winners (since 1955)

- David Neitz (2002)

Mark of the Year winners

- Shaun Smith (1995) (also informally dubbed *Mark of the Century*)
- Michael Newton (2007)
- Liam Jurrah (2010)

Goal of the Year winners

- Jeff Farmer (1998)

All-Australian players – AFL (since 1991)

- Jim Stynes (1991, 1993)
- Garry Lyon (1993, 1994, 1995)
- Stephen Tingay (1994)
- Todd Viney (1998)
- Jeff Farmer (2000)
- Adem Yze (2002)
- David Neitz (1995, 2002)
- Jeff White (2004)
- James McDonald (2006)
- James Frawley (2010)
- Mark Jamar (2010)

All-Australian players – Interstate Carnivals (1953–1988)

- Ron Barassi (1956, 1958, 1961)
- Brian Dixon (1961)
- Hassa Mann (1966)
- Gary Hardeman (1972)
- Robert Flower (1980, 1983)
- Danny Hughes (1988)

National team representatives (since 2003)

- Clint Bizzell (2003)
- Aaron Davey (2005, 2006)
- Brent Moloney (2005)
- Russell Robertson (2005)
- James McDonald (2006)

See also

- List of Melbourne Football Club players
- Melbourne Football Club/Hawthorn Football Club planned merger
- Sport in Victoria
- Sport in Australia

Footnotes

Notes

1. In recess owing to war.

2. Sacked mid-season.

3. Caretaker coach.

4. Retired after Round 13.

5. Resigned after Round 11.

References

External links

- Official Website of the Melbourne Football Club [1]
- "Around the Grounds" – Web Documentary – MCG [2]

Transportation

Transport in Melbourne

Transport in Melbourne consists of extensive networks and a wide variety of transport services in the city of Melbourne, Australia, including:

- The world's largest tram network.
- Bus (which consist of 323 routes) and coach services.
- The suburban railway network (consisting of 16 lines, the second largest in Australia).
- Inter-city railway services.
- Interstate railway services.
- The largest freeway network in any Australian city.
- Two major passenger airports (including Tullamarine, the second busiest in Australia)
- Port of Melbourne (Australia's busiest port for containerised and general cargo).
- Multiple taxi services.
- Public bike-hire system (since mid 2010)

The dominant mode of transport in Melbourne is the private motor vehicle with 91% mode share of motorised trips in 2005. Melbourne has more roadspace per capita than any Australian city and its network of freeways is comparable with cities including Los Angeles and Atlanta. Melbourne is also home to much of Australia's Automotive industry. In 2002, the state government set an "aspirational goal" as part of Melbourne 2030 for this mode share to decrease to 80%, however the Eddington Report released in 2008 concluded that the mode share of private vehicles is likely to stay the same (or increase) to over 90% in 2005. This is despite booming figures for public transport growth in recent years and despite studies into road congestion in 2008, official Vicroads figures showed no growth in car travel on Melbourne's roads, possibly due to roads reaching full capacity.

Public transport

Trams pass trains on the Flinders Street
Viaduct in the Melbourne CBD

Melbourne is served by a public transport system integrating rail, light rail and bus services. Its extensive tram network is one of the largest in the world, integrated into both bus and train networks. Almost 300 bus routes and a train system comprising 16 lines service Melbourne, Greater Melbourne and suburban regions. Metropolitan, rural and interstate railway networks link together at Southern Cross Station, in Melbourne's WCBD (Western Central Business District).

A Space Syntax Approach Multiple Centrality Analysis of Melbourne's public transport network (excluding buses which were deemed too inefficient) in 2009, found that approximately 8.8% of the greater urban area and approximately 448,000 residents were serviced within 30 minutes of anywhere in the greater Melbourne area. This concluded that only 10-15% of the residents in Melbourne are serviced by appropriate and timely public transport.

The public transport system in Melbourne carries 7% of all trips within the metropolitan area. In early 2009 this figure increased to 9%.

Since World War II, Melbourne urban form changed to a dispersed city, car-oriented pattern which caused a decline in public transport use by commuters. Yet the old pattern of transport still reflected the Melbourne's urban form.

In 1999, operation of the city's public transport system was privatised. In 2006, privitisation was estimated to have cost taxpayers $1.2 billion more than if the system had remained publicly operated. With the franchise extensions in 2009, taxpayers will pay an estimated $2.1 billion more by 2010.

Unlike many major cities in the world, Melbourne has an integrated public transport ticketing system, called Metcard. Metcard enables passengers to buy one ticket for use on suburban bus, train and tram services for a specified time period.

A public bike-hire system is expected to come into service by mid 2010.

Tram

Main article: Trams in Melbourne

See also: List of Melbourne tram routes

Melbourne has the world's largest tram network, consisting of 245 kilometres of track, nearly 500 trams on 28 routes, and 1,813 tram stops. Two light-rail routes are also a part of the tram network. The tram network is a part of the Metlink network and a part of the Metcard ticketing system.

D1 class tram operated by Yarra Trams

The tram network is operated by KDR Melbourne, a private company trading as Yarra Trams. Trams operate on many of the major roads in the inner suburbs, but only some trams operate on roads in middle and outer suburbs.

Heritage trams operate on the free City Circle route, intended for visitors to Melbourne, and privately-run Colonial Tramcar Restaurant trams travel through the city during the evening.

Train

Main article: Railways in Melbourne

See also: List of Melbourne railway stations

Melbourne's suburban train network is operated by Metro Trains Melbourne, a private company, which took over from Connex Melbourne on 30 November 2009. The rail network consists of 16 railway lines and is a part of the Metlink network and a part of the Metcard ticketing system. Several sections of lines which are part of the V/Line network and which fall into the metropolitan area are also covered by Metcard.

X'Trapolis 100 train operated by Connex Melbourne, the previous operator

With the exception of the Stony Point line and the greater metropolitan lines served by V/Line, the rest of the suburban railway network is electrified and services are operated by a fleet of 326 EMU trains.

Bus

Main article: Buses in Melbourne

See also: List of Melbourne bus routes and List of bus companies#Victoria

The bus network is run by several bus companies (approximately 50) under a franchise from the State Government. There are approximately 300 routes in operation with a varying range of service frequencies. A NightRider bus system operates on Friday and Saturday nights, and a Smart Bus orbital bus network is being set up, which is intended to

National Bus Company operated bus

facilitate cross city travel, while the current network is predominantly a radial network. Most of the bus network is a part of the Metlink network and a part of the Metcard ticketing system. The Skybus Super Shuttle is a non-Metcard based airport bus service. In addition, several local government councils operate free local community bus services within their local areas.

Taxi

Taxis in Melbourne are regulated by the State government through the Victorian Taxi Directorate. [1] They are required to be painted canary yellow, but since October 2008 those that operate only at peak times, at night and special events must have green tops. Taxis operate and charge on a meter. There are 3,774 licensed taxis in Melbourne (including 235 wheelchair-accessible taxis).[2] Taxi licenses are estimated to be valued at around $464,000, at October 2008.

Regional rail

Main article: Rail transport in Victoria

Melbourne is the centre of a state-wide railway network, consisting of various lines used for both freight and passenger services.

Intrastate passenger services are operated by V/Line and a fleet of locomotive hauled trains and Diesel Multiple Units. There are seven passenger railway lines connecting

V/Line operated VLocity diesel train

Melbourne to various towns and cities in Victoria. Four of these lines were upgraded as part of the Regional Fast Rail project. The centre of the regional passenger railway network is Southern Cross Station located in the Melbourne CBD.

Melbourne is also connected to Sydney by the CountryLink XPT and Adelaide by Great Southern Railway's *The Overland*.

Passenger Mode share

Melbourne metropolitan trips in 2008	
Public Transport	9%
Car	91%

Trips to Melbourne CBD in 2006Wikipedia:Disputed statement	
Public Transport	80%
Car	20%

Passenger trips by motorised mode	
Mode	Million Trips
Private Car (driver or passenger)	2190
Metro Train	201.2
Tram	170
Bus	91.3

Rail freight

Main article: Freight railways in Melbourne

The Port of Melbourne is Australia's largest container and general cargo port. Regular shipping lines operate to around 300 cities around the world and 3200 ships visit the port each year. The Port of Melbourne is located in the inner west of Melbourne, near the junction of the Maribyrnong and Yarra rivers.

Pacific National locomotive at the
Melbourne Steel Terminal

Container crane and ship at Swanson Dock
East

On 8 February 2008 the Port Phillip Channel Deepening Project, a dredging project to deepen Melbourne's shipping channels, began.

Melbourne also has an extensive network of railway lines and yards to serve freight traffic. The lines are of two gauges - 5 ft 3 in (1600 mm) broad gauge and 4 ft 8 $\frac{1}{2}$ in (1435 mm) standard gauge, and are not electrified. In the inner western suburbs of the city, freight trains have their own lines to operate upon, but in other areas trains are required to share the tracks with Metro Trains Melbourne and V/Line passenger services. The majority of freight terminals are located in the inner suburbs about the Port of Melbourne, located between the Melbourne CBD and Footscray.

Until the 1980s a number of suburban stations had their own goods yards, with freight trains running over the suburban network, often with the E or L class electric locomotives.

Airports

Melbourne Airport, located in the north-western suburb of Tullamarine, is the nation's second busiest airport. Over 30 airlines and 22 million international and domestic passengers are served and service there each year. The airport is a hub for passenger airlines Qantas, Jetstar, Tiger Airways Australia and Virgin Blue and cargo airlines Australian air Express and Toll Priority.

Melbourne Airport

Melbourne's second major passenger airport, Avalon Airport (Melbourne Avalon), is south-west of Melbourne, and north-east of Geelong. Avalon Airport is primarily used by Jetstar and operates flights to Brisbane, Sydney and Perth. AirAsia X was expected to commence flights from Avalon to Kuala Lumpur in October 2009, providing a low-cost service. This provides Melbourne with a second international airport, unique among all capital cities in Australia.

Melbourne's first major airport, Essendon Airport, is no longer used for scheduled international flights, though a small number of scheduled domestic flights operate from there. The airport is also home to the state's Air Ambulance service and services private aviators.

Moorabbin Airport is located to the south of Melbourne, and is primarily used for recreation flying and for flying lessons, conducted in Piper and Cessna aircraft. Moorabbin is also used for a small number of scheduled passenger services, most notably to King Island. Moorabbin is a GAAP airport and its code is YMMB.

Airbase RAAF Point Cook, where the Australian Air Force originated, is located near the city's south-western limits.

Car

See also: List of highways in Melbourne, List of freeways in Victoria, and List of old road routes in Melbourne, Victoria

Motor vehicles are the predominate travel mode, as a result the freeways and roads in Melbourne are critically congested during peak hours. Many residents are car dependent due to minimal public transport outside of the inner city - the city is one of the most car-dependent cities in the world. The freeway network is the largest of any Australian city, with an extensive grid of arterial roads; the locations of which date back to the initial surveying of the city.

Eastern Freeway, looking towards the City

The total urban road area in Melbourne is 21,381 kilometres.

The beginnings of the freeway network was the 1969 Melbourne Transportation Plan, which included a grid of freeways that would cover the entire metropolitan area. In 1973 these plans were reviewed, with a large number of inner city projects deleted.

Freeways that were built throughout the 1960s and '70s included the South Eastern Arterial (now part of the Monash Freeway), the Tullamarine Freeway, the Lower Yarra Freeway (now West Gate Freeway) and the Eastern Freeway.

Further expansion occurred over the next thirty years, with the 'missing links' between the existing freeways built - completion of the Monash Freeway, CityLink, and the Western Ring Road. This period also saw further freeway expansion into suburbia with the Mornington Peninsula Freeway, Eastern Freeway extension, and the South Gippsland Freeway being constructed.

2008 saw the construction and opening of the EastLink radial freeway, as well as further extensions of existing freeways.

Despite government figures slowed growth in road travel since 2006 and zero growth in 2008/09 and the government's goal to reduce road use to 80% of all motorised trips, the State government announced a massive road infrastructure investment, continuing to complete some of the road projects from the 1969 Transport plan including Peninsula Link and North-East Link.

Bicycle

Main article: Cycling in Melbourne

Melbourne has an extensive network of bicycle paths and bicycle lanes on roads. These paths are used for both recreation and for commuting.

Around 2 per cent of all journeys in Melbourne are made by bicycle.[*citation needed*]

On 31 May 2010 the first public bicycle sharing system in Australia was launched in Melbourne. On completion the system will consist of 50 docking stations with 600 bikes, situated around the Melbourne CBD.

Melbourne Bike Share station on Macarthur St

Ferry

Station Pier in Port Phillip Bay is where cruise ships and ferries dock; the Spirit of Tasmania which crosses Bass Strait to Tasmania docks here. Ferries and cruises travel from Southbank along the Yarra River and around the bay to Williamstown, and also across Port Phillip Bay.

Timeline

During Melbourne's history, the transport system and infrastructure has been subject to strategic planning at several levels of government.

1837

- Hoddle grid is laid out, forming Melbourne's first street system which is used almost solely for horse and cart transport and pedestrians.

1844

- First bridge over the Yarra River opened: Princes Bridge on St Kilda Road as a toll bridge

1849

- Melbourne's principal streets are paved.

1850

- Princes Bridge reopened as a free bridge

1854

- Flinders Street railway station opened
- First railway opened to Sandridge (Port Melbourne)

1858

- Spencer Street Station built connecting Melbourne to regional Victoria

1885

- First cable tram to Hawthorn

1889

First electric tram

1890

- Doncaster railway line first proposed

1912

- Electrification of the suburban railway network

1919

- Current Flinders Street Station opened as the main suburban railway terminus

1934

- Flinders Street station declared the busiest in the world

1940

- Ashworth Improvement Plan details proposed improvements to the number of improvements to suburban railways in the inner city.

1966

- St Kilda Junction remodelled and Queens Way underpass created, much cutting and demolition to create way for new highways at Dandenong Road and Punt Road.

1969

- Melbourne Transportation Plan commissioned, includes recommendation for Western Ring Road

1970

- West Gate Bridge collapses

1971

- Melbourne Underground Rail Loop project begins

1977

- First section of Eastern Freeway opened with land reserved for a Doncaster railway line
- $202 million West Gate Bridge opened, with tolls
- Hoddle Highway created from widening of Hoddle Street by 4 lanes and demolishing buildings on eastern side of Hoddle Street.

1980

- Lonie Report recommends closing half of tram system and replacing it with buses. This is rejected.

1981

- First stage of Melbourne Underground Rail Loop opened.

1985

- Tolls on the West Gate Bridge abolished.

1989

- Construction of $631 million Western Ring Road begins.

1994

- Free City Circle Tram opened

1995

- Dandenong to Cranbourne rail extension opened.

1996

- Construction of $2 billion CityLink tollway begins.

1997

- Privatisation of the public transport network

1999

- Opening of Western Ring Road
- Opening of the Bolte Bridge forming the second major roadway over the Yarra River.
- State government commissions the *Linking Victoria* study and allocates $510 of budget toward the initiatives.

2002

- Transport minister Peter Batchelor announced that Airport rail link to Tullamarine not viable for another 10 years. Commits to upgrading Skybus Super Shuttle services to the airport.
- State government commissions *Melbourne 2030* planning report aimed at addressing population growth of up to a million new residents also contained recommendations for transport including the expansion major *activity centres* such as Dandenong and Camberwell with access to public transport and the triplication of the Dandenong line. The document contained a controversial aim of 20% of trips in Melbourne made by public transport by 2020.

2003

- $23 million Box Hill tram/light rail extension opened.

2004

- *Linking Melbourne: Metropolitan Transport Plan* released. The report summarised findings from the Inner West Integrated Transport Study, North East Integrated Transport Study, Outer Western Suburbs Transport Strategy, Whittlesea Strategic Transport Infrastructure Study and Northern Central City Corridor Strategy and recommended investment to the tune of $1.5 billion. Much subsequent infrastructure investment. The Southern Cross Station redevelopment (which ran late and over budget), Docklands light rail extension and the Regional Fast Train system were aimed for the Commonwealth Games. The Eastlink freeway was also not in this report.

- $30.5 million Vermont South tram extension begins.

2005

- $2.5 billion EastLink Freeway project begins.

2006

- State government released a $10 billion plan to improve both public transport and roads, *Meeting our Transport Challenges*. It included the "Think Tram" project aimed at speeding up tram travel times and contained recommendations for a new SmartBus system for the outer eastern suburbs. The Smartbus system had several delays.

2007

- A new public transport ticketing system - Myki was to be launched. The project experienced several technical complications and was significantly delayed and over budget.
- State government commissions East-West transport plan
- Public transport ticketing Zone 3 abolished
- First "Copenhagen style" cycleways in Australia implemented in Swanston Street, Carlton.
- Tim Pallas rejects Melbourne City Council plan for Copenhagen style cycleway on St Kilda Road.

2008

- The Port Phillip Channel Deepening Project, a dredging project to deepen Melbourne's shipping channels, begins.
- Release of the $18 billion Eddington Transport Report, commissioned by the government in 2007 due to revised population growth estimates and increasing congestion problems. The report was aimed at reducing traffic congestion, particularly focused on East-West routes and included a controversial 18 kilometre road tunnel and 17 kilometre rail tunnel and a new rail line from Werribee to Deer Park, Victoria but did not address greenhouse emissions.
- Eastlink freeway tunnel opened
- Monash-CityLink-West Gate freeway upgrade begins
- Australian Greens Victoria party transport plan, The People Plan, released.
- Public Transport minister Lynne Kosky pushes back Airport link by another 20 years.
- Victorian Transport Plan unveiled - the State Government's fourth "long-term" transport statement since 2002.
- New Melbourne Lord Mayor Robert Doyle proposes returning vehicle traffic to Swanston Street

2009

- Myki officially in late December to meet a State Government election promise, however it was launched to operate on suburban trains only

2010

- A public bike-hire service is planned to be introduced by mid year.

Recent statistics

Between 2001 and 2006 - census data shows that Melbourne has had:

- 7.6% population growth
- 8.6% employment growth
- 15% increase in the number of passenger vehicles on the road
- 6% increase in the total number of kilometres driven by those vehicles
- 7.3% increase in CO_2 emissions from passenger vehicles

Further reading

- Dodson, Jago; Sipe, Neil (December 2005), *Oil Vulnerability in the Australian City*, Australia: Urban Research Program, Griffith University, ISBN 1 920952 50 0

External links

- Metlink Melbourne [3]
- Metro Trains Melbourne [4]
- Yarra Trams [5]
- V/Line [6]
- Victorian Department of Transport [7]
- Public Transport Users Association [8]
- City Link [9]
- VicRoads [10]
- Melbourne Bike Share [11]

Melbourne Airport

Melbourne Airport Tullamarine Airport	
 The tower at Melbourne Airport with a United Airlines 747 taking off.	
IATA: MEL – ICAO: YMML	
Summary	
Airport type	Public
Owner	Australia Pacific Airports Corporation Limited
Operator	Australia Pacific Airports (Melbourne) Pty Ltd
Serves	Melbourne
Location	Melbourne Airport, adjacent to Tullamarine
Hub for	Qantas Jetstar Airways (Main) Tiger Airways Australia (Main) Virgin Blue
Elevation AMSL	434 ft / 132 m
Coordinates	37°40′24″S 144°50′36″E
Website	www.melbourneairport.com.au [1]

Runways			
Direction	**Length**		**Surface**
	m	**ft**	
09/27	2,286	7,500	Asphalt
16/34	3,657	11,998	Asphalt
Statistics (2009–2010)			

Passengers	26,287,000
Aircraft Movements	195,018

Source: En Route Supplement Australia
Passengers from Melbourne Airport
Movements from Airservices Australia

Melbourne Airport (IATA: **MEL**, ICAO: **YMML**), also known as **Tullamarine Airport**, is the primary airport serving the city of Melbourne and the second busiest in Australia. It was opened in 1970 to replace the nearby Essendon Airport. Melbourne Airport is the sole international airport of the four airports serving the Melbourne metropolitan area.

The airport is 23 kilometres (14 mi) from the city centre. The airport has its own postcode—Melbourne Airport, Victoria (postcode 3045). This is adjacent to the suburb of Tullamarine.

The Melbourne—Sydney air route is the third most-travelled passenger air route in the world and the busiest in the Asia Pacific region. The airport features direct flights to destinations in all states and territories of Australia in addition to numerous destinations in Oceania, Asia, Africa, Europe and North America. Melbourne is the most common destination for the airports of five of Australia's seven capital cities.[N1] Melbourne serves as a major hub for Qantas and Virgin Blue, while Jetstar Airways and Tiger Airways Australia utilise the airport as home base. Melbourne is the busiest airport for international export freight as of September 2010, while second busiest for import freight. Domestically, Melbourne serves as headquarters for Australian air Express and Toll Priority and handles more domestic freight than any other airport in the nation.

In 2003, Melbourne received the International Air Transport Association Eagle Award for service and two National Tourism Awards for tourism services. Skytrax, an airline consultancy company, classifies Melbourne as a four-star airport. The airport comprises four terminals: one international terminal, two domestic terminals and one budget domestic terminal.

History

Before the opening of Melbourne Airport, Melbourne's international airport was Essendon Airport. By the 1960s, Essendon's limitations as Melbourne's main airport had become apparent. Essendon Airport's facilities were insufficient to meet the increasing demand for air travel; the runways were too short to handle the then new jet airliners and the terminals failed to handle the increase in passengers. Due to the encroachment of the urban boundary, the airport had become surrounded by residential housing, meaning that expansion of Essendon Airport was not possible. In October 1964, Ansett Australia launched the Boeing 727, the first jet aircraft used for domestic air travel in Australia, placing further strain on Essendon and increasing the need for a new airport.

But advances had been made before the launch of the new jet aircraft in Australia. On 27 November 1962, Prime Minister Robert Menzies announced a five-year plan to provide Melbourne with a AU$45 million "jetport" by 1967. A site in Tullamarine was chosen, maintaining proximity to Essendon.

In line with the five-year plan, the airport was ready to handle aircraft by 1967, but not passenger flights. Air Force One landed at the airport on 22 December 1967, carrying United States President Lyndon B. Johnson. Prime Minister John Gorton officially opened the airport to international operations on 1 July 1970 to much fanfare. Essendon still was home to domestic flights for one year, until they were transferred to new airport on 26 June 1971, and the first arrival of a Boeing 747 occurred later that year. In the first year of operations, Melbourne handled six international airlines and 155,275 international passengers.

In 1988, the Australian Government formed the Federal Airports Corporation (FAC) and placed Melbourne Airport under operational control of the FAC along with 21 other airports around the nation. The domestic terminals were significantly upgraded in 1990, and an upgrade of the international terminals began in 1991. In April 1994, the Australian Government announced that all airports operated by Federal Airports Corporation would be privatised in several phases. The carparks were upgraded between 1995 and August 1997.

Australian Airlines aircraft at Melbourne Airport in 1988.

Melbourne Airport was privatised on 2 July 1997 when it was leased to the newly formed Australia Pacific Airports Corporation Limited. In July 1997, the Melbourne Airport website was launched, providing Australia's first real-time flight operations data over the internet. Since privatisation, further improvements to infrastructure have begun at the airport, including expansion of runways, car parks and terminals.

Melbourne Airport was originally called *Tullamarine Airport*, after the adjacent suburb of the same name. Tullamarine derives from the indigenous name Tullamareena. *International* has sporadically been used in the name of the airport. After privatisation, the name changed to *Melbourne Airport*, following the lead of most other major Australian airports. Locally, the airport is commonly referred to as *Tullamarine* or simply as *Tulla* to distinguish the airport from the other Melbourne airports: Avalon, Essendon and Moorabbin.

Terminals

Melbourne Airport's terminals have 56 gates: 40 domestic and 16 international. There are six dedicated freighter parking positions on the Southern Freighter Apron. The current terminal numbering system was introduced in July 2005; they were previously known as Qantas Domestic, International, and South (formerly Ansett Domestic).

Terminal 1

Qantas logo at the front of T1

Qantas operations at Terminal 1

Terminal 1 hosts domestic services for Qantas Group airlines, Qantas, Jetstar and QantasLink and is located to the northern end of the building. Departures are located on the first floor, while arrivals are located on the ground floor. The terminal has 15 parking bays served by aerobridges; 11 are served by single aerobridges whilst 4 are served by double aerobridges.

In late 1999, an expanded Qantas terminal was opened, featuring a second pier, a new access roadway and the expansion of the terminal. The works cost $50 million and took two years to complete. Today, a wide range of shops and food outlets are situated at the end of the terminal near the entrance into Terminal 2. Qantas has a Qantas Club, Business Class and a Chairmans lounge in the terminal.

Terminal 2

T2 International arrivals

Terminal 2 handles all international flights out of Melbourne Airport with the exception of Jetstar's flight to Singapore, which operates via Darwin. The terminal has 15 gates with aerobridges, (although gates 18 & 20 are yet to be fitted). The terminal also has 2 standoff (non aerobridge) gates. Cathay Pacific, Malaysia Airlines, Qantas (which includes two lounges in Terminal 2, a First lounge and a Business lounge/Qantas Club), Singapore Airlines, Air New Zealand/United Airlines and Emirates Airline all operate airline lounges in the terminal. The international terminal, completed in 1996, contains works by noted Australian Indigenous artists including Daisy Jugadai Napaltjarri and Gloria Petyarre.

A $330 million expansion programme for Terminal 2 was announced in 2007. The objectives of this project include new lounges and retail facilities, a new satellite terminal, increased luggage capacity and a redesign of customs and security areas. A new satellite terminal features floor-to-ceiling windows offers views of the North-South runway. The new concourse includes three double-decker aerobridges, each accommodating an A380 aircraft or two smaller aircraft and one single aerobridge. The baggage handling capacity will be increased, and two new baggage carousels will cater to increased A380 traffic. Work commenced in November 2007 and will be completed in 2011.

Although described as a satellite terminal, the terminal building is connected by an above-ground corridor to Terminal 2. Departures take place on the lower deck (similar to the A380 boarding lounges currently in use at Gates 9 and 11), with arrivals streamed on to the first floor to connect with the current first floor arrivals deck.

Gates 12, 14 & 16 are now accepting passengers, whilst gates 18 & 20 will open in November 2010.

Terminal 3

Terminal 3 - Originally the Ansett Australia terminal is now owned by Melbourne Airport. Terminal 3 is home to Virgin Blue and Regional Express. It currently has eleven parking bays served by single aerobridges and eight parking bays not equipped with aerobridges.

Gate 13 used by Virgin Blue at T3

An expansion of the terminal was approved in 1989 and completed in 1991 when a second pier was added by Ansett to the south for use by smaller regional airline Kendell. The terminal was used exclusively by the Ansett Group for all its domestic activities until its collapse in 2001. It was intended to be used by the "New" Ansett, under ownership of Tesna — however, following the Tesna group's widthdrawl of the purchase of Ansett in 2002, the terminal was sold back to Melbourne Airport by Ansett's administrators. as a result, Melbourne Airport undertook a major renovation and facelift of the terminal, following which Virgin Blue moved in from what was then called Domestic Express (now Terminal 4), and has since began operating The Lounge in the terminal, using the former Ansett Australia Golden Wing Lounge area. Regional Express also operate an airline lounge in the terminal.

Terminal 4

Terminal 4—originally called the Domestic Express or South Terminal—is dedicated to budget airlines and is the first facility of its kind at a conventional airport in Australia. Originally constructed for Virgin Blue and Impulse Airlines. Virgin Blue eventually moved into Terminal 3 following the demise of Ansett. A $5 million refit began in June 2007 along the lines of the budget terminal model at Singapore Changi Airport and Kuala Lumpur International Airport. Lower landing and airport handling fees are charged to airlines due to the basic facilities, lack of aerobridges, and fewer amenities and retail outlets compared to a conventional terminal. However, the terminal is located next to the main terminal building, unlike in Singapore and Kuala Lumpur. The terminal was rebuilt by Tiger Airways Australia, who have used it as their main hub since they operated their first domestic flight on 23 November 2007.

Jetstar Airways confirmed its involvement in discussions with Melbourne Airport regarding the expansion of terminal facilities to accommodate for the growth of domestic low-cost services. The proposed expansion of Terminal 4 includes infrastructure to accommodate Tiger Airways Australia and Jetstar Airways flights. These plans are currently in development, and the expansion of Terminal 4 would include the relocation of the current freight centre. If approved, the development is expected to cost hundreds of millions of dollars and take five years to complete.

Southern Freighter Apron

The Southern Freighter Apron has five dedicated freighter parking positions which host 21 dedicated freighter operations a week. In August 1997, the fifth freighter parking position and the apron was extended.

Airlines and destinations

rgin Blue Boeing 737 during a turn-around at T3

Overview of Terminal 1 with Qantas and Jetstar aircraft

rways Australia A320 taxiing from T4

Jetstar Airbus A321-200 ready to take off from Runway 27

100 parked at Melbourne
a turn-around

Airlines	Destinations	Terminal
AirAsia X	Kuala Lumpur	2
Air China	Beijing-Capital, Shanghai-Pudong	2
Air Mauritius	Mauritius	2
Air New Zealand	Auckland, Christchurch, Wellington **Seasonal:** Dunedin, Queenstown	2
Air Pacific	Nadi	2
Air Vanuatu	Port Vila	2
Cathay Pacific	Hong Kong[1]	2
China Eastern Airlines	Shanghai-Pudong	2
China Southern Airlines	Guangzhou	2
Emirates	Auckland, Dubai, Kuala Lumpur, Singapore	2
Etihad Airways	Abu Dhabi	2
Garuda Indonesia	Denpasar/Bali, Jakarta	2
Jetstar Airways	Adelaide, Brisbane, Cairns, Darwin, Gold Coast, Hamilton Island, Hobart, Launceston, Newcastle, Perth, Singapore[2] [ends 15 December], Sunshine Coast, Sydney, Townsville	1
Jetstar Airways	Auckland [begins 13 December], Bangkok-Suvarnabhumi, Christchurch, Denpasar/Bali, Honolulu , Queenstown [begins 16 December], Singapore [begins 16 December], Sydney	2
Korean Air	Seoul-Incheon	2
Malaysia Airlines	Kuala Lumpur	2

Norfolk Air operated by Our Airline	Norfolk Island	2
Philippine Airlines	Manila[1]	2
Qantas	Adelaide, Alice Springs, Brisbane, Cairns, Canberra, Darwin [begins May 2], Hobart, Karratha, Perth, Port Hedland , Sydney **Seasonal:** Broome	1
Qantas	Adelaide, Auckland, Hong Kong, London-Heathrow, Los Angeles, Singapore **Seasonal:** Queenstown	2
Qantas operated by Jetconnect	Auckland, Wellington	2
Qantas operated by QantasLink	Adelaide, Canberra, Devonport, Launceston, Mildura	1
Qatar Airways	Doha	2
Regional Express	Albury, Burnie, Griffith, King Island, Merimbula, Mildura, Mount Gambier, Wagga Wagga	3
Skywest Airlines	Kalgoorlie, Perth	3
Singapore Airlines	Singapore	2
Thai Airways International	Bangkok-Suvarnabhumi	2
Tiger Airways Australia	Adelaide, Alice Springs [ends 9 November][citation needed], Brisbane, Cairns, Canberra, Darwin, Gold Coast, Hobart, Mackay [ends 8 November][citation needed], Perth, Rockhampton [ends 9 November], Sunshine Coast, Sydney	4
United Airlines	Los Angeles[1]	2
Vietnam Airlines	Ho Chi Minh City	2
Virgin Blue	Adelaide, Brisbane, Cairns, Canberra, Coffs Harbour, Darwin, Gold Coast, Hobart, Launceston, Mildura, Newcastle, Perth, Sunshine Coast, Sydney	3
Virgin Blue operated by Pacific Blue	Auckland, Christchurch, Denpasar/Bali, Nadi	2
Virgin Blue operated by V Australia	Johannesburg [ends 24 February], Los Angeles, Phuket [ends 24 February]	2

Notes

- **1** These flights may make an intermediate stop en route to their listed final destination; however the airlines have no traffic rights to carry passengers solely between Melbourne and the intermediate Australian stop.

- **2** Despite this being an international destination, the flight departs from the domestic terminal and makes an intermediate stop enroute for processing.

Prospective flights

- Air India - announced an intent to start direct flights from Delhi in November 2010

Cargo services

The following airlines operate cargo-only services from Melbourne Airport's Southern Freighter Apron:

Atlas Air Boeing 747 on the Southern
Freighter Apron

Airlines	Destinations
Australian air Express	Adelaide, Brisbane, Cairns, Canberra, Gold Coast, Hobart, Launceston, Perth, Sydney, Townsville
Cathay Pacific Cargo	Hong Kong, Sydney
MASkargo	Kuala Lumpur, Jakarta, Sydney
Qantas Freight	Auckland
Qantas Freight operated by Atlas Air	Auckland, Chicago-O'Hare, Hong Kong, Honolulu, New York-JFK
Singapore Airlines Cargo	Adelaide, Auckland, Singapore
Toll Priority	Brisbane, Perth, Sydney
Toll Priority operated by Jetcraft Aviation	Adelaide, Brisbane, Sydney

Other facilities

Melbourne Airport is served by four hotels. A Hilton is located 100 metres (330 ft) from Terminal 2 atop the multi-level carpark. Work commenced on the six-story 280 room hotel in January 1999, which was completed in mid-2000. Holiday Inn has an outlet located 400 metres (1300 ft) from the terminal precinct. Motel Formule 1 offers lodgings located 600 metres (2000 ft) from the terminals. Mantra Tullamarine opened in 2009, 2 kilometres (1.2 mi) from the terminal precinct.

Hilton Melbourne International Airport

Operations

The T2 sign

Melbourne is the second busiest airport in Australia after Sydney. The airport is curfew-free and operates 24 hours a day, although between 2 am and 4 am, freight aircraft are more prevalent than passenger flights. In 2004, the environmental management systems were accredited ISO 14001, the world's best practice standard, making it the first airport in Australia to receive such accreditation.

Airbus A380

Construction works have been undertaken to prepare the airport for the arrival of the double-decker Airbus A380. The A380 has been purchased by several airlines using the airport, namely Malaysia Airlines, Qantas, Qatar Airways, Thai Airways, Vietnam Airlines, China Southern Airlines, Singapore Airlines, Korean Air, Etihad Airways and Emirates. The improvements included the construction of dual airbridges (Gates 9 and 11) with the ability to board both decks simultaneously to reduce turnaround times, the widening of the North-South runway and remote stands and

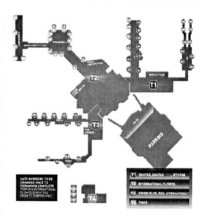

Melbourne Airport terminal precinct

taxiways by 15 metres (49 ft), the extension of the international terminal building by 20 metres (66 ft) to include new penthouse airline lounges, and the construction of an additional baggage carousel in the arrivals hall. As a result the airport was the first in Australia to be capable of handling the A380. The A380 made its first test flight into the airport on 14 November 2005. On 15 May 2008 the A380 made its first passenger flight into the airport when a Singapore Airlines Sydney-bound flight was diverted from Sydney Airport because of fog.

Beginning 20 October 2008, Qantas was the first airline to operate the A380 from the airport, flying nonstop to Los Angeles International Airport twice a week. This was the inaugural route for the Qantas A380. Qantas was followed by Singapore Airlines, who now opearates the A380 daily to Singapore Changi Airport. Singapore Airlines services began on September 29 2009. Emirates intend to fly the A380 to Dubai International Airport in 2011.

The A380 at the airport for the first time as part of the testing programme

Runways

Melbourne Airport has two intersecting runways: a 3657 metres (11998 ft) North-South runway and a 2286 metres (7500 ft) East-West runway. Due to increasing traffic, several runway expansions are planned, including an 843 metres (2766 ft) extension of the North-South runway to lengthen it to 4500 metres (14800 ft), and a 1214 metres (3983 ft) extension of the East-West runway to a total of 3500 metres (11500 ft). Two new runways are also planned: a 3000 metres (9800 ft) runway parallel to the current North-South runway and a 3000 metres (9800 ft) runway south of the current East-West runway. Traffic movement is expected to reach 248,000 per annum by 2017, necessitating a third runway.

On 5 June 2008, it was announced that the airport intends to install a Category III landing system, allowing planes to land in low visibility conditions, such as fog, by the end of 2008. This system will be the first of its kind in Australia.

Awards and accolades

Melbourne Airport has received numerous awards. The International Air Transport Association ranked Melbourne among the top five airports in the world in 1997 and 1998 and, in 2003, presented it with the Eagle Award. The Australian Airport Association named it the Airport of the Year in 1999, while *Business Traveller Magazine* and Airports Council International have ranked Melbourne in the top ten every year from 1996 to 2000 and in the top five for airports that handle between 15 and 25 million passengers. Melbourne is classified as a four-star airport by Skytrax.

Aerial shot of the airport showing runway, taxiway and terminal layout

The airport has received recognition in other areas. It has won national and state tourism awards, and Singapore Airlines presented the airport with the Service Partner Award and Premier Business Partner Award in 2002 and 2004, respectively. In 2006, the airport won the Australian Construction Achievement Award for the runway widening project, dubbed "the most outstanding example of construction excellence for 2006".

Melbourne Centre

Main article: Melbourne Centre

In addition to the onsite control tower, the airport is home to Melbourne Centre, an air traffic control facility that is responsible for the separation of aircraft in Australia's busiest Flight Information Region, Melbourne FIR. Melbourne FIR monitors airspace over Victoria, Tasmania, southern New South Wales, most of South Australia, the southern half of Western Australia and airspace over the Indian and Southern Ocean. In total, the centre controls 6% of the world's airspace. The airport is also the home of the Canberra Approach and Melbourne Approach facilities, which provide control services to aircraft arriving and departing at those airports.

Traffic and statistics

Melbourne Airport recorded more than 26.3 million passengers in 2009-10. 5.54 million of those were international, with the remaining 20.63 million being domestic. There were 193,826 aircraft movements, the vast majority being domestic passenger services. In the long term, the compounded average annual growth rate (CAAGR) for passenger movements is between 3.3% and 4.3%. For aircraft movements, the CAAGR is between 1.8% and 2.6%. This firmly entrenches Melbourne as

Australia's second busiest airport, ahead of Brisbane and behind Sydney.

The following table lists passenger statistics for Melbourne Airport. Forecast statistics are in dark grey.

Annual passenger statistics for Melbourne Airport

Year	Passenger movements (millions)	Aircraft movements (thousands)
1997–98	14.20	154.13
1998–99	14.58	156.80
1999–00	15.57	164.67
2000–01	17.24	187.36
2001–02	16.48	157.60
2002–03	16.92	157.92
2003–04	19.16	165.26
2004–05	20.78	180.51
2005–06	21.43	179.51
2006–07	22.50	180.16
2007–08	24.26	193.826
2008–09	24.77	195.018
2009–10	26.28	195.018
2012–13	27.4–29.8	203.0–217.0
2017–18	32.5–37.1	223.9–247.4
2022–23	38.5–45.8	243.9–281.7
2027–28	43.9–54.9	263.2–316.5

Busiest international freight routes out of Melbourne Airport (FY 2009)

Rank	Airport	Freight tonnes handled	% Change
1	Singapore Changi Airport	50,751.8	▼3.3
2	Hong Kong International Airport	36,450.4	▲4.7
3	Auckland Airport	24,105.8	▼22.8
4	Kuala Lumpur International Airport	19,712.7	▼6.4
5	Suvarnabhumi Airport	17,237.8	▲4.3
6	Dubai International Airport	13,692.6	▲4.1

7	Los Angeles International Airport	5,663.1	▼15.8
8	O'Hare International Airport	3,189.5	▼52.5
9	▬ Shanghai Pudong International Airport	2,902.5	▲22.3
10	▬ Ngurah Rai International Airport	2,456.0	▼18.9

Busiest international passenger routes out of Melbourne Airport (Year ending December 2009)

Rank	Airport	Passengers handled	% Change
1	▬ Singapore Changi Airport	874,617	▲0.8
2	▬ Auckland Airport	759,476	▲6.9
3	▬ Hong Kong International Airport	501,856	▲0.0
4	▬ Kuala Lumpur International Airport	498,182	▲45.3
5	▬ Suvarnabhumi Airport	380,530	▼0.9
6	▬ Dubai International Airport	348,573	▲15.7
7	Los Angeles International Airport	333,535	▲9.5
8	▬ Christchurch International Airport	296,834	▲7.1
9	▬ London Heathrow Airport	171,442	▼19.8
10	▬ Ngurah Rai International Airport	159,164	▲16.6

Busiest domestic passenger routes out of Melbourne Airport (YE July 2010)

Rank	Airport	Passengers handled	% Change
1	▬ Sydney Airport	7,721,700	▲13.6
2	▬ Brisbane Airport	2,833,900	▲5.0
3	▬ Adelaide Airport	2,118,100	▼2.9
4	▬ Perth Airport	1,685,200	▼3.6
5	▬ Gold Coast Airport	1,673,700	▲5.0
6	▬ Hobart International Airport	1,206,100	▲0.1
7	▬ Canberra International Airport	1,123,200	▲2.3
8	▬ Launceston Airport	833,300	▲0.2
9	▬ Cairns Airport	392,600	▼12.5
10	▬ Sunshine Coast Airport	391,500	▼4.5

Access

Car

Melbourne Airport is 23 kilometres (14 mi) from the city centre and is accessible via CityLink and the Tullamarine Freeway. One freeway offramp runs directly into the airport grounds, and a second to the south serves freight transport, taxis, buses and airport staff. Melbourne Airport has five car parks, all of which operate 24 hours a day, 7 days a week. The short-term, multi-level long-term, business and express carparks are covered, while the long-term parking is not. The main multi-level carpark in front of the terminal was built in the late 1990s, replacing the pre-existing ground-level car parking. It has been progressively expanded ever since.

Tullamarine Freeway at the Calder Freeway turnoff

A Skybus Super Shuttle leaving a bus terminal at Melbourne Airport.

Public transport

The Skybus Super Shuttle service is the main public transport link to the airport, taking approximately 20 minutes to reach Southern Cross Station in the Melbourne central business district. From Southern Cross, travellers can access V/Line regional and Metro Trains Melbourne suburban trains, Yarra Trams and interstate train and bus services.

There are four local bus services to Melbourne Airport.

Moonee Ponds - Melbourne Airport via Essendon RS, Airport West Shoppingtown,
[2]   Tullamarine
        Bus service operating Monday to Friday (peak), Saturday to Sunday by Tullamarine Bus Lines

Moonee Ponds - Sunbury RS via Essendon RS, Airport West Shoppingtown, Melbourne Airport, City (weekends
[3]   only)
        Bus service operating every day by Tullamarine Bus Lines

Broadmeadows - Sunbury via Westmeadows, Gladstone Park, Melbourne Airport, Sunbury
[4]   RS
        Bus service operating Monday to Friday by Tullamarine Bus Lines

Frankston - Melbourne Airport via Dandenong, Knox City SC, Ringwood, Greensborough, South Morang,
[5] Broadmeadows
SmartBus service operating every day by Grenda's Bus Services, East West Bus Company, Tullamarine Bus Lines and
Invicta Bus Services

There are nine other bus companies serving the airport, with services to Ballarat, Bendigo, Dandenong, Frankston, Mornington Peninsula, Geelong, Melbourne's suburbs, Shepparton and the Riverina. These negate the need to transfer onto V/Line services.

Rail link

The possibility of installing a rail link from what was known as the Broadmeadows (now the Craigieburn Suburban Line) to the airport was debated in the 1960s, but little progress was made.

The rail link was an Australian Labor Party 1999 Victorian Election promise.

In 2001, the state government investigated the construction of a heavy rail link to the airport under the Linking Victoria programme. Two options were considered; the first branched off the Craigieburn Suburban Line to the east, and the second branched off the Albion Goods Line, which passes close to the airport's boundary to the south. The second option was preferred. Market research concluded most passengers preferred traveling to the airport by taxi or car, and poor patronage of similar links in Sydney and Brisbane cast doubt on the viability of the project. This led to the project being deferred until at least 2012. On 21 July 2008, the Premier of Victoria reaffirmed the government's commitment to a rail link and said that it would be considered within three to five years. To maximise future development options, the airport is lobbying for the on-grounds section of the railway to be underground.

In 2010, new public transport minister announced that the rail link had been taken off the agenda with new freeway options being explored instead.

Accidents and incidents

- On 29 May 2003, Qantas Flight 1737—en route to Launceston Airport—was hijacked shortly after takeoff. The hijacker, a passenger named David Robinson, intended to fly the plane into the Walls of Jerusalem National Park, located in central Tasmania. The flight attendants and passengers successfully subdued and restrained the hijacker, and the plane turned around and landed safely at Melbourne.

- On 21 February 2005, a mystery illness caused the evacuation and closure of what was then the South Terminal. The incident began at 7:10 am when a female collapsed in the terminal building. The terminal was closed at 10:10 am because several individuals exhibited symptoms and were hospitalised. In all, 57 individuals were treated by ambulance officers, 47 of whom were hospitalised. All flights landing at the affected terminal were bused to the Patrick Freight facility and unloaded. The South Terminal reopened at 6 pm. The mystery illness was never determined.

- On 20 March 2009, Emirates Airline Flight 407—en route to Dubai International Airport, an Airbus A340-500 was taking off from Melbourne Airport on Runway 16 and failed to become airborne. When the plane was nearing the end of the runway, the crew pulled up sharply causing the tail of the plane to scrape along the runway during which smoke was observed in the cabin. The crew dumped fuel and returned to the airport. The damage caused to the plane was considered substantial. The ATSB is continuing its investigation into the accident. It is believed the plane damaged a strobe light at the end of the runway as well as a antennae on a small building.

Avalon Airport

Main article: Avalon Airport

When Jetstar was established in 2004, it decided to operate flights to Adelaide, Brisbane, Perth and Sydney from Avalon rather than Melbourne Airport. This made Melbourne the only city in Australia with two commercially served airports and generated airport competition for the first time in an Australian city. To compete with Avalon, Melbourne established the Budget Terminal and lowered landing fees, which made it the cheapest arrival point in Australia and one of the cheapest international airports in the world. Since then, Jetstar has moved its Perth and Adelaide flights to Melbourne Airport.

AirAsia X was widely expected to launch international flights to Kuala Lumpur from Avalon in October 2008. However, Linfox's proposal to upgrade Avalon's international facilities was rejected on 5 June 2008, which prompted AirAsia X to announce flights from Melbourne Airport on 20 August 2008. Linfox vowed to resolve the Government's concerns and build the terminal, but on 14 November 2008, announced that upgrading Avalon to handle international flights would no longer be viable due to the government's resistance. Then on 10 March 2009, Linfox announced that Avalon would indeed handle international flights within two years and the Government would approve of a $50 million terminal by the end of 2009.

See also

- City of Keilor – the former local government area of which Melbourne Airport was a part
- List of airports in Australia
- Transport in Australia
- Avalon Airport
- Moorabbin Airport
- Essendon Airport

Notes

1. The airport is the number one destination for Perth, Adelaide, Hobart, Canberra and Sydney airports. It is not the number one destination for Brisbane or Darwin airports, where it falls second.

External links

- Melbourne Airport website [6]
- Skybus website [7]
- Accident history for MEL [8] at Aviation Safety Network

Avalon Airport

Avalon Airport Linfox Field	
Avalon's Control tower and offices	
IATA: AVV – ICAO: YMAV	
Summary	
Airport type	Public
Owner	Linfox
Operator	{{{operator}}}
Serves	Melbourne, Geelong
Location	Avalon, Victoria
Hub for	{{{hub}}}
Elevation AMSL	35 ft / 11 m
Coordinates	38°02′22″S 144°28′10″E
Website	www.avalonairport.com.au [1]

Runways			
Direction	**Length**		**Surface**
	m	**ft**	
18/36	3,048	10,000	Asphalt

Statistics	
Total Passengers	1,400,000
Aircraft Movements	9,026

Avalon Airport (IATA: **AVV**, ICAO: **YMAV**) is the second busiest of the four airports serving Melbourne (in passenger traffic) and is located in Avalon, Victoria, Australia. It is located 23 kilometres (14 mi) north-east of the city of Geelong and is 55 kilometres (34 mi) to the south-west of the state's capital city of Melbourne.

The airport is designed to cater for jet aircraft, and comprises a single runway. It is used for scheduled passenger services by Jetstar Airways and Sharp Airlines and as a heavy maintenance facility by Jetstar's parent company, Qantas. It is also the site of the biennial Australian International Airshow. Previously, air traffic control was only provided on request, but on 16 May 2008 it was announced that regular air traffic control facilities would now be provided at Avalon.

The land on which Avalon Airport lies is part of the Lara Lea escarpment which is bounded by the You Yangs, Corio Bay and Melbourne Water sewage treatment agistment paddocks. The airport continues to fall under the jurisdiction of the Australian Department of Defence.

History

Avalon Airport was opened in 1953, to cater for the production of military aircraft. Previously the Government Aircraft Factory located at Fishermans Bend, Melbourne had used a runway beside their factory. However, newer jet aircraft required a longer runway length for safe operations, and the Fishermans Bend runway was being encroached upon by development. Land near Lara was purchased by the Commonwealth Government for a new facility. The site of the airport was originally part of the Avalon homestead and sheep station.

A 10000 feet (3000 m) runway was built by Country Roads Board, with the first plane landing on 3 April 1953 - a 4 engined Avro Lincoln bomber flown from Fishermans Bend. The Canberra jet bomber was under construction at same time at the new airport. In 1959, Qantas established a training base at the site.[citation needed]

In 1985 the Government Aircraft Factory changed its name to Aerospace Technologies of Australia (ASTA). Aircraft produced during this time had included the Sabre jet fighter, Jindavik remotely-piloted aircraft, and Nomad civil aircraft. Under the ASTA banner engines for the Dassault Mirage III jet fighters were produced, as well as assembly of the F/A-18 fighter jets for the RAAF.

October 1988 saw ASTA Aircraft Services division take delivery of the first Boeing 747 to Avalon for servicing and maintenance. By December 1993 fifty 747 aircraft had been through the Avalon facility, and 820 people were employed at the site. October 1995 saw a Cathay Pacific Lockheed L-1011 flown to Avalon for scrapping by ASTA Aircraft Services, in what was a one off event.

Training of pilots from Japan's All Nippon Airways commenced at Avalon on 8 September 1993.

On 27 June 1995 Aerospace Technologies of Australia was privatised by the Commonwealth Government, selling the aircraft divisions to Rockwell Australia Limited, and the airport operations to Avalon Airport Geelong Pty Ltd. The ASTA airliner overhauling facility was closed in 1997.

The first scheduled passenger flights out of Avalon were operated by Hazelton Airlines, who commenced flights between Avalon Airport and Sydney in February 1995. 36 seat SAAB 340 aircraft were used for the service. The service was discontinued after a short time due to a lack of patronage.

In 1997 the Australian government decided Avalon was no longer needed [citation needed] and it was leased to Linfox, a company owned by transport tycoon Lindsay Fox.

Aircraft hangars at the airport. The tail of H-EBU *Nalanji Dreaming* can be seen in the second hangar

Today

Scheduled passenger flights

Jetstar Airways, a low cost subsidiary of Qantas, is the current major user of Avalon Airport. Although its main base is Melbourne-Tullamarine, Jetstar service Brisbane and Sydney from Avalon. Adelaide and Perth were previously serviced, but these have since been moved to Tullamarine. Nearly all other Melbourne services use Tullamarine Airport as to compete with rivals Tiger Airways and Virgin Blue.

Jetstar announced that they would use Avalon as the origin of flights to Sydney and Brisbane in 2004. Avalon was chosen in preference to Melbourne Airport due to relatively lower operating costs. A new terminal, consisting of three check-in counters and a departure lounge, was constructed to cater for the airline. Since that time, Avalon Airport has expanded its facilities and is now recognised as a major hub for travel to Melbourne and Geelong. The domestic terminal is currently being expanded at a cost of A$4 million. A new departure gate, additional lounge seating, new retail outlets and an enlarged arrivals hall is under construction.

Tiger Airways Australia announced it was basing two aircraft at the airport from 10 November 2010, expanding its services which presently operate only from Melbourne Airport.

Currently, the only other airline operating passenger services is Sharp Airlines, operating regional flights to Portland Airport and Hamilton Airport.

Qantas maintenance facility

Avalon is the site of one of Qantas' heavy maintenance and engineering facilities. The facility opened in the late 1990s, and currently employs 1000 people.

Other uses

Avalon Airport hosts the Australian International Airshow, which is held every two years.

Future

C-17 Globemaster III at Avalon Airport, Australia, March 2005

Avalon Airport was one of three sites considered for the Wholesale Fruit and Vegetable Markets which will be moved from West Melbourne to allow development of the Port of Melbourne. A site in Epping was ultimately chosen as the preferred site.

Linfox hopes Avalon will capture 10% of the Melbourne domestic passenger market by 2010, increasing to 20% by 2017. This represents up to 3.4 million passengers each year in the next decade. Further expansion plans involve international passenger and freight flights to the Asia-Pacific rim and Europe.

Malaysian long haul budget airline AirAsia X has been awarded rights to operate to Avalon Airport from Kuala Lumpur,. Avalon was considered the preferred option, however the need to construct customs facilities ruled it out for the first Australian destination. The current terminal is planned to be upgraded to handle AirAsia X and future international passenger airline flights. This new facility will provide Avalon with customs, immigration, quarantine and retail facilities and will be approximately 8000 square meters in size. In a bid to attract potential airlines, airport owner Lindsay Fox embarked on an overseas tour to attract carriers. Airlines from India, Macau and Australia's Jetstar have been named as possible users. In June 2008, the initial proposal for the international terminal was rejected by the Federal Government for a number of unspecified reasons. This setback will mean Avalon cannot meet AirAsia's timetable of flying into Avalon from early 2009 although Linfox were prepared to continue to work with the Federal Government to sort out those issues. Currently, passenger volumes at Avalon are 1.4 million per annum. However, on 14 November 2008, Lindsay Fox announced that upgrading Avalon Airport to handle international flights would no longer be viable due to the government's resistance. Then on 10 March 2009, Linfox announced that Avalon would indeed handle international flights within two years and the Government would approve of a $50 million terminal by the end of 2009.

India's Kingfisher Airlines has also expressed interest in flying from Avalon to Bangalore non stop utilising Airbus A330-200 or Airbus A340-500 aircraft. This speculation has been formulated around the opening of an international terminal at Avalon Airport.[*citation needed*]

Airlines and destinations

Airlines	Destinations
Jetstar Airways	Brisbane, Sydney
Sharp Airlines	Adelaide, Portland
Tiger Airways Australia	Adelaide [begins 10 November], Alice Springs [begins 11 November], Gold Coast [beings 10 November], Mackay [begins 10 November], Perth [begins 12 November], Rockhampton [begins 11 November], Sydney [begins 10 November]

Gallery

Arrival and baggage collection

Inside arrivals building

Check in counters

Inside of departure terminal

Departure gate

Jetstar's Airbus A320 VH-VQY at Avalon Airport

See also

- Australian International Airshow
- Commonwealth Aircraft Corporation
- List of Australian airports
- Transport in Australia

References

- Peter Begg (1990). *Geelong — The First 150 Years*. Globe Press. ISBN
0-9592863-5-7

External links

- Avalon Airport [1]
- Australian International Airshow [1]
- Avalon Airport is at coordinates 38°02′22″S 144°28′10″E

Moorabbin Airport

Moorabbin Airport Harry Hawker Airport Melbourne/Moorabbin Airport	

King Island Airlines plane at Moorabbin	
IATA: MBW – ICAO: YMMB	
Summary	
Airport type	Public
Operator	Moorabbin Airport Corporation
Serves	Melbourne
Location	Mentone, Victoria, Australia
Hub for	{{{hub}}}
Elevation AMSL	50 ft / 15 m
Coordinates	37°58′36″S 145°06′06″E
Website	www.moorabbinairport.com.au [1]

Runways			
Direction	Length		Surface
	m	ft	
04/22	571	1,873	Asphalt
13R/31L	1,060	3,478	Asphalt
13L/31R	1,150	3,772	Asphalt
17R/35L	1,240	4,069	Asphalt
17L/35R	1,335	4,379	Asphalt
Source: Enroute Supplement Australia from Airservices Australia			

Moorabbin (Harry Hawker) Airport (IATA: **MBW**, ICAO: **YMMB**) is a general aviation airport for light aircraft located in Mentone, Victoria. The airport grounds are treated as their own suburb, designated the postcode *3194*. The airport opened in December 1949. Originally the intent was to name the airport "Mentone" but this was abandoned after a potential clash with the then French airport Menton. Similarly, Cheltenham was discarded due to similarities to the UK airport Gloucester/Cheltenham. Moorabbin Airport is the third busiest airport in Australia by aircraft movements.

Overview

Moorabbin Airport has 5 intersecting runways, an air museum, helicopter terminals, a control tower, several flight training facilities, and a Direct Factory Outlets shopping centre on its land. It serves the general aviation needs for the south-eastern suburbs of Melbourne.

Getting there

The nearest train station is Cheltenham, approx 3 km (1.9 mi) from the airport. The following bus routes operating around the area:

Hampton - Berwick via Southland SC, Parkmore SC, Dandenong RS, Fountain Gate
[2] SC
Bus service operating every day by Moorabbin Transit & Grenda's Bus Services

Hampton - Berwick RS via Southland SC, Parkmore SC, Dandenong RS, Fountain Gate
[3] SC
Bus service operating every day by Moorabbin Transit & Grenda's Bus Services

These bus services run along Centre Dandenong Rd at the northern boundary connecting to a number of rail stations including Hampton, Highett and Dandenong. Nearest freeway is Eastlink approx 6 km (3.7 mi) to the east.

Airlines and destinations

Passenger airlines operating in Melbourne-Moorabbin Airport

Airlines	Destinations
King Island Airlines	King Island

Awards

In 2006 Moorabbin Airport was named "Australian Regional Airport of the Year"

Master plan

The Master Plan for Moorabbin Airport was approved by the Minister for Infrastructure, Transport, Regional Development and Local Government, Anthony Albanese MP, on 25th June 2010. The Master Plan provides a twenty year horizon detailing the development of the airport and associated infrastructure. It will be published on the airport website.

External links

- Moorabbin Airport website [1]

See also

- List of Australian airports
- Transportation in Australia
- Royal Victorian Aero Club

Essendon Airport

Essendon Airport is also the name of a 'post-punk' Melbourne band.

Essendon Airport Melbourne/Essendon	
IATA: MEB – ICAO: YMEN	
Summary	
Airport type	Public
Owner	Zavanti Holdings Pty. Ltd.
Operator	Essendon Airport Pty. Ltd.
Serves	Melbourne
Location	Essendon
Hub for	{{{hub}}}
Elevation AMSL	282 ft / 86 m
Coordinates	37°43′41″S 144°54′07″E
Website	www.essendonairport.com.au [1]

Runways			
Direction	Length		Surface
	m	ft	
08/26	1,921	6,302	Asphalt
17/35	1,503	4,931	Asphalt

Statistics (2006)	
Movements	60,000+

Source: Enroute Supplement Australia from Airservices Australia
Statistics from Essendon Airport

Essendon Airport (IATA: **MEB**, ICAO: **YMEN**) is located at Essendon, in Melbourne's northern suburbs, Victoria, Australia. It is located next to the Tullamarine Freeway on 305 ha (750 acres), 13 kilometres (8.1 mi) from the Melbourne Central Business District and 7 kilometres (4.3 mi) from Melbourne Airport.

History

The area of the airport was originally known as St Johns, after an early landowner. The airport was proclaimed by the Commonwealth Government in 1921. For some time prior to Proclamation, the airfield had been used by the Victorian Chapter of the Australian Aero Club (renamed the Royal Victorian Aero Club), having initially been based at Point Cook. The Aero Club remained at Essendon until the late 1940s when it transferred to Moorabbin Airport.

Originally the airport had grass runways with the first tenants moving in from December 1921, including J. H. Larkin, Captain Matthews, Bob Hart and Major Harry Shaw.

The 1920s period saw the great pioneering aviation flights of Sir Charles Kingsford Smith who visited the airport on several occasions. In August 1926, 60,000 people swarmed across the grassy fields of Essendon Airport upon the arrival of aviation pioneer Alan Cobham when he landed his de Havilland DH.50 floatplane, flown from England to Australia.

Expansion

The airport was extended with additional land during the 1930s. The grass was finally upgraded to concrete tarmac in 1946. The first international commercial flight arrived from New Zealand in 1951. Commercial international flights were transferred nineteen years later to the new Tullamarine International Airport in 1970, with Commercial domestic flights following in 1971. The short runways at Essendon, and the surrounding housing, made the airport unsuitable for long range pure jet operations (such as Boeing 707s and Douglas DC-8s). The only pure jet to use Essendon commercially was BOAC's Comets, which were withdrawn in late 1965.

A BOAC Bristol Britannia at the airport in 1959.

Qantas ran a Super Constellation, and later Lockheed Electra turboprop service from Sydney to Johannesburg, via Essendon, Perth, Cocos Island, and Mauritius. By 1969 this had been replaced by a Boeing 707 which overflew Melbourne - and with it, went the airport's last long range international service, leaving it only with trans-Tasman operations. Qantas and Air New Zealand operated the service with Lockheed Electras.

A large variety of aircraft were used through Essendon in the 1960s - Lockheed Electras, Vickers Viscounts, Fokker Friendships, Douglas DC-3s, DC-4s, and DC-6s, De Havilland Comets, and from 1964, Boeing 727s. Douglas DC-9s were introduced later in the decade. International flights departed mainly from Sydney during Essendon's years of operation, and there were regular daily flights between the two largest metropolitan areas in Australia.

Some notable arrivals at the airport include:

- 1956 - Olympics and arrival of Queen Elizabeth II. Airport staff directed 206 international flights down safely during one week at Essendon airport.
- 1964 - The Beatles, upon arrival, waved to thousands of teenagers from the viewing deck of Essendon Airport's main terminal building.
- 1967 -United States President Lyndon B. Johnson for funeral of Prime Minister Harold Holt.Air Force One landed at Essendon airport on 22 December 1967. Air Force One then flew empty to Tullamarine Airport as its weight when refuelled was too haevy for Essendon Airport.
- 1973 - Sir Robert Helpmann co-directed with Rudolph Nureyev, the Australian Ballet film of Don Quixote in F hangar.
- 1987 - Kylie Minogue films her first ever music video for her debut single Locomotion here.

Post 2000

In 2001, the Commonwealth Government sold its management rights for the airport to Edgelear Pty. Ltd., a consortium of the Linfox transport group owned by transport tycoon Lindsay Fox (which also owns Avalon Airport), and the Becton group of companies. Executive, corporate and privately owned aircraft are based here along with charter, freight and regional Victorian airlines who currently operate from the airport as well as several flight training schools. The airport also provides warehousing facilities, and a home to the Victorian Air Ambulance, Royal Flying Doctor Service and the Victoria Police Air Wing.

Recent history

In 2007, the airport was re-designed under a new master plan, as part of the Essendon Fields development. This master plan caters for the future of the site for both aviation and non-aviation use. A new access road and off ramp was constructed from the Tullamarine Freeway to enter the airport precinct from the north, rather than the common Matthews Avenue entry point. This has necessitated the construction of an Aero-Crossing as the new access road crosses a taxiway. Most of the aviation users of the former 'Northern Hangars' have moved to other sites on the airport with the notable exceptions of the Victoria Police Air Wing and Executive Airlines. The Police Air Wing are due to move to a new facility in the future as the former 'Northern Hangars' are scheduled to be removed as non-aviation businesses purchase sites in that area. Executive Airlines will continue to operate from their present building and are the only company that uses the Aero-Crossing site. Of course the Air Wing Helicopters are not affected by the insertion of the roadway.

The airfield itself also has undergone a major upgrade with the installation of lighting and signage systems to bring the airport to International Civil Aviation Organization standards. There are now taxiway signs, and the taxiway and runway lighting has been upgraded to new units. The runway lighting is now medium intensity on runway 17/35 and upgraded to high intensity on 26/08. This alleviates the loss of the approach lighting system previously. Also during this upgrade the old Fixed

Distance Lighting and Visual Approach Slope Indicator systems were decommissioned and replaced with new Precision Approach Path Indicator systems on the left side of all runways. A new Pilot Activated Lighting or PAL system was also installed to allow the lighting system to remain off when not required for use by aircraft.

In November 2007 Essendon Airport released its latest Master Plan. The Master Plan details further proposals to expand aviation activities. These plans have been opposed by the local residents group 'Close Essendon Airport' and local political representatives Kelvin Thomson MP and Judy Maddigan. A competing group known as 'Save Essendon Airport' wants the airport to stay open for air ambulance services.

Aviation users

Airlines

Passenger airlines operating in Melbourne-Essendon Airport

Airlines	Destinations
Airlines of Tasmania	Flinders Island
Sharp Airlines	Hamilton, Portland

Charter Operators

- Direct Air (Charter)
- Shortstop Jet Charter ('Gooney Bird' Flights, Charter, FBO)
- Executive Airlines (Charter, FBO)
- General Aviation Maintenance (Freight, FBO)

Flying schools

- InterAir
- National Aerospace Training (NAT)
- Pearson Aviation
- Conair Aviation

Other operators

- Royal Flying Doctor Service (RFDS)
- Air Ambulance Victoria
- Victoria Police Air Wing
- Prestige Aero Detailing (Aircraft Detailing - fixed and rotary wing)

See also

- Transportation in Australia
- United States Army Air Forces in Australia (World War II)

References

🌐 *This article incorporates public domain material from websites or documents* [2] *of the Air Force Historical Research Agency.*

- Essendon Airport History on Strathmore Community Website [3]
- Register of the National Estate entry [4]

External links

- Essendon Airport Website [1]
- Airways Museum [1]
- Save Essendon Airport Campaign [2]
- Close Essendon Airport Campaign [3]

Port of Melbourne

Port of Melbourne	
Container crane and ship at Swanson Dock East	
Facility information	
Location	West Melbourne
Constructed	1889
Land area	143,000m²
Operator	DP World Patrick
Annual TEU	1.9 million
Shipping information	
Number of berths:	30+
Rail information	
Number of platforms	16
Rail gauge	Dual gauge
Road information	
Street access	Docklands Highway

The **Port of Melbourne** is Australia's busiest port for containerised and general cargo. It is located in Melbourne, Victoria on the mouth of the Yarra River, which is at the head of Port Phillip Bay. It is owned by the Port of Melbourne Corporation, a statutory corporation owned by the State of Victoria.

The majority of the port is in the suburb of West Melbourne and should not be confused with the Melbourne suburb of Port Melbourne although Webb Dock, part of the Port of Melbourne, is in Port Melbourne.

Port Melbourne (or Sandridge as it was known until 1884) was a busy port early in the history of Melbourne, but declined as a cargo port with the development of the Port of Melbourne in the late 19th century. It retains Melbourne's passenger terminal however, with cruise ships and ferries using Station Pier.

History

In the early days in Melbourne, large ships were unable to navigate the Yarra River so cargo destined for Melbourne was unloaded at either Hobsons Bay (now Williamstown) or Sandridge and transferred either by rail or by cargo lighter to warehouses which were concentrated around King Street. This was an expensive and inefficient process.

In 1877, Victoria's colonial government resolved to make the Yarra more navigable and engaged English engineer Sir John Coode to devise a solution. He decided to change the course of the river by cutting a canal to the south of the existing course of the river. This shortened it by a mile and made it much wider. It also created Coode Island, a name still used today although the northern course of the river has long since disappeared. Ships were now able to sail as far up the river as Queensbridge where a turning basin was constructed.

Coode also oversaw the construction of Victoria Dock in swampland to the west of the city. This opened in 1889.

Over time the docks moved progressively downstream as ships became larger and road bridges were built across the Yarra. The construction of the Spencer Street Bridge in 1928 and the Charles Grimes Bridge in 1975 each closed access to docks to the east. The barque *Polly Woodside* lying in the old Duke and Orr drydock , the warehouses of South Wharf and the Mission to Seafarers building are now the only reminders of the maritime history of this area.

Expansion

Development slowed during the Great Depression and World War II but resumed after the war with construction of Appleton Dock (1956), Webb Dock (1960) at the mouth of the Yarra and Swanson Dock, the first container terminal, on what was Coode Island.

Three container ships berthed at Swanson Dock West

Eventually Victoria Dock became too small to handle large container ships and was closed. Its fate was permanently sealed by the construction of the Bolte Bridge, part of CityLink, across its entrance in 1999. It now forms the centrepiece of the Melbourne Docklands redevelopment.

In 1991 a large fire at the Coode Island bulk liquid handling facility blanketed much of Melbourne in toxic fumes. The public outrage forced the government to investigate relocating the facility. Point Lillias   near   Geelong   was   considered.

However due to the high cost involved and local opposition the facility has remained at Coode Island.

Train loaded with containers at Swanson Dock East

The Port of Melbourne was also the scene of a watershed industrial battle in 1998 between Patrick Corporation and the Maritime Union of Australia (MUA).

Recently further controversy has resulted from plans to dredge Port Phillip Bay to deepen shipping channels to allow larger ships into the Port of Melbourne. This process commenced in 2008 and was completed in November 2009. It involved removing more than 22 million cubic metres of sand and silt to provide a minimum 14 metre draught at all times. Opposition to this project stems from potential environmental damage due to silting and loss of amenity for bayside residents due to the noise produced by the dredges. The project was subject to the strictest environmental testing and monitoring requirements in the world at the time. These activities will continue on for many years to help protect the Port Phillip Bay ecosystems.

In the future the Victorian Government will redevelop the Port of Melbourne to better integrate it with other modes of transport. The Melbourne wholesale fruit and vegetable market will be relocated to Epping and Footscray Road raised so that port users will have improved access to the rail facilities at South Dynon.

Facts and Figures

The Port of Melbourne is made up of the following:

- Swanson Dock West has four berths and is used for containerised cargo. It is managed by D.P.World a division of DUBAI WORLD
- Swanson Dock East has four berths and is used for containerised cargo. It is managed by Patrick Terminals.
- Appleton Dock berths B,C and D are used for general cargo. They are managed by D.P.World.

Roll-on/roll-off ship at Webb Dock

- Appleton Dock E is used for general cargo destined for or from Tasmania.

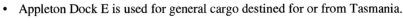

- Appleton Dock F is used for bulk dry cargo.
- Maribyrnong (Coode Island) is a bulk liquid facility.
- Webb Dock West is a roll-on-roll-off facility for motor vehicles. It is managed by Toll Stevedores.
- Webb Dock East 1 is managed by Toll Shipping for Tasmanian general cargo.
- Webb Dock East 2 is also for general Tasmanian cargo but managed by Patrick.
- Webb Dock East 3,4,5 are managed by Patrick for general and automotive cargo.
- Gellibrand Pier is operated by Mobil and has a direct pipeline to their refinery at Altona
- Holden Dock handles refined petroleum products.
- South Wharf berths 26 to 33 handle general cargo.

Container Straddle carriers at Swanson Dock

From May 2003 till May 2004, approximately 3,400 ships from 42 different lines called at the Port of Melbourne. The port handled 64.4 million tonnes of cargo, including a throughput of 1.9 million Twenty-foot equivalent units (TEU) of cargo. In 2006-07 it became the first Australian port to handle two million TEU in a year.

Rail access

Railway goods sidings serve both Swanson Dock East and West, permitting the transfer of shipping containers between sea and rail transport. Originally provided in the 1960s with the development of the port, they were later removed and not restored until 2003 as a 1500 metre long siding. Rail sidings at Appleton Dock reopened in 2000 to serve a new export grain terminal at the port. Dual gauge access is provided to the majority of sidings in the area. Extensive sidings once served the Victoria Dock area, as well as Webb Dock which had a dedicated line.

See also

- Port Phillip Channel Deepening Project
- Port of Geelong

External links

- Port of Melbourne website [1]

Railways in Melbourne

Melbourne rail network
City Loop
Caulfield group
Frankston line
Pakenham line
Sandringham line
Cranbourne line
Northern group
Upfield line
Werribee line
Craigieburn line
Sydenham line
Williamstown line
Flemington Racecourse line
Burnley group
Lilydale line
Glen Waverley line
Belgrave line
Alamein line
Clifton Hill group
Hurstbridge line
Epping line
Greater-metropolitan
Stony Point line

| Melton line |
| Sunbury line |
| **List of stations** |
| **Freight railways**
 Closed railways
 Proposed railways |
| **Alternate Map** |

The **Melbourne rail network** is operated by Metro Trains Melbourne under franchise from the Government of Victoria. The network is based on a commuter rail model centred on the Melbourne Central Business District (CBD) and Flinders Street Station, rather than a rapid transit model, with a focus on services at peak periods. Melbourne's suburban railway network consists of 16 electrified lines, the central City Loop subway, and 200 stations, with a total length of 372 km of electrified lines. The suburban network operates between approximately 5.00 am and midnight. The network is

The pre 1910 Flinders Street Station building on Swanston Street

primarily at ground level, with a number of level crossings, and tracks shared with freight trains and V/Line regional services.

In the 2008–2009 financial year, the Melbourne rail network recorded 213.9 million passenger trips, the highest in its history.

History

Melbourne's first railway line opened in 1854, when only 20 years earlier Melbourne itself did not exist. The network was extended with lines being built to the suburbs, reaching a peak by the 1900s. Electrification of the system commenced from 1919, with electric multiple unit operation commencing at the same time.

In 1839 the Government Surveyor Robert Hoddle provided for a railway linking Melbourne and Hobsons Bay.

On 7 September 1851 a public meeting called for a railway linking Melbourne to Port Melbourne (then called Sandridge) which led to the establishment on 20 January 1853 of the Melbourne and Hobson's Bay Railway Company. On 8 February 1853 the Government also approved the establishment of the Geelong and Melbourne Railway Company and the Melbourne, Mount Alexander and Murray River Railway Company.

In 1855 the Government conducted enquiries and carried out surveys into country railways. On 1 April 1856, the Railway Department was established as part of the Board of Land and Works with George Christian Darbyshire being appointed Engineer in Chief. On 23 May of that year the Melbourne, Mount Alexander and Murray River Railway Company was taken over by the Government.

The first train

Work began on laying the first railway in Victoria on March 1853, the line stretching 4 km. from the Melbourne (or City) Terminus (on the site of modern day Flinders Street Station) to Sandridge (now Port Melbourne). As with many of Australia's early railways, it was owned and operated by a private company - the Melbourne and Hobson's Bay Railway Company, which was formed in 1853.

Trains were ordered from Robert Stephenson and Company of the United Kingdom. The first train was locally built by Robertson, Martin and Smith, however, owing to delays in shipping. Australia's first steam locomotive was built in ten weeks and cost £2,700. Forming the first steam train to travel in Australia, it made its maiden voyage on 12 September 1854.

The opening of the line occurred during the period of the Victorian gold rush - a time when both Melbourne and Victoria undertook massive capital works, each with its own gala opening. The inaugural journey on the Sandridge line was no exception. According to the Argus newspaper's report of the next day: "*Long before the hour appointed ... a great crowd assembled round the station at the Melbourne terminus, lining the whole of Flinders Street*". Lieutenant-Governor Sir Charles Hotham and Lady Hotham were aboard the train - which consisted of two first class carriages and one second class - and were presented with satin copies of the railway's timetable and bylaws.

The trip took 10 minutes, none of the later stations along the line having been built yet. On arriving at Station Pier (onto which the tracks extended), it was hailed with gun-salutes by the warships HMS *Electra* and HMS *Fantome*.

By March 1855, the four engines ordered from the UK were all in service, with trains running every half-hour. They were named *Melbourne*, *Sandridge*, *Victoria*, and *Yarra* (after the Yarra River over which the line crossed).

Early privateers

Melbourne's second railway line opened 13 May 1857, when the Melbourne and Hobson's Bay Railway Company opened their 4.5 km line from the Melbourne (or City) Terminus (on the site of modern day Flinders Street Station) to St Kilda. This line was later extended by the St Kilda and Brighton Railway Company, which opened a line from St Kilda to Brighton in 1857.

Country lines were also built in 1857, with the Geelong and Melbourne Railway Company opening a line from Geelong to Newport. In 1859 the Williamstown railway line opened, connecting Williamstown and Geelong to Spencer Street Station.

More country lines followed in 1859 when Victorian Railways opened a line from the Williamstown line at Footscray, to Sunbury, taking over from the Melbourne, Mount Alexander and Murray River Railway Company that was established in 1853 to build a railway to Echuca, but failed to make any progress.

The first line to Melbourne's south-eastern suburbs was opened in 1859 by the Melbourne and Suburban Railway Company, which ran from Princes Bridge railway station to Punt Road (Richmond), South Yarra, and Prahran. This line was extended to Windsor in 1860, connecting with the St Kilda and Brighton Railway Company line from St Kilda. The new line replaced the indirect St Kilda and Windsor line to the city, which was closed in 1867.

Another suburban line was built by the Melbourne and Essendon Railway Company in 1860, with their line running from North Melbourne to Essendon, with a branch line from Newmarket to Flemington Racecourse opening in 1861. On the eastern side of town, the Melbourne and Suburban Railway Company opened a branch line from Richmond to Burnley and Hawthorn in 1861.

By this point, the railways of Melbourne was a disjointed group of city centric lines, with various companies operating from three separate city terminals - Princes Bridge, Flinders Street, and Spencer Street stations.

Some of the smaller companies were encountered financial problems. The St Kilda and Brighton Railway Company and Melbourne and Suburban Railway Company were absorbed by the Melbourne and Hobson's Bay Railway Company in 1865, forming the Melbourne and Hobsons Bay United Railway Company. The Melbourne and Essendon Railway Company was taken over by the Victorian Government in 1867. The Melbourne and Hobsons Bay United Railway Company was not taken over by the Victorian Government until 1878.

The terminals themselves were linked in 1879, when track was built along the southern side of Flinders Street at street level to connect with Spencer Street Station, although this was only used for freight traffic at night. It was not until 1889 that the two track Flinders Street Viaduct was built between the two city terminus stations.

Outwards expansion also continued, with major trunk lines being opened into rural Victoria. Victorian Railways extended their line to Broadmeadows in 1872 as part of the line to Seymour and Albury-Wodonga. In 1879 the Gippsland line was opened from South Yarra to Caulfield, Pakenham and Bairnsdale.

Land boom lines

The 1870s and 1880s were a time of great growth and prosperity in Melbourne. Land speculation companies were formed, to buy up outer suburban land cheaply, and to agitate for suburban railways to be built or extended to serve these land holdings and increase land values. By 1880 the "Land Boom" was in full swing in Victoria, with the passing of the Railway Construction Act 1884, later known as the *Octopus Act* for the 66 lines across the state that were authorised in it.

New suburban railways were opened, the Frankston line begun with the opening of a line from Caulfield to Mordialloc in 1881, reaching the terminus in 1882. A second new suburban railway line was opened from Spencer Street Station to Coburg in 1884, and extended to Somerton in 1889, meeting the main line from Spencer Street to Wodonga. Land developers opened a private railway from Newport to Altona in 1888, but it was closed in 1890, due to lack of demand.

The line from Hawthorn was extended, to Camberwell in 1882, Lilydale in 1883, and Healesville in 1889. In addition, a branch line (now known as the Belgrave line) was opened from Ringwood to Upper Ferntree Gully in 1889. A short branch two station was also opened from Hawthorn to Kew in 1887. The Brighton Beach line was also extended to Sandringham in 1887.

In 1888, railways came to the north eastern suburbs with the opening of the Inner Circle line from Spencer Street Station via Royal Park station to what is now Victoria Park station, and then on to Heidelberg. A branch was also opened off the Inner Circle in Fitzroy North, to Epping and Whittlesea in 1888 and 1889. Trains between Spencer Street and Heidelberg reversed at Victoria Park until a link was opened between Victoria Park and Princes Bridge in 1901.

The Outer Circle line opened in 1890, linking Oakleigh (on the Gippsland line) to Riversdale (with a branch to Camberwell on the Lilydale line) and Fairfield (on the Heidelberg line). Originally envisigaed to link the Gippsland line with Spencer Street Station in the 1870s, this reason disappeared with the building of a direct link via South Yarra before the line had even opened. The line saw little traffic as it traversed empty paddocks, and with no though traffic, the Outer Circle was closed in sections between 1893 and 1897. The Camberwell to Ashburton stretch of the Outer Circle re-opened as the Ashburton line in 1899, and in 1900, part of the northern section of the Outer Circle reopened as a shuttle service between East Camberwell and Deepdene station. This line closed in 1927.

At the same time as the Outer Circle, a railway was opened from Burnley to Darling and a junction with the Outer Circle at Waverley Road (near the modern East Malvern). A stub of the future Glen Waverley line, it was cut back to Darling in 1895.

The land boom railway building hit a peak with the construction of the Rosstown Railway between Elsternwick and Oakleigh. Built by William Murry Ross, the line was planned from the 1870s to serve a sugar beet mill near Caufield. Construction commenced in 1883, followed by rebuilding in 1888. Ross's debt grew, and he attempted to sell the line many times without success. The line never opened to traffic and was later dismantled.

The stock market crash of 1891 lead to an extended period of economic depression, and put an end to railway construction until the next decade.

By the 1900s, the driving force for new railway lines was the farmers in what is now Melbourne's outer suburbs. In the Dandenong Ranges a narrow gauge 762 mm line was opened from Upper Ferntree Gully to Belgrave and Gembrook in 1900 to serve the local farming and timber community. In the Yarra Valley a branch was opened from Lilydale to Yarra Junction and Warburton in 1901.

Ripponlea railway station is an older station in the southern suburbs

On the other side of the valley, the Heidelberg line was extended to Eltham in 1902 and Hurstbridge in 1912. The freight only Mont Park line was also opened in 1911, branching from Macleod. Finally on the Mornington Peninsula, a branch was built from Bittern to Red Hill in 1921.

Electrification

Planning for electrification was started by Victorian Railways chairman Thomas James Tait, who engaged English engineer Charles Hesterman Merz to deliver a report on the electrification of the Melbourne suburban network. His first report in 1908 recommended a three stage plan over 2 years, covering 200 route km. of existing lines and almost 500 suburban carriages (approximately 80 trains). The report was considered by the Government and the Railway Commissioners, and Merz was engaged to deliver a second report based on their feedback.

Four car Tait train at the Spring Vale Cemetery platform

Delivered in 1912, this second report recommended an expanded system of electrification to 240 route km. of existing lines (463 track km.), and almost 800 suburban carriages (approximately 130 trains). The works were approved by the State Government in December 1912. It was envisaged that the first electric trains would be running by 1915, and the project was completed by 1917; World War I restrictions prevented electrical equipment being imported from the United Kingdom, so progress fell behind.

Rolling stock construction continued, with a number of older suburban carriages converted for electric use as the Swing Door trains, while the first of the Tait trains were introduced as steam hauled carriages. Track expansion was also carried out, with four tracks being provided between South Yarra and Caulfield, as well as grade separation from roads.

The first trials did not occur until October 1918 on the Flemington Racecourse line. Driver training continued on this line until the night of Sunday 18 May 1919, when the first electric train ran between

Sandringham and Essendon, simulating revenue services. Electric services were inaugurated on May 28, 1919 with the first train running to Essendon, then to Sandringham. Full services started the next day.

The Burnley - Darling line, the Fawkner line, the re-opened branch to Altona, and the Williamstown line followed in 1920.

The line to Broadmeadows, the Whittlesea line to Reservoir, the Bendigo line to St. Albans, and the inner sections of the Hurstbridge line were electrified in 1921.

The Gippsland line to Dandenong and Frankston line were electrified in 1922, as was the inner sections of the Ringwood line due to regrading works.

1923 was the completion of the original electrification scheme, but over the next three years a number of short extensions were carried out. The Ashburton line was electrified in 1924, final works on the Lilydale line were completed in 1925, as was electrification on the line to Upper Ferntree Gully. Electrification on the outer ends of the Hurstbridge line were completed by 1926, the Whittlesea line to Thomastown was electrified in 1929, and the Burnley - Darling line was extended to Glen Waverley in 1930 to become the Glen Waverley line.

Post war rebuilding

Railways experienced increased patronage into the 1940s, but railway improvements recommended in the Ashworth Improvement Plan were delayed until after World War II. It was not until 1950 that the Victorian Railways were able to put their Operation Phoenix rebuilding plan into action. The delivery of the Harris trains, the first steel suburban trains on the network, enabled the retirement of the oldest of the Swing Door trains.

A retired Harris train

Railway lines were extended during this period to encompass Melbourne's growing suburban footprint. The Ashburton line

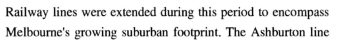

was extended along the old Outer Circle track formation to Alamein station in 1948. The Fawkner line to Upfield and the Reservoir line to Lalor were both electrified in 1959, the Epping line reaching its current terminus in 1964. A great deal of track amplification was also undertaken, with a number of single line sections eliminated.

The Upper Ferntree Gully to Belgrave section of the Gembrook narrow gauge line was converted to broad gauge and electrified in 1962. The remainder of the line was closed in 1954, but has been progressively reopened by the Puffing Billy Railway. The Pakenham line was electrified in 1954 as part of the works being carried out on the Gippsland line, but suburban services to Pakenham did not start until 1975.

During this rebuilding, a number of little used lines were closed on the edges of Melbourne. The Bittern to Red Hill line closed in 1953, the line between Epping and Whittlesea closed in 1959, and the Lilydale to Warburton line closed in 1964. The final stages of the rebuilding stretched into the 1970s, with track amplification carried out to Footscray, and Box Hill, and the first deliveries of the stainless steel Hitachi trains. Detailed planning for the Doncaster line also commenced in this period, and by 1972 the route was decided upon. Despite rising costs, the state governments of the period continued to make assurances that the line would be built, but by 1984 land for the line had been sold.

Modernisation

By the late 1970s, the state of Melbourne's railway network was very run down. The last major investment on the suburban tracks had taken place fifty years earlier with the completion of Glen Waverley line in 1930 and extensions of all suburban services on existing non-electrified lines during the 1950s. Sixty year old Tait trains (known colloquially as "red rattlers") were still in operation, and inner city congestion at Flinders Street led to peak hour delays.

Melbourne Central railway station in the underground City Loop

The Lonie Report, delivered in 1980, called for financial rationalisation and the closure of the Port Melbourne, St. Kilda, Altona, Williamstown, Alamein and Sandringham lines, and their replacement with buses. These recommendations and cuts were not enacted. However, many uneconomic branch lines were closed throughout the rest of the state. The line between Lilydale and Healesville was closed in 1980, now used by the Yarra Valley Tourist Railway. The branch from Baxter to Mornington was closed in 1981, but the line south of Moorooduc is now operated by the Mornington Railway as a tourist route.

Comeng train on the Werribee line

In the 1980s, the government authority overseeing Victorian Railways became VicRail and was restructured along corporate lines. The Metrol train control centre was opened in 1980 to coordinate trains throughout the network. Public transport in Melbourne was also reorganised, with the Metropolitan Transit Authority (MTA) formed in 1983 to coordinate all train, tram and bus services in the city. Between 1981 and 1985 the underground City Loop line was opened around central Melbourne to improve the capacity of Flinders and Spencer Street stations to handle suburban trains and to offer a better choice of stations to users.

In 1983 the Werribee line was electrified, followed two years later by an extension of the Altona line to Laverton. The Port Melbourne and St Kilda lines were converted to standard gauge light rail in 1987, to accommodate tram routes 111 (now route 109) and 96.

Privatisation

The early 1990s saw further changes, with the MTA reborn as the Public Transport Corporation, trading as "The Met".

State Governments of both sides of politics began to push for reform of the railway network, proposing conversion of the Upfield, Williamstown and Alamein lines to light rail. These proposals failed, with the Upfield line instead receiving a series of upgrades to replace labour intensive manual signalling systems. Federal government funding was made available for the electrification of the Cranbourne line in

The modern Southern Cross Station

1995. Rationalisation of the Jolimont Railyards commenced, allowing the creation of Melbourne Park and the later Federation Square.

The Kennett Government also initiated a number of reforms to the operation of the railway system, with guards being abolished from suburban trains and train drivers taking over the task of door operation. Stations were de-manned, and the Metcard ticketing system was introduced to cut the need for staff even further.

The biggest change was privatisation. In 1997 'The Met' was split into two operating units - 'Hillside Trains' and 'Bayside Trains', each to be franchised to a different private operator. In 1999 the process was complete, with Connex Melbourne and M>Train each operating half of the network. By 2004 the parent company of M>Train (National Express) withdrew from operating public transport in Victoria, and their half of the suburban network was passed to Connex as part of a renegotiated contract.

The franchising contracts contained provisions for the new operators to refurbish the Comeng trains, and to replace the older Hitachi trains - Connex chose the Alstom X'Trapolis while M>Train chose Siemens. Since privatisation the Victorian Government has funded expansions to the suburban network - the electrification of the St. Albans line was extended to Watergardens (near the former Sydenham station) in 2002, and the Broadmeadows line was extended to Craigieburn in 2007.

In 2006, Professor Paul Mees and a group of academics estimated that privatisation had cost taxpayers $1.2 billion more than if the system had remained both publicly owned and operated. With the franchise extensions in 2009, taxpayers will pay an estimated $2.1 billion more by 2010. However the Institute of Public Affairs has released its own report into Melbourne's privatisation citing it as a modest success and pointing out that patronage had returned to Melbourne's railways (37.6% increase) after ballooning deficits and the use of old rolling stock had deterred patronage . The Auditor General of Victoria also performed a comprehensive audit report into the franchises and found that 'the franchises represent reasonable value for money.'

In November 2007, Singapore's SMRT Transit and Hong Kong's MTR Corporation Limited expressed interest in taking control of Melbourne's suburban rail network from Connex in November 2009, when their contract was to be reviewed.

On June 25, 2009, Connex lost its bid to renew its contract with the Victorian Government. Hong Kong backed and owned MTR Corporation took over the Melbourne train network on 30 November 2009, operating as a locally-themed consortium Metro Trains Melbourne. MTR is a non-public railway owner and operator in Hong Kong where it is well known for constructing Transit Oriented Developments (TODS) around its stations.

Recent years

During 2005 to 2006 patronage of Melbourne's trains increased over 18 per cent. This increase was partly attributed to increased petrol prices prompting commuters to travel by train rather than by car[citation needed]. As early as 2003 there were union calls to restaff all stations by 2006, primarily for safety reasons. Then-Transport Minister Lynne Kosky said the Government's $10.5 billion 10-year major transport plan announced in May 2006 had significantly underestimated the usage of public transport.

In response to this the State Government undertook to purchase new trains and introduced a new ticketing option where commuters could pay a reduced fare if they completed their journey by 7 am.

In 2006, the Victorian Government announced plans to spend $2 billion on 'the biggest investment in the rail network since the construction of the City Loop 25 years earlier. The initiative is expected to substantially boost the carrying capacity of Melbourne's rail network. It also contains plans for a third rail line between Caulfield and Dandenong which is designed to expand the capacity of, and relieve congestion on, the Pakenham line.

This was followed by an announcement of the introduction of more than 200 new weekly train services, set to tackle overcrowding on the city's busiest train lines, which had been attributed to a lack of trains and falling reliability. In a period of three years, from 2005–2008, rail patronage grew by 35 per cent.

Future expansion

See also: Proposed Melbourne rail extensions

In December 2008, the Brumby Government announced a $14.1 billion Victorian Transport Plan to augment Melbourne's rail network. The plan includes:

- Regional Rail Link, a new railway line at a cost of more than $4 billion, providing new tracks to separate regional trains from Metro trains, which will deliver "extra capacity on the network"
- A metro rail tunnel, costing more than $4.5 billion, from Dynon to Domain, to "relieve overcrowding on the busy suburban lines from Melbourne's west"
- Rolling stock, $2.65 billion for up to 70 new trains, including 32 "new generation" trains which will carry 30 per cent more passengers
- Rail extensions to Cranbourne East, South Morang and electrification to Sunbury and Melton, more than $2.4 billion
- Improvements to train operations, at a cost of $200 million
- Upgrades to metro stations, costing $50 million, and new stations in growth areas at a cost of $220 million
- A Park & Ride expansion package costing $60 million.

On May 1, 2009 the State Government announced that they had committed $562.3 million in the 2009 State Budget for the extension of the Epping line 3.5 kilometres north to South Morang. Construction will start in 2010 and be completed by 2013.

Operations

Melbourne's suburban electrified railway system consists of 16 interdependent lines all feeding into Flinders Street station. Some of these lines share track with regional lines, and also carry diesel-hauled passenger and goods trains to locations beyond the suburban network. Melbourne railways are built to 5 ft 3 in (1600 mm) Irish broad gauge. Interstate lines and the tram system (including former railway lines converted to light rail) are 4 ft 8 $\frac{1}{2}$ in (1435 mm) standard gauge.

Power is supplied by catenary-style overhead wiring at 1500 volts DC.

Before 1999, the network was operated by the Victorian Government, under a number of names. Until the early 1980s it was known as Victorian Railways. This was shortened to Vicrail in the early 1980s and then later in the decade the metropolitan system became known as Metropolitan Transit. This was at the same time that regional services became known as V/Line. In the 1990s this was shortened to The Met. In preparation for privatisation the system was split into Bayside Trains and Hillside Trains.

Timeline of Private Operators

- **1999 - 2009** Connex (Operated the Clifton Hill and Burnley groups and the Showgrounds services only)
- **1999 - 2004** M>Train (National Express Group)(Operated the remaining groups)

- **2009 - current** Metro Trains Melbourne (MTR Corporation Joint Venture)

Infrastructure

The Melbourne suburban rail network consists of 16 electrified lines, the central City Loop subway, and 200 stations, with a total length of 372 km of electrified lines. It operates on 1600 mm (5 ft 3 in) broad gauge track. The network is primarily at ground level, with a number of level crossings, and shared trackage with freight trains and V/Line regional services. The suburban network uses power catenary-style overhead wiring at 1500 volts DC.

Quadruple track near Caulfield station, showing signalling and overhead wiring

All but a handful of the lines include at least one single-track section, and except for flyovers at North Melbourne, Burnley, and Camberwell, all junctions are flat junctions. These restrictions hinder the performance of the system, as delays tend to "knock on" to other services. Two lines have three-track sections (the centre line being signalled for two-way operation and used for up trains in the morning peak period and down trains at other times). Where two or more lines come together in the inner area, there are four or more tracks.

Operationally, the 16 lines are divided into four groups of lines. The Clifton Hill Group comprises the two lines that branch at Clifton Hill station. The Burnley Group comprises the four lines that go through Burnley station. The Caulfield Group comprises the three lines that go through Caulfield station, plus the Sandringham line. The Northern Group comprises the remaining lines, which all go through North Melbourne station.

The City Loop consists of four single-track underground lines, one for each group, allowing trains arriving in the city from each group to circle the central business district then head out again to a destination on the same group. Trains generally operate within one of the four groups, although there is some interworking between the Burnley and Clifton Hill groups and between the Caulfield and Northern Groups.

Safeworking

Most lines in Melbourne operate under an automatic block system of safeworking with three-position power signalling. This permits signals to operate automatically with the passage of trains, enforcing the distance between them. At junctions signals are manually controlled from signal boxes, with interlockings used to ensure conflicting paths are not set. The Flemington Racecourse line has two-position automatic signalling, a variant of the three-position system.

A signal with associated train stop in the raised position to the right

The outer end of the Hurstbridge line is operated with token based systems and two-position manual signalling, where access to the line is based upon possession of a token.

Train stops are used to enforce stop indications on signals - should a train pass a signal, the train's brakes will automatically be applied. Trains are also fitted with pilot valves, a form of dead man's switch that applies the brakes should the driver fail to maintain a foot or hand pilot valve in a set position. The "VICERS" vigilance control and event recorder system is also being currently fitted to suburban trains to provide an additional level of safety.

Train control

The main control room for the rail network is Metrol. Located in the Melbourne CBD, it controls signals in the inner suburbs, tracking the location of all trains, as well as the handling the distribution of real time passenger information, and manages disruptions to the timetable. Additional signal boxes are located throughout the network, and in direct communication with Metrol.

Suburban services

Fleet

Hitachi train

Comeng train

X'Trapolis 100 train

Siemens train

All trains on the Melbourne suburban network are electric and are driver-only operated. Guards on suburban trains were discontinued between 1993 and 1995.

All trains are fitted with power-operated sliding doors which are closed by the driver, but opened by passengers. The doors of newer model X'Trapolis 100 and Siemens trains are opened by a button, but the Hitachi and Comeng trains are opened using handles. Stiff doors, sometimes found on the older Hitachi models, are often difficult to open by hand for some.

Trains also have inter-car doors to enable passengers to change carriages while in transit. All trains except the older Hitachi trains are fitted with air conditioning, closed-circuit cameras, and emergency intercom systems. Trains are fixed into three car units, and may operate alone or in pairs.

There are four types of trains in operation, each type being unable to operate coupled to another train type. The rolling stock currently consists of (numbers are number of 3-carriage units):

- 14 Hitachi Electric Multiple Units (EMU), built by Martin & King using Hitachi-designed electrical components during the 1970s. The Hitachi fleet was to be replaced by the X'trapolis and Siemens trains, but 12 (plus and additional two on long term hire from preservation group Elecrail) have been kept to cater for a growth in traffic. The Hitachi sets are all coupled semi-permanently in 6-car configuration, so effectively there are only seven sets.
- 187 Comeng EMUs, built by Commonwealth Engineering from 1981–1989, refurbished by EDi Rail and Alstom for M>Train and Connex respectively from 2000-2003.
- 81 X'Trapolis EMUs, built by Alstom from 2002-2004, 2009-current.
- 72 Siemens EMUs, built by Siemens AG from 2003-2006.

The Hitachi trains, the oldest in the fleet, and the Comeng trains can operate throughout the network, but the X'Trapolis trains can only operate on the Burnley and Clifton Hill Groups of lines, and the Siemens trains can only operate on the Caulfield and Northern Groups of lines. Although both the Siemens and X'Trapolis have been known to run without passengers on the lines they are not usually permitted on in order to access workshops, or for testing purposes.

Classification and configuration

Since shortly after the introduction of suburban electric trains in Melbourne, their carriages have been classified as follows. All fleet types have used these classifications, with different fleet types using different number ranges for the carriages.

- **M** indicates a motorised carriage, with a driving compartment.
- **T** indicates a trailer carriage.
- **D** indicated a trailer carriage with a driving compartment. Only Swing-door, Tait, and Hitachi trains had these.
- **G** indicated a trailer carriage fitted with both gas and electric lighting, for use on country services. Only Tait trains had these.
- **BT** indicated a second class trailer carriage. Prior to the abolition of first class suburban travel in 1958, motorised carriage were generally second class and trailer carriages were generally first class.

An exception to the above classifications was the trial double-deck train, which used **T** to indicate a trailer carriage with a driving compartment, and **M** to indicate a motorised carriage without a driving compartment.

Currently, all trains are assembled into a symmetrical **M-T-M** arrangement. Trains comprise either one or two such *units*. All peak period services and some off-peak services comprise two units. The few remaining Hitachi trains operate in fixed two-unit sets.

Service patterns

Melbourne uses "clock-face" timetables in off-peak periods, but generally not in peak periods, due to operating near to the capacity of the infrastructure and having to accommodate single-line sections, flat junctions, and regional diesel-hauled trains. Even in off-peak periods, however, frequencies vary according to time of day and day of week, and by line. In some places, services on two lines combine to provide more frequent services on common sections of tracks. Saturday and Sunday services are identical during the day, but differ during the evening on some lines. Sunday morning services however start later than on Saturdays, and run less frequently until around 10am.

Melbourne, along with other Australian railways, uses the British terminology of "up" and "down", with "up" being defined as toward Flinders Street Station.

Burnley Group

All trains run via the City Loop (in one direction depending on time of day and day of week), with the exception of Alamein and Blackburn services. With minor exceptions, Lilydale and Belgrave trains do not stop at East Richmond station, which is served by Glen Waverley trains.

During peak hours express trains operate from the outer ends of the Lilydale and Belgrave lines in the direction of peak travel, utilising the third track from Box Hill and the City Loop. Alamein trains run direct to Flinders Street, in addition to stopping all stations trains from the intermediate terminus of Blackburn.

All off-peak trains run via the City Loop in one direction, with the exception of Alamein services which are shuttles to and from the junction at Camberwell.

Caulfield Group

All trains on the Pakenham, Cranbourne, and Frankston lines operate via the City Loop (in one direction depending on time of day and day of week), with the exception of a small number of peak hour services. Sandringham trains also operate via the underground loop on weekends, but not weekdays.

The Frankston line has a number of peak hour express services in the direction of peak travel, utilising the third track from Moorabbin. The Pakenham and Cranbourne lines have a smaller number of peak expresses, and all Sandringham trains stop at all stations.

Clifton Hill Group

From 9 November 2008, all trains (with the exception of those departing the city after midnight, all services after midnight run direct from Flinders Street) operate via the City Loop (in a clockwise direction from Jolimont station on weekdays and anti-clockwise on weekends and public holidays). On most occasions, Hurstbridge line trains operate express between Jolimont and Clifton Hill, with the Epping trains serving the intermediate stations.

Northern Group

All trains operate via the City Loop (in one direction depending on the time of day and day of week), except for the Williamstown services. All off-peak Williamstown services are shuttles to and from the junction at Newport, while in peak they run direct from Flinders Street. Since 9 November 2008, Werribee trains do not run through the Loop during morning and afternoon peaks.

Greater metropolitan lines

Stony Point line services operate as shuttles from Frankston station with advertised connections between trains. Melton (Ballarat line) and Sunbury (Bendigo line) services are operated by V/Line and depart from Southern Cross Station, but metropolitan tickets can be used.

Special services

There are no regularly-scheduled services on the Flemington Racecourse line, but services are run to the Racecourse whenever race meetings are held at the racecourse. Services are also operated to the Showgrounds platform during the Royal Melbourne Show every September.

Fares and Tickets

Main article: Metcard

Melbourne's railway network is part of the integrated fare and ticketing system, known as *Metcard*, which covers all public transport services in Melbourne.

Metcard operated barrier gates

Fares are charged on the basis of zones and are time-based. There are two concentric zones (which was reduced from three on March 4, 2007), with fares applicable to one or two zones. Tickets are valid for two hours, all day and for longer periods, such as weekly and monthly. Within the time periods, tickets can be used on an unlimited number of services and all modes (train, tram, and bus). There is no extra fee for transfers. Various discounts are also available, such as for off-peak travel and buying tickets in bulk.

Tickets are credit-card in size with a magnetic stripe, and must be inserted in a validator before each use. Only the busier stations have ticket-operated barrier gates. At other stations, enforcement is based on honesty with random checks. Tickets are available from machines at all stations and on trams, from station ticket offices at manned stations, from bus drivers, from various retail outlets such as newsagents and convenience stores, and via the Internet. As the tickets have to be validated before use (except when bought on trams, which are sold pre-validated), they may be bought in advance and used when required.

The Metcard ticket system was due to be replaced in 2008 with a new system of smartcards, known as Myki. As of January 2010 the Myki system is being gradually implemented, and is in use on Melbourne's train network. In July 2010, the use of Myki was extended to Melbourne Metropolitan Trams and Buses.

Passenger information

Timetable information is available to passengers at stations through the **PRIDE II** system, which is an electronic timetable and announcement system, and stands for Passenger Real-time Information Dissemination Equipment. The system consists of:

- The control system, situated at Metrol.
- Control stations, at which staff update information, and announcements and CCTV recordings are dealt with for nearby stations.
- Public address systems at each station on the network. The PRIDE system automatically announces when a train is due soon, delayed, or cancelled; this is done via the rail telephone network.
- PRIDE "talking boxes" installed on each platform of all stations.
- Electronic information displays.

Control data comes from two locations: Metrol, and control stations. Next train data and times are automatically updated by the train control systems, with manual overrides also possible.

All stations are provided with "talking boxes" which have two buttons and a small speaker. The green button, when pressed, contacts the PRIDE controller over the rail telephone network, identifying itself by the DTMF tones that correspond to the ID number assigned to the box. The system then reads out times and destinations for the next two services to depart that platform (or, in the case of stations with a single island platform with departures either side, both platforms). The red button when pressed, gives the user two way communication with the closest control station.

Busy stations are often provided with an electronic LED PIDs, which indicate the destination, time, stopping pattern summary, and minutes to departure for the next train on the platform.

Finally stations on the City Loop, in addition to North Melbourne, Richmond, and Box Hill stations, have CRT screen PIDs, although some of these have recently been replaced by widescreen LCD screens. These displays show in detail the destination, scheduled and actual departure time, and all stations the next train stops at. Also shown is the destination and time of the following train, and the system is capable of providing suggested connections and warn of service interruptions.

On Sunday, 26th of September 2010, the PRIDE system was upgraded with new voice announcements. The voice is now female, and now advises to touch on and off when using Myki.

Regional passenger services

V/Line regional services share tracks with suburban trains from the outskirts of Melbourne to the central regional railway service terminus at Southern Cross Station. The Pakenham line has the longest shared line section, used by V/Line services to the Latrobe Valley. The Werribee, Sydenham and Craigieburn lines also share tracks. The Regional Rail Link project is intended to separate suburban services from all regional trains except those to the North-East and then Latrobe Valley, a ceremonial start of construction held in August 2009.

Freight services

Main article: Freight railways in Melbourne

Melbourne also has an extensive network of railway lines and yards to serve freight traffic. The lines are of two gauges - 5 ft 3 in (1600 mm) broad gauge and 4 ft 8 $\frac{1}{2}$ in (1435 mm) standard gauge, and are not electrified. In the inner western suburbs of the city, freight trains operate on dedicated lines, but in other areas freight trains share tracks with the suburban Metro Trains Melbourne and regional V/Line passenger services. The majority of freight terminals are located in the inner suburbs around Port of Melbourne, others are located between the Melbourne CBD and Footscray.

NR class locomotive at the Melbourne Steel Terminal, off Footscray Road

Until the 1980s a number of suburban stations had their own goods yards, with freight trains running over the suburban network, often with the E or L class electric locomotives.

See also

- Metro Trains Melbourne
- Rail transport in Victoria

Further reading and reviews

- *A review of Melbourne's Rail Franchising reforms* Currie, Graham (2009) Journeys, Singapore Land Transit Authority Academy [1]
- *Refranchising Melbourne's metropolitan train and tram networks* Deloitte Touche Thomatsu (2007), Department of Infrastructure [2]
- *The reliability of Melbourne's trains 1993-2007* Mees, Dr. Paul (2007); University of Melbourne Urban Planning Program paper [3]

Railways in Melbourne

External links

- Metlink [3] - official website of Melbourne's public transport
- Official map of Melbourne's modern railway network [4]
- Vicsig [5] - Victorian railways enthusiast website
- Railpage Australia [6] - enthusiast website
- V/LineCars.com [7] - Comprehensive V/Line carriage information & enthusiast website
- Dallas Delta Corporation [8] – producer of the PRIDE "talking boxes".

Buses in Melbourne

Buses in Melbourne, Australia, are a major form of public transport in Melbourne, with an extensive bus network. The network of 323 bus routes (including NightRider, excluding Kew School Services) is operated by a number of privately owned bus companies.

The Melbourne bus network is run by approximately 50 privately-owned bus corporations under a franchise from the State Government. There are approximately 300 routes in operation with a varying range of service frequencies. A NightRider bus system operates on Friday and Saturday nights, and a Smart Bus orbital bus network is being set up, which is intended to facilitate cross city travel, while the current network is predominantly a radial network. Most of the bus network is a part of the Metlink network and a part of the Metcard ticketing system.

The Skybus Super Shuttle is a non-Metcard based airport bus service. There are nine other bus companies serving Melbourne airport, with services to Ballarat, Bendigo, Dandenong, Frankston, Mornington Peninsula, Geelong, Melbourne suburbs, Shepparton and the Riverina. A daily return service from the states north—starting in Shepparton, passing through Nagambie, Seymour and Broadford—is operated by Airport Direct.

In addition, several local government councils operate free local community bus services within their local areas. In addition, there are free tourist bus services in the CBD and other tourist attractions.

While the city relies predominantly on an inner-city tram network and radial train network, the outer suburbs of Melbourne are primarily serviced by bus. Melbourne's buses also provide a local feeder to Melbourne's train and tram network. Unlike Melbourne's train and tram networks, up until the 1970s, buses in Melbourne were operated in a largely deregulated free market by private companies.[citation needed]

Bus use in Melbourne peaked in 1953 at 158 million passenger trips four years after the introduction of the network, but fell dramatically in subsequent years and three decades later passenger numbers had halved. In 2007, a total of 86.7 million passenger trips were recorded on Melbourne's buses and in recent years patronage has recovered to 1970s levels.

History

Early history

Many of Melbourne's private bus operators began by running jitney style 7 seat-buses. The use of these small buses may have been an attempt to circumvent State government regulations. While some of these early operators ran fixed routes or regular timetables, there was no State Government agency to regulate, or officially recognise these routes. Many attempted to compete with trams, running along tram routes but charging lower fares. The Motor Omnibuses Acts of 1924 and 1925 removed competition from buses on tramway routes.

The Ventura Bus Lines was founded in 1924 by Harry Cornwall, who began operating a bus route between Box Hill and the city, and later running buses along dirt tracks between Box Hill and Mentone, which roughly equates to the 700 bus route which was integrated into the orbital 903 [1] bus route. Its first depot was the petrol station on the corner of Station Street and Canterbury Road, in Box Hill South.

In 1925, Melbourne and Metropolitan Tramways Board introduced the first tramways buses. Their first bus routes ran down Swanston Street from La Trobe Street, and along Glen Huntly Road to Elsternwick Station.

After World War II, unlike other Australian cities which began to replace their trams with buses, Melbourne was by the 1960s the only Australian city with a major tram network (there is one tramline in Adelaide, and there are also trams in Bendigo). Melbourne resisted the trend because Melbourne's wide streets and geometric street pattern made trams more practicable than in many other cities. There was also resistance from the unions, and the Chairman of the MMTB, Sir Robert Risson, successfully argued that the cost of ripping up the concrete-embedded tram tracks would be prohibitive.

1950s - 1960s

From the 1950s onwards, Melbourne's bus operators began replacing jitneys with full-size buses.

Between 1952 and 1969, Ventura purchased Clarinda Transport, High Street Road Bus Service and Knibbs Bus Service. It also added a service between Blackburn and Clayton (roughly equivalent to the current 703 [2] service), added Waverley and East Burwood services, and (in 1957) opened its Oakleigh South depot at the corner of Centre and Warrigal Roads. Also during this time-frame, Ventura closed its Box Hill South depot and replaced it with a new depot at Mahoney's Road, East Burwood.

During the 1960s, the MMTB took over services in the north-eastern suburbs, after the bankruptcy of the private operator. The services would eventually be onsold to the National Bus Company. The Tramways Board took the unprecedented step of running its buses to the same level of service as its trams - every 10 to 20 minutes until midnight seven days a week.

In 1969 Ventura purchased several bus routes around Mitcham from C Young.

1970s

In 1970, Ventura acquired Boronia Bus Lines; the two purchases added 12 route services to the company.

Kefford Corporation entered the Victorian bus market in January 1976, when it acquired Point Cook - Werribee Passenger Service Pty. Ltd.

Regulation

The collapse of many bus companies led to State Government intervention in Melbourne's bus network in the 1970s. Buses would eventually fall under the responsibility of the Public Transport Corporation. The Public Transport Corporation would take over running ticketing for Melbourne's bus network, and would contract out the operation of routes to various private operators.

1980s

In December 1981, Kefford Corporation expanded its bus business beyond Melbourne, when it acquired H. A. Davis Motor Service Pty. Ltd. in Ballarat.

In July 1983, the Metropolitan Transit Authority, was formed to integrate Melbourne's tram, train, and bus services. The Metropolitan Transit Authority, commonly known as "The Met", would manage Melbourne's bus network through its Bus and Tram Division, as well as operating the tramways bus services.

The reforms included the integration of bus, train, and tram tickets. From 1983 onwards, the State Government began collecting all revenue from the multi-modal tickets, with private bus operators receiving money for costs one month in advance. Unfortunately, the State Government had trouble increasing the fixed-ticket subsidies in line with inflation. The State Government would introduce a moratorium on new bus purchases, as well as make attempts at forcing the consolidation of the numbers of private bus operators, in attempt to overcome the subsidy problem.

Go or Grow

In an attempt to cut costs, the Cain Government wanted to reduce the number of private operators, while increasing the number of cross-city bus routes. At this stage Melbourne's bus network (aside from the MET buses) was run by a large number of small, family operators which ran no more than a handful of routes each. The Cain Government reasoned that it would be more efficient, and cost effective, to have bus services provided by no more than about half a dozen large companies than dozens of small ones: larger operators would bring in economies of scale on bus purchases, repair costs, staffing, and would require fewer depots. The State Government also believed that it would be easier to negotiate contracts with a smaller number of large bus companies than with a large number of small bus companies. Thus the government put pressure on many of the small operators, in 1986, to either "Go or Grow."

In response to the State Government's "Go or Grow" policy, particularly between 1986 and 1988, there was consolidation in the bus industry. 1986 saw Driver Bus Lines amalgamate with Shave Bus Service to form Waverley Transit. The consolidation of small family operators continued into 1987, when Ventura acquired Bentleigh Bus Lines, Rennies Bus Services, Willis Bus Services and Hawthorn Bus Services. As a result of these purchases, Ventura sold its East Burwood depot and replaced it with its larger Knoxfield depot. In August 1987, Kefford Corporation acquired the Bono Bus Services which served Footscray, Highpoint City, and East Keilor. Also in 1987, Cunningham Bus Lines (who operated route 503 [3], Essendon to East Brunswick) was taken over by Moonee Valley Bus Lines.

The consolidations continued when, in January 1988, Kefford Corporation acquired Sitch Bus Services (which served Sunshine, North Sunshine, St Albans, Footscray, Yarraville, Altona, Laverton, and Williamstown), as well as Sinclair Bus Services (which served Monash University, Elwood, and Gardenvale). August 1988 saw Southland Bus Service (which operated the 645 Southland - Mentone - Sandringham, 652 Southland - Beaumaris, 654 Moorabbin - Dingley, 655 Chadstone - Murrumbeena - Southland, 656 Moorabbin - Clayton, and shared the 636 Chadstone - Hughesdale - Southland with Ventura) was taken over by the Grenda Group. Southland bus lines, along with other Grenda Group acquisitions including Blue & Silver Bus Lines, Hampton Red, Hampton Green, and Camden Bus Lines were amalgamated into Moorabbin Transit.

New bus moratorium

The bus operators now funded their operations via a State Government subsidy, partially funded by the sale of multi-modal Met Tickets (rather than each bus company issuing their own tickets). In another attempt to reduce costs beyond the 'go or grow' policy, the State Government refused to subsidise new capital investment into the private bus companies (for instance, spending on new depots) and put a moratorium on the subsidies on bus replacement. Any new additions to the fleets of bus companies would have to be covered out-of-pocket by the bus companies themselves. This policy led to the dilapidation of the bus fleet through the late 1980s and into the 1990s, though would later be lifted.

Quince's

In 1988, the then Metropolitan Transit Authority called for tenders on all of Melbourne's bus routes. Prior to the completion of tenders, Met employees reportedly told Waverley Transit 'not to bother' entering tenders for some of their existing routes. At the completion of the tender process, seven bus routes previously operated by Ventura, and three previously operated by Waverley Transit were tendered out to a company called Quince's, which had 60 buses used mostly for charter and school services.

In the case Waverley Transit V Metropolitan Transit Authority, Waverley Transit launched a Supreme Court challenge to the results of the tendering process. The verdict deemed that the State Government had acted inappropriately during the tendering process, and as the contract between the State Government and Quince's was illegal, thus restored the bus routes to Ventura and Waverley Transit. In the wake of this verdict, the Met launched an appeal, with Waverley Transit launching a counter-appeal; the cases lasted into the early 1990s. The final verdict of these cases pointed out that the licenses to operate bus routes, as well as the bus routes themselves, were legally the property of the respective bus companies and not the State Government.

In spite of this, Quince received the rights to operate a number of new cross-suburban bus routes cutting across a number of bus operator territories, including a route from Brighton to Lilydale.

1990s

By the 1990s Melbourne's public transport network was making huge losses and costing the Victorian state government many millions of dollars. In 1990 the Labor government of Premier John Cain tried to introduce economies in the running of the system, which provoked a long and crippling strike by the powerful transport unions in January 1990. When Cain resigned suddenly in August 1990, Joan Kirner was elected Labor leader and thus became Victoria's first female Premier. In October 1992 the Liberals came to power under Premier Jeff Kennett in a landslide, as a result of the public's complete disillusionment with the Labor government, which was held responsible for the state's economic and budgetary crisis. The Kennett Government pledged corporatisation of Melbourne's public transport network, however policy shifted to supporting the privatisation of the tram system in the wake of a series of public transport union strikes.

The route 401 prepaid shuttle from North Melbourne railway station to the University of Melbourne

Sita Buslines route service bus

Deregulation and Privatisation

Under the government of Jeff Kennett, the state government-run bus routes were privatised. Using the NationalBus brand, British operator National Express purchased the Public Transport Corporation's bus services in the Northern and Northeastern suburbs of Melbourne, centred around Doncaster.

Ventura Bus Lines bus parked at the Chadstone Shopping Centre bus terminus

National Bus Company commenced operations on the 27th December 1993 with a fleet made up of former Government owned buses including MAN SL200s and Volvo B59s. The company acquired two depots located at Doncaster and Fitzroy North.

In 1994, National introduced the first of 56 Mercedes-Benz LO812 mini buses. These buses were introduced under National's plan to introduce bus services in local areas previously not serviced by bus routes.

In addition, between 1997 and 2005, National has undergone extensive fleet modernisation programs in order to phase out Volvo B59s and early model MAN SL200s. This has involved the purchase of 68 Mercedes-Benz O405 series buses along with 53 low floor MAN AG buses.

A 1997 press release from then Transport Minister Robin Cooper announced that a consortium of Reservoir Bus Company and Dyson's Bus Services were the preferred bidders for the remainder of the Public Transport Corporation's bus routes (particularly in the inner city). In 1998, the routes were sold to the consortium, which operated under the name Melbourne Bus Link.

In 1998, Quince's lost their bus routes. Ironically, Quince's long cross-suburban bus routes were broken up, with sections divided between Ventura, Moorabbin Transit and Driver (for instance, the Monash University - Brighton leg of one Quince's route became part of Ventura route 703, the Glen Waverley - Mitcham section became part of Ventura route 736 [4]).

2000s

In 2000, Ventura purchased Mount Dandy Bus, while in June of that same year, Kefford Corporation acquired Geelong's Benders Buslines. In September 2003, Dyson's Bus Services acquired the Nixon Group, which was the parent company of Bell Transit, Cobb & Co., and Rambler Tours.

2002 saw the sale of Sandringham Charter Coaches to the Dineen Group, it now operates under the Sandringham & Brighton Coaches brand.

National Bus Company MAN 15.220

In 2004, Ventura purchased the National Bus Company from the National Express Group for A\$45 million, becoming the largest private bus operator in Melbourne. While the company has announced that it will continue to use the National Bus Company brand until bus contracts come under re-tender in July 2008, new National Buses are painted in the Ventura livery. Through National Express, Ventura purchased what remains of the old government fleet, which is often of particular interest to railfans, though this section of the fleet will be phased out over the coming years. Also in 2004, in September, Chris' Coaches (which also traded under the 'Melbourne on the Move' brand, and formerly operated Hope Street Bus Line) changed its name to Olympic Coaches.

Recent developments

Since the Kennett Government left office in 1999, a number of new policy initiatives have been undertaken in regards to Melbourne's bus network, as spelled out in the Melbourne 2030 and Melbourne Transport Plan documents.

These include:

- Improvements to passenger information through Metlink signage
- The introduction of higher-frequency cross-suburban SmartBus routes
- Proposals for a series of orbital bus routes, based on existing and proposed SmartBus routes.
- Progressively upgrading 250 local routes to specified minimum service levels by the state government's Department of Transport. These upgrades will mean that most local routes will run until at least 9 pm seven days a week.
- Coordinating bus service reviews based on discussions between local councils, public transport operators and community groups to address issues for service improvements.

Bus usage dropped sharply in 2006, in contrast to rail use which rose sharply, however it has since recovered.

A series of television advertisements for Metlink since 2008 have promoting public transport in Melbourne, in particular buses featured prominent comedian Frank Woodley.

SmartBus

Main article: SmartBus

The first SmartBus service begun on 5 August 2002 and will eventually establish a series of key suburban bus routes, and orbital bus routes, around Melbourne.

Key aspects of this program include longer operating hours, higher service frequency, improved information at bus stops, wheelchair accessible services and priority at traffic lights. Current Melbourne SmartBus routes are:

A bus heading towards Mordialloc in silver and orange livery.

- 703 [2] Middle Brighton - Blackburn via Bentleigh Railway Station, Clayton Railway Station, Monash University, Syndal Railway Station and Forest Hill Chase Shopping Centre
- 900 [5] Caulfield - Rowville/Stud Park S/C via Chadstone Shopping Centre, Oakleigh Railway Station, Huntingdale Railway Station, Monash University, and Waverley Park
- 901 [5] Melbourne Airport - Frankston via Broadmeadows, Roxburgh Park, Epping, Greensborough, The Pines Shopping Centre, Blackburn, Ringwood, Knox City Shopping Centre and Dandenong
- 902 [6] Airport West - Chelsea via Broadmeadows, Keon Park, Greensborough, Eltham, Doncaster Shoppingtown, Donvale, Nunawading, Glen Waverley, Springvale, Keysborough and Edithvale
- 903 [1] Altona - Mordialloc via Sunshine, Essendon, Coburg, Northland Shopping Centre, Heidelberg, Doncaster Shoppingtown, Box Hill, Holmesglen, Chadstone Shopping Centre, Oakleigh and Mentone
- 905 City - The Pines SC via Eastern Fwy and Templestowe
- 906 City - Warrandyte via Eastern Fwy and Doncaster East
- 907 City - Mitcham via Eastern Fwy, Doncaster and Bulleen
- 908 City - The Pines SC via Eastern Fwy and Doncaster East

SmartBus services typically run every 15 minutes on weekday, 30 minutes during evenings (hourly beyond 10pm on routes 703 and 888/889) and every 20 to 40 minutes on weekends. The last SmartBus services depart around midnight on weeknights, except on weekends, when services finish earlier, an example could be the 703 and 888/889 weeknight services compared to Saturday/Sunday. The final 703 departing Blackburn is 12:04am, while on Saturdays, the final service is 9:00pm, and on Sundays, the final service is 8:40pm. On the 888/889, the final service to depart Nunawading on a weeknight is 11:35pm, on Saturdays 8:23pm while on Sundays, 8:30pm. The southern portions of routes 703, 888 and 889 are not considered part of SmartBus and may receive less frequent services. An extreme example of this is the 703 does not run to/from Middle Brighton on Sundays and Public Holidays. All

Sunday and Public Holiday 703 services terminate early at Bentleigh Railway Station.

SmartBus 900, is the first truly dedicated SmartBus service. This service only stops at dedicated stops along the route from Caulfield railway station to Stud Park Shopping Centre in Rowville. SmartBus 900 was introduced to alleviate some of the pressure on the State Government to introduce a rail service to Rowville.

NightRider

Main article: NightRider

Melbourne also has a series of 13 dedicated routes which operate after midnight on Friday and Saturday nights, a time when the suburban rail network does not run. The buses fall under the standard Metcard ticketing system, until March 2007 they were covered by their own premium fares. All NightRider buses are fitted with CCTV Surveillance equipment, and mobile phone for arranging pick ups and taxis. These routes are operated under the NightRider brand by private companies under contract to the Department of Transport. Over half of all NightRider routes are operated by Dysons, but Grenda's also run three, Ventura run two, and McKenzie's operates one.

NightRider routes are typically radial in nature, which more services commencing from City Square in Swanston Street, and running to the outer suburbs. A number of loop services were introduced in November 2008 to connect with these routes in the outer suburbs to provide a night service to those who lacked them previously. A new service to Doncaster was also introduced at the same time.

See also

- List of Victorian Bus Companies
- List of Melbourne bus routes
- Transportation in Australia
- Transport in Melbourne

External links

- Department of Transport Victoria [7]
- Bus Association Victoria - BusVic [8]

Trams in Melbourne

See also: List of Melbourne tram routes

KDR Melbourne Trading as: Yarra Trams	
 Melbourne Tram Network	
Locale	Melbourne, Victoria, Australia
Dates of operation	2009–
Predecessor	Transdev TSL Trading as: Yarra Trams
Track gauge	Standard Gauge
Headquarters	Melbourne

Trams in Melbourne, Australia, are a major form of public transport and Melbourne is home to the largest tram network in the world, (following the dismantling of much of Saint Petersburg's tramway tracks early in the 21st century). Melbourne's network consists of 245 km (152.2 mi) of track, 500 trams, 28 routes, and 1,813 tram stops.

In terms of overall boardings, trams are the second most used form of public transport in Melbourne after the commuter railway network with a total of 178 million passenger trips a year. The network carries 83% as many passengers as

W6.983 in The Met livery on Victoria Parade

metropolitan rail despite having less than half the range. As of 2009, trams had the fastest growing patronage of any mode of transport in Melbourne, despite having less overall spent on extension than the rail or freeway network in the last decade.

Melbourne is the only city in Australia where, at some intersections, motor vehicles are required to perform a hook turn, a manoeuvre designed to give trams priority. To further improve tram speeds on congested Melbourne streets, trams also have priority in road usage, with specially fitted traffic lights and exclusive lanes being provided either at all times or in peak times, as well as other measures.

Trams are a distinctive part of Melbourne's character and trams feature heavily in tourism and travel advertising.

Melbourne's tram network is based on standard gauge tracks and powered by overhead wires at 600 volts DC. The infrastructure and rolling stock is owned by the Victorian Government and operated under contract, the current private operator being KDR Melbourne, operating as Yarra Trams. Melbourne's trams are a part of the Metlink marketing brand and the Metcard integrated ticketing system.

History

The interior of a W Class Tram in City Circle service

C.3010 in Transdev TSL livery on Spencer Street

C2 class tram in Transdev TSL livery

Cable trams

Main article: Melbourne cable tramway system

In 1885 the Melbourne Tramway and Omnibus Company was granted a 30-year monopoly franchise for the entire cable tram network in Melbourne, with no competing lines being permitted. The system was so comprehensive within its area of operation, that there was no way for a competing electric tram service to get into the city centre. Electric trams, when they started in Melbourne after 1906, were for the most part acting as feeders to the cable system. The only alternative form of public transport into the city centre were the railways which had been in operation since 1854.

Cable tram dummy and trailer passing the Queen Victoria Hospital on Swanston Street in Melbourne en route between Carlton and St Kilda in 1905

The cable tram network in Melbourne was progressively built after 1885 by local tramway trusts composed of local councils and municipalities, and was operated by the Melbourne Tramway and Omnibus Company. The first service ran from Spencer St/Flinders St, to Hawthorn Bridge, using the 1435 mm (4 ft 8 $\frac{1}{2}$ in) gauge, which was to become the standard tramway gauge. By 1891, the cable tramway network consisted of 17 lines running from the city to nearby suburbs. However, as the city grew, the technical limits of the cable tram system became apparent, and after 1906 electric trams were being built to radiate from the ends of some cable tram lines to more distant suburbs.

Cable tram dummy and trailer outside Melbourne Town Hall in 1910

When the franchise ended in 1916, the operation of the entire cable network was taken over by the State government.[1] The Melbourne and Metropolitan Tramways Board (MMTB) was formed in 1918, and took over the cable tram network and the tramway trusts by 1920.

The cable tram lines were progressively converted by the MMTB to electric trams from the 1920s, with the last Melbourne cable tram operating on October 26, 1940.

Electric trams

The earliest electric tram in Melbourne was operated by a group of land developers from Box Hill railway station along Tram Road to Doncaster from 1889 using equipment left over from the Great Exhibition of 1888. The venture failed and the service ceased in 1896.

Z.199 in The Met livery on Swanston Street

After this ultimately failed experiment, electric trams first returned in 1906, operated by the North Melbourne Electric Tramway and Lighting Company, which operated a line from the terminus of the cable tram to Essendon, until it was taken over by the MMTB in 1922, the last private company taken over by the MMTB. By that time the MMTB had also taken over all Melbourne's cable and electric tram companies.

The Victorian Railways also operated their 'Electric Street Railway' from St Kilda to Brighton. The Victorian Railways line came about when Thomas Bent became Premier of the State. It was alleged that he used his position to enhance the value of his property interests in Brighton by forcing the VR to build and operate a tram service in 1906.

Z1.95 in The Met livery on Swanston Street

However, it has also been said, the reluctant VR insisted that the tram be called a "Street Railway" and built it using the Victorian railway 1600 mm (5 ft 3 in) broad gauge instead of the proposed tramway standard gauge of 1435 mm (4 ft 8 $\frac{1}{2}$ in), and connected it with the St Kilda railway station instead of the cable tram terminus. The line was opened in two stages, from St Kilda railway station to Middle Brighton on 7 May 1906 and to Brighton Beach terminus on 22 December 1906. The St Kilda to Middle Brighton section was the first successful electric tramway in Melbourne.

A fire at the Elwood tram depot on 7 March 1907 destroyed the depot and all the trams. Services resumed on 17 March using four C class trams and three D class trams from Sydney, which were altered to run on VR trucks salvaged from the fire. These trams apparently sufficed until Newport Railway Workshops built 14 new trams. (The St Kilda to Brighton Beach Electric Street Railway closed on 28 February 1959 and was replaced by buses.)

When the MMTB took over Melbourne's cable and electric trams network (other than the St Kilda-Brighton street railway line) in early 1920s it inherited a system with many types of cable cars and trams. To solve the operational and maintenance problem, it introduced in 1923 the iconic W-class tram and phased out the other models, while the cable car network was converted to electric trams.

The last cable trams were replaced by electric trams in 1940, after a 55-year history.

Network under MMTB

In the "golden era" of the 1920s and 1930s, loadings were heavy, a tram conductor earned more than a schoolteacher or a policeman, and the rolling stock was well maintained. The MMTB generated further patronage by establishing the enormous Wattle Park and the Vimy House private hospital for tramways staff.

After World War II other Australian cities began to replace their trams with buses.

Melbourne's tram usage peaked at 260 million trips in 1949, before dropping sharply to 200 million the following year in 1950, the same year as the introduction of Melbourne's bus network. However usage defied the trend and bounced back in 1951, but began a gradual decline in usage which would continue until 1970. Closure of some of Melbourne's tram lines continued and replaced by buses. Despite this, during the same period bus use also went into decline and has never proved as popular with passengers as trams at any time in Melbourne's history.

By the 1970s Melbourne was the only Australian city with a major tram network. Melbourne resisted the trend to shut down the network partly because the city's wide streets and geometric street pattern made trams more practicable than in many other cities, partly because of resistance from the unions, and partly because the Chairman of the MMTB, Sir Robert Risson, successfully argued that the cost of ripping up the concrete-embedded tram tracks would be prohibitive. Also, the infrastructure and vehicles were relatively new, having only replaced Cable Tram equipment in the 1920s-1940s. This destroyed the argument used by many other cities, which was that renewal of the tram system would cost more than replacing it with buses.

Rebirth

By the mid 1970s, as other cities became increasingly choked in traffic and air pollution, Melbourne was convinced that its decision to retain its trams was the correct one, even though patronage had been declining since the 1950s in the face of increasing use of cars and the shift to the outer suburbs, beyond the tram network's limits.

The first tram line extension in over twenty years took place in 1978, along Burwood Highway. The W-class trams were gradually replaced by the new Z-class trams in the 1970s, and by the A-class trams and the larger, articulated B-class trams in the 1980s. However, in 1980, the controversial Lonie Report recommended the closure of about half of the network, in favour of buses. Public protest resulted in these closures not being carried out.

Hook turn sign

By 1990, the tram network was making losses of many millions of dollars, which was borne by the Victorian state government. In 1990, the Labor government of Premier John Cain tried to introduce economies in the running of the system, which provoked a long and crippling strike by the powerful tramways union in January 1990. Use of the network slumped to its lowest point - below 100 million trips for the first and only time since trams were in operation. In 1992, the Liberals came to power under Premier Jeff Kennett and pledged to corporatise Melbourne's public transport network. However, the policy shifted to supporting the privatisation of the tram system in the wake of a series of public transport strikes. The government abolished tram conductors and replaced them with ticketing machines, shortly before the system was privatised. This move was highly unpopular with the travelling public and led to the loss of millions of dollars in revenue through fare evasion. However, use of the system began a gradual increase. The increase in patronage, beginning in the mid 1990s was solely due to the revival of the inner urban population.[citation needed]

Privatisation

On 1 July 1998, in preparation for privatisation of the Public Transport Corporation, Melbourne's tram network was split into two businesses – Met Trams 1 Corporation (trading as Swanston Trams) and Met Trams 2 Corporation (Yarra Trams). After a tendering process with the businesses awarded as 12-year franchises, on 25 July 1999, Premier Kennett announced that the Swanston Trams business was won by National Express Group PLC, a European mass passenger transport company, and the Yarra Trams business by MetroLink Victoria Pty Ltd, a consortium with French company Transdev, Australian company Transfield Services, and French infrastructure project management company Egis Projects. Following a transitional period, the two tram businesses were officially transferred (sold) from the government to the private sector on 29 August 1999.

B2.2078 class tram in the M>Tram livery

Metlink tram stop signage outside Flinders Street Station

National Express renamed Swanston Trams as M>Tram, similarly along with its M>Train suburban train business, on 28 March 2001. After several years of failing to make a profit, more than a year of negotiations over revised financing arrangements with the government, and grave concern over its future viability, National Express Group announced on 16 December 2002, its decision to walk away from all of their Victorian contracts and hand control back to the state government, with funding for its operations to stop on 23 December 2002. The government ran M>Tram until negotiations were completed with Yarra Trams for it to take-over responsibility of the whole tram network from 18 April 2004.

On 25 June 2009, it was announced that Keolis/Downer EDI will be the operator of the Melbourne tram network from December 2009. Their contract is for 8 years with an option of a further 7 years.

Modernisation

As a part of the privatisation process, franchise contracts between the state government and both private operators included obligations to extend and modernise the Melbourne tram network. This included the purchase of new tram rolling stock, as well as the refurbishment of the current fleet which, built in the 1980s, were ready for mid-life refurbishing. The Swanston Trams (M>Tram) business invested A$175million into 59 new low-floor Combino trams by Siemens AG, and A$7.2 million to refurbish their existing trams, while the Yarra Trams consortium invested A$150 million in 31 Citadis low-floor light rail vehicles from Alstom.

In 2003 the marketing and umbrella brand Metlink was introduced to co-ordinate the promotion of Melbourne's public transport and the communications from the separate privatised companies. This was to, in turn, better integrate the three modes of transport and provide passengers with more information about connecting services provided by several operators under just one name with a unified appearance.

Recent extensions

Extensions were again made to the tram network. In 2003, the Box Hill tram/light rail extension was opened, followed by the Vermont South and Docklands tram extensions in 2005.

Fleet

W class trams

Main article: W class Melbourne tram

- **748** trams built in total 1923-1956, in service 1923–present
  - **230** total currently, 200 in storage, 26 in full service, 12 on city circle

W class trams were introduced to Melbourne in 1923 as a new standard design. They had a dual bogie layout with a distinctive 'drop centre' section, allowing the centrally placed doors to be lower to the ground. They are a simple rugged design, with a substantially timber frame, supplanted by a steel under-frame, characterised by fine craftsmanship. The W Class was the mainstay of Melbourne's tramways system for 60 years. A total of 748 trams of all variants were built, the last in 1956.

It was not until the 1980s that the W Class started to be replaced in large numbers, and by 1990 their status as an icon for the city was recognised, leading to a listing by the National Trust. Public outrage over their sale for tourist use overseas led to an embargo on further export out of the country in 1993, though recently some have been given or loaned to various Museums. Approximately 200 of the W class trams retired since then remain stored, and the future use of these trams is unknown.

By 2006 the number of operating W Class trams has been gradually reduced to about 45, running regularly on the North Richmond to Prahran / St Kilda Beach route (Route:78/79), and a short shuttle along La Trobe Street in the CBD. The zero-fare City Circle route also operates using the W class. The oldest W class tram remaining in service run this route, dating from 1936. There are also three others converted into mobile restaurants which cruise the suburbs in the evening.

Of the W-class trams that have been sent overseas, five went to Seattle between 1978 and 1993, where they operated as Seattle's George Benson Waterfront Streetcar Line, starting in 1982 but suspended in 2005. Another nine are now part of the downtown Memphis tourist service, while many other US cities have one or two.

As of 2010, there are 230 W-class trams, 200 of which are in storage, 12 run on the city circle loop and 26 are used on two inner city routes. A proposal exists to better utilise the unused W-class trams by refurbishing and leasing them as "roving ambassadors" to other cities, generating revenue which could then be invested back into the public transport system. In January 2010, it was announced by the new transport minister that the 26 W-class trams running the two inner city routes, would be phased out by 2012, prompting a new campaign from the National Trust of Australia.

Z class trams

Main article: Z class Melbourne tram

- Z1 - **100** built, made in Australia, slowly being withdrawn from service
- Z2 - **15** built, made in Australia, slowly being withdrawn from service
- Z3 - **115** built, made in Australia, 114 currently in service

The development of new rolling stock to replace the W Class finally began in 1975 with a complex and expensive Swedish design that was ill-suited to Melbourne's hot summers and heavy loadings.

The Z-class trams, built by Comeng, were introduced from the mid-late 1970s, starting with the Z1 class, built from 1975 to 1979. 100 trams were built, most of which are now being withdrawn. Those withdrawn are usually sold at auction. Some have also been donated to tram museums in places such as Bendigo.

In 1978 and 1979, fifteen Z2 class trams—having little difference from the Z1 classes—were built. As with the Z1 class, Z2 class trams are now being withdrawn from service.

From 1979 to 1984, Z3 class trams were introduced, being a significant improvement on the Z1 and Z2 class trams. They had an additional door each side and much smoother acceleration and braking. 115 were built, 114 of which are in service (Z3.149 was destroyed in a fire). All are re-liveried in either Yarra Trams or all-over advertising livery.

A class trams

Main article: A class Melbourne tram

- A-class - **70** built, all still in service, made in Australia

These trams, again built by Comeng, were introduced between 1984 and 1987. This model did away with the concept of a seated conductor, which was characteristic of the Z class trams. 70 were built and are still in service today.

A C class tram at the St Vincent's Plaza
stop in East Melbourne

B class trams

Main article: B class Melbourne tram

- B1 - **2** built, made in Australia, both still in service
- B2 - **130** built, made in Australia, all currently in service, air conditioned

The B-class trams (also known as light rail vehicles) were first introduced to Melbourne in 1984 with the prototype B1 class trams, which were a significant improvement over the Z1-classes. The B class tram was a lengthened version of the A class tram. Only 2 were built and they remain in service today.

B2 class trams were built from 1988–1994, by Comeng, and later ABB Transportation. They were an improvement over the B1-classes. 130 were built (No 2003-2132), all of which remain in service today. B2-classes are often spotted in all-over advertising livery. The B2 class was notable for the long overdue introduction of air-conditioning.

All of the B2-classes, and B1.2002 have been repainted in Yarra Trams livery (B1.2001 is in all-over advertising livery, but was also in Yarra Trams livery).

Citadis (C-class) and Combino (D-class)

See also: C class and D class

- C1 - **36** in service, made in France
- C2 - **5** in service, leased from Mulhouse, France ("Bumblebees")
- D1 - **38** in service, made in Germany, owned by Yarra Trams
- D2 - **21** in service, made in Germany, owned by Yarra Trams

The Citadis and Combino trams were introduced following privatisation of Melbourne's tram system. The private operators were obliged under their franchises to replace older Z class trams, although this has not fully taken place. Yarra Trams introduced the Citadis or C class, manufactured in France by Alstom. It is a three section articulated vehicle. Thirty-six are in service. The now defunct M>Tram purchased the German made Siemens Combino. The Combino is a three (D1 class) or five (D2 class) section articulated vehicle. Ownership of the D class trams has now passed to Yarra Trams. Currently 38 D1 and 21 D2 section vehicles are in service. The Combinos are generally favored over the Citadis by tram drivers, as they are easier on the wrist when driving and make it much easier to answer passenger queries.

The five C2 class trams are another low floor tram, introduced in 2008 after being leased from Mulhouse in France. They have been dubbed 'Bumblebees' due to their distinctive yellow colour, and exclusively run on route 96. In a newspaper report titled 'Bees to stay on track' says that the State Government is poised to purchase the 5 C2 trams from France.

Popular culture

Melbourne's tram system has been celebrated across several media. The city's system is the central theme of the movie *Malcolm*. A flying Melbourne tram was also a feature of the 2006 Commonwealth Games Opening Ceremony. Among songs devoted to Melbourne's Tram, is "Toorak Tram", by Bernard Bolan

The "flying tram" featured in the Opening Ceremony, sitting on a Melbourne street map.

Network expansion

Mode Connectivity Links

In response to the State Government's 2001 Melbourne 2030 planning policy, the Public Transport Users Association lobbied for extensions (most of which are in line with the Melbourne 2030 planning policy to provide links between different modes of transport) including:

- East Malvern (route 3) to the East Malvern railway station or Chadstone Shopping Centre.

- High Street (route 6) to Ashburton station
- Toorak (route 8) to Hartwell station (serving two rail lines and the Coles Group headquarters)
- Cotham Road Kew (route 16) to Kew Junction in Kew. (Which would not require a rail extension, it merely requires the tram to travel further)
- Camberwell (route 72) to North Kew or Ivanhoe (connecting with the proposed East Doncaster rail line), and also south to Caulfield.

Balwyn - Heidelberg

The Victorian Greens 'The People Plan' proposes an extension of the Route 72 from Burke Road, Balwyn to Heidelberg.

Burwood - Doncaster Hill

The Victorian Greens 'The People Plan' proposes a route from Doncaster, via Box Hill, to Burwood.

Sunshine - Highpoint

The Victorian Greens 'The People Plan' proposes an extension from Highpoint, via Maidstone, to Sunshine.

Moonee Ponds - Clifton Hill

The Victorian Greens 'The People Plan' proposes an extension from Moonee Ponds, along Ormond and Brunswick Roads, to Clifton Hill station.

South Melbourne - Toorak

In 2006 there were strong calls by a joint council project and the (Inner Melbourne Action Group) to provide an inner south tram link between City of Port Phillip and City of Stonnington by connecting route 112 with route 8 via Park Street. This would require less than 100 metres of track to be laid along the Park Street gap to create the new route.

Carnegie Tram-Train link

An extension of the (route 67) to the Carnegie station would require just under 2 kilometres of track and would increase patronage on the tram route, greatly reduce walking distance for mode transfer and service the busy Koornang Road in the Carnegie shopping precinct. The extension has been a campaign of the Public Transport Users Association since 2006.

Knox City

Route 75 was originally proposed by the State government to terminate at Knox City Shopping Centre, however it did not complete the construction, instead terminating at Vermont South with the option of a future extension.

Doncaster

Light rail routes to service Doncaster have been raised on numerous occasions as an alternative to the overloaded bus system and expensive heavy rail proposals.

The Public Transport Users Association has been lobbying for an extension of the North Balwyn (route 48) to Doncaster Shopping Centre, other proposals include extension along Doncaster Road to Donvale or Mitcham.

The Doncaster Light Rail has been made reference to in several reports and studies since 2000, including the Rowville Rail Pre-feasibility Study.

Eastlink Light Rail Reservation

When the Eastlink roadway was in planning, the State Government created a reservation for a future heavy or light rail corridor and conducted a feasibility study into a light rail system to service the outer eastern suburbs. However the road became tolled and light rail did not eventuate. A SmartBus system was implemented instead. However the reservation remains which would have potentially provided a link between the Belgrave/Lilydale, Pakenham/Cranbourne and Stony Point railway groups.

Port Melbourne proposals

There have been a number of proposals for tram and light rail extension in Port Melbourne.

St Kilda-Port Melbourne link

A 5 kilometre tram link between St Kilda, Victoria and Port Melbourne along Beaconsfield Parade was first raised by the City of Port Phillip in 2005. The City of Port Phillip's 2007 feasibility study into the route found that the high density population could sustain around 200,000 annual commuter trips and that the link would be financially viable if tourists were charged $6 per one-way trip.

To address residents concerns over possible loss of beachfront views, the council investigated the possibility of a new high-tech line, involving wire-free operation. Critics argued that it would be duplicating the 112 route, with the two routes running in parallel just 200 metres apart for about 2 kilometres along Beaconsfield Parade. However a direct tram journey between St Kilda and Port Melbourne is not possible and currently requires a change of routes at Southbank which is a 20 kilometre round trip.

Fisherman's Bend proposal

During the Australian Greens 2007 federal election campaign a call was made for more federal funding of public transport projects including a proposal for a new light rail route from Melbourne to Port Melbourne and/or Garden City via Lorimer Street to service the once industrial inner city suburb's fast growing business and residential areas and to open up the possibility of future high density residential development along the route.

Melbourne - Footscray Light Rail Reservation

The Melbourne City Council first proposed extending Route 86 from the Docklands along Footscray Road to Footscray station in 2004. The proposal was to be grade separated along almost the entire length of Footscray Road.

The extension became part of the official Inner Melbourne Action Plan adopted by the Cities of Melbourne, Stonnington, Port Phillip and Yarra in December 2005 as a "long term" goal.

Since 2007 plans have progressed, with the City of Melbourne attempting to source funding.

In response to the Eddington Plan in July 2008, the City of Melbourne included a request for consideration as a key East-West transport solution.

The Victorian Greens also included the route in its 'The People Plan' election proposal.

However the propopsal it suffered a setback in late 2008 when it met State Government opposition. The Department of Infrastructure recommended the removal of the Footscray Road reservation to reduce the cost of constructing a overpass to ease congestion on the CityLink freeway off-ramp. The State Government's plan was rejected by the City of Melbourne who passed the flyover project in council on the provision that it would retain the light-rail reservation, at additional State Government expense whilst also adding to the future cost of the tram link.

Williamstown

In 2005, a proposal was considered by the Victorian state government and the City of Hobsons Bay including four options for a new Williamstown tramway, including a line from North Williamstown station running along Ferguson St to the Strand operated by heritage cars; closing Williamstown railway line and replacing with a tram service ; Constructing a line from Newport station to Williamstown via Melbourne Road and Ferguson St; Rebuilding a short section of line from Williamstown to Williamstown Pier

Fawkner Extension

A proposal to extend the route 19 North Coburg-Elizabeth Street tram to Fawkner, a suburb in the northern suburbs of Melbourne has been suggested by many lobby groups. About 3 kilometres of track would need to be laid along Sydney Road and Hume Highway from North Coburg to Fawkner.

In 1993 plans were made to demolish most of the Upfield Railway Line and install a light rail service. Due to the unpopularity of the plan, the idea was scrapped and the railway line still exists today.

The Public Transport Users Association called for the extension in 2006. The proposal was also included as part of the Victorian Greens 2008 'The People Plan'.

See also

- Buses in Melbourne
- List of Melbourne tram routes
- List of tram and light-rail transit systems
- Railways in Melbourne
- Tram controls
- Trams in Australia
- Tramway Museum Society Of Victoria

External links

Official

- Official map of Melbourne's tram network [2]
- Metlink - official website of Melbourne's public transport [3]
- Yarra Trams [5]
- 100 Years of Electric Trams in Melbourne [4]

Enthusiast

- VICSIG - Victorian tramway infrastructure and rollingstock information [5]
- Melbourne's Trams To The Millennium [6]
- Trams of Australia : history [7] and current [8]
- Unofficial Public Transport Guide to Melbourne [9]
- Tram People Down Under: DVD Video Documentary [10]
- Prince of Rails [11] The IET. 2009-01-19.
- Geographically accurate map on Google Maps [12]

Article Sources and Contributors

Melbourne *Source*: http://en.wikipedia.org/?oldid=390654469 *Contributors*: Mattinbgn

History of Melbourne *Source*: http://en.wikipedia.org/?oldid=381841035 *Contributors*: 1 anonymous edits

Melbourne City Centre *Source*: http://en.wikipedia.org/?oldid=389455607 *Contributors*: Biatch

Hoddle Grid *Source*: http://en.wikipedia.org/?oldid=389437738 *Contributors*: Biatch

Docklands, Victoria *Source*: http://en.wikipedia.org/?oldid=390609962 *Contributors*: Wcrosbie

Southbank, Victoria *Source*: http://en.wikipedia.org/?oldid=377199232 *Contributors*: Erianna

South Melbourne, Victoria *Source*: http://en.wikipedia.org/?oldid=381987135 *Contributors*: Crusoe8181

Fitzroy, Victoria *Source*: http://en.wikipedia.org/?oldid=390172105 *Contributors*: WalkingMelbourne

Carlton, Victoria *Source*: http://en.wikipedia.org/?oldid=390197811 *Contributors*: WalkingMelbourne

Caulfield North, Victoria *Source*: http://en.wikipedia.org/?oldid=384228443 *Contributors*: 1 anonymous edits

Heide Museum of Modern Art *Source*: http://en.wikipedia.org/?oldid=388834710 *Contributors*: Hmains

Melbourne Museum *Source*: http://en.wikipedia.org/?oldid=382533246 *Contributors*: George Burgess

Immigration Museum, Melbourne *Source*: http://en.wikipedia.org/?oldid=333156786 *Contributors*: Simeon

Australian Centre for Contemporary Art *Source*: http://en.wikipedia.org/?oldid=379469094 *Contributors*: R'n'B

Gertrude Contemporary Art Spaces *Source*: http://en.wikipedia.org/?oldid=371692359 *Contributors*:

The Arts Centre (Melbourne) *Source*: http://en.wikipedia.org/?oldid=387856934 *Contributors*: Diannaa

National Gallery of Victoria *Source*: http://en.wikipedia.org/?oldid=387165058 *Contributors*:

State Library of Victoria *Source*: http://en.wikipedia.org/?oldid=371159560 *Contributors*: Elekhh

St Paul's Cathedral, Melbourne *Source*: http://en.wikipedia.org/?oldid=385369729 *Contributors*:

Collins Street Baptist Church *Source*: http://en.wikipedia.org/?oldid=378188552 *Contributors*: Hugo999

East Melbourne Hebrew Congregation *Source*: http://en.wikipedia.org/?oldid=371617212 *Contributors*:

Scots' Church, Melbourne *Source*: http://en.wikipedia.org/?oldid=388525426 *Contributors*:

St Francis Catholic Church (Melbourne) *Source*: http://en.wikipedia.org/?oldid=367762724 *Contributors*: Curleyellen

St Patrick's Cathedral, Melbourne *Source*: http://en.wikipedia.org/?oldid=389811527 *Contributors*: 1 anonymous edits

Wesley Church, Melbourne *Source*: http://en.wikipedia.org/?oldid=378146248 *Contributors*: Douglasmiller

Bishopscourt, East Melbourne *Source*: http://en.wikipedia.org/?oldid=358191171 *Contributors*: 1 anonymous edits

Shrine of Remembrance *Source*: http://en.wikipedia.org/?oldid=386554576 *Contributors*: Figaro

South Melbourne Town Hall *Source*: http://en.wikipedia.org/?oldid=361049112 *Contributors*: Biatch

Melbourne Town Hall *Source*: http://en.wikipedia.org/?oldid=371706313 *Contributors*: Look2See1

Box Hill Town Hall *Source*: http://en.wikipedia.org/?oldid=243767407 *Contributors*: Nsk92

Brighton Town Hall *Source*: http://en.wikipedia.org/?oldid=386540975 *Contributors*: Jllm06

Brunswick Town Hall *Source*: http://en.wikipedia.org/?oldid=348259160 *Contributors*: RL0919

Camberwell Town Hall *Source*: http://en.wikipedia.org/?oldid=348435510 *Contributors*: RL0919

Coburg City Hall *Source*: http://en.wikipedia.org/?oldid=385288802 *Contributors*: Twp

Collingwood Town Hall *Source*: http://en.wikipedia.org/?oldid=356914146 *Contributors*: Mattinbgn

Fitzroy Town Hall *Source*: http://en.wikipedia.org/?oldid=348435562 *Contributors*: RL0919

Footscray Town Hall *Source*: http://en.wikipedia.org/?oldid=360856756 *Contributors*: 1 anonymous edits

Heidelberg Town Hall *Source*: http://en.wikipedia.org/?oldid=384376540 *Contributors*: Melburnian

Northcote Town Hall *Source*: http://en.wikipedia.org/?oldid=379099335 *Contributors*: MRSC

North Melbourne Town Hall *Source*: http://en.wikipedia.org/?oldid=384365542 *Contributors*: Billingd

Victorian Trades Hall *Source*: http://en.wikipedia.org/?oldid=366675361 *Contributors*:

Parliament House, Melbourne *Source*: http://en.wikipedia.org/?oldid=382698461 *Contributors*: 1 anonymous edits

Hamer Hall, Melbourne *Source*: http://en.wikipedia.org/?oldid=386802386 *Contributors*: Waacstats

Federation Square *Source*: http://en.wikipedia.org/?oldid=386604895 *Contributors*: Kevlar67

Clocktower Centre *Source*: http://en.wikipedia.org/?oldid=348433330 *Contributors*: RL0919

Victoria Barracks, Melbourne *Source*: http://en.wikipedia.org/?oldid=388045012 *Contributors*: 1 anonymous edits

HM Prison Pentridge *Source*: http://en.wikipedia.org/?oldid=389115361 *Contributors*: Muhandes

City Baths, Melbourne *Source*: http://en.wikipedia.org/?oldid=380668884 *Contributors*: Ewawer

Old Melbourne Gaol *Source*: http://en.wikipedia.org/?oldid=390612242 *Contributors*: Purrum

Newport Workshops *Source*: http://en.wikipedia.org/?oldid=389961064 *Contributors*:

Queen Victoria Market *Source*: http://en.wikipedia.org/?oldid=378612887 *Contributors*:

Hotel Windsor (Melbourne) *Source*: http://en.wikipedia.org/?oldid=387293596 *Contributors*:

Bali Memorial, Melbourne *Source*: http://en.wikipedia.org/?oldid=373370194 *Contributors*: Millahnna

Spencer Street, Melbourne *Source*: http://en.wikipedia.org/?oldid=381442538 *Contributors*: Orderinchaos

Rippon Lea Estate *Source*: http://en.wikipedia.org/?oldid=378304406 *Contributors*: Eleworth

Valentines Mansion *Source*: http://en.wikipedia.org/?oldid=371215475 *Contributors*: Quartic

Rialto Towers *Source*: http://en.wikipedia.org/?oldid=388256109 *Contributors*:

Royal Exhibition Building *Source*: http://en.wikipedia.org/?oldid=389986509 *Contributors*: SMasters

La Mama Theatre (Melbourne) *Source*: http://en.wikipedia.org/?oldid=384370914 *Contributors*: Billingd

State Theatre (Melbourne) *Source*: http://en.wikipedia.org/?oldid=336122548 *Contributors*: LilHelpa

Princess Theatre, Melbourne *Source*: http://en.wikipedia.org/?oldid=353957577 *Contributors*: Boweneer

Regent Theatre, Melbourne *Source*: http://en.wikipedia.org/?oldid=390302251 *Contributors*: And1987

Forum Theatre *Source*: http://en.wikipedia.org/?oldid=373737605 *Contributors*: Shyguy1991

Palace Theatre, Melbourne *Source*: http://en.wikipedia.org/?oldid=371616663 *Contributors*:

Comedy Theatre, Melbourne *Source*: http://en.wikipedia.org/?oldid=371736687 *Contributors*:

Melbourne Athenaeum *Source*: http://en.wikipedia.org/?oldid=369341233 *Contributors*: Bduke

Her Majesty's Theatre, Melbourne *Source*: http://en.wikipedia.org/?oldid=390678739 *Contributors*: McAusten

Capitol Theatre, Melbourne *Source*: http://en.wikipedia.org/?oldid=388729350 *Contributors*:

Malthouse Theatre, Melbourne *Source*: http://en.wikipedia.org/?oldid=378745179 *Contributors*: 1 anonymous edits

Victorian Opera (Melbourne) *Source*: http://en.wikipedia.org/?oldid=376547742 *Contributors*: Design

Melbourne Symphony Orchestra *Source*: http://en.wikipedia.org/?oldid=389451818 *Contributors*: JackofOz

Centre for Contemporary Photography *Source*: http://en.wikipedia.org/?oldid=371684577 *Contributors*:

Melbourne International Arts Festival *Source*: http://en.wikipedia.org/?oldid=343298146 *Contributors*: MelbFest

Melbourne International Film Festival *Source*: http://en.wikipedia.org/?oldid=386432915 *Contributors*:

Melbourne International Comedy Festival *Source*: http://en.wikipedia.org/?oldid=390369508 *Contributors*: Wcrosbie

Melbourne Fringe Festival *Source*: http://en.wikipedia.org/?oldid=377655987 *Contributors*: LilHelpa

Melbourne International Flower and Garden Show *Source*: http://en.wikipedia.org/?oldid=371743791 *Contributors*:

Royal Melbourne Show *Source*: http://en.wikipedia.org/?oldid=382193531 *Contributors*: BD2412

Melbourne International Animation Festival *Source*: http://en.wikipedia.org/?oldid=371689729 *Contributors*:

Melbourne Spring Racing Carnival *Source*: http://en.wikipedia.org/?oldid=382608232 *Contributors*:

Melbourne Jazz Festival *Source*: http://en.wikipedia.org/?oldid=371617865 *Contributors*:

Melbourne Underground Film Festival *Source*: http://en.wikipedia.org/?oldid=384964287 *Contributors*: 1 anonymous edits

Centro Box Hill *Source*: http://en.wikipedia.org/?oldid=389272832 *Contributors*: Lakeyboy

Block Arcade, Melbourne *Source*: http://en.wikipedia.org/?oldid=384351324 *Contributors*: 1 anonymous edits

Royal Arcade, Melbourne *Source*: http://en.wikipedia.org/?oldid=368015907 *Contributors*: Deor

Werribee Park *Source*: http://en.wikipedia.org/?oldid=374704929 *Contributors*:

Luna Park, Melbourne *Source*: http://en.wikipedia.org/?oldid=390012075 *Contributors*: Teles

Princes Park (stadium) *Source*: http://en.wikipedia.org/?oldid=384543176 *Contributors*: Melbourne.sport

Albert Park, Victoria *Source*: http://en.wikipedia.org/?oldid=383022423 *Contributors*: Crusoe8181

Footscray Park *Source*: http://en.wikipedia.org/?oldid=360083849 *Contributors*: Deor

Fawkner Park, Melbourne *Source*: http://en.wikipedia.org/?oldid=361727743 *Contributors*: Deor

Edinburgh Gardens, Melbourne *Source*: http://en.wikipedia.org/?oldid=378854767 *Contributors*: Interscan

Carlton Gardens, Melbourne *Source*: http://en.wikipedia.org/?oldid=382113076 *Contributors*: Yousou

St Vincent Gardens, Melbourne *Source*: http://en.wikipedia.org/?oldid=361729384 *Contributors*: Deor

Royal Botanic Gardens, Melbourne *Source*: http://en.wikipedia.org/?oldid=382427848 *Contributors*: Bracteantha

Queen Victoria Gardens, Melbourne *Source*: http://en.wikipedia.org/?oldid=360812202 *Contributors*: Deor

Alexandra Gardens, Melbourne *Source*: http://en.wikipedia.org/?oldid=387331901 *Contributors*:

Treasury Gardens *Source*: http://en.wikipedia.org/?oldid=384371881 *Contributors*: Billingd

Fitzroy Gardens, Melbourne *Source*: http://en.wikipedia.org/?oldid=355493263 *Contributors*: Aaroncrick

Flagstaff Gardens *Source*: http://en.wikipedia.org/?oldid=385314647 *Contributors*: Billingd

Hedgeley Dene Gardens *Source*: http://en.wikipedia.org/?oldid=361728672 *Contributors*: Deor

Melbourne Zoo *Source*: http://en.wikipedia.org/?oldid=389524123 *Contributors*: Donlammers

Batman's Hill *Source*: http://en.wikipedia.org/?oldid=387120307 *Contributors*: Billingd

Melbourne Aquarium *Source*: http://en.wikipedia.org/?oldid=388759223 *Contributors*:

Morell Bridge *Source*: http://en.wikipedia.org/?oldid=389697210 *Contributors*:

Princes Bridge *Source*: http://en.wikipedia.org/?oldid=385194475 *Contributors*: Muhandes

Sandridge Bridge *Source*: http://en.wikipedia.org/?oldid=385335119 *Contributors*: Muhandes

Melbourne Victory FC *Source*: http://en.wikipedia.org/?oldid=390221796 *Contributors*: Camw

Melbourne Storm *Source*: http://en.wikipedia.org/?oldid=390487656 *Contributors*: 1 anonymous edits

Melbourne Cricket Club *Source*: http://en.wikipedia.org/?oldid=381331990 *Contributors*: Jenks24

Melbourne Football Club *Source*: http://en.wikipedia.org/?oldid=390044282 *Contributors*: Jenks24

Transport in Melbourne *Source*: http://en.wikipedia.org/?oldid=386553644 *Contributors*:

Melbourne Airport *Source*: http://en.wikipedia.org/?oldid=390641505 *Contributors*: Bidgee

Avalon Airport *Source*: http://en.wikipedia.org/?oldid=389077194 *Contributors*: 1 anonymous edits

Moorabbin Airport *Source*: http://en.wikipedia.org/?oldid=387696020 *Contributors*:

Essendon Airport *Source*: http://en.wikipedia.org/?oldid=390583616 *Contributors*: 1 anonymous edits

Port of Melbourne *Source*: http://en.wikipedia.org/?oldid=388009287 *Contributors*:

Railways in Melbourne *Source*: http://en.wikipedia.org/?oldid=387955787 *Contributors*: Daduzi

Buses in Melbourne *Source*: http://en.wikipedia.org/?oldid=390420880 *Contributors*: 1 anonymous edits

Trams in Melbourne *Source*: http://en.wikipedia.org/?oldid=390234145 *Contributors*: 1 anonymous edits

Image Sources, Licenses and Contributors

File:Melbourne montage six frame infobox jpg.jpg *Source*: http://bibliocm.bibliolabs.com/mwAnon/index.php?title=File:Melbourne_montage_six_frame_infobox_jpg.jpg *License*: Creative Commons Attribution-Sharealike 3.0 *Contributors*: User:AshGreen, User:Diliff

File:Australia location map.svg *Source*: http://bibliocm.bibliolabs.com/mwAnon/index.php?title=File:Australia_location_map.svg *License*: unknown *Contributors*: -

File:Red pog.svg *Source*: http://bibliocm.bibliolabs.com/mwAnon/index.php?title=File:Red_pog.svg *License*: unknown *Contributors*: -

File:Landing at melbourne 1840.jpg *Source*: http://bibliocm.bibliolabs.com/mwAnon/index.php?title=File:Landing_at_melbourne_1840.jpg *License*: unknown *Contributors*: -

File:Canvas town south melbourne victoria 1850s.jpg *Source*: http://bibliocm.bibliolabs.com/mwAnon/index.php?title=File:Canvas_town_south_melbourne_victoria_1850s.jpg *License*: unknown *Contributors*: -

File:Melbourne international exhibition 1880.jpg *Source*: http://bibliocm.bibliolabs.com/mwAnon/index.php?title=File:Melbourne_international_exhibition_1880.jpg *License*: unknown *Contributors*: -

File:Yarra River railway bridge 1928.jpg *Source*: http://bibliocm.bibliolabs.com/mwAnon/index.php?title=File:Yarra_River_railway_bridge_1928.jpg *License*: Public Domain *Contributors*: Original uploader was Wongm at en.wikipedia

File:Melbourne skyline, 1959.jpg *Source*: http://bibliocm.bibliolabs.com/mwAnon/index.php?title=File:Melbourne_skyline,_1959.jpg *License*: unknown *Contributors*: -

File:Melbourne docklands twilight.jpg *Source*: http://bibliocm.bibliolabs.com/mwAnon/index.php?title=File:Melbourne_docklands_twilight.jpg *License*: unknown *Contributors*: -

File:Greater Melbourne Map 4 - May 2008.png *Source*: http://bibliocm.bibliolabs.com/mwAnon/index.php?title=File:Greater_Melbourne_Map_4_-_May_2008.png *License*: Creative Commons Attribution-Sharealike 3.0 *Contributors*: User:Diliff

File:Victoria Avenue - Canterbury.jpg *Source*: http://bibliocm.bibliolabs.com/mwAnon/index.php?title=File:Victoria_Avenue_-_Canterbury.jpg *License*: unknown *Contributors*: -

File:Melbourne Skyline from Rialto Crop - Nov 2008.jpg *Source*: http://bibliocm.bibliolabs.com/mwAnon/index.php?title=File:Melbourne_Skyline_from_Rialto_Crop_-_Nov_2008.jpg *License*: GNU Free Documentation License *Contributors*: User:Diliff

Image:Centre Place.jpg *Source*: http://bibliocm.bibliolabs.com/mwAnon/index.php?title=File:Centre_Place.jpg *License*: unknown *Contributors*: -

Image:Melbourne CBD (View from the top of Shrine of Remembrance).jpg *Source*: http://bibliocm.bibliolabs.com/mwAnon/index.php?title=File:Melbourne_CBD_(View_from_the_top_of_Shrine_of_Remembrance).jpg *License*: Creative Commons Attribution-Sharealike 2.5 *Contributors*: User:Donaldytong

File:Neighbours Pinoak Court.jpg *Source*: http://bibliocm.bibliolabs.com/mwAnon/index.php?title=File:Neighbours_Pinoak_Court.jpg *License*: Public Domain *Contributors*: Gareth

File:Victorian terrace on canterbury road, Middle Park.jpg *Source*: http://bibliocm.bibliolabs.com/mwAnon/index.php?title=File:Victorian_terrace_on_canterbury_road,_Middle_Park.jpg *License*: Attribution *Contributors*: User:Donaldytong

File:Litter trap.jpg *Source*: http://bibliocm.bibliolabs.com/mwAnon/index.php?title=File:Litter_trap.jpg *License*: unknown *Contributors*: -

File:Leonard French National Gallery of Victoria 1968 01.jpg *Source*: http://bibliocm.bibliolabs.com/mwAnon/index.php?title=File:Leonard_French_National_Gallery_of_Victoria_1968_01.jpg *License*: unknown *Contributors*: -

File:Princess Theatre, Melbourne, Australia.jpg *Source*: http://bibliocm.bibliolabs.com/mwAnon/index.php?title=File:Princess_Theatre,_Melbourne,_Australia.jpg *License*: unknown *Contributors*: -

Image:Etihad Stadium crop.jpg *Source*: http://bibliocm.bibliolabs.com/mwAnon/index.php?title=File:Etihad_Stadium_crop.jpg *License*: Creative Commons Attribution-Sharealike 3.0 *Contributors*: User:Invincible

Image:Docklands 9984.jpg *Source*: http://bibliocm.bibliolabs.com/mwAnon/index.php?title=File:Docklands_9984.jpg *License*: unknown *Contributors*: -

Image:Aust.-Synchrotron-Interior-Panorama,-14.06.2007.jpg *Source*: http://bibliocm.bibliolabs.com/mwAnon/index.php?title=File:Aust.-Synchrotron-Interior-Panorama,-14.06.2007.jpg *License*: unknown *Contributors*: -

Image:St pauls, melbourne.jpg *Source*: http://bibliocm.bibliolabs.com/mwAnon/index.php?title=File:St_pauls,_melbourne.jpg *License*: Creative Commons Attribution-Sharealike 2.5 *Contributors*: User:Adam.J.W.C.

Image:St Patrick's Cathedral - Gothic Revival Style.jpg *Source*: http://bibliocm.bibliolabs.com/mwAnon/index.php?title=File:St_Patrick's_Cathedral_-_Gothic_Revival_Style.jpg *License*: unknown *Contributors*: -

Image:Federation Square (SBS Building).jpg *Source*: http://bibliocm.bibliolabs.com/mwAnon/index.php?title=File:Federation_Square_(SBS_Building).jpg *License*: Public Domain *Contributors*: User:Donaldytong

Image:Victoria Parliament Melbourne (Colonnades & Stairs).jpg *Source*: http://bibliocm.bibliolabs.com/mwAnon/index.php?title=File:Victoria_Parliament_Melbourne_(Colonnades_&_Stairs).jpg *License*: unknown *Contributors*: -

Image:Melbourne Town Hall-Collins Street.JPG *Source*: http://bibliocm.bibliolabs.com/mwAnon/index.php?title=File:Melbourne_Town_Hall-Collins_Street.JPG *License*: GNU Free Documentation License *Contributors*: Original uploader was Adz at en.wikipedia

File:State Library of Victoria La Trobe Reading room 5th floor view.jpg *Source*: http://bibliocm.bibliolabs.com/mwAnon/index.php?title=File:State_Library_of_Victoria_La_Trobe_Reading_room_5th_floor_view.jpg *License*: Creative Commons Attribution 2.5 *Contributors*: User:Diliff

Image:Scotch College Melbourne chapel 2.jpg *Source*: http://bibliocm.bibliolabs.com/mwAnon/index.php?title=File:Scotch_College_Melbourne_chapel_2.jpg *License*: unknown *Contributors*: -

File:BolteBridge.jpg *Source*: http://bibliocm.bibliolabs.com/mwAnon/index.php?title=File:BolteBridge.jpg *License*: unknown *Contributors*: -

File:Southern-cross-station-melbourne-morning.jpg *Source*: http://bibliocm.bibliolabs.com/mwAnon/index.php?title=File:Southern-cross-station-melbourne-morning.jpg *License*: unknown *Contributors*: -

image:St. Paul's Cathedral Tower.jpg *Source*: http://bibliocm.bibliolabs.com/mwAnon/index.php?title=File:St._Paul's_Cathedral_Tower.jpg *License*: Public Domain *Contributors*: Akinom, Bidgee, Donaldytong, 2 anonymous edits

image:St. Paul's Cathedral (Stained Glass Window).jpg *Source*: http://bibliocm.bibliolabs.com/mwAnon/index.php?title=File:St._Paul's_Cathedral_(Stained_Glass_Window).jpg *License*: Creative Commons Attribution-Sharealike 2.5 *Contributors*: User:Donaldytong

Image:St. Paul's Cathedral Interior (Candle light).jpg *Source*: http://bibliocm.bibliolabs.com/mwAnon/index.php?title=File:St._Paul's_Cathedral_Interior_(Candle_light).jpg *License*: Public Domain *Contributors*: Bidgee, Donaldytong, Mike.lifeguard, 1 anonymous edits

Image:St. Paul's Cathedral (the chapel in west wing of the cathedral).jpg *Source*: http://bibliocm.bibliolabs.com/mwAnon/index.php?title=File:St._Paul's_Cathedral_(the_chapel_in_west_wing_of_the_cathedral).jpg *License*: unknown *Contributors*: -

image:Interior of st pauls melb02.jpg *Source*: http://bibliocm.bibliolabs.com/mwAnon/index.php?title=File:Interior_of_st_pauls_melb02.jpg *License*: unknown *Contributors*: -

image:Interior of st pauls melb.jpg *Source*: http://bibliocm.bibliolabs.com/mwAnon/index.php?title=File:Interior_of_st_pauls_melb.jpg *License*: unknown *Contributors*: -

Image:Collins Street Baptist Church Melbourne.jpg *Source*: http://bibliocm.bibliolabs.com/mwAnon/index.php?title=File:Collins_Street_Baptist_Church_Melbourne.jpg *License*: unknown *Contributors*: -

File:East Melbourne Synagogue.JPG *Source*: http://bibliocm.bibliolabs.com/mwAnon/index.php?title=File:East_Melbourne_Synagogue.JPG *License*: Creative Commons Attribution-Sharealike 3.0 *Contributors*: User:Spud770

File:Scots Church Collins Street Melbourne.jpg *Source*: http://bibliocm.bibliolabs.com/mwAnon/index.php?title=File:Scots_Church_Collins_Street_Melbourne.jpg *License*: Public Domain *Contributors*: Simeon87

File:Olderfleet buildings Collins Street Melbourne.jpg *Source*: http://bibliocm.bibliolabs.com/mwAnon/index.php?title=File:Olderfleet_buildings_Collins_Street_Melbourne.jpg *License*: unknown *Contributors*: -

Image:Scots' Church in Collins Street.jpg *Source*: http://bibliocm.bibliolabs.com/mwAnon/index.php?title=File:Scots'_Church_in_Collins_Street.jpg *License*: Public Domain *Contributors*: User:Donaldytong

Image:Treasure and Pearl.jpg *Source*: http://bibliocm.bibliolabs.com/mwAnon/index.php?title=File:Treasure_and_Pearl.jpg *License*: Public Domain *Contributors*: User:StAnselm

Image:Scot's Church Tower.jpg *Source*: http://bibliocm.bibliolabs.com/mwAnon/index.php?title=File:Scot's_Church_Tower.jpg *License*: unknown *Contributors*: -

Image:Scots 10 Commandments.jpg *Source*: http://bibliocm.bibliolabs.com/mwAnon/index.php?title=File:Scots_10_Commandments.jpg *License*: unknown *Contributors*: -

File:St Patrick's Cathedral-Gothic Revival Style (Central Tower).jpg *Source*: http://bibliocm.bibliolabs.com/mwAnon/index.php?title=File:St_Patrick's_Cathedral-Gothic_Revival_Style_(Central_Tower).jpg *License*: unknown *Contributors*: -

File:St Patrick's Cathedral (Gothic Revival Style).jpg *Source*: http://bibliocm.bibliolabs.com/mwAnon/index.php?title=File:St_Patrick's_Cathedral_(Gothic_Revival_Style).jpg *License*: unknown *Contributors*: -

File:St Patrick's Cathedral, Irish Nationalist Leader Daniel O'Connell Statue.jpg *Source*: http://bibliocm.bibliolabs.com/mwAnon/index.php?title=File:St_Patrick's_Cathedral,_Irish_Nationalist_Leader_Daniel_O'Connell_Statue.jpg *License*: unknown *Contributors*: -

File:St Patrick's Cathedral - Gothic Revival Style.jpg *Source*: http://bibliocm.bibliolabs.com/mwAnon/index.php?title=File:St_Patrick's_Cathedral_-_Gothic_Revival_Style.jpg *License*: unknown *Contributors*: -

File:St Patrick's Cathedral-Gothic Revival Style.jpg *Source*: http://bibliocm.bibliolabs.com/mwAnon/index.php?title=File:St_Patrick's_Cathedral-Gothic_Revival_Style.jpg *License*: unknown *Contributors*: -

File:St Patrick's Cathedral-Gothic Revival Style (East Side).jpg *Source*: http://bibliocm.bibliolabs.com/mwAnon/index.php?title=File:St_Patrick's_Cathedral-Gothic_Revival_Style_(East_Side).jpg *License*: unknown *Contributors*: -

File:St Patricks Cathedral East Side.jpg *Source*: http://bibliocm.bibliolabs.com/mwAnon/index.php?title=File:St_Patricks_Cathedral_East_Side.jpg *License*: unknown *Contributors*: -

File:St Patricks Cathedral St Catherine of Siena Statue.jpg *Source*: http://bibliocm.bibliolabs.com/mwAnon/index.php?title=File:St_Patricks_Cathedral_St_Catherine_of_Siena_Statue.jpg *License*: unknown *Contributors*: -

File:St Patricks Cathedral St Francis of Assisi Statue.jpg *Source*: http://bibliocm.bibliolabs.com/mwAnon/index.php?title=File:St_Patricks_Cathedral_St_Francis_of_Assisi_Statue.jpg *License*: unknown *Contributors*: -

File:St Patricks Cathedral River From the Throne of God of the Lamb.jpg *Source*: http://bibliocm.bibliolabs.com/mwAnon/index.php?title=File:St_Patricks_Cathedral_River_From_the_Throne_of_God_of_the_Lamb.jpg *License*: unknown *Contributors*: -

File:St Patricks Cathedral River Fall.jpg *Source*: http://bibliocm.bibliolabs.com/mwAnon/index.php?title=File:St_Patricks_Cathedral_River_Fall.jpg *License*: Creative Commons Attribution-Sharealike 2.5 *Contributors*: User:Donaldytong

File:St Patricks Cathedral Entrance Interior.jpg *Source*: http://bibliocm.bibliolabs.com/mwAnon/index.php?title=File:St_Patricks_Cathedral_Entrance_Interior.jpg *License*: unknown *Contributors*: -

File:St Patricks Cathedral Interior.jpg *Source*: http://bibliocm.bibliolabs.com/mwAnon/index.php?title=File:St_Patricks_Cathedral_Interior.jpg *License*: unknown *Contributors*: -

File:StPatrick_9801.jpg *Source*: http://bibliocm.bibliolabs.com/mwAnon/index.php?title=File:StPatrick_9801.jpg *License*: unknown *Contributors*: -

File:St Patrick's Cathedral - Music Organ.jpg *Source*: http://bibliocm.bibliolabs.com/mwAnon/index.php?title=File:St_Patrick's_Cathedral_-_Music_Organ.jpg *License*: unknown *Contributors*: -

Image:commons-logo.svg *Source*: http://bibliocm.bibliolabs.com/mwAnon/index.php?title=File:Commons-logo.svg *License*: logo *Contributors*: User:3247, User:Grunt

Image:Shrine of Rememberence.jpg *Source*: http://bibliocm.bibliolabs.com/mwAnon/index.php?title=File:Shrine_of_Rememberence.jpg *License*: unknown *Contributors*: -

Image:Federation-square-sandstone-facade.jpg *Source*: http://bibliocm.bibliolabs.com/mwAnon/index.php?title=File:Federation-square-sandstone-facade.jpg *License*: Creative Commons Attribution-Sharealike 2.1 *Contributors*: Seo75

Image:Fed square tiles.jpg *Source*: http://bibliocm.bibliolabs.com/mwAnon/index.php?title=File:Fed_square_tiles.jpg *License*: Public Domain *Contributors*: User:Farsouth

Image:FederationSquare-panorama.jpg *Source*: http://bibliocm.bibliolabs.com/mwAnon/index.php?title=File:FederationSquare-panorama.jpg *License*: Creative Commons Attribution-Sharealike 3.0 *Contributors*: User:Invincible

Image:Australian Centre for the Moving Image.jpg *Source*: http://bibliocm.bibliolabs.com/mwAnon/index.php?title=File:Australian_Centre_for_the_Moving_Image.jpg *License*: Creative Commons Attribution 3.0 *Contributors*: User:Bidgee

File:Federation Square Overview, Melbourne.jpg *Source*: http://bibliocm.bibliolabs.com/mwAnon/index.php?title=File:Federation_Square_Overview,_Melbourne.jpg *License*: unknown *Contributors*: -

File:City of Melbourn.jpg *Source*: http://bibliocm.bibliolabs.com/mwAnon/index.php?title=File:City_of_Melbourn.jpg *License*: Creative Commons Attribution-Sharealike 2.5 *Contributors*: User:Adam.J.W.C.

File:Federation Square (SBS Building).jpg *Source*: http://bibliocm.bibliolabs.com/mwAnon/index.php?title=File:Federation_Square_(SBS_Building).jpg *License*: Public Domain *Contributors*: User:Donaldytong

File:Melbourne Federation Square Theatre.jpg *Source*: http://bibliocm.bibliolabs.com/mwAnon/index.php?title=File:Melbourne_Federation_Square_Theatre.jpg *License*: Public Domain *Contributors*: Bidgee, Donaldytong, 2 anonymous edits

Image: Clocktower Centre 01a.jpg *Source*: http://bibliocm.bibliolabs.com/mwAnon/index.php?title=File:Clocktower_Centre_01a.jpg *License*: GNU Free Documentation License *Contributors*: Melburnian

File:Victoria Barracks Melbourne.jpg *Source*: http://bibliocm.bibliolabs.com/mwAnon/index.php?title=File:Victoria_Barracks_Melbourne.jpg *License*: Public Domain *Contributors*: Original uploader was Donaldtong at en.wikipedia

Image:Image-(VIC) Victoria Barracks.jpg *Source*: http://bibliocm.bibliolabs.com/mwAnon/index.php?title=File:Image-(VIC)_Victoria_Barracks.jpg *License*: unknown *Contributors*: -

Image:Pentridge.jpg *Source*: http://bibliocm.bibliolabs.com/mwAnon/index.php?title=File:Pentridge.jpg *License*: unknown *Contributors*: -

Image:ned kelly day before execution photograph.jpg *Source*: http://bibliocm.bibliolabs.com/mwAnon/index.php?title=File:Ned_kelly_day_before_execution_photograph.jpg *License*: Public Domain *Contributors*: Original uploader was Robert Merkel at en.wikipedia

Image:Pentridgeentrancesteps.jpg *Source*: http://bibliocm.bibliolabs.com/mwAnon/index.php?title=File:Pentridgeentrancesteps.jpg *License*: Public Domain *Contributors*: Jean Baptiste Charlier

File:City Baths Melbourne.jpg *Source*: http://bibliocm.bibliolabs.com/mwAnon/index.php?title=File:City_Baths_Melbourne.jpg *License*: unknown *Contributors*: -

File:Old Melbourne Gaol - Melbourne (76468479).jpg *Source*: http://bibliocm.bibliolabs.com/mwAnon/index.php?title=File:Old_Melbourne_Gaol_-_Melbourne_(76468479).jpg *License*: unknown *Contributors*: -

File:Calico hood.JPG *Source*: http://bibliocm.bibliolabs.com/mwAnon/index.php?title=File:Calico_hood.JPG *License*: Creative Commons Attribution-Sharealike 2.5 *Contributors*: User:Ciell

File:Long drop gallow.JPG *Source*: http://bibliocm.bibliolabs.com/mwAnon/index.php?title=File:Long_drop_gallow.JPG *License*: unknown *Contributors*: -

File:RMITAlumniCourtGates.jpg *Source*: http://bibliocm.bibliolabs.com/mwAnon/index.php?title=File:RMITAlumniCourtGates.jpg *License*: unknown *Contributors*: -

Image:Newport-workshops-west-block-assortment.jpg *Source*: http://bibliocm.bibliolabs.com/mwAnon/index.php?title=File:Newport-workshops-west-block-assortment.jpg *License*: unknown *Contributors*: -

Image:Newport-workshops-loco-shop.jpg *Source*: http://bibliocm.bibliolabs.com/mwAnon/index.php?title=File:Newport-workshops-loco-shop.jpg *License*: GNU Free Documentation License *Contributors*: User:Wongm

Image:QueenVictoriaMarketBuildingFacade.jpg *Source*: http://bibliocm.bibliolabs.com/mwAnon/index.php?title=File:QueenVictoriaMarketBuildingFacade.jpg *License*: unknown *Contributors*: -

Image:Melbourne Windsor Hotel Lobby.jpg *Source*: http://bibliocm.bibliolabs.com/mwAnon/index.php?title=File:Melbourne_Windsor_Hotel_Lobby.jpg *License*: Creative Commons Attribution-Sharealike 3.0 *Contributors*: User:Donaldytong

File:Greg Barber Bob Brown Brian Walters.jpg *Source*: http://bibliocm.bibliolabs.com/mwAnon/index.php?title=File:Greg_Barber_Bob_Brown_Brian_Walters.jpg *License*: Creative Commons Attribution-Sharealike 3.0 *Contributors*: User:Peter Campbell

Image:Bali Memorial,Carlton, Victoria, Australia.jpg *Source*: http://bibliocm.bibliolabs.com/mwAnon/index.php?title=File:Bali_Memorial,Carlton,_Victoria,_Australia.jpg *License*: Creative Commons Attribution 2.5 *Contributors*: User:Matnkat

File:Australian_State_Route_50.svg *Source*: http://bibliocm.bibliolabs.com/mwAnon/index.php?title=File:Australian_State_Route_50.svg *License*: unknown *Contributors*: -

File:Australian_Tourist_Route_2.svg *Source*: http://bibliocm.bibliolabs.com/mwAnon/index.php?title=File:Australian_Tourist_Route_2.svg *License*: unknown *Contributors*: -

file:Southern-cross-station-melbourne-morning.jpg *Source*: http://bibliocm.bibliolabs.com/mwAnon/index.php?title=File:Southern-cross-station-melbourne-morning.jpg *License*: unknown *Contributors*: -

Image:Rippon_Lea_front_gates.JPG *Source*: http://bibliocm.bibliolabs.com/mwAnon/index.php?title=File:Rippon_Lea_front_gates.JPG *License*: unknown *Contributors*: -

Image:VictorianBuilding0013.jpg *Source*: http://bibliocm.bibliolabs.com/mwAnon/index.php?title=File:VictorianBuilding0013.jpg *License*: unknown *Contributors*: -

Image:Rippon Lea front door.jpg *Source*: http://bibliocm.bibliolabs.com/mwAnon/index.php?title=File:Rippon_Lea_front_door.jpg *License*: unknown *Contributors*: -

Image:Rippon Lea lawn.jpg *Source*: http://bibliocm.bibliolabs.com/mwAnon/index.php?title=File:Rippon_Lea_lawn.jpg *License*: unknown *Contributors*: -

Image:Rippon Lea house.jpg *Source*: http://bibliocm.bibliolabs.com/mwAnon/index.php?title=File:Rippon_Lea_house.jpg *License*: unknown *Contributors*: -

Image:Rippon Lea swimming pool.jpg *Source*: http://bibliocm.bibliolabs.com/mwAnon/index.php?title=File:Rippon_Lea_swimming_pool.jpg *License*: unknown *Contributors*: -

Image:Rippon Lea hallway.jpg *Source*: http://bibliocm.bibliolabs.com/mwAnon/index.php?title=File:Rippon_Lea_hallway.jpg *License*: unknown *Contributors*: -

Image:Rippon Lea ground floor.jpg *Source*: http://bibliocm.bibliolabs.com/mwAnon/index.php?title=File:Rippon_Lea_ground_floor.jpg *License*: unknown *Contributors*: -

Image:Rippon Lea back garden.jpg *Source*: http://bibliocm.bibliolabs.com/mwAnon/index.php?title=File:Rippon_Lea_back_garden.jpg *License*: unknown *Contributors*: -

Image:Rippon LEa fernery.jpg *Source*: http://bibliocm.bibliolabs.com/mwAnon/index.php?title=File:Rippon_LEa_fernery.jpg *License*: unknown *Contributors*: -

Image:Rippon Lea boat house.jpg *Source*: http://bibliocm.bibliolabs.com/mwAnon/index.php?title=File:Rippon_Lea_boat_house.jpg *License*: unknown *Contributors*: -

Image:Rippon Lea lake seat.jpg *Source*: http://bibliocm.bibliolabs.com/mwAnon/index.php?title=File:Rippon_Lea_lake_seat.jpg *License*: unknown *Contributors*: -

File:Rialto Towers 1.png *Source*: http://bibliocm.bibliolabs.com/mwAnon/index.php?title=File:Rialto_Towers_1.png *License*: Creative Commons Attribution-Sharealike 3.0 *Contributors*: User:Samekh

File:Rialto old.....jpg *Source*: http://bibliocm.bibliolabs.com/mwAnon/index.php?title=File:Rialto_old.....jpg *License*: unknown *Contributors*: -

File:Rialto view night.jpg *Source*: http://bibliocm.bibliolabs.com/mwAnon/index.php?title=File:Rialto_view_night.jpg *License*: Creative Commons Attribution-Sharealike 2.0 *Contributors*: Original uploader was Abdominator at en.wikipedia

Image:royal exhibition building tulips straight.jpg *Source*: http://bibliocm.bibliolabs.com/mwAnon/index.php?title=File:Royal_exhibition_building_tulips_straight.jpg *License*: unknown *Contributors*: -

Image:Royal Exhibition Building 2003-05-17.jpg *Source*: http://bibliocm.bibliolabs.com/mwAnon/index.php?title=File:Royal_Exhibition_Building_2003-05-17.jpg *License*: unknown *Contributors*: -

Image:Melbourne Royal Exhibition - East Buildings.jpg *Source*: http://bibliocm.bibliolabs.com/mwAnon/index.php?title=File:Melbourne_Royal_Exhibition_-_East_Buildings.jpg *License*: unknown *Contributors*: -

Image:Royal Exhibition Building inside1.JPG *Source*: http://bibliocm.bibliolabs.com/mwAnon/index.php?title=File:Royal_Exhibition_Building_inside1.JPG *License*: unknown *Contributors*: -

File:La_Mama_Theatre,_Carlton,_Victoria,_Australia.jpg *Source*: http://bibliocm.bibliolabs.com/mwAnon/index.php?title=File:La_Mama_Theatre,_Carlton,_Victoria,_Australia.jpg *License*: Creative Commons Attribution 2.5 *Contributors*: User:Matnkat

Image:Melbourne Princess Theatre.jpg *Source*: http://bibliocm.bibliolabs.com/mwAnon/index.php?title=File:Melbourne_Princess_Theatre.jpg *License*: Public Domain *Contributors*: Aconcagua, Donaldytong, Elekhh, Ingolfson, Mattinbgn, 2 anonymous edits

File:Regent Theatre Melbourne.jpg *Source*: http://bibliocm.bibliolabs.com/mwAnon/index.php?title=File:Regent_Theatre_Melbourne.jpg *License*: unknown *Contributors*: -

File:Forum Theatre Melbourne.jpg *Source*: http://bibliocm.bibliolabs.com/mwAnon/index.php?title=File:Forum_Theatre_Melbourne.jpg *License*: GNU Free Documentation License *Contributors*: Melburnian

File:ComedyTheatreMelbourne1.JPG *Source*: http://bibliocm.bibliolabs.com/mwAnon/index.php?title=File:ComedyTheatreMelbourne1.JPG *License*: Creative Commons Attribution-Sharealike 3.0 *Contributors*: User:AshGreen

File:ComedyTheatreMelbournefresco1.JPG *Source*: http://bibliocm.bibliolabs.com/mwAnon/index.php?title=File:ComedyTheatreMelbournefresco1.JPG *License*: Creative Commons Attribution-Sharealike 3.0 *Contributors*: User:AshGreen

File:ComedyTheatreMelbournefresco2.JPG *Source*: http://bibliocm.bibliolabs.com/mwAnon/index.php?title=File:ComedyTheatreMelbournefresco2.JPG *License*: Creative Commons Attribution-Sharealike 3.0 *Contributors*: User:AshGreen

File:ComedyTheatreMelbournefresco3.JPG *Source*: http://bibliocm.bibliolabs.com/mwAnon/index.php?title=File:ComedyTheatreMelbournefresco3.JPG *License*: Creative Commons Attribution-Sharealike 3.0 *Contributors*: User:AshGreen

File:ComedyTheatreMelbournewindows.JPG *Source*: http://bibliocm.bibliolabs.com/mwAnon/index.php?title=File:ComedyTheatreMelbournewindows.JPG *License*: Creative Commons Attribution-Sharealike 3.0 *Contributors*: User:AshGreen

File:Melbourne Athenaeum.jpg *Source*: http://bibliocm.bibliolabs.com/mwAnon/index.php?title=File:Melbourne_Athenaeum.jpg *License*: Creative Commons Attribution-Sharealike 3.0 *Contributors*: User:Canley

File:Capitol Theatre, Swanston Street, Melbourne.JPG *Source*: http://bibliocm.bibliolabs.com/mwAnon/index.php?title=File:Capitol_Theatre,_Swanston_Street,_Melbourne.JPG *License*: Creative Commons Attribution-Sharealike 2.5 *Contributors*: me (w:User:pfctdayelise)

File:Acca and malthouse theatre southbank.jpg *Source*: http://bibliocm.bibliolabs.com/mwAnon/index.php?title=File:Acca_and_malthouse_theatre_southbank.jpg *License*: unknown *Contributors*: -

Image:Melb symphony orchestra.jpg *Source*: http://bibliocm.bibliolabs.com/mwAnon/index.php?title=File:Melb_symphony_orchestra.jpg *License*: unknown *Contributors*: Ejdzej, Fir0002, Magister Mathematicae, Thuresson

Image:Melbourne symphony orchestra.jpg *Source*: http://bibliocm.bibliolabs.com/mwAnon/index.php?title=File:Melbourne_symphony_orchestra.jpg *License*: unknown *Contributors*: Ejdzej, Fir0002, Magister Mathematicae, Yann

File:Australian Centre for the Moving Image.jpg *Source*: http://bibliocm.bibliolabs.com/mwAnon/index.php?title=File:Australian_Centre_for_the_Moving_Image.jpg *License*: Creative Commons Attribution 3.0 *Contributors*: User:Bidgee

Image:Secondary college carcase comp - weekly times pavillion - melbourne show 2005.jpg *Source*: http://bibliocm.bibliolabs.com/mwAnon/index.php?title=File:Secondary_college_carcase_comp_-_weekly_times_pavillion_-_melbourne_show_2005.jpg *License*: unknown *Contributors*: -

Image:Horse riding in coca cola arena - melbourne show 2005.jpg *Source*: http://bibliocm.bibliolabs.com/mwAnon/index.php?title=File:Horse_riding_in_coca_cola_arena_-_melbourne_show_2005.jpg *License*: unknown *Contributors*: -

Image:Lama head - melbourne show 2005.jpg *Source*: http://bibliocm.bibliolabs.com/mwAnon/index.php?title=File:Lama_head_-_melbourne_show_2005.jpg *License*: unknown *Contributors*: -

Image:Sheep - melbourne show 2005.jpg *Source*: http://bibliocm.bibliolabs.com/mwAnon/index.php?title=File:Sheep_-_melbourne_show_2005.jpg *License*: unknown *Contributors*: -

Image:Hereford cow - carcase comp.jpg *Source*: http://bibliocm.bibliolabs.com/mwAnon/index.php?title=File:Hereford_cow_-_carcase_comp.jpg *License*: unknown *Contributors*: -

Image:Rides at melbourne show 2005.jpg *Source*: http://bibliocm.bibliolabs.com/mwAnon/index.php?title=File:Rides_at_melbourne_show_2005.jpg *License*: unknown *Contributors*: -

Image:Dodgem cars - melbourne show 2005.jpg *Source*: http://bibliocm.bibliolabs.com/mwAnon/index.php?title=File:Dodgem_cars_-_melbourne_show_2005.jpg *License*: unknown *Contributors*: -

Image:Collins Street - The Block Arcade.jpg *Source*: http://bibliocm.bibliolabs.com/mwAnon/index.php?title=File:Collins_Street_-_The_Block_Arcade.jpg *License*: unknown *Contributors*: -

Image:Collins Street (The Block Arcade).jpg *Source*: http://bibliocm.bibliolabs.com/mwAnon/index.php?title=File:Collins_Street_(The_Block_Arcade).jpg *License*: Public Domain *Contributors*: Bidgee, Donaldytong, Simeon87

Image:Gog&Magog-2,-Royal-Arcade,-Melb,-11.08.2008.jpg *Source*: http://bibliocm.bibliolabs.com/mwAnon/index.php?title=File:Gog&Magog-2,-Royal-Arcade,-Melb,-11.08.2008.jpg *License*: GNU Free Documentation License *Contributors*: User:Jjron

Image:Royal Arcade, Melbourne, Australia - April 2004.jpg *Source*: http://bibliocm.bibliolabs.com/mwAnon/index.php?title=File:Royal_Arcade,_Melbourne,_Australia_-_April_2004.jpg *License*: Creative Commons Attribution-Sharealike 2.5 *Contributors*: User:Diliff

Image:Gog&Magog-1,-Royal-Arcade,-Melb,-11.08.2008.jpg *Source*: http://bibliocm.bibliolabs.com/mwAnon/index.php?title=File:Gog&Magog-1,-Royal-Arcade,-Melb,-11.08.2008.jpg *License*: GNU Free Documentation License *Contributors*: User:Jjron

File:Luna st kilda.jpg *Source*: http://bibliocm.bibliolabs.com/mwAnon/index.php?title=File:Luna_st_kilda.jpg *License*: unknown *Contributors*: -

Image:Melbourne Luna Park.jpg *Source*: http://bibliocm.bibliolabs.com/mwAnon/index.php?title=File:Melbourne_Luna_Park.jpg *License*: unknown *Contributors*: -

Image:Luna Park Melbourne scenic railway.jpg *Source*: http://bibliocm.bibliolabs.com/mwAnon/index.php?title=File:Luna_Park_Melbourne_scenic_railway.jpg *License*: unknown *Contributors*: -

Image:Luna Park St. Kilda.JPG *Source*: http://bibliocm.bibliolabs.com/mwAnon/index.php?title=File:Luna_Park_St._Kilda.JPG *License*: Public Domain *Contributors*: User:Erin Silversmith

Image:Princes park from air.jpg *Source*: http://bibliocm.bibliolabs.com/mwAnon/index.php?title=File:Princes_park_from_air.jpg *License*: Public Domain *Contributors*: User:Rulesfan

File:Port Melbourne Bayside Foreshore Promenade.jpg *Source*: http://bibliocm.bibliolabs.com/mwAnon/index.php?title=File:Port_Melbourne_Bayside_Foreshore_Promenade.jpg *License*: unknown *Contributors*: -

Image:Heidfeld and Rosberg - 2008 Melb GP.jpg *Source*: http://bibliocm.bibliolabs.com/mwAnon/index.php?title=File:Heidfeld_and_Rosberg_-_2008_Melb_GP.jpg *License*: unknown *Contributors*: -

Image:Albert Park Lake 2005-11-06.jpeg *Source*: http://bibliocm.bibliolabs.com/mwAnon/index.php?title=File:Albert_Park_Lake_2005-11-06.jpeg *License*: unknown *Contributors*: -

Image:Footscray Park path.jpg *Source*: http://bibliocm.bibliolabs.com/mwAnon/index.php?title=File:Footscray_Park_path.jpg *License*: Creative Commons Attribution 2.5 *Contributors*: Melburnian

Image:Footscray Park plan detail.jpg *Source*: http://bibliocm.bibliolabs.com/mwAnon/index.php?title=File:Footscray_Park_plan_detail.jpg *License*: unknown *Contributors*: -

Image:Footscray Park entrance.jpg *Source*: http://bibliocm.bibliolabs.com/mwAnon/index.php?title=File:Footscray_Park_entrance.jpg *License*: unknown *Contributors*: -

Image:Fawkner Park, South Yarra, Victoria, Australia.jpg *Source*: http://bibliocm.bibliolabs.com/mwAnon/index.php?title=File:Fawkner_Park,_South_Yarra,_Victoria,_Australia.jpg *License*: unknown *Contributors*: -

Image:Fitzroy Memorial Rotunda.jpg *Source*: http://bibliocm.bibliolabs.com/mwAnon/index.php?title=File:Fitzroy_Memorial_Rotunda.jpg *License*: unknown *Contributors*: -

Image:Fitzroy Cricket Ground Grandstand.jpg *Source*: http://bibliocm.bibliolabs.com/mwAnon/index.php?title=File:Fitzroy_Cricket_Ground_Grandstand.jpg *License*: unknown *Contributors*: -

Image:Carlton gardens.jpg *Source*: http://bibliocm.bibliolabs.com/mwAnon/index.php?title=File:Carlton_gardens.jpg *License*: unknown *Contributors*: -

Image:St vincent garden albert park.jpg *Source*: http://bibliocm.bibliolabs.com/mwAnon/index.php?title=File:St_vincent_garden_albert_park.jpg *License*: Public Domain *Contributors*: Original uploader was Biatch at en.wikipedia

Image:St_vincent_garden_albert_park.jpg *Source*: http://bibliocm.bibliolabs.com/mwAnon/index.php?title=File:St_vincent_garden_albert_park.jpg *License*: Public Domain *Contributors*: Original uploader was Biatch at en.wikipedia

Image:Melb botanical gardens03.jpg *Source*: http://bibliocm.bibliolabs.com/mwAnon/index.php?title=File:Melb_botanical_gardens03.jpg *License*: unknown *Contributors*: -

Image:Royal Botanic Gardens (The National Herbarium Victoria - Founded in 1853).jpg *Source*: http://bibliocm.bibliolabs.com/mwAnon/index.php?title=File:Royal_Botanic_Gardens_(The_National_Herbarium_Victoria_-_Founded_in_1853).jpg *License*: unknown *Contributors*: -

Image:Eels at melbourne botanical gardens.jpg *Source*: http://bibliocm.bibliolabs.com/mwAnon/index.php?title=File:Eels_at_melbourne_botanical_gardens.jpg *License*: unknown *Contributors*: -

Image:Melbourne Australia Royal Botanical Garden.JPG *Source*: http://bibliocm.bibliolabs.com/mwAnon/index.php?title=File:Melbourne_Australia_Royal_Botanical_Garden.JPG *License*: unknown *Contributors*: -

Image:Melb botanical gardens.jpg *Source*: http://bibliocm.bibliolabs.com/mwAnon/index.php?title=File:Melb_botanical_gardens.jpg *License*: unknown *Contributors*: -

Image:Nympheas Lake 2003-05-24.jpg *Source*: http://bibliocm.bibliolabs.com/mwAnon/index.php?title=File:Nympheas_Lake_2003-05-24.jpg *License*: unknown *Contributors*: -

Image:BGM Herb Garden.jpg *Source*: http://bibliocm.bibliolabs.com/mwAnon/index.php?title=File:BGM_Herb_Garden.jpg *License*: unknown *Contributors*: -

Image:Royal Botanic Gardens (Entrance Gate).jpg *Source*: http://bibliocm.bibliolabs.com/mwAnon/index.php?title=File:Royal_Botanic_Gardens_(Entrance_Gate).jpg *License*: unknown *Contributors*: -

Image:Queen Victoria Gardens.jpg *Source*: http://bibliocm.bibliolabs.com/mwAnon/index.php?title=File:Queen_Victoria_Gardens.jpg *License*: unknown *Contributors*: -

Image:Floral Clock, Queen Victoria Gardens, Melbourne.JPG *Source*: http://bibliocm.bibliolabs.com/mwAnon/index.php?title=File:Floral_Clock,_Queen_Victoria_Gardens,_Melbourne.JPG *License*: Public Domain *Contributors*: Original uploader was Josh Parris at en.wikipedia

Image:Alexandra Gardens Boathouses.jpg *Source*: http://bibliocm.bibliolabs.com/mwAnon/index.php?title=File:Alexandra_Gardens_Boathouses.jpg *License*: unknown *Contributors*: -

Image:ATB2009alexandergardens.JPG *Source*: http://bibliocm.bibliolabs.com/mwAnon/index.php?title=File:ATB2009alexandergardens.JPG *License*: Creative Commons Attribution-Sharealike 3.0 *Contributors*: User:Unwicked

Image:Melbourne Treasury Gardens.jpg *Source*: http://bibliocm.bibliolabs.com/mwAnon/index.php?title=File:Melbourne_Treasury_Gardens.jpg *License*: unknown *Contributors*: Original uploader was Stevage at en.wikipedia

Image:Treasury gardens 2.jpg *Source*: http://bibliocm.bibliolabs.com/mwAnon/index.php?title=File:Treasury_gardens_2.jpg *License*: unknown *Contributors*: -

Image:Treasury gardens 1.jpg *Source*: http://bibliocm.bibliolabs.com/mwAnon/index.php?title=File:Treasury_gardens_1.jpg *License*: unknown *Contributors*: -

Image:Brushtail possum stroked.jpg *Source*: http://bibliocm.bibliolabs.com/mwAnon/index.php?title=File:Brushtail_possum_stroked.jpg *License*: Public Domain *Contributors*: Original uploader was Godnose at en.wikipedia

Image:Melbourne Capt Cooks Cottage - outer00.jpg *Source*: http://bibliocm.bibliolabs.com/mwAnon/index.php?title=File:Melbourne_Capt_Cooks_Cottage_-_outer00.jpg *License*: GNU Free Documentation License *Contributors*: Andy king50, Ausxan, Patche99z

Image:Fitzroy Gardens Fairy tree.jpg *Source*: http://bibliocm.bibliolabs.com/mwAnon/index.php?title=File:Fitzroy_Gardens_Fairy_tree.jpg *License*: GNU Free Documentation License *Contributors*: Original uploader was Tirin at en.wikipedia

Image:English Elm avenue.jpg *Source*: http://bibliocm.bibliolabs.com/mwAnon/index.php?title=File:English_Elm_avenue.jpg *License*: Creative Commons Attribution 2.5 *Contributors*: Melburnian

Image:Fitzroy Gardens.jpg *Source*: http://bibliocm.bibliolabs.com/mwAnon/index.php?title=File:Fitzroy_Gardens.jpg *License*: GNU Free Documentation License *Contributors*: Original uploader was Tirin at en.wikipedia

Image:Scarred tree Fitzroy Gardens.jpg *Source*: http://bibliocm.bibliolabs.com/mwAnon/index.php?title=File:Scarred_tree_Fitzroy_Gardens.jpg *License*: unknown *Contributors*: Original uploader was Tirin at en.wikipedia

Image:Flagstaff Gardens Melbourne.jpg *Source*: http://bibliocm.bibliolabs.com/mwAnon/index.php?title=File:Flagstaff_Gardens_Melbourne.jpg *License*: GNU Free Documentation License *Contributors*: Original uploader was Two stripe at en.wikipedia

file:Zoo_melb_entrance_1940.jpg *Source*: http://bibliocm.bibliolabs.com/mwAnon/index.php?title=File:Zoo_melb_entrance_1940.jpg *License*: Public Domain *Contributors*: Original uploader was Longhair at en.wikipedia

Image:Tiger - melbourne zoo.jpg *Source*: http://bibliocm.bibliolabs.com/mwAnon/index.php?title=File:Tiger_-_melbourne_zoo.jpg *License*: unknown *Contributors*: User:Fir0002

Image:Batmans-hill-melbourne.jpg *Source*: http://bibliocm.bibliolabs.com/mwAnon/index.php?title=File:Batmans-hill-melbourne.jpg *License*: GNU Free Documentation License *Contributors*: User:Wongm

file:MelbourneAquariumEast.JPG *Source*: http://bibliocm.bibliolabs.com/mwAnon/index.php?title=File:MelbourneAquariumEast.JPG *License*: GNU Free Documentation License *Contributors*: User:Uncke Herb

Image:Feeding time melb aquarium.jpg *Source*: http://bibliocm.bibliolabs.com/mwAnon/index.php?title=File:Feeding_time_melb_aquarium.jpg *License*: unknown *Contributors*: -

Image:Melbourne Aquarium.jpg *Source*: http://bibliocm.bibliolabs.com/mwAnon/index.php?title=File:Melbourne_Aquarium.jpg *License*: GNU Free Documentation License *Contributors*: User:Bidgee

Image:Giant squid melb aquarium03.jpg *Source*: http://bibliocm.bibliolabs.com/mwAnon/index.php?title=File:Giant_squid_melb_aquarium03.jpg *License*: unknown *Contributors*: Fir0002, Liné1, Pristigaster, 2 anonymous edits

File:Melbourne Skyline and Princes Bridge - Dec 2008.jpg *Source*: http://bibliocm.bibliolabs.com/mwAnon/index.php?title=File:Melbourne_Skyline_and_Princes_Bridge_-_Dec_2008.jpg *License*: Creative Commons Attribution 3.0 *Contributors*: User:Diliff

Image:Princes Bridge, Flinder Street Station, Federation Square and St. Paul's Cathedral and Melbourne CBD on the background from the Yarra river.JPG *Source*: http://bibliocm.bibliolabs.com/mwAnon/index.php?title=File:Princes_Bridge,_Flinder_Street_Station,_Federation_Square_and_St._Paul's_Cathedral_and_Melbourne_CBD_on_the_background_fro *License*: unknown *Contributors*: -

Image:Princes Bridge (Melbourne) underside.jpg *Source*: http://bibliocm.bibliolabs.com/mwAnon/index.php?title=File:Princes_Bridge_(Melbourne)_underside.jpg *License*: unknown *Contributors*: -

Image:Princes Bridge Melbourne lamp.jpg *Source*: http://bibliocm.bibliolabs.com/mwAnon/index.php?title=File:Princes_Bridge_Melbourne_lamp.jpg *License*: unknown *Contributors*: -

Image:Eureka_Tower_01.jpg *Source*: http://bibliocm.bibliolabs.com/mwAnon/index.php?title=File:Eureka_Tower_01.jpg *License*: unknown *Contributors*: -

File:Sandridge Bridge (Built in 1888).jpg *Source*: http://bibliocm.bibliolabs.com/mwAnon/index.php?title=File:Sandridge_Bridge_(Built_in_1888).jpg *License*: Creative Commons Attribution-Sharealike 2.5 *Contributors*: User:Donaldytong

Image:Former Sandridge Railway Bridge over the Yarra River Melbourne, 1959.jpg *Source*: http://bibliocm.bibliolabs.com/mwAnon/index.php?title=File:Former_Sandridge_Railway_Bridge_over_the_Yarra_River_Melbourne,_1959.jpg *License*: Creative Commons Attribution-Sharealike 2.0 *Contributors*: Peter Forster

Image:Sandridge Bridge Built in 1888 (Historical Site).jpg *Source*: http://bibliocm.bibliolabs.com/mwAnon/index.php?title=File:Sandridge_Bridge_Built_in_1888_(Historical_Site).jpg *License*: Public Domain *Contributors*: User:Donaldytong

Image:SandridgeBridge-1.jpg *Source*: http://bibliocm.bibliolabs.com/mwAnon/index.php?title=File:SandridgeBridge-1.jpg *License*: Creative Commons Attribution-Sharealike 2.5 *Contributors*: User:Invincible

CPSIA information can be obtained
at www.ICGtesting.com
Printed in the USA
LVOW09s1347040218
565249LV00010B/322/P